SolidWorks® Surfacing and Complex Shape Modeling Bible

SolidWorks® Surfacing and Complex Shape Modeling Bible

Matt Lombard

Wiley Publishing, Inc.

SolidWorks® Surfacing and Complex Shape Modeling Bible

Published by
Wiley Publishing, Inc.
10475 Crosspoint Boulevard
Indianapolis, IN 46256
www.wiley.com

Copyright © 2008 by Wiley Publishing, Inc., Indianapolis, Indiana

Published by Wiley Publishing, Inc., Indianapolis, Indiana

Published simultaneously in Canada

ISBN: 978-0-470-25823-1

Manufactured in the United States of America

10 9 8 7 6 5 4 3 2 1

For general information on our other products and services or to obtain technical support, please contact our Customer Care Department within the U.S. at (800) 762-2974, outside the U.S. at (317) 572-3993 or fax (317) 572-4002.

Library of Congress Control Number: 2008924089

About the Author

Matt Lombard holds a mechanical engineering degree from Rochester Institute of Technology in Rochester, New York. Matt has worked as a design and manufacturing engineer in the medical and microelectronics industries. Currently, through his company Dezignstuff, he works mainly as a consumer product modeling consultant and technical writer.

Before becoming an engineer, Matt went to music school for two years and performed with the U.S. Navy band for four years. He still plays in local community groups for fun. Having grown up in the Adirondack Mountains of northeastern New York, he now calls the Shenandoah Valley of Virginia home. Contact Matt directly at matt@dezignstuff.com, or visit his blog at www.dezignstuff.com/blog.

This book is dedicated to my parents, Jim and Carol Lombard. Dad is the consummate punster and word play addict, as well as a former math teacher. Mom is a retired music teacher. Between these influences, it isn't any surprise that I have written this book that straddles between the analytical and aesthetic.

Credits

Senior Acquisitions Editor
Stephanie McComb

Project Editor
Sarah Hellert

Technical Editor
Mark Matthews

Copy Editor
Marylouise Wiack

Editorial Manager
Robyn Siesky

Business Manager
Amy Knies

Senior Marketing Manager
Sandy Smith

Special Help
Alissa Birkel
Jama Carter
Sarah Cisco

Vice President and Executive Group Publisher
Richard Swadley

Vice President and Publisher
Barry Pruett

Project Coordinator
Erin Smith

Graphics and Production Specialists
Stacie Brooks
Carl Byers

Quality Control Technicians
John Greenough
Dwight Ramsey

Media Development Coordinator
Jenny Swisher

Proofreading and Indexing
Broccoli Information Management

Cover Design
Michael Trent

Cover Illustration
Joyce Haughey

Preface

Welcome to the *SolidWorks Surfacing and Complex Shape Modeling Bible*. I know, that is quite a mouthful for the title of a book. To just call it the "SolidWorks Surfacing Bible" does not do the topic justice because much of the content deals with solids. There was also the temptation to use "Swoopy Shapes" in the title, but editors have little sense of humor when it comes to abusing the English language in that way, so I had to compromise with the phrase "Complex Shape Modeling". The "Bible" part of course comes from the name of the series of books from the publisher, Wiley Publishing, and is not meant to be blasphemous or to put me up on a supernatural pedestal.

This book is intended for intermediate to advanced SolidWorks users. Everyone has a different idea of what those two levels mean, but I'm assuming the reader of this book has a complete understanding of solid functions in SolidWorks, and at least a passing familiarity with surfacing. If you know nothing about surfacing, a surfacing primer is included in the early chapters to help familiarize you with some terminology. Surface modeling requires a completely different way of looking at geometry. Surfacing is essentially building a model one face at a time.

You might look at the *SolidWorks 2007 Bible* as a good pre-requisite for this book. If you understand things at the level of the *SolidWorks 2007 Bible*, you are ready for this book. Assembly topics are used minimally in this book, and there are no sheet metal or weldment topics used here.

The *SolidWorks Surfacing and Complex Shape Modeling Bible* is written from the point of view of an engineer who has to precisely re-create concept shapes provided by artistic professionals in a way conducive to the manufacture of the part. I do not discuss artistic design issues here; I prefer to use the term "modeling" rather than "design". In this case, modeling is the main difficult task, and it is difficult enough without also considering design.

The book is written from the point of view of an engineer primarily because I am an engineer, and it would be difficult for me to write it from another point of view. The information contained in the book is certainly useable by artistic professionals, hobbyists, CNC programmers, drafters, entrepreneurs, students, or others. The goal in most of the examples is to work from some sort of input, which could be point cloud data, digital photos, or scanned hand sketches, and to produce high quality finished geometry.

As in the *SolidWorks 2007 Bible*, the *SolidWorks Surfacing and Complex Shape Modeling Bible* takes the approach that to talk about the capabilities of the software completely, you must also understand its limitations. Discussions of limitations, bugs and work-arounds are not intended to belittle the software or its creators, only to help align your expectations; what should you expect the software to do, and what is beyond the capabilities of the software.

Acknowledgments

The information in this book came from several sources. Most of it came from reverse engineering the software to figure out what certain functions actually did, but there are several individuals whom I must credit for either specific or general information that got me on the right track. Mark Matthews of Essential Design in Boston, MA is an Industrial Design professional who acted as my technical editor for this book. Mark kept me in touch with the ID side of issues, and offered several ideas that I added to the book. Mark Biasotti of SolidWorks certainly deserves much credit as well. He was able to arrange conversations with developers to try to get a better understanding of what was actually going on behind the scenes. Other individuals who contributed ideas or encouragement include Ricky Jordan, John "Muggs" Ferguson, Kim Hardy, Stan Kujawski, and the guys from Spark Engineering. I would be remiss if I didn't also list materials provided to the general SolidWorks user community by people like Mike Wilson, Keith Pedersen, and Ed Eaton; they have made contributions to the SolidWorks surfacing topic long before this book became available.

Contents at a Glance

Contents

Contents

Part I

Laying the Groundwork

Chapter 1

Understanding Basic Concepts

IN THIS CHAPTER

Assumed basic skills

Concepts, tools, techniques, and strategies

Understanding the difference between design and modeling

Everyone has a different idea of what the words "basic" and "advanced" mean. In general terms, some users might consider everything in this book advanced, and others might consider it basic. Still, in order to progress, the concepts have to start from somewhere, and so the initial concepts will form the basis for the more advanced material to come later.

SolidWorks probably has more surface and complex shape functionality than you realize, especially if you are coming to this book from a machine design background. Some of the tools are matured, having been available for quite some time, and some are newly added to the software, with some occasional kinks still left to work out.

Regardless of how you have arrived here, surfacing and complex shapes are areas of the SolidWorks software that have been flourishing in recent years, and improve with each new release of the software. Still, it is an area that doesn't get as much traffic as, say, the extrudes, revolves and fillets, and so bugs, or quirky functionality, can still be found from time to time.

Figure 1.1 shows an example of some of the modeling that you will find in the pages of this book. This is a SolidWorks model of the SolidWorks Roadster, a Shelby Cobra kit car built by SolidWorks employees, and displayed at SolidWorks World 2007. This rendering was done by Matt Sass for the PhotoWorks contest on Rob Rodriguez's site, www.robrodriguez.com.

FIGURE 1.1

Model of the SolidWorks Roadster

Rendering by Matt Sass

Assumed Basic Skills

The *SolidWorks Surfacing and Complex Shape Modeling Bible* is intended for a diverse cross-section of readers. The first type of reader is the SolidWorks user who is otherwise knowledgeable about the software, but wants to learn about surfacing and complex shape-creation techniques. This reader may have come from another type of design, and is more mechanical than artistic in method. The second is the user of another surfacing program who has learned SolidWorks basics and wants to transfer surfacing skills from the other program to SolidWorks. This reader is more likely an industrial designer or otherwise artistically inclined. This book assumes you already have a good grasp on the basics, such as sketching and sketch relations, the basics of parametric relations between features, and commonly used terminology in SolidWorks. The *SolidWorks Bible* can help bring you to this level, and is a great companion to this book for reference on the more basic concepts.

You will find a small amount of overlap between the current edition of the *SolidWorks Bible* and the *SolidWorks Surfacing and Complex Shape Modeling Bible*. The overlapping topics are splines and multi-body modeling. Both of these skills are essential to working with surfaces and complex shapes, which is why you find them again here, although discussed from a slightly different perspective.

This book was written using early versions of SolidWorks 2008, but most of the concepts discussed can be effectively applied to versions earlier and later. I have tried to make minimal references to version-specific aspects of the interface, but have pointed out where necessary the functional differences if any between features in prior versions.

Assemblies are only discussed in this book in a couple of areas, such as master modeling techniques and multi-body techniques. You will find no reference to any of the specialty techniques such as sheet metal or weldments.

Beyond that, a firm grasp of high school geometry concepts and terminology is necessary. Analytical geometry and simple calculus concepts come into play in the form of tangency, rate of change, and derivatives discussions. Because this book is primarily for actual users of the SolidWorks software, and actual users may or may not have an engineering math background, I will not involve any math or equations directly except for c = 1/r (curvature equals the inverse of radius).

You will find plastic-molded part terminology sprinkled throughout this book, with common references to parting lines, draft, and direction of pull. I have assumed that the reader has a passing familiarity with some form of plastic molding process such as thermoforming, injection molding, rotational molding, or blow molding. A background in metal injection molding, casting, or even forging may also be helpful, as many of the same concepts employed by these manufacturing techniques are also applicable to plastics processes.

Although you will not find drawings discussed in this book, basic mechanical drawing skills are required to get the most out of this book. You must understand basic terminology, such as section, projected view, and orthogonal views.

I intend this book to be primarily for the use of professional CAD operators, whether artist or technical, as opposed to casual or hobbyist users. If you are looking to make characters or equipment for games, SolidWorks may not be your best option. One of the polygonal modelers would be a better bet. Any type of casual user will probably find that complex shapes are easier to create in other software because, as CAD software, SolidWorks tends to require more precision than a tool like Maya or modo, or any of the freeware mesh modelers available.

Concepts, Tools, Techniques, and Strategies

The SolidWorks Surfacing and Complex Shape Modeling Bible is organized into four parts that discuss the concepts and tools (two sections are dedicated to the tools), and finally combine techniques and strategies into a series of longer hands-on model walk-throughs. I believe that this approach answers the how and why questions in addition to explaining and demonstrating what individual button clicks do. Tutorials on their own do not explain the decision-making process, but they do demonstrate the workflow. Lectures on their own do not demonstrate the tools in action. Concepts, of course, are useless without application to realistic scenarios.

Demonstrating techniques and strategies gives you, the reader, a head start with visualizing the application of the tools to real-world modeling scenarios. Most of the models used as examples have been adapted from real-world work projects, to keep them as realistic as possible. Techniques in particular will cover topics such as capping rounded ends, making blends at complex intersections, making sharp edges fade into smooth faces, how to use images as reference, how to deal with draft at the edges of complex surfaces, and many other commonly encountered situations.

Strategies refer to some of the bigger picture questions, like "Where do I start?" On a complex model, it is often difficult to know where to start. Also, if you need to make an assembly where the parts all contain an overall shape, how does modeling of that sort work? The model walk-through chapters in Part 4 answer these questions for you and are meant to spark your imagination to come up with new applications for the tools and techniques, and your own modeling strategies.

SolidWorks corporate documentation explains where to find the tools and generally what they do in the Help documentation. The official SolidWorks training materials offered by resellers are basically instructor-guided tutorials, which are valuable, but they stop short of arming the student with the ability to make modeling decisions based on thorough knowledge of the options. The training materials are also not generally available without paying for the reseller class.

You may also find tutorials on the Web that are either simplistic step-by-step instructions or heady and difficult to comprehend. Again, this book fills the gap between them and tries to do it in a more conversational language that conveys the necessary concepts without talking over your head or down to you.

In the course of talking about concepts, tools, techniques, and strategies, most of the individual topics are covered twice, or even three times from different angles. For example, the Fill surface is a tool that I discuss in Chapter 2 to illustrate the concept of trimmed surfaces, again in detail in Chapter 6, and again in multiple chapters of Part 3 as a practical application in tutorials.

As important as knowing positively what types of features work in which types of situations, it is also important to know the kinds of things that do not work the way you might expect. The purpose of talking about limited functionality is not to be derisive to the software or the parent company, but rather to offer the reader of this book as complete a picture as possible of the capabilities of the software. Often when using software, I have felt that if limitations were spelled out completely in the documentation, I could save a lot of time by avoiding figuring out the limitations for myself. In this book, I have made every attempt to be fair to the software, and if it works, I want to tell the story of how well it works and how to use it to its best advantage. On the other hand, if it doesn't work as you might expect, I feel the obligation to do my readers the service of letting them know where the reliable limits of the software lie.

The point is that whether you use this book as a text to read straight through, or as a reference to look up topics as needed, I hope you find the information well presented and laid out logically. It is not possible to arrange all of the topics in sequential order.

Understanding the Difference Between Design and Modeling

The SolidWorks Surfacing and Complex Shape Modeling Bible, as the name suggests, focuses on modeling parts in SolidWorks with the purpose of manufacturing those parts. This is not a book about design. The act of modeling assumes that the design (or a starting place for the design) already exists. The design may exist in one of many forms. It could be sketched on paper, scanned into a digital image format, or modeled in clay or foam. It could be taken from a digital camera, the back of an envelope or napkin, or a whiteboard. It could already be drawn or modeled in a different 2D or 3D software, it could exist as a 3D point cloud from a 3D scanner, or it may simply exist only in your head. Wherever the design comes from, it probably exists somewhere else before it shows up in SolidWorks.

Dividing the tasks into design and modeling reflects the way that some companies divide their work force. Industrial designers often create a design in a given media, and modelers build a manufacturing model from the design data. There are some industrial design folks who can do their own manufacturing models, but this usually requires some form of engineering input. The modeler is often an engineer, or from a mechanical discipline in any case.

My background is as a mechanical engineer, and in my work as a consultant/contractor, I have often taken conceptual data from industrial designers and converted it to an engineering or manufacturing model. My point of view throughout this book will be just that: as an engineer re-creating or interpreting design data to prepare it for manufacturing. I avoid using the term design when what I am really talking about is simply modeling. While making the interpretations sometimes necessary in this kind of work, it is always important to remain sensitive to the original intent of the design. Other groups within an organization may also have some input into the design, such as branding established by marketing, stacking features introduced by shipping, material or finish costs driven by accounting, geometrical changes driven by molders, or structural changes made by mechanical engineers. Designs very rarely originate from only a single source. In this book, the design data is treated as if it is complete, and all that is required is the 3D CAD model.

In the course of this book, most of the modeling you will do centers around copying an existing form in one of the media mentioned above into a detailed model in SolidWorks. In some cases the models you finish will be ready for prototyping or manufacturing, and in others you will complete only a sampling of a certain technique.

In many of the tutorials in this book, the designer did not execute the provided design information perfectly. This is often also the case in the real world, where the designer creating two orthogonal views of a shape has drawn views that are incompatible with one another. In many cases, the modeler has to make subjective interpretations. I recommend consulting the original designer in cases when there is some discrepancy, but in situations of this sort encountered in this book, you will apply your own judgment to the model to fill in the gaps.

Summary

SolidWorks software is in many areas surprisingly full of powerful functionality to help you with your surfacing and complex shape modeling. This book will help you understand which functions are available, which to use in certain situations, and which to avoid through describing the underlying concepts at play with surfacing and complex shape modeling, the functions of specific individual tools and options, how the tools can be strung together into techniques, and how to plan out an overall strategy to accomplish your modeling goal efficiently.

You should also be clear that this is not a book about design in general. I do not cover how design should progress, the sources of design inspiration or design styles, but rather the details of creating 3D models with SolidWorks. The end goal in mind is creating models that are ready for manufacture or prototyping. Sample designs are presented in this book to be used as practice, creating 3D parametric models that update reliably through changes.

Chapter 2

Surfacing Primer

Solid modeling has introduced an entire generation of engineers and designers to working in 3D. Today you can find younger users who have never drawn on the drawing board with a pencil and instruments, or even done much work in 2D CAD applications. Solid-modeling software takes the underlying power of surface modeling and automates its application to common types of mechanical geometry. In addition to modeling mechanical parts more quickly, this also allows many more people to gain entry into the world of 3D design because less specialized knowledge is required. Solid modeling removes many of the tedious modeling tasks that you would otherwise need to go through by using a surfacing approach.

SolidWorks users who are just beginning to venture into the use of surfacing techniques may find that a new world awaits them. Learning the concepts, tools, and language of the trade can initially be a daunting task, but one that ultimately pays off in many ways. This surfacing primer aims to introduce you to the things you need to know when using surfacing functions in SolidWorks.

What are Surfaces?

In the early days of automobiles, an integral part of knowing how to drive a car was knowing how to tinker with the engine. Modern design and manufacturing now allow us to drive a car without knowing how it works. These days you might still tinker with the engine if you want to improve the performance. Think of surfacing as "tinkering with the engine" with both goals in mind — troubleshooting the inner workings, and getting it to do things it otherwise would not have been able to do.

If up until now you have worked exclusively in solids, the use of surfaces may be a bit of an eye opener for you. If you are already a surfacing veteran from another CAD software, you may be surprised at some of the underlying power of SolidWorks for this type of work.

The answer to the question, "what are surfaces?" is that surfaces serve as the infinitely thin boundary of faces that encloses a solid. A solid could not exist without something to separate the inside from the outside. In the same way that endpoints are the boundaries of a line or edge, and edges form the boundary around a surface, surfaces are the boundary around a solid. So, surfaces are derived from two aspects — infinitely thin boundaries and stand-alone faces.

Infinitely thin

Although surfaces exist in 3D space, they do not take up any volume. They are infinitely thin, mathematically-represented skins. Even when a surface is a closed loop, such as the face of a cylinder, the surface itself does not have any thickness. Surface models in themselves cannot have the property of volume; volume is a property that only solids have. A surface can only have the property of area.

With the exception of a shape such as a sphere, more than one surface is usually required to enclose a volume. A single surface is usually but not always created by a single feature, and each new feature creates a body.

CROSS-REF Working with bodies is an integral part of surface modeling. You can find information about the concept of bodies in Chapter 13

Stand-alone faces

Another way of thinking about surfaces is to think of them as stand-alone faces. When working with solid models, you are already familiar with the difference between the model and a face of the model. Surfaces can be thought of as a single face taken out of the context of the rest of the faces of the solid. Thinking of surfaces as stand-alone faces is probably conceptually better than thinking of surfaces as abstract infinitely thin boundaries, because it more closely reflects how practical surface features are used in real modeling.

When SolidWorks first added surfacing capabilities in SolidWorks 1997, the commands fell under the Reference Geometry header. In my view, this reflected how surfaces are used in real-world modeling. Surfaces are not an end to themselves, but are a means to create a finished solid model. Thinking of surfaces as reference geometry works well when combined with seeing them as stand-alone faces, because individual faces are of little use unless combined with other faces to make a complete solid model.

Surfacing: One Stop in the Evolution of CAD

Surfaces are one of the stops in the evolution of CAD. The practice of representing mechanical objects as lines on paper had been around for thousands of years, before the 2D process was replicated on a computer in the 1960s or thereabouts. From 2D computer representations, the state of the art moved to 3D wireframe, where sharp edges of objects were represented by lines in space. To represent the area between the edges of the wireframe, we started using surfaces. Wireframe models are sufficient to represent faces with curvature in only one direction but cannot fully describe more complex curvature. Representing this more complex curvature is really where the first necessity of 3D surface models came from.

Surface modeling represents the area between the wireframe edges in 3D space, giving even more information about a part that cannot be conveyed with a drawing in sand or on paper. One of the shortcomings of surface modeling, however, is that the model does not understand the inside from the outside, and does not guarantee that enough faces exist to fully represent an actual object. Taking this a step further created solid modeling, where the volume between the surfaces is represented. Solid modeling just turns out to be surface modeling with a lot of automated rules built into it, and so it makes sense to understand solids in terms of surfaces. The automation maintains the enclosed volume and the other solid aspects of the surface model.

Surfaces can be used in several different ways to achieve the end goal, which is usually to create a solid. One common method in which surfaces are used is to build a shape, face by face. Solid features build all of the faces needed to enclose a solid, all at the same time. However, this can be limiting sometimes because the shape that you need to build does not lend itself nicely to that method; adjacent faces may need to be created by using different feature types or techniques. In situations like this, surfaces are used to build a model one face at a time, and then knit the faces together into a single body.

CROSS-REF   Knitting is described in detail as a method for joining surface bodies in Chapter 11.

Another method for using surfaces is to deconstruct a solid into surfaces, then make changes to the surface body by removing, changing, adding, or replacing faces, and finally to knit the surface body back into a solid body.

A third method that is used frequently is to use surface bodies to alter the solid body directly. Solids may be cut with a surface, faces of the solid can be replaced with faces of a surface, or a surface can be used as an end condition for a solid using an Extrude Up To option. Modeling techniques that make use of both solid and surface geometry are often called *hybrid* modeling.

CROSS-REF **Hybrid modeling is described as combining solid and surface techniques in Chapter 10.**

An example of using a surface as reference geometry would be copying a face of a solid early on in the feature tree, so that the whole face can be reused later after cuts, bosses, or fillets may have broken it up. Figure 2.1 shows an example of using surface geometry as reference geometry.

FIGURE 2.1

Using a surface as reference geometry

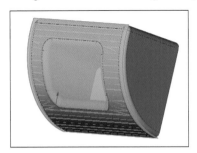

An example of using a surface as construction geometry would be to create a skirt surface around the parting line of a plastic part so that the faces of the part may be created with the appropriate draft on them. Figure 2.2 shows a ruled surface created as a skirt around a complex part, where it has been used as construction geometry.

CROSS-REF **The skirt technique is shown in Chapter 9.**

FIGURE 2.2

Using a surface as construction geometry

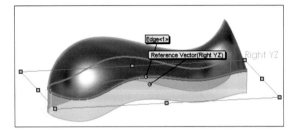

In the end, your goal is usually to end up with a solid model.

Choosing Solids or Surfaces

Surface modeling is clearly a lot more work than solid modeling. Surface modeling forces you to work face by face, and faces must be manually fit together. These actions are all performed automatically in solid modeling. Where surfacing techniques become beneficial is in situations where solid modeling becomes clumsy or inefficient, or when a given modeling task is simply impossible with solids.

Assessing strengths and weaknesses

When learning surface modeling, it can be difficult to tell the difference between situations where surfacing should be used and where it is simply overkill. Learning to differentiate the strengths and weaknesses of the two methods is important.

One of the strengths of solids is prismatic shapes. A series of prismatic shapes is shown in Figure 2.3. Any shape that can be created with an extrude or revolve operation typically offers a great opportunity for using a solid feature. Solid features usually (although not always) produce shapes with flat-capped ends. In some situations this is a strength, while in others it can be considered a weakness. In the realm of creating complex, curvy models, it is usually seen as undesirable.

FIGURE 2.3

Examples of prismatic shapes

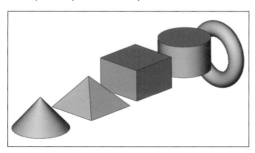

In the same way, the main strength of surfaces can also be described as its main weakness: Shapes and volumes can (or must, depending on your point of view) be created piece by piece. Although the "can" side of that statement offers additional capabilities by *allowing* you to build a model face by face and giving you ultimate control over the finished solid, the "must" side forces you into certain obligations, *requiring* you to work face by face, which can be a slow and tedious process. A common choice when working with surface model is control or speed.

How to choose

Sometimes, you don't have to choose; you can use both solids and surfaces. You can choose a workflow that works exclusively in solids *or* surfaces, completely transforming your model from one to the other, or you can work with solids *and* surfaces at the same time.

The use of both solids and surfaces is often called *hybrid* modeling. Most of the mainstream CAD modeling tools available today fit into this category, such as SolidWorks, Solid Edge, Pro/ENGI-NEER, Unigraphics NX, and Catia. There are few modelers that use exclusively solids *or* surfaces. Rhino is an example of a surface-only modeler. Alibre is an example of a solid-only modeler.

Many people have told me that looking at SolidWorks as a hybrid modeler rather than just a solid modeler, and coming to grips with what surfacing brings to the table, has changed the way they approach almost every modeling task. Several of the examples that you see in this book are not complex shapes at all, but certainly benefit from surfacing techniques. By that I mean that surface modeling can be used for more than just complex shapes, but also for certain types of features on simple prismatic geometry.

Still, for many tasks, you must choose one method or the other. One sign that you are using solids when you should be using surfaces is when you find yourself drawing extra sketch lines that don't actually create any geometry, or creating clumsy and awkward cuts to get rid of little bits of extra geometry. The sketch lines are still creating geometry, but it is geometry that is inefficiently swallowed up by other parts of the model.

Consider the model in Figure 2.4. The goal is to make a rectangular hole with a hemi-spherical bottom. This can be accomplished by using a combination of a cut-revolve and an extrude with the clumsy sketch as shown, or by simply cut-extruding to a hemi-spherical surface feature.

FIGURE 2.4

Extra sketch elements indicate a possible need for a surface technique

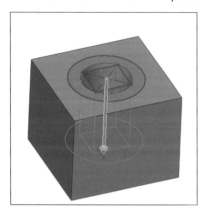

The reason that the extra sketch elements indicate the need for a different technique is that these extra lines actually create geometry. The way this works is that the shape is created as defined by the extrude feature *as a separate body*, and then that body is either joined to or subtracted from the main body, depending on the feature type. The processing time depends on the number of faces, the curvature of faces, and the types of features used to create the faces.

NOTE Much of this behind-the-scenes manipulation is taken care of by the Parasolid kernel, the geometry engine behind SolidWorks. The SolidWorks application turns out to be predominantly a user interface for the Parasolid kernel.

Another sign to indicate that you should be using surfaces is when you find yourself wanting a solid feature that could cut away part of the model created by another feature that ended awkwardly.

In the image of the coffee mug shown in Figure 2.5, notice that the handle breaks through to the inside of the mug when the handle is created. The use of surface features can avoid or repair this awkward geometry.

FIGURE 2.5

Surface functions can be used to avoid awkward modeling situations

Awkward geometry

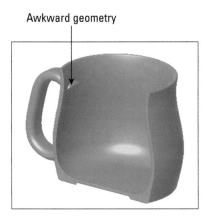

A more efficient way to deal with cutting off this little extra nub of material is either to use a Cut with Surface tool using a memory surface, or to use the Delete Face tool.

CROSS-REF The Cut with Surface and Delete Face tools are described in more detail in Chapters 10 and 12, respectively.

If you need to model a shape, and cannot identify a solid feature that enables you to create all of the faces at once, this may be another indication that you need some surface modeling.

It takes some practice, but after you have worked with a few techniques, you will begin to recognize models that you have already done where you could have benefited from surface techniques.

Surfacing is not just a set of esoteric functionality that is used by elitists who want to make things look more difficult than they really are. In some cases surfacing can actually save you a lot of work, and in other cases it simply makes something possible that otherwise would not be possible.

One of the little secrets about solids and surfaces is that geometrically, they are (or can be) identical. Also, when a solid model is translated into a neutral file format such as IGES, there is absolutely no difference between the solid model and a surface model. What it becomes when read by the second CAD system is completely up to that CAD system, as long as it follows the rules for solid models. Simply put, a solid model has certain requirements:

- The faces form a fully watertight boundary (no gaps or overlaps).
- It is composed of a single body.
- All of the face normals point the same direction (the *inside* is distinguished from the *outside*).

A face normal is a vector, or arrow, that points to one side of the face. Because faces can only have two sides, there are only two options for the direction of the arrow. For example, notice that if you use shaded planes in SolidWorks, one side of the plane is green and the other is red. Other than this, face and plane normals cannot be directly observed or manipulated in SolidWorks.

NOTE   The watertight condition is more technically referred to as *manifold*. A surface body that does not meet the watertight condition is referred to as *non-manifold*. In this book I use the watertight terminology because it is a more intuitively understandable term, and due to the ambiguity that may be associated with various meanings of the word manifold. A model can be exported from one software as a surface and imported into another as a solid, and vice versa, as long as it meets the requirements. The only real difference is in how the modeling software treats the data. That needs to be said once more for emphasis. The only real difference between a solid and a surface model is how the modeling software treats it. They are otherwise geometrically identical.

Even in the SolidWorks import options, shown in Figure 2.6, you find the option to import IGES models as solids, knit surfaces, or un-knit surfaces.

To you, the user, this means that a solid model is really just a surface model where the software is automating many of the otherwise manual surfacing tasks that you would need to go through, and automatically maintains the conditions that define the solid. Features that cannot maintain those conditions result in model errors. Sometimes the conditions aren't met due to the geometry-checking feature, allowing something to slip through the automated checking routines. This can in turn cause geometry errors that are unseen and yet may cause other features to fail.

FIGURE 2.6

SolidWorks import options enable you to choose between solids and surfaces.

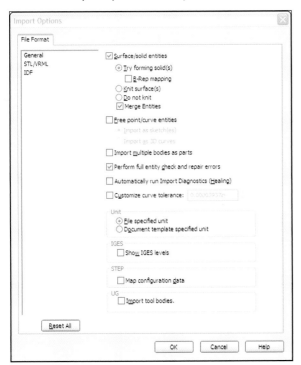

Surfacing Theory and Concepts

Surface geometry breaks into several general categories, but this book is mainly concerned with two of them. Two of those types are called *algebraic* (sometimes referred to as *analytical*) and NURBS surfaces.

Algebraic and NURBS surfaces

Algebraic surfaces are defined by fairly simple mathematical expressions. In SolidWorks, this translates into shapes that can be created using lines and arcs in operations such as extrude and revolve. Planar, cylindrical, spherical, conical, toroidal, and other types of surfaces are examples of this type of geometry. Algebraic surfaces are attractive because they are fast for the software to calculate, they offer exactly predictable and perfectly extensible geometry, and certain types have special properties. Planar faces can be selected to sketch on, or used in other ways like reference planes. Cylindrical faces produce a temporary axis, and can be used for concentric mates in assemblies.

On the other hand, algebraic surfaces are limited in the types of shapes they can create, and in particular are not very useful when you want to build complex shapes. In product design, algebraic shapes are often avoided, and are often described using words like boxy or harsh.

The other type of geometry is referred to as *NURBS surfaces*. NURBS stands for non-uniform rational b-spline. NURBS is a method of using math to interpolate curves and surfaces between control points. In SolidWorks and many other CAD programs, NURBS is used to create shapes that fall outside of the algebraic regime, which is to say general complex shapes.

U-V isoparameter curves

NURBS works by interpolating a surface between curves in two roughly perpendicular directions. These curves are called the *U-V isoparameters*, which are roughly similar to the longitude and latitude lines on a globe. The term *isoparameter* simply means that the curves in the U direction lie along a fixed parameter of the V direction. When all of these curves are displayed, it looks like a grid. Figure 2.7 shows a Fill surface preview that displays these curves on the surface being created.

FIGURE 2.7

U-V isoparameter curves shown in a Fill surface preview

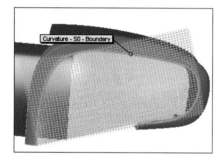

Curvature - S0 - Boundary

CROSS-REF The Fill surface is described in more detail in Chapter 6.

The U and the V stand for the two directions of the grid — where one direction is called U and the other is called V. Positions along the U and V directions are called the parameter of the curve, and range from 0 to 1. The curve shown in Figure 2.8 is on the .5 isoparameter of the V direction.

The U-V isoparameter curves for any face can be seen by using the Face Curves tool on the Sketch toolbar. Understanding the orientation of the U-V grid of the existing faces can be instrumental in fitting other surfaces to closely match the existing faces.

You don't need to know any of this in order to simply run the software, but knowledge of the inner workings can often help you troubleshoot features that are not working as you might expect.

FIGURE 2.8

Curve at the .5 isoparameter of the V direction

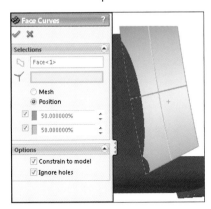

CROSS-REF **Transitions between surfaces are discussed in more detail in the chapters of Part 4, in particular Chapters 18 and 19. Face Curves are described in more detail in Chapters 4 and 14.**

The degenerate condition

One of the implications of creating surfaces from a grid of curves in perpendicular directions is that the resulting surfaces have the tendency to be four-sided. This is in fact a common limitation of NURBS that CAD designers and programmers struggle against. Because it is a NURBS limitation, it affects all CAD programs that use NURBS, not just SolidWorks.

In reality, though, surfaces come in all shapes, including shapes that are not four-sided. One option for creating non-four-sided surfaces is to use *trimmed* surfaces, which are discussed later in this chapter. Another way is to collapse all of the U-V lines on one side into a single point. When this happens, that side of the four-sided patch is said to be a zero-length side. Zero-length sides are called *degenerate*, or it may be said to contain a *singularity*. Fillet features commonly create geometry of this type, as shown in Figure 2.9, where you can see what happens to the U-V grid when faces of 3, 2, or even zero are created.

The problem with degenerate faces is the number zero. Mathematics and computers have difficulty with the number zero, and of course these surfaces are made using both. Degeneracies may cause features such as shells, fillets, offsets, scales, or moves to fail because the surrounding geometry cannot deal with the singularity. Sometimes in SolidWorks, you can identify degenerate faces visually, without showing the face mesh because there is an odd discoloration or shading at or near the singularity.

Recent versions of SolidWorks have become much better at handling degeneracies, but they still can cause problems.

FIGURE 2.9

Degenerate faces

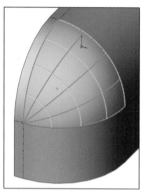 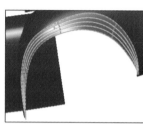 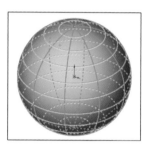

CROSS-REF An example of working past degeneracies is shown in Chapter 16, as a part of capping off a handle.

Trimmed surfaces

Surfaces want to be four-sided, but they are sometimes forced into other shapes. Surfaces that must be some other shape have one of two options: degenerate condition or trimmed surfaces. Trimmed surfaces are the preferable choice, because of the problems I have just outlined with degenerate surfaces.

Understanding the B-rep

Trimmed surfaces offer a lot of advantages. Essentially, trimmed surfaces are composed of two elements: the underlying surface and some definition of its boundary. This combination of surface and boundary is sometimes referred to as the boundary representation, or *b-rep*.

A working understanding of the b-rep is important for three reasons. First, when building surfaces, it is common practice to overbuild the surface (meaning to make it bigger than it needs to be), and then to trim it back to fit. This is a technique unique to working with surfaces that is not used with solid modeling. Many reasons exist for using this technique. A surface that is too small is difficult to work with, but a surface that is too large, once trimmed, is never a problem. Also, making a surface larger than it needs to be helps to prevent extra edges from showing up in the model. The one thing that gives SolidWorks surfacing users the most problems is building smooth transitions between faces and across edges. The best way to eliminate this difficulty is to eliminate the edges as much as possible.

One of the best ways to visualize trimmed surfaces in action is to observe the Fill surface. The Fill surface builds a four-sided patch, fits it into whatever shaped gap is to be filled, and then trims the surface to fit the gap. The situations in which this tool works are sometimes amazing. Figure 2.10

shows the Fill surface automatically overbuilding a surface that will be trimmed back when the feature is accepted.

The Fill surface overbuilds a four-sided patch and trims it to fit the gap.

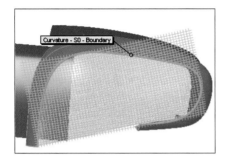

CROSS-REF Continuity of curvature across edges is treated in the last section of this chapter, and also in most of the chapters of Part 4. More information on the Fill surface is in Chapter 6 and interspersed throughout Part 4.

Imported geometry and Untrim

The second reason why a working understanding of the b-rep concept is important is something that turns out to be an unexpected benefit for many users, in particular, users who frequently deal with imported geometry. When geometry is written to an IGES file, for example, for each face of the model, the IGES file describes the underlying surface and its boundary. The implication here is that the underlying surface exists independently from its boundary. The boundary can be removed, and you can see just the underlying surface. What does this mean from a practical usage standpoint? It means that you can sometimes remove features from imported models by using surfacing tools in such a way that no edges remain on the model where the feature once stood. Figure 2.11 shows the before and after images of an imported surface model.

Before and after images of an imported surface after editing takes advantage of the underlying b-rep

A set of features in SolidWorks enables you to do this kind of work, where it almost seems as if you are getting some sort of history along with the imported model. These features are Untrim, Delete Face, and Delete Hole.

CROSS-REF The features Trim, Untrim, Delete Hole, and Delete Face are covered in depth in Chapters 10 and 11, and also throughout the chapters of Part 3. Working with imported geometry is covered in Chapters 11 and 22.

Extending faces

When you place a fillet on a part, and the end of the fillet causes a face to be extended, it is the b-rep that is being extended. Extending analytical faces is easy, because as I mentioned earlier, analytical faces can be extended indefinitely, but when the adjacent faces that need to be extended are complex, this can cause a problem. If the face to be extended started as a face that you overbuilt using a surface feature, the problem is automatically taken care of.

Mesh and subdivision surfaces

Another type of geometry creation and display method is known as *mesh* or *subdivision surfaces*. This type of data is used extensively by 3D graphic artists in animations, games, and other forms of 3D graphic arts. The advantage of this type of surfacing is that it is not really surfacing at all; it is simply a collection of 3D points, and so it is much faster for the computer to calculate than also calculate the surface area between all of the points. It is also much faster to display this kind of data because mesh data is the same type of data used by computer graphics cards to display even the highly accurate NURBS surfaces. The display uses facets created by groups of three or four adjacent points. The meshes of points are made to look like surfaces because they are so close together, but if you were to zoom in to the mesh, you would see that it is made of a collection of flat triangular or rectangular faces. The display of subdivision surfaces can be refined when necessary by interpolating or approximating additional mesh points. This makes subdivision modeling efficient for many types of uses within the 3D graphic arts genre. Rarely do you see graphic artists going to all of the bother to use parametric CAD tools to create content. It is simply overkill, and too difficult to get the organic-type shapes and fluid motion of those shapes in animation.

Figure 2.12 shows the same mesh data in three formats: point cloud, mesh, and surfaced.

This technique works well for animations and games where there is a lot of motion and the calculations need to be fast, and where detail and accuracy can be sacrificed. But in CAD applications, the surfaces need to be mathematically correct, and so the faceted approximations do not work.

Point cloud, mesh, and surfaced model

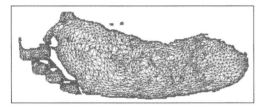

Figure 2.13 shows the detail of a faceted (tessellated) mesh model.

Detail of a mesh model

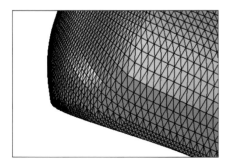

The mesh model is what you get when you use the STL or WRL file formats. The STL format is a stereolithography format, used to transmit data to rapid prototyping machines. It is also used by scanning equipment to transmit point cloud data from a 3D digitizer.

CROSS-REF Chapter 21 deals with working with digitized data, which revisits mesh or point cloud data. Rapid prototyping is discussed in Chapter 23.

The WRL format is known as the Virtual Reality Markup Language format, and has been used in a lot of game character and environment development. Both of these formats are terrible to work with in SolidWorks, unless you have the ScanTo3D software, which is a part of SolidWorks Office Premium mainly intended to assist in working with scanned data from a 3D digitizer.

CROSS-REF ScanTo3D and working with tessellated models and point cloud data are discussed in more detail in Chapter 21.

Converting mesh data types

Mesh data does not convert easily into NURBS data. This is a continuing source of frustration for users trying to share data between SolidWorks and 3ds Max or Maya. Again, this is something ScanTo3D can help with, as can RapidForm or Geomagic's Raindrop software. These are not push-button solutions, but they may prevent you from needing to rebuild a model.

Displaying surface data

Another aspect of tessellated meshes is that the technique is always used for display of even highly accurate NURBS models on the computer monitor. Regardless of how accurate the math for the surface is, the display is represented by very small flat triangles. Models made of entirely flat faces do not require much subdivision of the faces in order to be represented by triangles. The more highly curved a surface is, the smaller the size of the triangles and the greater the number of the triangles has to be to approximate the display to a given accuracy.

One easy way to see the effects of this method of displaying curved data is to turn down the Image Quality display settings found at Tools ➪ Options ➪ Image Quality. Move the slider to the left, then exit the dialog box and zoom in to a curved face on the model. Circular edges can be displayed to look hexagonal. Additional accuracy in the display comes at the expense of computer power, which can translate into sluggish performance while rotating the model. Figure 2.14 demonstrates the difference that the resolution of the display tessellation can have on the appearance of a curvy model in SolidWorks.

Mesh models are used by 3D graphic artists because it gives a more direct access to the actual display format. This means that display calculations happen much faster for applications that use mesh data such as games, animated movies, and animated 3D graphics. With CAD data, there is a translation that needs to happen between the highly accurate NURBS model and the display mesh.

Interestingly, mesh models, in the form of STL format files, are often used for low-resolution manufacturing of several varieties of rapid prototyping processes. This is not the kind of data you would grind precision gears from, but it is very useful for cheap physical prototypes with an accuracy of, for example, 0.01 inch rather than the 0.000001 inch of the NURBS model.

FIGURE 2.14

FIGURE 2.14

Effect of Display Quality settings on visible model tessellation

Understanding Curvature Continuity

The one quality that can make the difference between a very nice model and an unacceptable one is the question of curvature continuity of surfaces across edges. In SolidWorks it is simply not possible in most situations to create a complex model without any edges, or breaks between faces. Your eye can pick up imperfections in reflective surfaces very easily, like a crack in a mirror or a dent in a car door can cause a distinct break in the reflection. Bad transitions can be seen easily on a CAD model, and can translate into edges or reflective breaks on molded parts.

It is primarily at the edges that we are concerned about curvature continuing smoothly from the face on one side of an edge to the face on the other side. Figure 2.15 contrasts a model with good continuity across edges against a model with poor continuity.

FIGURE 2.15

Comparing good and bad curvature continuity across edges

 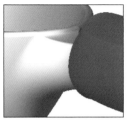

What causes edges?

Understanding what causes edges on a model is a good place to start the discussion on continuity. Edges separate faces created by different math. For example, the math behind a planar face is different than the math behind a cylindrical face, and so every time you see a planar face next to a cylindrical face, there is an edge between them. Even the math between planar faces at different angles causes an edge, and cylindrical faces of different radii, even if they are tangent, are separated by an edge.

Notice that some types of faces merge together. For example, a planar face created by an extrude, and a planar face created as the end of a revolve merge together into a single face with no edge between them, as shown in Figure 2.16.

The co-planar faces of an extrude and a revolve merge to form a single face.

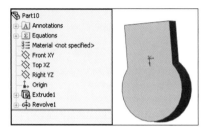

> **NOTE** This face merging behavior has not always been the case in SolidWorks. In early versions, faces such as those shown in Figure 2.16 would produce an edge between them. I mention this to call attention to the fact that SolidWorks is often improving features that are not immediately obvious, but which have a very positive effect on the overall software.

Armed with information about why faces merge or don't merge into single faces in SolidWorks, let's look at a slightly more complex case. Figure 2.17 shows two sweeps that appear identical. They are both created with a profile that is an oval, with two straight lines and two arcs. The difference between them is that the path for one of the sweeps is a series of lines and arcs, while for the other, a spline has been fitted over the lines and arcs, and the spline is used as the path.

FIGURE 2.17

Comparing sweeps

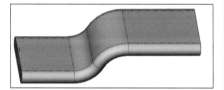 

Notice that the sweep along the spline is not divided up by edges in the same way that the sweep along the lines and arcs is. This is because a spline is a single piece of geometry, and thus the sweep is created from a single piece of math. Lines and arcs are each individual pieces of geometry, and so the sweep is segmented accordingly.

The first thing you need to take from this is that lines and arcs are going to chop up the faces of your models. Splines make them smooth. Sometimes edges between faces are appropriate, but when smoothness is required, you want to create as few edges as possible.

Types of curvature transitions

Transitions between surfaces and curves can be identified by one of three conditions in SolidWorks, and in fact in other CAD software as well.

- **Contact:** The surfaces simply intersect at the edge without being tangent.
- **Tangent:** The surfaces are tangent at the edge, but do not share the same radius at the edge.
- **Curvature Continuous:** The surfaces are tangent at the edge, and have the same radius of curvature at the edge.

Curvature is defined as the inverse of radius, and so $c = 1/r$. The larger the radius, the smaller the curvature. Infinite curvature is zero radius is a sharp corner, and infinite radius is zero curvature is a straight line.

I have already described one of the differences between lines/arcs and splines. In the area of curvature, this difference becomes more important and more pronounced. An arc by definition has a single, constant radius. A spline typically has a constantly changing curvature. This is best demonstrated using the tool in SolidWorks called *curvature comb*. The curvature comb graphs the curvature of the sketch element. Figure 2.18 shows that the curvature comb for an arc or circle is a constant height. For a spline, the curvature comb varies in height. Notice at the end that the curvature comb reduces to nothing, which means that at the end, the spline is curvature continuous to a straight line.

FIGURE 2.18

Curvature combs on an arc and a spline

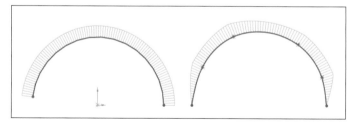

Learning to interpret the significance of curvature combs may take a little practice, but if you are going to do much development of complex shapes in SolidWorks, it is a skill you need to possess.

Algebraic versus interpolated geometry

Many beginning users ask if it is possible to model complex shapes, but just with lines and arcs, because they are simpler and can be dimensioned more easily. The answer is no, lines and arcs give you a 1983 K-car. What you want to create is a flowing sexy shape, like the Shelby Cobra. Figure 2.19 makes this appeal visually.

FIGURE 2.19

Lines and arcs or splines?

I do not mean to say here that you can *never* use lines and arcs in a complex model, but complex faces are made smooth by interpolated geometry — splines and complex surfaces.

CROSS-REF **Splines are specifically covered in Chapter 3, and also throughout the chapters of Part 4.**

Interpolation, as it relates to splines, means that you specify the spline by placing points, and SolidWorks calculates the curve between the points by interpolating according to appropriate

NURBS math. In the same way that splines are interpolated between points, surfaces are interpolated between splines. This is to say that splines and complex surfaces react the same way to their respective controls. Figure 2.20 shows that a spline going through points is shaped exactly the same as a lofted surface going through lines at every spline point.

FIGURE 2.20

Similarities between 2D and 3D interpolated geometry

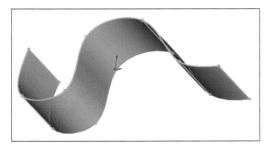

This concept comes in handy when adjusting the shape of interpolated features, and when trying to understand how lofted surfaces will react to moving a profile sketch.

Summary

Surface modeling is a study in building model faces individually. These stand-alone faces may be used together with other faces, in combination with a solid model, or as reference or construction geometry to assist in modeling the rest of the part. Surface modeling is usually not an end in itself, but a stepping-stone to a solid model, which is simply a single surface body that is watertight and follows special rules.

Complex shapes are best achieved when transitions between surfaces across edges maintain a smoothly continuous change in curvature. The smoothest shapes are produced by interpolated geometry, meaning splines and surface features such as Loft, Fill, Boundary, and others.

Part II

Understanding the Tools

Chapter 3

Sketching with Splines

plines are sketch entities that offer almost infinite possibilities to create shapes. They can imitate other sketch entities and at the same time give incredible flexibility with curvature, as well as curvature matching of other entities. Splines can match edges or complex curves either in 2D or in 3D. You can drive splines dimensionally by using better-behaved lines and arcs as reference geometry. When you are working with complex shapes, you must also work with splines.

A little history of the word "spline" may help you understand part of what it is all about. Dictionary.com defines spline as "a long, narrow, thin strip of wood, metal, etc.; slat." The origin of this word comes from the eighteenth-century shipbuilding trade. Think of the slats of wood used to create the outer skin of a wooden ship. Think of the way that these slats had to bend, and yet were held firmly in place at points, being nailed to the frame. (The word "loft" also comes from the shipbuilding trade, and is closely related to splines).

A second definition of spline from Dictionary.com is as follows: "a long, flexible strip of wood or the like, used in drawing curves." When designers drafted with a pencil, flexible lengths of wood or metal could be pinned down in various locations, and the shape occurring naturally due to the bending of the material would be traced by pencil. Again, the natural bending of a material pinned at points created natural-looking, smooth shapes used for both engineering and aesthetic applications. In this way, the mathematics of bending has influenced what we think of as desirable, natural shapes.

33

Why Splines?

Ultimately, splines are all about curvature. They are the only sketch entity that can bend in almost limitless ways, with constantly changing curvature. When you look at a sheet-metal enclosure of a machine and compare it to the sheet metal on the body of a stylish automobile, this is how you characterize the difference between lines/arcs and splines.

Splines are driven by math that naturally smoothes curvature by interpolating the shape between spline points. Often when modeling shapes, you depend more on the interpolation than on placing spline points precisely where you need them. You may be tempted to create splines with densely packed control points to get the most control over the shape, but you will eventually come to the same conclusion through experience; use fewer control points and let the spline do the smoothing for you.

Many users who are new to complex shape creation in SolidWorks assume that they can continue working with familiar and easy-to-use line-and-arc sketch geometry. Lines and arcs are fine for certain purposes, but the more you get into shape creation, the more you understand the role that splines play in making attractive curvature that blends smoothly between shapes.

Of course, different types of complex shapes have different requirements. If you are creating mainly aesthetic shapes for consumer products, precisely-shaped splines are probably not a big priority. However, for airfoil shapes in compressor turbines or aircraft, or for certain medical applications such as replicating bones or teeth, the shapes are both complex and precise. You have the opportunity to work with both aesthetic and technically complex-shaped models during the course of this book, although the bulk of the information concerns aesthetic-type surfaces.

Types of splines

Splines are all the same in their underlying mathematics and how you work with them, but some of them come into being or are controlled through different methods.

2D and 3D

You can draw splines in both 2D and 3D. 3D splines are very powerful, but can also be very difficult to control.

CROSS-REF   3D splines and other 3D sketch topics are covered in detail in Chapter 4.

User-drawn splines

Aren't all splines user-drawn? Who else would draw a spline? SolidWorks can sometimes create splines automatically, and the user can even create splines unintentionally. User-drawn splines are simply splines drawn by the user.

Converted splines

Some splines are created through the Convert Entities sketch command. If you select an edge and that edge does not project into the 2D sketch plane as one of several pre-defined types, SolidWorks automatically converts it into a spline. The pre-defined types are straight line, circular arc, ellipse, and parabola. SolidWorks handles general curves as splines.

Face curves

Face curves are the U-V curves for a given face. The Face Curves tool is in the Sketch Tools, and it creates a series of 3D sketches, each containing a single 3D spline.

CROSS-REF Face curves are covered in more detail in Chapter 14.

Auto Trace

Auto Trace is an add-in provided with SolidWorks starting in 2008, which traces over sketch pictures. It may create any sketch entity, including lines, arcs and splines. As of this writing, SolidWorks 2008 is at service pack 2.0, and the Auto Trace tool is still clearly in its infancy; I would not depend on it to create sketch geometry that you can work with,

CROSS-REF You can find more information about Auto Trace and Sketch Pictures in various tutorials of Part 4. Auto Trace is new to SolidWorks 2008, but you can find information about Sketch Pictures in the current edition of the *SolidWorks Bible*.

Intersection curves

Intersection curves do not always create splines; they can create any type of sketch entity. However, the point of using an intersection curve is frequently to find a complex intersection that is not simply defined, which usually indicates a spline. You can create intersection curves in 2D or 3D sketches. In a 2D sketch, SolidWorks creates the curve at the intersection of the current sketch plane and the selected faces. In a 3D sketch, SolidWorks creates the curve at the intersection of selected faces, bodies, surfaces, or planes (only one of the selected entities may be a plane).

Fit spline

The Fit spline is a spline which fits over a number of selected entities within a user-specified tolerance. A spline cannot fit some things exactly — for example, a sharp corner created by two lines intersecting at an angle — and so the spline fits by rounding off the corner. The elements that drive the fit spline do not necessarily have to touch one another end to end, but the spline can act as a bridge between them.

When you make a fit spline from several sketch elements, the user has the option to turn the original elements into construction geometry. This can be very useful if dimensions drive the original sketch; it gives you the ability to drive a spline using dimensions.

CROSS-REF Various tutorials of Part 4 demonstrate several advantages of fit splines.

Anatomy of a Spline

Splines in SolidWorks have many different controls for shape creation and also for evaluation or visualization of curvature characteristics. Getting a handle on the terminology for the different parts of the anatomy of the spline is essential to getting the most out of this book. You may not see all of the elements of a spline when you first create one. This is because the default installation settings of SolidWorks do not have all of the elements turned on. This is a good thing, because when you turn everything on, it becomes a cacophonous mess. More typically, you will use various elements independently at different times, and then turn them off so that they do not become too distracting.

Figure 3.1 shows the default display of basic elements for all splines. All splines have either one or two endpoints. Closed-loop splines have a single endpoint, and open-loop splines have two. Two types of splines do not have interior control points: two-point splines (consisting only of endpoints) and splines created automatically by some process such as Convert Entities, Face Curves, Intersection Curves, or Offset Sketch.

FIGURE 3.1

Identifying spline elements shown by default

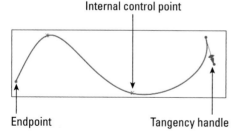

Use the spline control points to directly manipulate the shape of the spline. You can use dimensions and sketch relations to control the points.

Tangency Handle

The next level of spline controls is the Tangency Handle control. Handles are actually multiple controls all in one. You can find handles at endpoints and internal control points. Handles are essentially the tangency vector of spline points. Handles control the direction and weighting (weighting is sometimes also referred to as magnitude) of the tangency. You can dimension both the angle and the weighting of the handle. The diamond shape on the arrow leader is the control for the direction only. The arrow head at the end of the leader controls weighting only. The dot at the very end of the arrow controls both direction and weight simultaneously. SolidWorks displays handles if the spline is selected, if you have applied a tangent or equal curvature relation to the ends of a spline, or if you have edited the handle to change the default tangency direction or weighting.

When you select a spline, all of the handles appear, whether they are active or passive. (Passive handles are simply handles which do not have user-assigned values, and still maintain their default settings.) Active spline handles appear blue or black, depending on whether they are under- or fully defined. Passive spline handles appear gray when you select the spline itself or a control point. Selecting a spline control point or endpoint enables you to see only the handle for that point. Figure 3.2 shows a spline with handles in various states.

FIGURE 3.2

Spline handles shown in fully defined, under defined, and passive states

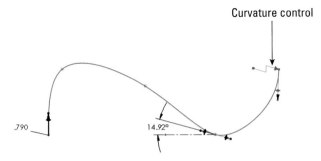

NOTE Some users prefer to use handles to control the shape of splines; they usually use fewer internal control points as a result.

CROSS-REF The next section, Controlling Splines, describes in detail the ways in which you can use spline handles to control the shape of splines.

The arrow that looks like a foreshortened radius leader in Figure 3.2 is called a Curvature Control, and is usually created by the Equal Curvature sketch relation. The Equal Curvature sketch relation matches the tangencies, the radius at the end of the spline, and the concavity (which side of the spline the center of curvature is on).

You can also add curvature and tangency handles separately at any location along the spline, and so these controls are not limited to end and control points.

You can control whether or not you can access spline handles through the System Options, on the Sketch page, by using the Enable Spline Tangency and Curvature Handles setting. Turning this setting on does not automatically show all handles; it simply enables them. Turning it off completely disables the use of spline handles, even when sketch relations exist to the spline. I do not recommend turning this setting off.

An additional viewing option is available through the right mouse button (RMB) menu, called Show Spline Handles. This option is on by default, and displays any active handles. When it is off, handles are only visible when you select the spline or points.

Control Polygon

The next element of the spline anatomy is the Control Polygon. The name may seem misleading, because it only actually forms a polygon when the spline is a closed loop. Activate the Control Polygon from the spline RMB menu or through the Sketch page of System Options using the Show Spline Control Polygon By Default setting. Figure 3.3 shows Control Polygons.

Dragging the nodes of the Control Polygon adjusts the shape of the spline, and may also move any internal spline points. Some users find this sort of spline editing — moving points which are not directly connected to the spline — to be somewhat awkward, but this is a commonly used technique, both in SolidWorks and in other software tools that use splines. I have heard many people claim that the smoothest splines are controlled using the Control Polygon rather than other options. You should try all the available methods and decide for yourself which ones to use.

FIGURE 3.3

Spline Control Polygons

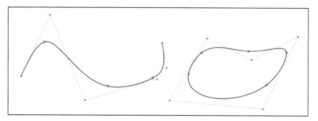

Spline evaluation tools

Several tools are available to help you evaluate splines in SolidWorks. Specifically, the tools I am referring to here are the Curvature Comb, Inflection Points, and Minimum Radius. These tools are all available from the RMB menu.

TIP   You could easily customize the Sketch Shortcut Bar (in SolidWorks 2008) to contain some of these tools if you find you use them frequently, although this does not save any mouse-clicks as compared to simply using the RMB menu. Fortunately, these tools are available to make hotkeys, and so it would be useful to have a hotkey that toggles curvature combs for selected splines.

For more information on setting up hotkeys please refer to Chapter 2 of the *SolidWorks 2007 Bible*.

Curvature Comb

The Curvature Comb is an essential tool in evaluating your splines. The Curvature Comb is essentially a graph of the curvature of the spline, where SolidWorks plots the curvature value along the length of the spline itself. The Curvature Comb is also valid for 3D splines, arcs, circles, parabolas, and ellipses. Several options govern the appearance of Curvature Combs.

You can activate the Curvature Comb for a selected spline from the Show Curvature selection in the Options panel of the Spline PropertyManager, from the spline RMB menu, or by using a custom user-defined hotkey.

Immediately upon activating the Curvature Comb, the Curvature Scale PropertyManager appears, which enables you to control the height and density of the comb.

TIP The Curvature Scale PropertyManager window cannot be accessed for an existing comb; it can only be accessed when the comb is turned on. To adjust an existing comb, you just turn it off and then back on.

Figure 3.4 shows a Curvature Comb, its PropertyManager, Inflection Points, and a Minimum Radius indicator.

FIGURE 3.4

A Curvature Comb, the Curvature Comb PropertyManager, Inflection Points, and a Minimum Radius indicator

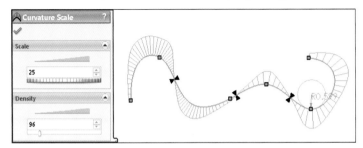

NOTE As shown in Figure 3.4, the spline is displayed with its bounding curve. Bounding curve display is off in a default installation. To turn on the display of the bounding curve, go to Tools ⇨ Options ⇨ Sketch ⇨ Show Curvature Comb Bounding Curve.

Also note that the default colors are different in the image to help ensure visibility. The Web site for this book contains a SolidWorks Options file that enables you to use the same settings that I used to create the screen shots for this book.

You can use Curvature Combs to detect wobbles in splines that are more difficult to detect with your eye. Usually the goal is to get the cap of the comb to be as smooth as possible. Because the Curvature Comb is charting curvature of the spline, and curvature is the inverse of radius (c = 1/r), the tighter the curve, the larger the comb. This also means that if the comb is at a constant height, the curve is a constant radius, like a circular arc. If the comb is flattening out and ramping down to touch the spline at the endpoint, it is tangent to a straight line (zero curvature is a straight line).

Inflection Point indicator

If the comb crosses the spline itself, it means that the curvature has changed direction. This is known as an inflection point, where concavity changes from one side of the spline to the other. The Inflection Point indicators display a small, bow tie-like symbol indicating curvature inflections. Inflection points on a spline are at times undesirable. For example, you do not want to have a surface which is nearly flat waffling back and forth between barely concave and barely convex. It is a good idea to use this tool to check all splines that approach flat.

Minimum Radius indicator

Minimum Radius indicators are another important evaluation tool. When you run into difficulties offsetting, shelling, or filleting a part, you can sometimes trace the problem to a small radius in some spot on the model. Using the Minimum Radius indicator can help you check for this in real time as you edit a spline used to create a particular face. You can only show a single indicator on any given spline, but you can use a Curvature Control to precisely specify the radius value in a particular spot along a spline. The next section of this chapter, Controlling Splines, demonstrates the use of Curvature Controls.

Spline PropertyManager

Although the Spline PropertyManager is not an actual part of the displayed spline, it does contain several of the settings, options, and controls for the spline, and becomes an integral part of interacting with the spline. Figure 3.5 shows the Spline PropertyManager. The next section shows the functions of all of the available options.

FIGURE 3.5

Spline PropertyManager

Controlling Splines

An almost dizzying array of controls, tools, and indicators come with splines. You need to be intimately familiar with a few of them and at least be aware of the existence of the rest. Sometimes problems can arise with splines. You can easily deal with these problems if you only know which option to change in your particular situation. The more you use splines, the more familiar the tools become, and the more adept you become with the entire process.

Drawing splines

You may have heard the old saying that you "draw once, edit ten times." Nowhere is this truer than when dealing with splines in the context of complex shapes. In fact, many SolidWorks users who model with splines get into the habit of first simply creating a spline with the desired number of control points using a random shape, and then dragging each point to its destination.

Click-click or click-drag?

Like other sketch entities, you can use one of two methods to draw a spline from scratch: click-click and click-drag. I personally find the click-click method to be the easiest; you click and release the mouse button for each control point. Where people often get into trouble is when they start going too fast, and use a click-drag where they meant to click-click. In particular, the biggest trouble comes when you start a spline by click-dragging and then switch to click-clicking. This typically causes breaks between splines when you intend to create a single spline.

To avoid this problem, I recommend that you settle the mouse before starting the spline. You can create the internal points of the spline while the mouse is moving, but for effective click-click spline drawing, you should start with the mouse stationary if you can. Practice drawing a few splines of random shape to become familiar with the technique. Whichever method you select is fine; the main thing is that you are comfortable with the method you select.

Ending a spline

To end the spline, again, there are several techniques that work. The one I like best is double-clicking. This creates the endpoint where the cursor is, and quits the spline. Finishing a spline on the first point also terminates the command, and creates a closed-loop spline.

You can also press Esc to quit the command, but the endpoint will be the last point you put down, not where your cursor is when you press Esc. The same thing applies for the techniques of clicking Select from the RMB menu or clicking the Spline toolbar button to toggle it off.

Users who are new to splines are sometimes unsettled by the way they change shape as you create additional points.

Draw a J

In the beginning of this chapter, I made the case for treating splines as if they were flexible slats of wood or metal. It might take some imagination to think of your cursor as flexing a physical piece of material and elongating it at the same time, but see if that visualization helps you when drawing and adjusting a spline to make a letter J. Make the J using only three spline points: the two endpoints and one interior control point.

Figure 3.6 shows a spline in progress, with two points already placed, and the third point in the act of being placed. Notice that as the third point is moved back and forth, the curve between the first and second points "teeter-totters" a little bit, with the second point as the pivot of the teeter-totter. This is behaving exactly the way a bit of flexible wire would behave if pinned at one end and the middle, and moved at the other end (except that the spline has no fixed length).

FIGURE 3.6

Drawing a letter J with the correct curvature

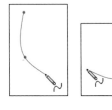

Notice this area is affected
by the position of the
point on the other
side of the internal point

Notice something else about the J. The interior point of the spline is closer to the end of the spline with the tighter curvature in it. The following tip illustrates one of the principles I try to follow when sketching a spline.

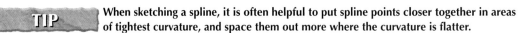

TIP   **When sketching a spline, it is often helpful to put spline points closer together in areas of tightest curvature, and space them out more where the curvature is flatter.**

If you draw another J and this time use five spline points, you will notice that this rule of thumb is often useful. It is not, however, the only or even the best way to create a shape like this.

Controlling end tangency

Instead of using more spline points, it is possible to create this J with *fewer* points. Fewer than three can only mean two. But a two-point spline creates a straight line. This is where using the handles to control the end tangency direction and weighting comes in.

After double-clicking to create the spline endpoint, SolidWorks shows the spline as selected, and the handles are still showing. Even though the Spline tool is still active, you can use the cursor to drag the diamond-shaped direction arrows on the handles. Try this, dragging both direction handles so that they point down. You may also try to adjust the weighting arrow-head control, especially for the uppermost handle. Following the analogy of the spline as a flexible metal slat, you can think of the tangency weighting handle as altering the local stiffness of the material, so that it more closely follows the tangency direction, bending either more or less, depending on whether you lengthen or shorten the arrow.

Figure 3.7 shows the result of manipulating the tangency direction handles of a two-point spline.

The quality of a curve is sometimes difficult to judge visually, because it is a somewhat subjective measure, and especially if you have a background in engineering rather than graphic arts. One tool that can help you in this regard is the Curvature Comb. Apply the Curvature Comb to your J either from the RMB menu or from the Spline PropertyManager. In the RMB menu, it is called Show Curvature Comb, while in the PropertyManager it is simply Show Curvature.

The goal for the comb on a shape like this is that the height of the comb changes smoothly, without lumps, dips, or sudden changes in height. One of the reasons for using a two-point spline and only controlling the curvature with the spline handles is that it naturally creates a very smooth and flowing shape, unless the weighting handles start interfering with one another. When you start introducing additional internal control points, these can easily break up the continuity or smoothness of the curve.

FIGURE 3.7
_____

Manipulating tangency direction handles of a two-point spline with a Curvature Comb

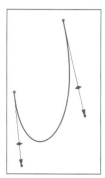

BEST PRACTICE When working with splines, many users consider it to be best practice to use the minimum number of internal spline points and the spline handles particularly at the endpoints to help control the shape. There is no general rule to define this; as with most things you will find when modeling complex shapes, it is open to interpretation.

You can also control end tangency by using sketch relations. Two relations that can do this for you are tangent and equal curvature. If you apply an equal curvature relation, it also automatically applies a tangent relation.

The use of the tangent relation should be obvious, but the equal curvature may not be. Because a spline can have any radius, and that radius changes along the length of the spline, it makes sense that you might want to transition smoothly from an existing edge or another sketch entity to the spline. The equal curvature relation ensures tangency, equal radius, and matching convexity (center of curvature of both elements is on the same side).

When the tangent relation is used, the tangency direction handle is constrained. When the equal curvature relation is used, SolidWorks displays the Curvature Control symbol identified earlier in this chapter on the spline.

> **TIP** You may occasionally encounter a situation in which, when you assign a tangent sketch relation, the spline is 180 degrees from the desired tangency direction (it is anti-tangent). In situations like this, aside from deleting the relation, repositioning, and trying again, there is only one (well-hidden) way to get around the problem. Select the spline with the incorrect tangent sketch relation, right-click the tangent relation in the Existing Relations box at the top of the Spline PropertyManager, and select Flip Relation.

Smooth corners

You are not always required to make only smoothly flowing shapes. Sometimes you may be required to make graceful corners which are neither sharp nor filleted in the normal sense of fillets. Smooth corners are simply small areas of the spline which have a much tighter curvature than the rest of the spline. If you go back to the J example, it is possible to create a J where the hook has a bit of a squared-off look, rather than the smoothly swooping look previously created.

Figure 3.8 shows a somewhat stylized J with corners of this sort. Notice that the corners use groups of three internal spline points placed closely together. This takes a little practice, and a little adjustment, but it is both useful and effective when a single spline needs to make a bit of a corner.

FIGURE 3.8

Creating a stylized J with tighter but still smooth corners

> **BEST PRACTICE** If a spline has areas of vastly different curvature, you may find that the best results come when the spline points are concentrated in the areas of the tightest curvature, and sparser in the flatter areas.

NOTE Corners of this sort are not always possible with a single sketch. Often, you must create corners using multiple features. Still, this is a useful spline sketching technique that you should master.

Adding internal spline points

You cannot always get away with making two-point splines. In fact, most of the time you will not be able to use two-point splines. Often, you will misjudge the number of internal spline points that you need to achieve a given shape. Fortunately, it is easy to edit the number of internal spline points.

To add internal spline points, select Insert Spline Point from the RMB menu for the spline. This allows you to put down multiple points. If the cursor displays the red circle with a line through it, this means that you cannot place a point where the cursor is currently located, probably because it would fall off of the spline or onto another point. You can even use this tool to place points on multiple splines — you do not have to restart the Insert Spline Point tool to put points on a spline other than the one that you initiated the command from.

I have discussed two-point splines and am now discussing adding points to splines, as well as cases in which adding points does not work. It therefore seems inevitable that the situation will arise where you are trying to add points to a two-point spline. While the difference between adding points to a general spline and adding points to a two-point spline seems trivial, it is not.

In the situation where a two-point spline has equal curvature relation on *both ends* of the spline, SolidWorks automatically *raises the degree* of the spline. SolidWorks does not do this with other types of splines under any other situation. Raising the degree of the spline is a mathematical operation that happens behind the scenes; it enables a smoother transition between entities (a good thing), but it disallows additional spline points to be added (a not-so-good thing).

So, if you are trying to add a spline point to a two-point spline with curvature controls on both ends, but the software is preventing you from doing this, use the Spline PropertyManager to select Standard rather than Raised Degree in the Options panel. Once the spline is set to Standard, you can add spline points again. This option is not available under any other circumstances. Changing from Raised Degree to Standard does change the shape of the spline somewhat, so be careful to check the rest of your sketch geometry when toggling between the options.

CAUTION Two-point splines with equal curvature relations on both ends are set to Raised Degree by default, and with this setting set, you cannot add spline points. To turn this option off, select the spline and select Standard from the Options panel of the Spline PropertyManager window.

Removing points, trimming and extending splines

Removing spline points is easy. Just select the spline point and press Delete on the keyboard. That method works unless you are trying to shorten a spline by deleting the endpoint. SolidWorks does not allow you to delete endpoints of sketch entities. One workaround is to delete the next-to-last control point and move the endpoint back to where the control point was. Another way to do this — if you are concerned about accuracy of moving back the endpoint — is to draw a construction line where you want the spline to end, and use the Trim function to cut off the end of the spline. You could also use the Split Entities point to break the spline where you want the new endpoint.

Another thing you need to know about trimming splines is that at the trim point, SolidWorks adds a tangency handle and assigns it values to maintain the shape of the original spline in that area. It also assigns a Coincident relation between the new endpoint of the spline and the trimming entity. The implication of this which catches some users off guard is that the newly created endpoint does not work like the endpoint of an untrimmed spline. Because the end tangency handle is active (has a set value), the handle maintains the direction value, regardless of how you move it. When moving an endpoint with a passive handle (no value set), the handle automatically changes in direction and weighting as you move it.

You run into the same problem for extending a spline. You cannot re-enter spline creation mode, when additional points simply extend the spline. SolidWorks provides two ways to lengthen a spline. One way is to simply drag the end of the spline farther, and then add internal points if necessary. Another approach that works in some but not all cases is to use the Extend sketch tool. Splines are unpredictable when it comes to extending them. It is easy to *interpolate* between existing points, but *extrapolating* means that the software has to try to guess where you would have taken the spline if you had done it. There is some algorithm involved which extrapolates the curve based on the existing curve, but this usually is good up to a certain point, at which point the spline may turn in an unpredictable direction.

> **TIP**   Using the Extend sketch tool on splines is usually only useful over short distances. Beyond that, it may become unpredictable.

Closed-loop splines

You can create closed-loop splines by ending a newly created spline at the first spline point. When editing an existing open-loop spline, you can close it by dragging one endpoint onto the other.

It is not as easy to make an open loop from a closed loop, however. I typically use one of two methods when I need to do this. One method is to draw a line and trim. The second method uses Split Entities points. Splines react a little differently to Split Entities points than other types of sketch entities do. If you place a single Split Entities point on a spline, the software ignores it unless you also place a second Split Entities point. When you place the second point, the first and second points become endpoints, and the software splits the spline into two splines. SolidWorks automatically converts the original endpoint to just another internal spline point.

This is a completely counterintuitive sequence of events, but it is the way it works. Fortunately, you will not encounter it often.

> **CROSS-REF**   Split Entities points are dealt with in detail in the current edition of the *SolidWorks Bible*.

Tangency handles on internal spline points

Tangency handles exist on all spline points — endpoints as well as internal control points. You can also use the handles on internal points to control tangency weighting (magnitude) and direction in the same way as endpoint handles, with the difference that internal handles have arrows in both directions along the spline. While the direction arrows are connected, pivoting about the control point to which they are attached, the weighting controls are independent in the two separate directions by default. If you want to move the weighting arrow such that it moves symmetrically, hold down the Alt key while dragging it.

As soon as you select a tangent control on an internal point the Control Polygon creates three new nodes (one of them being the edit point itself). If you want to go back to controlling with strictly the polygon controls, just using the Reset This Handle button in the PropertyManager window doesn't give you back the original polygon count. You must select the tangent control and delete it; the polygon nodes collapse to their original count, and the edit point is free to float.

> **TIP** To use internal weighting handles symmetrically, drag the arrow while holding down the Alt key on the keyboard.

The main problem with using internal weighting handles asymmetrically is that it can cause a sudden curvature discontinuity at the control point. To help control this problem, you may want to use a setting in the Spline PropertyManager Options panel called Maintain Internal Continuity. This is only available starting with SolidWorks 2008. The Curvature Comb in Figure 3.9 shows the abrupt change in curvature when an internal weighting handle is used asymmetrically.

FIGURE 3.9

Abrupt change in curvature when an internal weighting handle is used asymmetrically

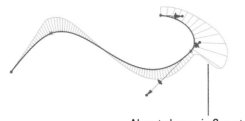

Abrupt change in Curvature Comb

PropertyManager controls

Figure 3.10 shows the Spline PropertyManager. You may see other items in the PropertyManager, for example, with 3D splines or two-point splines with equal curvature set to both ends you will see the Raised Degree option discussed earlier in this chapter.

FIGURE 3.10

The Spline PropertyManager controls

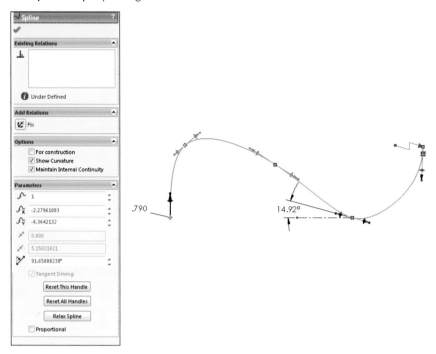

Existing Relations

The top panel of the Spline PropertyManager is the Existing Relations box. As for all sketch entities, it shows all sketch relations to the selected spline. Valid sketch relations for a spline are Tangent, Equal Curvature, Coincident, and Fix. Remember that the one unique use of this box is that by right-clicking a Tangent relation, you can flip the relation's direction (so that the tangency flips 180 degrees). Remember also that Fix can be useful to clamp a spline down temporarily, but if you (or someone else who works on your model at a later point) forget that a spline is Fixed, it may cause some confusion. I treat Fix as a limited-use tool, and tend not to leave anything with a Fix relation.

The Existing Relations panel also shows the status of the spline. Splines are generally left under-defined. I discuss this topic in more detail in the next section of this chapter.

Add Relations

The Add Relations panel of the Spline PropertyManager also allows you to add and remove sketch relations like any other sketch entity, with the valid relations mentioned previously.

Options

The Options panel of the Spline PropertyManager may have different options available to you, depending on the selection. For example, a converted spline will not give you the option to Maintain Internal Continuity. The Raised Degree option is also only available in special situations outlined earlier in this chapter.

The For Construction option simply turns the spline to construction geometry, which the software does not consider when creating any type of feature from the sketch. Construction geometry is useful in a wide variety of cases. Users sometimes forget about this tool for anything but lines.

Show Curvature turns on the Curvature Comb for the selected spline.

I discussed Maintain Internal Continuity earlier in this chapter. It is primarily necessary when you use internal weighting handles asymmetrically.

You can find more information on the Raised Degree/Standard toggle earlier in this chapter. SolidWorks only presents this option to the user when using a two-point spline with curvature controls on both ends.

Parameters

The Parameters panel of the Spline PropertyManager starts with several spin boxes that control numerical data.

Spline Point Number allows you to select the spline point by cycling through them with this spin box. The following X and Y coordinate-value spin boxes control the point selected in this box. The selected spline point highlights in a light-blue color in the graphics window. This color does not contrast well against the light-green selection color, and so you may have to look carefully to see which point highlights.

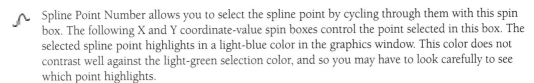

The X and Y coordinate boxes enable you to change the positions of the spline point selected in the top spin box. The increment settings at Tools ➪ Options ➪ Spin Box Increments control the increment the X or Y values for the selected spline point for every touch of the spin arrows. You can also manually enter values.

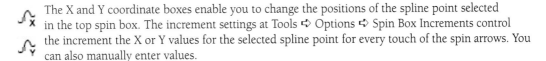

Tangent Weight 1 and 2 refer to the weighting, or weighting handles. These boxes only seem to become active when both end-tangency handles are active. The 1 and 2 refer to the different directions of the weighting setting. This is why at the ends only one direction has a value, and the other will always be zero. Remember that you can change the weighting symmetrically in the two directions by dragging the handle while holding down the Alt key.

Tangent Radial Direction enables you to specify the angle of the direction handle numerically. This spin box is only available for active handles which do not have tangent relations.

The Tangent Driving option controls whether or not the end handles are active. If either end handle of a spline is active, Tangent Driving becomes checked and grayed out. To turn it off, you need to delete the active handle or handles.

> **NOTE** Deleting an active handle simply sets it back to inactive with default values. It turns out that you will probably not actually use the Tangent Driving option very often.

Reset Handle does the same thing as deleting the currently selected handle, except that the handle remains visible and active (blue instead of gray).

The Relax Spline option can rescue splines that seem to become unmanageable. Splines can sometimes get kinks in them, or a section of spline that acts overly stiff right next to a section of spline that acts overly flexible; this usually causes a straight section with a sharp curve at the end of it that does not move as nicely as the rest of the spline. When this happens, select the spline and click the Relax Spline button in the PropertyManager; the spline is reparameterized (the equivalent of a rebuild for a spline) and the kink goes away. Figure 3.11 shows a spline with a kink before and after using Relax Spline.

FIGURE 3.11

Using Relax Spline to remove a kink from a spline

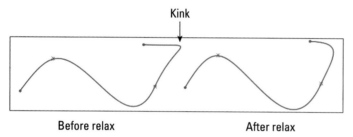

Kink

Before relax   After relax

> **NOTE** Moving a spline point to a substantially different position along the length of a spline in combination with handle manipulation is often the cause of this kind of kink. For example, if a point is roughly in the middle of a spline, pushing it to the end of the spline and changing tangency weighting might cause a kink, which can be fixed with the Relax Spline option.

Proportional is an option that disables shape changes to the spline, and only allows it to scale in size, or to move or rotate as a whole unit; its shape remains fixed. Manipulating endpoints or interior points only resizes or rotates the spline. A spline which you have created by using the Convert Entities tool, and for which you have then deleted the On Edge relation, might also have a fixed size as well as a fixed shape. Using the Proportional option with a spline like this (which likely has no interior spline points visible) can enable you to change the size of the spline.

You can turn on the Proportional option for most splines, but this option is particularly useful for sweeps where the path and a guide curve control the size and orientation of a shape along the length of the sweep. You cannot check the Proportional option if you have dimensions to internal points. This will over define the sketch. Checking Proportional will fully define the spline.

Simplify Spline

Simplify Spline is an option found in the RMB menu. Simplify Spline allows you to specify a tolerance value, and the function reduces the number of spline points to the minimum number while keeping within the tolerance value of the existing spline. You can use this function in two different ways: First, if you have a spline with a lot of points, and you need to edit the spline manually, you might want to simplify it first. Second, Simplify Spline can take a spline that has no control points (perhaps it was created using Convert Entities, but the On Edge relation was deleted), and add control points so that it can be manually edited.

Fully Defining Spline Sketches

Every time you hear someone talking about best practices and company standards, you are sure to hear someone recommend or demand fully-defined sketches. This is an essential best-practice recommendation for most kinds of modeling. However, splines tend to be a different subject. You cannot dimension splines like lines and arcs. A simple two-point spline has eight degrees of freedom, meaning that it would take eight dimensions to fully define it. Each interior point that you add, adds five more dimensions. If you fully dimensioned a spline with only three interior points, you could have as many as 31 dimensions.

Part of the reason for constraining most sketches is to help you establish parametric design intent to change predictably with related geometry. Generally speaking, for multi-point splines, it is not possible to establish this kind of parametric scheme. You usually place points freehand. It is unusual to have a way to drive all of the points in all of your splines with sketch relations to update with changes.

In most cases, most users leave spline sketches under-defined. It is possible to use the Fixed constraint on a spline to clamp it down, but this can cause problems with making changes to the model. It is also possible to use the Fully Define Sketch tool to add enough relations and dimensions to fully define a spline sketch, but the results of Fully Define Sketch are often arbitrary, and are more likely to cause problems with changes than prevent them.

So in the end, what do you do? I personally leave my spline sketches under-defined. It is too much work for too little benefit to do anything else. It is usually possible to fully constrain a two-point spline, because all you generally have to worry about is the tangency weighting. (Sketch dimensions can drive the arrow's length as well as angle.) Also it is often possible to use construction geometry to help constrain other interior points, but using construction geometry becomes unmanageable even at a relatively low number of points.

If you feel uncomfortable with leaving sketches under constrained and need to feel more secure with your data, clamp the sketches down using Fixed relations on splines, or use an exported Parasolid file to document the design as is. Trying to comply with general best-practice rules is usually counter-productive when dealing with spline data.

Tutorials

The purpose of these tutorials is to give the reader some practical hands-on experience with splines through a step-by-step process.

Tutorial 3.1: The S spline

When you perform operations with splines, they tend to be under-defined, and may not be exactly precise. Both creating your own shapes and being able to mimic source shapes are practices that have value, and you should practice and perfect both skills.

1. Open a new part, open a new sketch on the Front plane, and look normal to the Front plane.

2. Make sure the setting at Tools ⇨ Options ⇨ Sketch ⇨ Enable Spline Tangency and Curvature Handles is turned on, and that Show Spline Control Polygon By Default is turned off.

3. Sketch a spline with three internal points, as shown in Figure 3.12. You should have practiced drawing splines a little before now so that you have an intuitive feeling for the method you have chosen for sketching splines — either double-click or click-drag.

4. Select the spline to display the tangency handles, and then select the handle at the lower end and apply a Vertical sketch relation.

5. Draw two construction lines from the upper spline endpoint, as shown in Figure 3.12; one of the construction lines is vertical, and the other is at some angle from the first. Add an angle dimension between the lines and change it to 15 degrees.

FIGURE 3.12

Draw an S-shaped spline

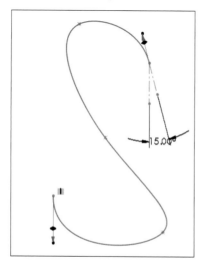

6. Select the spline and the angled line and apply a Tangent sketch relation between them.

7. Move the second and fourth spline points to make the top and bottom of the S more round and natural-looking. Also use the spline handles for direction and weighting to control the curvature. Notice that as you move spline points, a ghost image of the original position of the spline remains for reference. If you prefer to turn this option off, you can find the setting at Tools ➪ Options ➪ Sketch ➪ Ghost Image On Drag.

TIP Remember that using the Alt key while dragging internal weighting handles changes the weighting symmetrically on both sides of the internal point.

8. In the same sketch, draw another S, but this time with square corners, using the same technique from earlier in this chapter to bunch three points closely in a corner in order to create the stylized J. Imitate the sketch in Figure 3.13.

FIGURE 3.13

Draw a square-cornered, stylized S

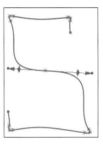

9. To get the curves in the middle of the S and prevent it from looking simply like a backwards Z, select the internal point in the middle of the S, hold down the Alt key, and drag the dot on the end of the tangency handle to approximately horizontal. Adjust the weighting to make the S look about right.

10. Zoom in to the lower right-hand corner of the stylized S and Ctrl-select the three points of the corner. Drag them together as a unit. Selecting multiple points makes it possible to maintain a local shape while editing the overall shape.

11. Open the SolidWorks part provided on the Web site called Chapter 3 – S spline (finished).sldprt to compare your spline against, or to examine the settings.

12. Save and close all files.

Tutorial 3.2: Tracing shapes

In this tutorial, you trace over shapes to try to get some practice with controlling the spline tool accurately. The Auto Trace function is not used here.

1. Open the part from the Web site named Chapter 3 – trace tutorial start.sldprt.

2. Show Sketch1 and then open a new sketch on the Front plane. Each of the sketches in this part comes from an actual model created in SolidWorks.

3. One of the techniques that you will use in the Part 4 tutorials is over-building splines. This simply means making splines longer than they need to be, which modelers do either to get the tangency correct at the actual start point of the feature, or for convenience. Try this technique here, as well. Try to extrapolate the spline about ten percent or about the space between average spline points before the beginning of the Sketch 1 spline, and continue it about the same distance past the end.

4. Once you start sketching, you can allow the spline points to snap to the sketch in the background, or for practice, you might try to hold down the Ctrl key while placing the points, which temporarily disables the automatic relations.

5. After you have finished the first sketch, close it and create another new sketch again on the Front plane. Show the next sketch (Sketch 2), and trace that in the same way. Do this for all four sketches.

6. Save and close all files.

Summary

Models with complex shapes present a number of challenges to SolidWorks users, with one of the most important challenges being maintaining curvature continuity between faces and between sketch entities. Splines are your main tool for creating smooth and continuous shapes, and you cannot hope to simulate their curvature by any combination of lines and tangent arcs.

All of this power to create shapes with splines does not come easily. Many different controls, settings, and options exist for splines, and it may not be necessarily obvious what the result of a particular setting is. With a little study, a little practice, and a little curiosity, you can learn to master this most complex sketch entity in the SolidWorks toolbox.

Chapter 4

Sketching in 3D

Most of the sketching you do in SolidWorks is in a 2D sketch on a plane or planar face. At times, 3D sketches are useful and even indispensible, but they are generally more difficult to control and temperamental at times. SolidWorks allows you to do all of your sketching in 3D sketches, but in most situations, not many users work this way because of the quirks and limitations of 3D sketches.

This chapter offers only a quick refresher on the basic concepts involved in working with 3D sketches, and deals in depth only with those aspects of 3D sketches that are specific to the creation of surfaces and complex shapes. For a more complete general reference on 3D sketching, please refer to the Weldments chapter, Chapter 31, and other locations throughout the *SolidWorks 2007 Bible* as identified in its index.

Many users assume that you would use 3D sketches primarily for complex freehand splines, but this is usually not the case. Freehand 3D splines are very difficult to work with, primarily because of the difficulties with visualization. 3D curves offer no way to judge depth without either rotating the model or seeing it from multiple points of view simultaneously. I use 3D sketches primarily for converted 3D edges, Intersection Curves, Face Curves, Spline on Surface, and less frequently for 3D sketch points that I use to control Fill Surface features. Granted, these may be mainly complex splines, but they are fully defined by the tools that create them automatically, and so there is little concern about controlling them manually.

Getting Started in a 3D Sketch

 Beginning a new 3D sketch does not require any preselection; just click the 3D sketch icon in the sketch toolbar. In SolidWorks 2008, the 3D sketch feature is not on the Sketch toolbar by default, and so you may want to add it yourself, or access it through the menus at Insert ⇨ 3D Sketch.

When you initially open a new 3D sketch, the red sketch origin simply replaces the blue part origin. When you activate a sketch tool such as a line or a spline, the larger red "space handle" appears along with a plane designation attached to the cursor, as shown in Figure 4.1. Remember that just because the cursor says XY doesn't mean that you are sketching *on* the XY plane. The only significance that you can take from the cursor is that you are sketching on a plane *parallel to* the XY plane.

FIGURE 4.1

The space handle and cursor in a 3D sketch

To change the plane indicated on the cursor, press Tab. Each time you press Tab, SolidWorks toggles through the XY, XZ, and YZ planes. Automatic relations and inferencing are different in 3D sketches from what you are familiar with in 2D sketches. For example, Horizontal and Vertical relations do not exist in a 3D sketch, only AlongX, AlongY, and AlongZ.

Using planes in a 3D sketch

While in a 3D sketch, it is sometimes beneficial to confine a section of your sketch to a plane. The purpose of 3D sketches is usually to get away from the need for planes, but in some situations, planar sections of a sketch can be useful. One example of this is the Loft feature. The Loft feature makes special functionality available when all of the loft profiles and guide curves exist inside a single 3D sketch. The special functionality in this case is called Drag Sketch, and is found in the Loft PropertyManager; it gives you the ability to interactively edit the sketch and watch the resulting feature update live.

 Creating a Loft feature from profiles and guide curves made in a single 3D sketch is demonstrated in Chapter 6.

NOTE   A similar type of sketch dragging and interactive update is also available if you use Move/Size Features (2007 and prior) or Instant3D (2008 and later).

Using standard reference planes

You can activate an existing reference plane listed in the FeatureManager by either double-clicking the plane in the graphics window or FeatureManager, or by right-clicking the plane and selecting 3D Sketch On Plane. This displays a small grid on the plane to remind you that you may only sketch on the activated plane. The sketch entities created while a plane is activated are still in the 3D sketch, but they get an On Plane sketch relation. To deactivate the plane and enable 3D sketching, either double-click in space, or right-click the plane and deactivate the 3D Sketch On Plane option.

Some highly useful functionality that is new in SolidWorks 2008 is 3D sketch mirroring. When you activate a plane in a 3D sketch, the Mirror Entities and Dynamic Mirror Entities sketch mirroring tools both work. This does not apply to general 3D sketches, or entities that are not on the active plane.

Additionally, you can manually apply the Symmetric sketch relation between sketch entities and non-sketch entities such as model corners (vertices) or edges.

3D planes

Sometimes the existing reference planes are not enough. You may need to create a plane based on geometry inside the 3D sketch. Doing this with standard reference planes would mean exiting the 3D sketch, making the plane, and then creating another 2D or 3D sketch. Of course, this creates multiple features in the history tree, and requires that you get in and out of sketches, and parent/child history problems may also limit the kinds of relations you can make between entities.

To avoid some of this clumsiness, you can create planes *inside* a 3D sketch using the option found through the menus at Tools ⇨ Sketch Entities ⇨ Plane. That's right; you can create a plane *inside* a 3D sketch. In this arrangement, the plane acts as just another sketch entity, meaning primarily that it follows sketch relations. You may sometimes hear these referred to as "3D planes" in the SolidWorks Help documentation. Of course the name is a misnomer; all planes are 2D by their nature.

The purpose of creating a plane inside a 3D sketch is to avoid *history* or parent/child problems that would otherwise arise by creating a 3D sketch, then a plane, and then a 2D sketch on the plane. Because you cannot use the familiar reference geometry plane-creation methods, and because the planes within a 3D sketch can move dynamically just like other sketch entities, it is important to understand ways in which you can align 3D sketch planes to other geometry in the part.

> **ON the WEB** A part demonstrating the concept of sketch relations driving 3D plane orientation is on the Web site in the folder for Chapter 4. The file is called Chapter 4 – 3D Sketch Planes.sldprt.

Figure 4.2 shows an image of this part. The three sketch lines and the plane are inside the same 3D sketch, and the plane is active. The PropertyManager calls the function the Sketch Plane, but the Help documentation calls it 3D Plane or 3D Sketch Plane. Just be aware that it has multiple names.

FIGURE 4.2

An example of a plane in a 3D sketch, with the PropertyManager

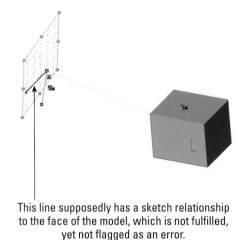

This line supposedly has a sketch relationship
to the face of the model, which is not fulfilled,
yet not flagged as an error.

After you use this PropertyManager to create the plane, you cannot return to it to edit the definition of the plane in the way that you would edit the definition of a standard reference plane in SolidWorks. You may edit the way the plane is positioned by editing the sketch relations between it and other sketch entities or other entities outside of the sketch, just like any other sketch entity. The plane does not show up in the FeatureManager, but you can reference it from outside the sketch by showing the 3D sketch and selecting it from the graphics window.

Open the part shown in Figure 4.2 (using SolidWorks 2008 or later), open the 3D sketch, and drag the sketch point where the three lines intersect. The part uses a sketch entity on the plane to control the orientation of the plane. The line with the 2.401 dimension has a Parallel relation to the face indicated in Figure 4.2. This makes the line lie on a plane parallel to the face.

If you drag the point where the three lines intersect, you may see that the orientation of the plane remains correct with respect to the model face, but it is difficult to keep the plane from flipping directions.

For these reasons, I recommend caution when using 3D planes unless you have a good way to keep them oriented and can deal with the quirks and limitations of the functionality, or your model is relatively static and not likely to change much. If the rotational orientation of a plane is critical, then I would recommend using the traditional but more stable method of using multiple sketch features with standard reference planes. In future releases, if this function becomes more stable and less quirky, it could certainly be a useful tool in building 3D sketches.

58

Editing and Visualization Techniques

Editing and visualizing 3D sketches can be tricky. Computer monitors are inherently 2D displays, and only offer a flattened view of a 3D curve or set of curves. For looking at real-life objects, humans use depth-of-field focus and perspective to help distinguish the depth of, say, a bent wire or a string tied into a bow. On the computer, it isn't as easy. Perspective does not mix well with sketches in SolidWorks, especially dimensioned sketches, and the display technology offers no way to experience depth of field in real time as the parts rotate on the screen, short of using 3D glasses. Also, curves and sketches do not have shading and specular highlights to help your eye distinguish the direction of curvature. Therefore users have to invent alternative methods to visualize curves in 3D.

Using the Shift-Arrow technique

When looking at either a single, complex 3D spline or a set of lines in 3D space, the only real way to get a sense of the geometry in 3D is to see it from multiple points of view. You can do this most easily by using standard orthogonal views like Front, Top, and Right. One easy way to shift quickly between views is to use the Shift-Arrow key combination to rotate the view 90 degrees.

CROSS-REF **Other view-manipulation techniques are covered in detail in the current edition of the** *SolidWorks Bible.*

Another important aspect of editing 3D sketches is that after you are done creating and you begin editing, when the sketch points move, they are not trying to move parallel to the standard orthogonal planes any longer; they are, unless otherwise constrained, trying to move in a plane parallel to the *display*. This means that if you are looking at a 3D spline with unconstrained control points from a Top view, and you move the points, the points move in a plane parallel to the Top plane. If you do the same from a random oblique view, the points are still trying to move parallel to the screen.

TIP **You can use this trait of unconstrained points in a 3D sketch always moving parallel to the screen as an advantage in some situations. For example, if you are in a random oblique view, and you would like to place a plane normal to the current view, there is no tool in SolidWorks that does this directly (although you may find a macro that does this on some Web sites).**

A useful tip to create this type of plane is to open a 3D sketch in a random oblique view, make three random sketch points that do not pick up automatic relations to anything, and then set the points all to be coincident to one another; then delete the coincident relations, and move the points apart. This creates three points that define a plane parallel to the current view, regardless of how random that view is.

Using viewports

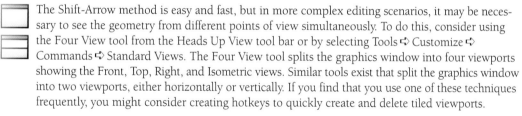

The Shift-Arrow method is easy and fast, but in more complex editing scenarios, it may be necessary to see the geometry from different points of view simultaneously. To do this, consider using the Four View tool from the Heads Up View tool bar or by selecting Tools ➪ Customize ➪ Commands ➪ Standard Views. The Four View tool splits the graphics window into four viewports showing the Front, Top, Right, and Isometric views. Similar tools exist that split the graphics window into two viewports, either horizontally or vertically. If you find that you use one of these techniques frequently, you might consider creating hotkeys to quickly create and delete tiled viewports.

To create the viewports manually in SolidWorks 2007, drag the splitter bars in the upper-right and lower-left corners, at the ends of the scroll bar areas. SolidWorks 2008 has removed this capability from the software, so use either the toolbar buttons or access the commands through the menus at Window ➪ Viewport ➪ Four View.

NOTE   In early versions of SolidWorks 2008 (prior to sp 2.0), the slider bars and splitter bars are not in the interface.

Two different methods exist to set the graphics window back to a single viewport: One method is to use the toolbar button or the menu selection in the same areas described earlier. A second method is to use the viewport dividers to either double-click at the intersection of the four viewports or just on the divider between two viewports, or to drag the divider or intersection between dividers back to the border of the graphics window.

Using the viewports enables you to see how moving a point in one view affects the rest of the views immediately. Also, items selected in one viewport display as selected in all views. Dynamic high-lighting also works across all viewports. This technique allows you to switch quickly and easily between views. Because SolidWorks automatically links the viewports created by the toolbar button method, panning the view in one viewport also pans the view in the others. Views can be unlinked by right-clicking anywhere in the viewport with the chain link symbol in front of the view name in the lower-left corner of the window, and then deselecting the Link Views option.

Figure 4.3 shows editing a 3D spline with four viewports to get the correct shape in all views.

FIGURE 4.3

Using viewports to edit a 3D spline

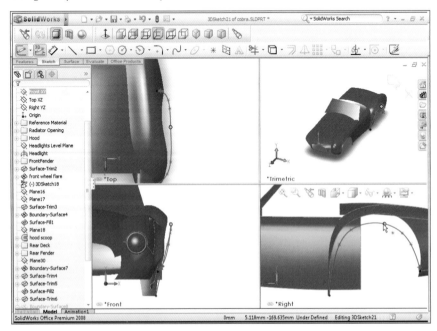

 The model shown in Figure 4.3 is available on the Web site in the folder for Chapter 4, and is called CSnS Cobra.sldprt. The sketch shown is called Rear Fender Flare Sketch.

Working within the Limitations of 3D Sketches

In software intended for more complex tasks, limitations tend to become more apparent than in software for simpler tasks. Three-dimensional sketching is a complex modeling task. It is difficult to visualize, and sometimes parametrically difficult to control. I believe that the way to be most successful with any tool is to understand both what it can and what it cannot do. Listing the limitations of 3D sketches is not a complaint against the software; it is simply a way to help users manage their expectations. If you go into 3D sketches believing that they are a single one-stop answer, you may be disappointed.

Limitations in 3D sketches

Three-dimensional sketches have a lot of sketch relations that you do not find in 2D sketches. I have already mentioned the AlongX, Y, and Z relations. The ParallelZX and YZ relations establish a line as parallel to a selected plane without needing to actually be on a plane.

NOTE The ParallelZX and YZ relations may not be as obvious as they first appear. If you set a line parallel to a plane or face, the ZX and YZ refer to the *local face* coordinates, not the part coordinates. The selected face or plane is XY by default, with the orientation being determined internally, invisible to the user. Positive Z is always out from a solid face and on the green side of a plane, and it would have to be determined experimentally for a planar surface.

Consequently, if you select the ZX (usually the Top) plane of a part and make a ParallelZX relation between it and a line in a 3D sketch, the line will actually be parallel to a plane perpendicular to the selected plane, because in this case, SolidWorks considers the selected ZX to be XY. If this seems confusing and counterintuitive, I agree. Please don't blame me: I didn't write the software.

Here are some additional limitations in 3D sketches.

- Mirroring does not work in a 3D sketch unless you have a plane activated.
- Patterning does not work in 3D sketches.
- The Modify Sketch tool does not work in 3D sketches.
- The Rotate, Scale, and Copy sketch tools do not work in the 3D sketch as of SolidWorks 2008 sp 2.0. This is important mainly because the combination of Scale and Modify Sketch not working in 3D sketches means that there is no way to scale an entire 3D sketch other than by using individual dimensions.
- The Line Format color and line style options work in 2D sketches, but not in 3D sketches.
- The Symmetric sketch relation is also unavailable unless you have a plane activated.

- The Polygon sketch entity does not work, even on a plane.

- You cannot create arcs and circles except on a plane. The one exception to this is that sketch fillets do not require a plane.

- You cannot create a sketch fillet between any entity and a non-planar spline, although you can create the fillet to a planar spline, and then edit the spline to be non-planar.

- The Equal Curvature relation between splines in a 3D sketch seems to be particularly susceptible to becoming over defined or unsolved. This is not to say that it doesn't work or that you should avoid it, but you just need to be careful when using it.

From time to time you may come across sketch relations that make logical sense, but that SolidWorks does not allow. The more exotic the example, the more likely you are to see a difficulty. For example, Figure 4.4 shows a Spline On Surface, where the internal control point of the spline is also coincident to the axis going through the part. This sketch relation fails.

CROSS-REF Spline On Surface is discussed in more detail later in this chapter.

FIGURE 4.4

This sketch relation between a Spline On Surface control point and axis fails.

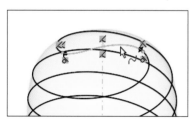

ON the WEB The part shown in Figure 4.4 is available on the Web site in the folder for Chapter 4 under the name Chapter 4 – Fluorescent Light Bulb.sldprt.

Dimensions are limited in several ways in 3D sketches. First, you cannot create horizontal and vertical dimensions as you can in 2D sketches. Also, you can only dimension the true length of a line so that the dimension is parallel to the line itself.

Angle dimensions in 3D sketches do not always allow you to get the angle you intend. For example, instead of dimensioning a 60-degree angle, it may default to a 300-degree angle, and not provide the option for the smaller angle.

If you want to force a dimension to a particular orientation, you need to use a construction line, axis, or plane to anchor one end of the dimension. Figure 4.5 shows this technique. You may want to open up the file shown in this figure for clarity.

FIGURE 4.5

Using reference geometry to orient dimensions

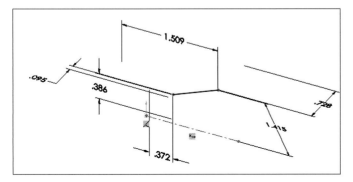

ON the WEB   **You may want to open the part shown in Figure 4.5 for clarity. It is on the Web site in the Chapter 4 folder and is called Chapter 4 – 3D Sketch Dimensioning.**

I am quite sure that with a little investigation, you can add a few of your own favorite limitations to this list.

Recently removed limitations

If you are a veteran SolidWorks user, you may remember that 3D sketches had many limitations, especially when it came to sketch relations. This list covers a few old limitations that no longer exist.

- You can now use Midpoint relations in a 3D sketch.
- You can now use Equal relations in a 3D sketch.
- Link Values now work for dimensions in a 3D sketch.

CROSS-REF   **Link Values are discussed in depth in Chapter 9 of the *SolidWorks 2007 Bible*.**

- You can now fillet between a line and a spline, as long as the spline is planar (it does not have to be *on* a plane, so long as it is planar). Still, this combination seems to become over defined if it is disturbed by the surrounding geometry being moved. It is not a robust or recommended method.
- Sketch Chamfer works in 3D sketch.
- Sketching on a plane within a 3D sketch has removed a great number of limitations, such as the ability to draw circles and to mirror.
- You can create all types of rectangles anywhere, parallel to the plane indicated on the cursor. This includes center point rectangles and parallelograms. The resulting sketch relations are different from what you get in a 2D sketch rectangle.

Using Special 3D Sketch Tools

Several special tools either automatically create 3D sketches or have special functions only in 3D sketches. Some of these special tools are extremely useful in making complex shapes, and, in fact, these tools form the bulk of the work I typically do in 3D sketches. The tools include Intersection Curve, Spline On Surface, Face Curves, and Convert Entities in a 3D sketch.

Intersection Curve

 Intersection Curve is found on the Sketch toolbar, or through the menus at Tools ⇨ Sketch Tools ⇨ Intersection Curve. In a 2D sketch, it creates sketch entities where the current sketch plane intersects selected faces. In a 3D sketch, Intersection Curve creates sketch entities at the intersection of surface or solid bodies, or faces and planes (although for some reason it does not create a line at the intersection of two planes).

Intersection Curve is a very powerful tool that was introduced into SolidWorks several releases ago, and it makes possible an entire range of things that were not possible before. I use it frequently to make sure a sketch is to one side of a certain face, especially when the face is irregularly shaped, or the sketch plane is at an angle to the face and no appropriate reference edges exist.

Figure 4.6 shows this functionality. Two surface bodies intersect, and at that intersection, the Intersection Curve tool has created a spline. This spline is associative, and updates when either of the surface bodies changes shape or position.

FIGURE 4.6

Demonstrating the Intersection Curve in a 3D sketch

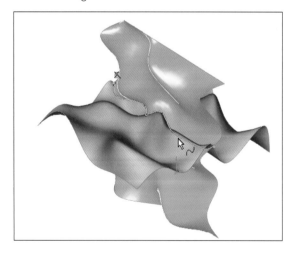

ON the WEB The part shown in Figure 4.6 is on the Web site in the folder for Chapter 4, and is named Chapter 4 – Intersection Curve 1.sldprt.

If you activate the Intersection Curve tool and a 3D sketch is not open, it automatically opens one. You can also preselect entities before activating the tool. The Intersection Curve is a *modal* tool, and so you need to deactivate it when you are done.

TIP Because Intersection Curve is a modal tool, the toolbar icon for it stays depressed while the tool is active. For this reason, I recommend that you put the Intersection Curve tool on your Sketch toolbar rather than accessing it through the menus or hotkeys, so that the tool is there as a visual reminder that it is active.

You may have difficulties with sketch entities created by the Intersection Curve tool if the entity changes type. For example, if you use the Intersection Curve tool to create a circle where a plane intersects a cylindrical face and the plane is perpendicular to the axis of the cylinder, and later the plane changes so that it is at some angle from the axis, the sketch entity created by the tool changes from a circle to a spline (ideally it would change to an ellipse). When this happens, any sketch relations made to the original circle become dangling relations.

The part shown in Figure 4.7 demonstrates this problem. Open the part from the Web site to help visualize what is happening. Change the angle of Plane1 to see the error.

FIGURE 4.7

Sketch entities created by Intersection Curve can cause problems when they change types.

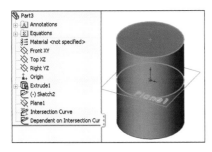
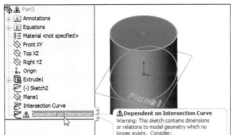

ON the WEB The part shown in Figure 4.7 is on the Web site in the folder for Chapter 4, and is named Chapter 4 – Change Types.sldprt.

Intersection Curve applies a sketch relation to the newly created sketch entity. The relation is called At Intersection Of Two Faces. If the sketch entity created by the Intersection Curve tool loses either of its references due to changes in the part, you cannot reapply or repair the relation. The only options are to delete the dangling relation and settle for a complex curve that is completely unde-fined, or delete the sketch entity and re-create it. Neither of these is a good option, and so I advise selecting your references with care.

The At Intersection Of Two Faces sketch relation is surprisingly resilient. If you change the sketch for the original extrude by deleting the circle and creating another circle, the relation still works. It even continues to work if you replace the circle with an ellipse or even a closed loop spline.

Spline On Surface

 The Spline On Surface tool is newer to SolidWorks than the Intersection Curve, and in fact, it has just received some additional functionality in SolidWorks 2008. Spline On Surface, as the name suggests, enables you to sketch a spline on any face in a 3D sketch. A better name for the tool is Spline On Face, because it is not limited to working on surfaces—it also works on solid faces.

The new functionality added to Spline On Surface in SolidWorks 2008 that makes this tool more useful is that the spline can now span multiple faces, as long as the edge between the faces is either tangent or curvature continuous, as shown in Figure 4.8.

FIGURE 4.8

Spline On Surface can cross tangent or curvature-continuous edges.

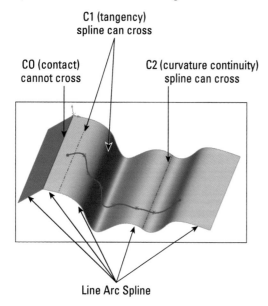

C1 (tangency) spline can cross

C0 (contact) cannot cross

C2 (curvature continuity) spline can cross

Line Arc Spline

ON the WEB To get a better look at the part shown in Figure 4.8, open the part from the Web site in the folder for Chapter 4. The part is called Chapter 4 – Spline On Surface.sldprt.

Additionally, the spline can go right up to the edge of the faces, but it sometimes exhibits strange behavior if relations at an edge go to another sketch entity off of the face.

Spline On Surface is not always my first choice when I need to make a curve entity of this sort. Frequently I find the Projected Curve to be more controllable and less prone to errors.

CROSS-REF You can find more information on the Projected Curve feature in Chapter 5.

Two highly useful applications of Spline On Surface are that you can use it to trim surfaces and split faces. Figure 4.9 shows both techniques. When creating a Split Line, use the Intersection option. With the Trim, select the sketch as the Trim tool.

ON the WEB You can find the parts shown in Figure 4.9 on the Web site in the Chapter 4 folder, named Chapter 4 – Spline On Surface Split.sldprt and Chapter 4 – Spline On Surface Trim.sldprt.

FIGURE 4.9

Using Spline On Surface to create Split Line and Trim features

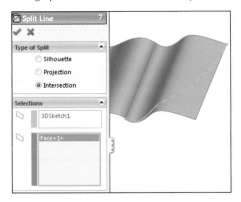
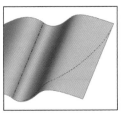
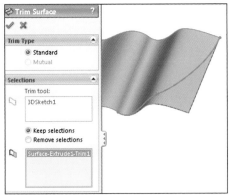

Face Curves

Face Curves has many potential uses, but in practice, it is generally used in one of two ways: as a diagnostic tool and as a shortcut to create a set of curves to parametrically re-create an imported face.

Face Curves exposes the underlying U-V structure of a face. This works for both analytical and NURBS type faces, and as Figure 4.10 shows, it can even bridge over holes in the face, regardless of whether the faces are solid or surface. You can use the PropertyManager for Face Curves to set the density of curves in either direction, whether you want to get the entire mesh or just the U and V curves at a particular position. You can also choose to constrain the curves to the face, or leave them unconstrained. Clicking the green check mark to accept the settings results in a series of 3D sketches, with one curve per sketch. Users frequently gather all of the sketches made by the Face Curves tool and put them into a single folder to minimize unnecessary clutter in the FeatureManager.

FIGURE 4.10

Using Face Curves

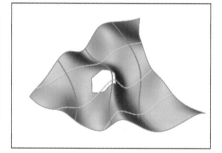

You can use curves obtained in this way to reconstruct a face. This technique is most commonly used on imported data where a face needs to be re-created or altered. The curves have an On Edge relation, the same as when Convert Entities is used. To edit splines created in this way, you can simply delete the On Edge relation, and use Simplify Spline from the right mouse button (RMB) menu to add control points back to the spline and make it editable. Both Loft and Boundary surfaces can make use of the mesh of curves created by the Face Curves tool.

The most common application for Face Curves is as a diagnostic tool. Because Face Curves exposes the underlying U-V structure of the face, it is a great tool to quickly check for singularities on model faces. Users also commonly use Face Curves to simply examine the orientation of the mesh to help with building surrounding faces. When used in this way, the preview is usually sufficient, and you need not actually create the curves.

Convert Entities

 Convert Entities is the same familiar tool that you use frequently in 2D sketches, but it has some interesting and useful applications when used in 3D sketches. The first difference between using Convert Entities in 2D and 3D is that in 2D, it projects entities onto the sketch plane, but in 3D, it just converts them to sketch entities exactly where they are in space. In addition, I frequently convert curve entities into the sketch for a number of reasons, which are illustrated in the tutorials at the end of this chapter.

At first, it may seem redundant to make a sketch entity directly on top of an edge or curve entity. I usually use this technique as a workaround for limitations with curve entities, which I discuss in detail in Chapter 5.

As an example, look at the model shown in Figure 4.11. This part exaggerates the techniques used for both curve generation and 3D sketches, but it can be useful to examine the construction of it. You see it again in the tutorials for both this chapter and Chapter 5.

I used Convert Entities in this model to convert the helical curve into sketch data. I did this because you cannot make sketch relations to the endpoints of curve entities. Neither can you make sketch entities tangent to curve entities. A convenient workaround is to convert the curve into a sketch, to which it is easy to make sketch relations.

FIGURE 4.11

Using Convert Entities in a 3D sketch

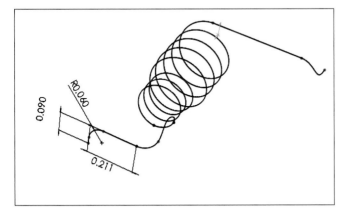

ON the WEB You can find the model shown in Figure 4.11 on the Web site in the Chapter 4 folder. It is called Chapter 4 – 3D Convert Entities.sldprt.

Open 3DSketch3 in the part shown in Figure 4.11. Notice that, aside from a couple of lines and an arc at the outer end of the spring, all of the entities in this sketch are converted entities. A helix, a projected curve, and even another 3D sketch have been converted into a 3D sketch.

> **NOTE** It is also possible to use a Fit Spline in the 3D sketch to merge all of the converted 3D sketch entities into a single spline, giving a single, smooth path to create a sweep without the edges between faces that this model has.

Tutorials

These tutorials demonstrate the use of 3D sketch tools and 3D sketches.

Tutorial 4.1: Fluorescent light bulb

This tutorial demonstrates the 3D sketch tools Intersection Curve, Spline On Surface, and simple 3D splines.

1. Begin by opening the part from the Web site in the Chapter 4 folder called Chapter 4 - Tutorial 4.1 Start.sldprt. Notice that a solid body and three surface bodies are showing. The surface bodies are construction surfaces, meant to help build the geometry needed to build the part, but these surfaces are not part of the finished part geometry. I commonly apply a contrasting color to reference geometry and make it transparent to keep it visually separate from real-part geometry.

2. Make sure the Surface Bodies folder is showing. If it is not, go to Tools ➪ Options ➪ FeatureManager and set the Surface Bodies folder to Show.

3. Ctrl-select all three surface bodies in the Surface Bodies folder.

4. If the Intersection Curve tool is not shown on your Sketch toolbar, go to Tools ➪ Customize ➪ Commands ➪ Sketch and drag it onto the Sketch toolbar. Close the Customize dialog box.

5. With the three surface bodies still selected, activate the Intersection Curve tool. The pink and blue surfaces do not intersect one another, but they both intersect the yellow. Where the surfaces intersect, the Intersection Curve tool creates a 3D spline. Two splines appear.

6. Deactivate the Intersection Curve tool.

> **NOTE** You may notice that when you activate the Intersection Curve tool, the Convert Entities toolbar button is also depressed. This can happen if the Convert Entities flyout toolbar button is on the toolbar. The Intersection Curve tool is also on the Convert Entities flyout.

7. Hide the helical construction surfaces (blue and pink) by Ctrl-selecting them from the Surface Bodies folder, and then right-clicking and selecting Hide Bodies. This leaves only the revolved, transparent yellow surface showing. Figure 4.12 shows the model at this point.

8. If the Spline On Surface toolbar button is not on your toolbar, go to Tools ➪ Customize and add it. It may be on the Spline flyout toolbar.

FIGURE 4.12

Construction surface with two intersection curves

9. Open a new 3D sketch, and activate the Spline On Surface tool. Draw a spline with only one internal spline point (a total of three points — two endpoints and one internal) near the top of the bulb area, being careful not to pick up automatic relations to anything other than the yellow construction surface. Also be careful to keep the sketch on the surface.

10. Drag the ends of the new spline onto the ends of the intersection curves. Assign tangent relations between the Spline On Surface and the intersection splines.

NOTE If the spline goes in the wrong direction when the tangent relation is added, select the spline, right-click the tangent relation in the PropertyManager, and select Flip Relation.

11. Orient the view into a Top view, and turn on Temporary Axes through the menu at View ⇨ Temporary Axes.

12. Drag the middle point of the spline onto the end view of the Temporary Axis. If this gives you an error, hold the Ctrl key while dragging, and drop the point in the same place.

NOTE Ctrl-dragging a spline point disables automatic relations. In cases like this where the correct relation causes errors, you may want to find a workaround such as placing a sketch point on the surface, giving it the On Surface sketch relation, and then making it coincident with the temporary axis; then make the spline point coincident with the sketch point.

13. Create a two-point spline from the lower end of one of the intersection curves, and pick up an automatic relation to the center of the extruded boss, as shown in Figure 4.13.

14. Add a Tangent relation between the intersection curve and the new spline, and on the other end, give the handle an AlongY relation. Repeat this step for the other side. Exit the 3D sketch when done.

15. Draw a circle on the face of the extruded boss, giving its centerpoint a Pierce relation to the 3D sketch spline. Exit the sketch.

16. Create a simple, solid sweep, using the circle as the profile and the 3D sketch as the path.

17. To preserve the original data, save the part with a new name using Save As. Close the part when finished.

Creating a two-point spline

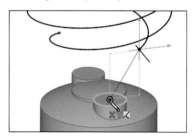

Tutorial 4.2: Complex spring

This tutorial demonstrates several techniques using 3D sketches, including a freehand 3D spline, using Convert Entities on 3D curves, and the Fit Spline tool. The Web site contains a part to start from that includes several curve entities. Figure 4.14 shows the finished part.

The finished part for Tutorial 4.2

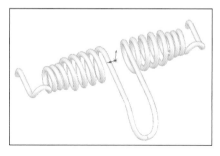

CROSS-REF Curve entities such as Helix, Projected Curve, and Composite Curve are covered in depth in Chapter 5.

1. Open the file Chapter 4 – Tutorial 4.2 Start.sldprt from the Chapter 4 folder on the Web site. Notice that it contains a complex helix and a projected curve.

2. Open a new 3D sketch. The first step is to draw the centerline for the middle portion of the spring. If you try to do this, you notice that you cannot assign a sketch relation between a sketch line or endpoint and a 3D curve entity. To overcome this limitation, Ctrl-select the helix and the projected curve, and click Convert Entities.

NOTE You can easily select the helix from the graphics window, but the projected curve is segmented, and so it is best to select it from the FeatureManager. If you choose to select the projected curve from the graphics window, you need to Ctrl-select all three segments of it.

3. Draw a line in the AlongZ direction, starting from the end of the converted helix nearest the origin. Dimension the length of this line at 0.50 inch.

4. Draw a two-point spline from the end of the line you just drew, putting the second point at a random, free location in space. You locate the second point in the next step.

5. Assign an On Plane relation between the second point of the spline and the Right reference plane.

6. For this step, it may be best to change to a Right view of the part. Make sure the second spline point is *below* the Top plane, and to the right of the first spline point (when seen from the Right view). With the Smart Dimension tool, select the Top plane from the FeatureManager, and then select the second spline point. This controls the distance below the origin of the point. If you select the origin for the dimension, you get a diagonal dimension from the origin to the point. Change the dimension to 0.075 inch.

7. Dimension from the Front plane to the second spline point. Change this dimension to 0.75 inch. The sketch now looks like Figure 4.15.

FIGURE 4.15
_____

The sketch at Step 7

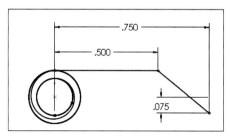

8. Rotate the view slightly so that you can see that the spline looks like a straight line. Select both the spline and the line it is attached to, and assign a Tangent sketch relation.

9. Select the spline; the spline handles appear. Select the handle at the unattached end of the spline and assign an AlongX sketch relation.

10. At the other end of the spring, at the end of the converted projected curve, draw two perpendicular lines on a plane parallel to the YZ plane. Dimension them as shown in Figure 4.16.

11. Place a sketch fillet of radius 0.06 inch between the two new lines. Exit the sketch.

FIGURE 4.16

Dimensions for Step 10

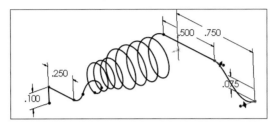

12. Open a 2D sketch on the Right plane, and draw a circle. Dimension the circle to have a 0.04-inch diameter, and give the center point of the circle a Pierce relation with the two-point spline in the 3D sketch. Exit the sketch.

13. Create a simple sweep using the circle as the profile and the 3D sketch as the path.

14. Right-click the Helix and Projected Curve features in the FeatureManager and hide them.

15. Notice that the face of the spring is broken into segments. Also, technically, the intersection between the straight line and the helix is not tangent. Expand the Sweep feature, and edit the 3D sketch used for the path.

16. Right-click any sketch element and click Select Chain. From the main menus, select Tools ➪ Spline Tools ➪ Fit Spline. Notice that the preview may not fit the existing sketch entities very well at the default tolerance. Lower the tolerance to see the preview more closely match the original sketch. Finally, set the tolerance value to 0.005 inch, and accept the Fit Spline.

17. Exit the sketch, and ensure that the spring sweep updates, has no face breaks along it, and is smooth.

18. Mirror the solid body about the face on the Right plane. The part now looks like Figure 4.14.

19. Save the part to a new name and close it.

Summary

3D sketches should not be your first choice in most cases, but they can be extremely valuable in some situations. 3D sketches are easier to work with if you use some simple visualization techniques using orthogonal views and viewports. Also, while SolidWorks has made significant progress in removing limitations, especially in the realm of 3D sketch relations, the relations can still be quirky, especially when working with spline end conditions.

Several familiar 2D sketch tools take on some additional capabilities when you use them in a 3D sketch. These add significant power and, at times, make up for shortcomings of other tools.

Chapter 5

Creating Curves

Curve features in SolidWorks are different from sketch entities. This might seem like an obvious statement, but as you work with curves, you may begin to wonder why curves are different from 3D sketches. You cannot manipulate the shape of curve features directly like you can with entities such as 3D splines; you must edit curves in dialog boxes or change the associative entities that drive the curves, such as sketches or other model edge, point, or vertex data.

Some additional factors can sometimes make curves difficult to deal with, and you need to be aware of these issues so you can work around them. Chapter 4 discusses using 3D sketches to work around some limitations with curves, and this chapter shows additional workaround techniques. As of SolidWorks 2008, SolidWorks Corporation has not paid much attention to enhancing curve features since the variable pitch helix several releases ago. It is hard to say what this means in terms of looking forward to new or improved functionality in future releases. Curve functionality is certainly due to receive some enhancement attention.

Regardless of what may or may not be happening in the future with curve functionality, curve features can be very useful in many situations, and in some cases, they are indispensable.

Using the Helix/Spiral Feature

 The most impressive of the curve features is the Helix/Spiral. Figure 5.1 shows the PropertyManager of the Helix/Spiral feature.

FIGURE 5.1

The PropertyManager for the Helix/Spiral feature

Helix feature options

All it takes to start a Helix feature is a sketch circle. The circle defines the center location, the start plane, and the initial diameter of the helix. A helix can be defined using one of four options:

- Pitch and Revolution
- Height and Revolution
- Height and Pitch
- Spiral

When you select one of the two types that are determined by pitch, Pitch and Revolutions or Height and Pitch, options become available in the Parameters panel of the Helix/Spiral PropertyManager that enable you to specify variable pitch and diameter values using a small chart. The variable pitch helix offers a lot of power and flexibility because you can vary both the pitch and the diameter of the helix at the same time using the chart.

TIP While the Helix feature is indeed a powerful tool, if all you need is a helical swept surface, a faster way to get there may be to simply use an option in the Sweep feature. Sweep features are arguably the most common area of use for curve features, although other 3D shape creation techniques can also make use of them, so it is interesting that a sweep is used as a workaround for a faster way to create a simple helix. While Chapter 6 covers the details of Sweep, I show this technique here because of its relationship to the Helix feature.

In addition to the various methods for defining the helix, you can flip the handedness, clockwise or counterclockwise, or the direction, up or down. You can also add a taper to the helix or change its angular starting location.

CROSS-REF For more information on the Sweep feature, see Chapter 6.

Figure 5.2 shows how a pair of straight lines in different sketches is transformed into a helical surface using the twist options in the Sweep feature.

ON the WEB For reference, the part shown in Figure 5.2 is on the Web site in the Chapter 5 folder under the name Chapter 5 – Twisted Sweep.sldprt.

FIGURE 5.2

Using straight lines to make a helical surface

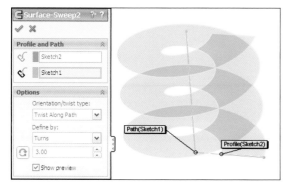

Spiral options

The Spiral option uses the same input as the Helix feature, namely a circle and a pitch value. However, the output is different. A spiral is a planar curve entity that lies in the plane of the parent circle, starts at the diameter of the circle, and becomes gradually larger (or smaller) with each turn. The pitch of a spiral is just the radial change of the curve for each turn. Figure 5.3 shows the PropertyManager and available parameters for the Spiral feature.

The Spiral PropertyManager

 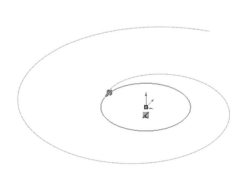

Creating a Projected Curve

 The Projected Curve feature has two options for projection: The default option is called Sketch Onto Sketch, by which two sketches may be projected onto one another. The other option is called Sketch Onto Face, by which a sketch can be projected from its sketch plane onto a face or set of faces.

Again, the name Projected Curve is a bit of a misnomer, which may contribute to some of the confusion among users new to this feature. The curve is not being projected, but it is the result of a sketch being projected in one of two ways, either onto another sketch or onto a selected face. Sketch Onto Sketch tends to be more difficult for people to grasp, and is explained in detail later in this chapter.

Sketch Onto Face

Sometimes users misinterpret the name of this option to mean that you actually sketch directly on a model face. That description more closely matches the Spline On Surface tool. When using the Sketch Onto Face option, a sketch is projected in a direction normal to its sketch plane onto a face or selection of faces as a curve feature. Figure 5.4 shows the PropertyManager for Sketch Onto Face.

When projecting a sketch onto a face, the sketch can only project in a single direction. If you find yourself in a situation where you need to project in both directions or where the sketch actually intersects a face you want to project it onto, you need to move the sketch so the sketch is completely to one side of the faces onto which you are projecting.

One of the reasons for using a Sketch Onto Face Projected Curve instead of a Spline On Surface is that a 2D sketch is often easier to control with dimensions and sketch relations than a 3D spline.

FIGURE 5.4

The Sketch Onto Face PropertyManager

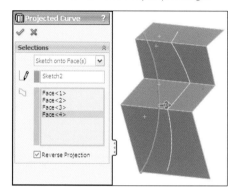

Sketch Onto Sketch

I have frequently seen people struggle to understand what the Sketch Onto Sketch Projected Curve option does. The problem seems to be that the name is not very descriptive, although I am not sure what else you could call it to make the function clearer. When the Sketch Onto Sketch option is used, two sketches — usually sketched on planes perpendicular to one another, but not necessarily so — are projected through space to the place where they intersect.

It may help you to visualize this by thinking of the projection of each sketch as if you were extruding a surface from each sketch. You can think of the Projected Curve as being where the Intersection Curve function would create sketch entities, or the edges where the surfaces would trim one another.

A second way to visualize the Sketch Onto Sketch Projected Curve is to think of it as the reverse of a 2D drawing in SolidWorks. In a 2D drawing, you start with a 3D object and create, or *project*, 2D views of its edges in orthogonal directions. With the Sketch Onto Sketch option, you start by drawing the 2D views, and then *project* those views back to create the 3D objects edges again. Using this method can also simplify the conceptualization of the curve, because you only need to think about what the curve looks like from one direction at a time. For this reason, Sketch Onto Sketch Projected Curves often replace freehand 3D splines because they are simpler to create and control.

Figure 5.5 shows the PropertyManager of a Sketch Onto Sketch Projected Curve. It also shows the result of projecting a J-shaped sketch onto a curved sketch. The sketches are on perpendicular planes, and I have included the transparent extruded surfaces to assist in the visualization.

ON the WEB If you would like to examine the part used to make the screenshot for Figure 5.5, look on the Web site in the folder for Chapter 5, for a part named **Chapter 5 – Sketch Onto Sketch.sldprt.**

FIGURE 5.5

The Sketch Onto Sketch Projected Curve PropertyManager

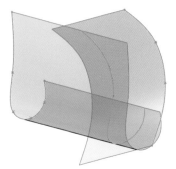

Sketch Onto Sketch projects both sketches in both directions, and the user is not given any control over the direction of the projection.

CROSS-REF Examples of Projected Curve methods are shown in various tutorials in Part 4.

Curve Through Reference Points

 In my experience, the Curve Through Reference Points is one of the least-used curve features available. The Curve Through Reference Points makes a spline type curve by selecting existing points. The points can be sketch points, endpoints, or spline points, as well as model vertices.

The most commonly used application of this feature is to create a straight-line curve from a two-point selection. This is particularly useful in closing off an open gap around a surface by selecting two vertices for the use of a Fill surface. Curve and sketch entities can be used to close the loop for a Fill, and the Curve Through Reference Points is extremely easy to create.

Figure 5.6 shows one use of the Curve Through Reference Points, along with the PropertyManager.

NOTE Several releases ago, this function was called Curve Through Free Points, for any old-timers looking for that function name.

Creating a Curve Through Reference Points

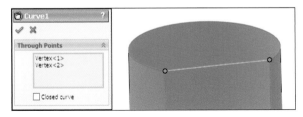

Curve Through XYZ Points

 The Curve Through XYZ Points feature makes a spline-like curve through points specified in a table of XYZ values. You can fill out the table manually, or import a tab- or space-delimited list of XYZ data in a file with the extension *.sldcrv or *.txt. Data of this sort can be generated manually or by using Excel. Well-defined curve information like this is frequently used in the course of creating engineered shapes such as airfoils, pump impellers, involutes, or propellers, among others. Examples of this kind of data are demonstrated in various chapters in Part 4 of this book.

Figure 5.7 shows the dialog box of the Curve Through XYZ Points in action, as well as the sample airfoil data. Notice that the interface is a dialog box instead of a PropertyManager. Whenever you find an interface that is not converted to the PropertyManager style, it usually indicates a feature that SolidWorks Corporation believes is less commonly used, the thinking being that these features are updated less frequently.

In this case, the data is the simple 2D profile of an airfoil, but it could be the leading edge of a compressor blade.

The Curve Through XYZ Points dialog box

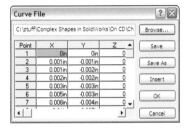 

NOTE You should be aware that just like splines without tangency assigned at the ends, curves created by the Curves Through XYZ Points method are also less likely to be accurate nearest the ends, due to the lack of proper tangency. The problem is that the curve you make using the Curve Through XYZ Points feature is tangent to a straight line at the end, and a curve feature does not allow you to set the tangency at the end. As a result, the more curvature your curve is supposed to have at the end, the more error you see using this method. In order to get an accurate curve, you should have data that extends at least two data points past where you need it to end.

Creating Composite Curves

 You can create Composite Curves from a combination of other curves, 2D and 3D sketches, and solid or surface model edges. The entities that together make up a Composite Curve must individually be open loops and touch end to end without gaps or overlaps. The completed Composite Curve may be a closed or open loop. It may have sharp corners, although the features you make from a sharp-cornered curve may have restrictions (Sweeps do not allow sharp-cornered paths if guide curves are used, and all guide curves must be entirely tangent within themselves).

You can use Composite Curves as sweep path or guide curve, loft guide curve, centerline or surface loft profile. Sometimes instead of creating a Composite Curve, users might use a 3D Sketch with Convert Entities or place a Fit Spline over the converted entities to smooth out the curve and join it into a single entity.

Split Lines

 Technically speaking, split lines are not curves; they are intentionally created edges used to break up existing faces. However, they are included on the Curves toolbar, and so I discuss them in this chapter.

Split lines are used for many reasons, including draft for plastic parts, coloring faces, identifying an area to be used in stress analysis, or to create other geometry in the place of the split face — for example, Fill surface, Dome, Shape, Freeform, Replace Face, and several others.

You can create split lines by splitting a face with one of several entities. Splitting entities are most commonly 2D sketches, but they may also be a Spline On Surface, another intersecting face, or a plane. Three different options exist for split lines: Silhouette, Projection, and Intersection. Projection is the default setting, and the most common type, created by projecting a sketch onto a face. You can use an Intersection split line if you want to break a face where a plane or surface crosses it, or you can use Intersection to split a face where a Spline On Surface exists. You can use a Silhouette split line to split a curved face at the silhouette when seen from a selected plane.

A splitting entity must create a closed loop split, which may include the existing boundary of the face to be split. The main limitation here is that a split line cannot create curve endpoints that do not intersect an edge — you cannot make a U-shaped split in the middle of the face if the open end of the U is not closed off by an edge. Limitations such as multiple closed loops and mixed open/closed profiles exist. For this reason, you cannot use sketch text with the Split Line feature.

As a work around if you have multiple loops that you need to split a face, I recommend extruding the sketch as a surface, and then using the surface bodies with the Intersection option of the Split Line command. This works on any type of surface, and any number of faces, with any number of closed loops, even if they are nested closed loops.

Figure 5.8 shows a part where several faces have been broken by Split Line features for various reasons and in various ways.

FIGURE 5.8

Various entities splitting faces

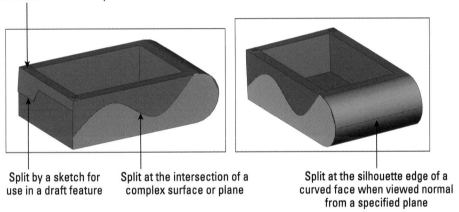

Split by a sketch for color markings or to denote an area for special FEA treatment

Split by a sketch for use in a draft feature

Split at the intersection of a complex surface or plane

Split at the silhouette edge of a curved face when viewed normal from a specified plane

ON the WEB The part used to create the screenshot in Figure 5.8 is on the Web site, located in the folder for Chapter 5, and called Chapter 5 – Split Line.sldprt. Open the part and examine it using the Rollback bar for a more detailed look at what the split lines are doing and how they were created.

Tutorial

This tutorial gives you a practical way to familiarize yourself with commonly used functionality of several curve features. In this tutorial, you create the geometry that was used as the starting point for the Chapter 4 tutorial.

1. Open the file from the Web site named Chapter 5 – Spring Tutorial start.sldprt. The only item in the FeatureManager is a 3D sketch. This 3D sketch is essentially the work you did in the tutorial of Chapter 4.

2. Create a reference plane using the Top plane and the non-construction straight line in the 3D sketch. Use the At Angle plane type, and use an angle of 90 degrees.

3. Start a new sketch on the new plane, and sketch a circle centered on the origin and coincident with the endpoint of the non-construction line in the 3D sketch that is nearest the origin.

4. Start the Helix/Spiral feature with the sketched circle selected. Use the Pitch and Revolution definition option, and in the Parameters panel, select the Variable Pitch setting. Enter the Region Parameters numbers from the table, as shown in Figure 5.9. Make sure the Counterclockwise option is selected and that the Start angle makes the end of the helix correspond with the end of the line in the 3D sketch. Accept the results of the Helix feature when it is complete.

FIGURE 5.9

Defining the helix

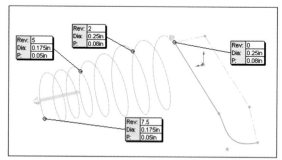

NOTE It is not possible at this time to drive the start angle of the helix through any means other than the number in the Start Angle field.

5. On the Right plane, sketch a semi-circle centered on the origin with a radius of 0.0875 inches. You can use a vertical construction line through the origin to help easily define the semi-circle. The arc should point in the –Z direction, as shown in Figure 5.10. Close the sketch when it is complete.

Depending on your template units settings for the number of places shown by the display, your computer may show 0.088 even if you key in 0.0875. The Modify dialog box always shows the correct number, out to eight decimal places, unless you have keyed in a number with fewer places. It may seem misleading, but when you use four-place values in a template that only displays three places, the software rounds the displayed number, although it retains the correct number.

6. Open a new sketch on the Front plane, and sketch the line-arc-line arrangement shown in Figure 5.10. Once all of the dimensions and sketch relations are in place, assign a Pierce relation between the line endpoint nearest the helix and the helix itself. The centerline in the sketch shows that it is symmetrical. All three entities snap into place when you create the relation. Exit the sketch when it is complete.

FIGURE 5.10

Setting up the projected curve

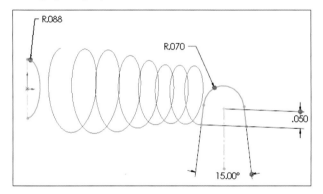

These two sketches may look totally unrelated, but they combine to form a single 3D curve. The 2D image in Figure 5.10 may be difficult to interpret, but the green-colored (selected) line-arc-line sketch is on a different plane than the gray semi-circle sketch. The 3D sketch has been hidden in the image for clarity.

7. Activate the Projected Sketch tool, select the Sketch On Sketch option, and select the semi-circle sketch and the line-arc-line sketch. Notice that a preview of the completed projected curve appears that touches the end of the helix. Click the green check mark to accept this result.

If you see a small gap between the helix and the projected curve, check to make sure that you didn't round off the 0.0875-inch value to 0.088. If you are using a template that shows only three decimal places, any four-place decimals are rounded to display only three places, regardless of the number you have entered.

8. Activate the Composite Curve tool, and select the 3D sketch, the helix, and the projected curve. You may select these from the graphics window or the FeatureManager. Figure 5.11 shows the Composite Curve PropertyManager and also the result of the sweep feature that will be created from this curve.

FIGURE 5.11

Creating a composite curve and half of the finished spring

 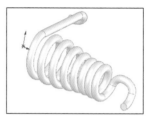

9. Open a sketch on the Right plane, and draw a circle with a diameter of 0.043 inches. Apply a Pierce relation between the center point and the composite curve.

10. Create a simple Sweep feature using the circle as the Profile and the composite curve as the Path.

11. Use the Mirror feature to mirror the solid body about the Right plane. Remember to activate the Bodies To Mirror panel in the PropertyManager to mirror bodies instead of features. Make sure the Merge Solids option is selected. Accept the result when the mirror feature is complete.

NOTE   You cannot mirror or pattern curve geometry. Also remember from Chapter 4 that you cannot mirror 3D sketch elements that are not on a plane. Sometimes an effective workaround is to simply mirror the finished solid geometry. Sometimes you can make a surface from the curve and mirror the surface, and then use the edge of the surface in the same way that you would have used the mirrored curve.

Remember also from Chapter 4 that to smooth out the spring somewhat, you can use Convert Entities on the curve in a 3D sketch to make sketch elements, then use a Fit Spline to smooth over the intersections, and sweep along the 3D fit spline.

Summary

Curve functionality has not received a lot of attention in the regular enhancement cycle, but curves remain an important part of modeling in SolidWorks. The most commonly used curve types are the Helix/Spiral and the Projected Curves, and these features are typically used primarily in conjunction with Sweep features. You may find a fair amount of overlap between curve functionality and 3D sketch functionality, with the curves offering more dimensional control, and 3D sketches allowing (or requiring) more freedom. Many of the limitations and quirks of curves can be overcome by converting them into 2D or 3D sketches, as appropriate.

The remaining curve features also have uses in niche applications. Overall, curves are easy to use, but they lack some of the sophistication found in other areas of the SolidWorks software.

Chapter 6

Using the Primary Shape Creation Features

SolidWorks has many options when it comes to surface feature types, but only a few distinguish themselves as primary shape creation features. For example, a loft is a primary shape creation feature, but a fillet is not. While fillets can make complex geometry, they are dependent on other existing geometry and in most cases take on a secondary role in overall shape creation. Also, the Freeform feature can shape major faces, but again, it is dependent on existing geometry.

The features that I consider to be primary shape creation features in SolidWorks surfacing are the Sweep, Loft, Boundary, and Fill features. There are certainly overlapping applications for these four features, which can make choosing between them confusing at times. The first part of this chapter helps you make the decision about which feature to use in which situation.

The second part of this chapter explains all of the available options for each of these features. Several examples show the options in action. If you are impatient with detailed descriptions of how things work, you may want to just skip directly to the chapters in Part 4, which are built on extensive model walk-throughs.

Choosing Which Feature to Use

When you first sit down with a brand-new complex surface modeling project, you may hesitate for a moment. "Where do I start?" is the question that goes through my mind at these times. Usually I start with a layout sketch, a sketch picture, or even a scanned 3D point cloud. Getting the first shaded face on the screen is always a bit of a relief for me because it feels like a more concrete starting point. After I have a more concrete starting point, everything else becomes much easier. There is something about going from sketches and curves to 3D geometry that somehow makes visualizing the end result somewhat easier.

What type of feature do you use for that first shaded face? Sometimes the first shaded face on the screen is just a construction surface, in which case it may be an Extruded or Ruled surface. Chances are that the first model face on the screen, if it is not something more mundane like an extrude or revolve, is a Loft, Sweep, Fill, or Boundary surface.

The decision of when to use a Sweep feature is usually easier to define than the other three. Sweeps have a consistent cross section, or at least a cross section that you can only change by using the path and guide curves.

Deciding between a Loft and a Boundary surface is often more difficult. The Boundary surface is still a relatively recent development in SolidWorks, and at first appearance they might appear to be the same; however, I assure you that once you start using the Boundary surface, you will see that it has power far beyond the Loft surface. Still, the Loft surface is easier to set up, and works in some situations when the Boundary surface will not.

The first section of this chapter briefly describes the essential elements of each of these four primary shape creation features in order to make it easier for you to recognize situations in which each is best applied. No foolproof set of rules exists that can make this decision for you.

Selecting a sweep

Sweep features are usually easy to identify. They are certainly the easiest to spot of the four mentioned here. The primary characteristic of a sweep is that it has a single profile (cross section) swept along a path. In the simplest sweeps, the profile does not change along the length of the sweep. This would include sweeps such as a spring, hose, or wire.

You can change the shape of the profile along the length of the path by driving a point on the profile with a guide curve. For example, a circle may change diameter. An ellipse may change axis direction or length.

Figure 6.1 shows some typical shapes of sweeps, as well as more sophisticated shapes like involute pump housings or spoon type shapes.

Sweeps tend to require you to follow more rules, and the shapes are limited in several ways. The primary limitation in a sweep is that the profile must be able to rebuild at every point along the path such that all of the sketch relations solve correctly. For this reason, you cannot use a sweep to flip the curvature of an arc such that the arc starts concave up and ends concave down (but you can do that using a three-point spline, as demonstrated in the spoon model shown in Figure 6.1).

The section of this chapter devoted to sweep functionality covers the rules for sweeps thoroughly.

FIGURE 6.1

Typical shapes achievable with sweeps

While this book talks more about surface than solid functionality, you should not forget that you can create complex shapes directly in solids in many situations. Sweep is available in both solid and surface features.

Another very specialized function of the sweep that no other feature in SolidWorks matches is that, starting in SolidWorks 2008, you can sweep a solid body as a cut. This is particularly useful when creating or simulating machining cutter paths in a piece of material. Prior to 2008, creating geometry of this sort was very difficult, both to execute and sometimes even to understand how to do correctly, particularly if the cutter moved in two axes simultaneously, and one of those was parallel to the axis of the cutter and the cutter had a flat end. Figure 6.2 shows a part where I have applied this technique.

FIGURE 6.2

A swept cut using a solid body as the profile

The geometry for this feature is not precise; SolidWorks approximates its shape to some extent, and use of this feature greatly affects your rebuild times. In the case of the solid sweep, what is normally referred to as the profile is referred to as the tool body instead. The cutting tool body is limited to revolved shapes.

Some users think of the sweep as an automated setup for a loft. When you create a sweep with guide curves, SolidWorks creates intermediate profiles behind the scenes by repositioning and solving your profile sketch in many locations along the length of the sweep. You can see these intermediate profiles by using the eyeglasses icon on the Guide Curves panel of the Sweep PropertyManager. SolidWorks then takes the intermediate profiles and lofts them together.

Selecting a loft

The lofted surface is a flexible and easy-to-use feature, and until the arrival of first the Fill and then the Boundary features, the Loft feature had been the primary staple of most complex surface creation. Even though the Fill and Boundary features have in many respects surpassed the Loft feature, Loft has improved continuously over each release; the newer features simply have more to offer. Because I have become more comfortable with the Boundary surface, my primary use for the Loft feature is either when I just use it by habit or as a backup for the Boundary or Fill features.

One type of situation does exist in which I would choose a loft over a boundary, and that is in the use of a centerline loft. A centerline loft is like a sweep in that it uses a path that does not need to directly touch the actual profile. Both sweeps and centerline lofts generate intermediate profiles. A centerline loft is more flexible than a sweep, however, because you can use multiple profiles instead of being limited to one. Centerline lofts are primarily useful in situations where the result can be approximate, because it does not necessarily follow the input curves exactly. Figure 6.3 shows a good application for a centerline loft. In this case, a 3D sketch around the outside of the part is the centerline and determines the overall shape for the feature in the same way that the path determines the overall shape of a sweep.

FIGURE 6.3

Application of a centerline loft

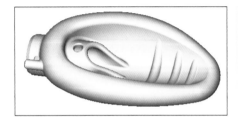 

ON the WEB   **The part in Figure 6.3 is on the Web site for this book, and is named Chapter 6 – Centerline Loft.sldprt. You may want to open it and examine how the first couple of loft features are made.**

The strengths of the Loft feature are primarily in its stability, interface, and familiarity. The loft interface is somewhat easier to manage than that of the boundary. Also, you can make solid or surface loft features, while the boundary can only make surface features.

The weaknesses of the loft when compared against the boundary include that the loft cannot give a curvature continuous condition across the guide curves. Also, the loft must have a profile at the beginning and the end of a feature, while the boundary can use curves in the middle, referred to in the next section as the "X" curve arrangement.

When you compare the Loft feature against the Fill feature, the loft can only create four-sided and degenerate patches, while you can create a fill from any number of sides. A fill has an entire range of functionality not available in other features, for which I simply refer you to the section on the Fill Surface feature later in this chapter.

Selecting the Boundary surface

The Boundary surface feature is quite an amazing and powerful tool in terms of real functionality and the quality of the surface produced. At the same time, it has some problems that cause it to issue warning messages that do not always seem to make sense, its interface is sometimes difficult to manage, and some of the option names do not seem descriptive. When it works, it produces very nice surfaces, and when it doesn't, you may waste a lot of time trying to figure out why.

It is difficult to clearly summarize the types of geometry you can create with the Boundary feature, but it is safe to say that almost anything you can create with a Loft surface you can also create with a Boundary surface. In fact, many things you can create with a simple sweep you can also create with a Boundary surface. This is partially because SolidWorks introduced the Boundary surface in SolidWorks 2007 (SolidWorks 2008 sp 2.1 is current at the time of this writing), and there is not a lot of available common public experience with the feature. In the course of writing this book and creating examples, I have gone out of my way to use the Boundary feature, which is where most of my observations have come from.

Generally, Boundary surfaces must be "bounded" on at least two sides by sketches, edges, or curves, but this is not always true, as the curves can be in the middle of the Boundary feature, rather than at the edges. This is the "X" curve arrangement mentioned in the section on lofts.

As I mentioned earlier, on the face of things, the Boundary surface bears a strong resemblance to the Loft feature. You select curves in one direction that act like loft profiles, and curves in a second direction, which can resemble loft guide curves. The boundary feature also enables you to limit the surface in one or both directions by using the Trim By Direction X option. The biggest distinction is that with the Boundary surface, you can set a curvature condition in both directions. With a loft, you can only set curvature at the profiles, and only tangent at the guide curves.

The Boundary feature works only on four-sided patches. However, like the loft, the boundary can create degenerate singularities, which means it can create three- or two-sided faces. While degenerate surfaces are not necessarily desirable, sometimes they are appropriate for the task at hand. For patches with a greater number of sides than four, you should consider a Fill surface.

Smoothness

The biggest advantage of the Boundary surface over the other primary shape creation features is the smoothness of the connections to other surrounding surfaces. You can measure the smoothness quantitatively using the Deviation Analysis tool. Even without any of the other advantages, this one alone would make the Boundary surface worth using.

CROSS-REF   Chapter 14 describes the Deviation Analysis tool in more detail.

Curve arrangements

The second-biggest advantage of the Boundary surface is the combination of possible arrangements of curves from which you can create a Boundary surface. For example, you can create a Boundary surface between two curves in Direction 1 separated by some distance, similar to a loft between two profiles. You can also create a boundary from an arrangement like the capital letter L, with one curve in Direction 1 and one in Direction 2. You could also use an arrangement like a capital letter T, where one curve is on the edge and the other curve is in the middle. The L and the T function somewhat like a Sweep feature, with a curve on the end of a path. Another option is an X, where both curves are in the middle of the surface. Figure 6.4 illustrates several of these curve arrangements, along with the resulting surface. Other potential letter-based comparisons include I, C, and O (these last two assume three- and four-sided boundaries, respectively).

FIGURE 6.4

Various profile arrangements that the Boundary surface can use

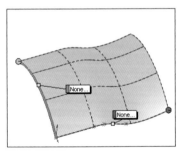
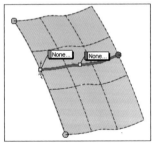
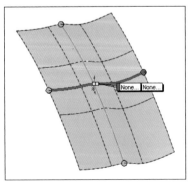

NOTE   I am using the word *curve* here generically, because that is the term that SolidWorks uses for what the Loft feature calls profiles and guide curves. The curves for the Boundary surface can be actual curve features, model edges, or sketches, and you can use the Selection Manager to make selections.

Trim with connectors

The third advantage of the Boundary surface that you can find in no other feature in SolidWorks is that you can dynamically trim back the profile selection using a sliding connector. So, if you select a single long edge to be a profile, but do not want to use the whole edge, you simply slide the connector back to the point where you want it. This avoids any of a number of workarounds for trimming edges that users frequently use with other features.

Of course, in addition to all of this, you can use as many profiles in either direction as you want, and yes, the order of selection matters in using the Boundary feature, just like it does in using the Loft feature. The main limitation is that all the curves in Direction 1 must intersect all the curves in Direction 2.

For all of these reasons, the Boundary feature is my first choice when modeling complex faces.

Other issues with the Boundary feature

Of course, in order to use the Boundary feature effectively, you also need to know how to work around some of the issues that you may encounter. Fortunately with this feature, most of the issues arise from the interface. The first problem you notice with the interface is that in each session, the curvature combs for the curves in the preview mesh are turned on. The combs in the two directions are different colors, and so when a tightly curved preview displays, the combs cover the screen with pink and purple spikes. You can turn these off, and they stay off for subsequent Boundary features in that session; however, when you quit and re-enter SolidWorks, the option is on again.

The second issue with the interface that can be difficult to deal with is that when assigning tangent types to the curves, you must select the curve, and then select the tangent type. In using the Loft feature, you just set the end condition for each end, and you can access both end condition settings at the same time. SolidWorks has probably done this to save interface space, but it means a lot of extra clicking and mouse travel to get the end conditions set.

Beyond these minor interface complaints, some more serious flaws exist. For example, when using the Curvature condition on an edge profile in a Boundary feature where you have selected curves in both directions that intersect at a sharp angle, SolidWorks often complains that the curvature in the two directions is not compatible. To be fair, sometimes this is a valid warning, but in many situations, such as when the profiles in opposite directions are actually edges that both lie on the same smooth surface, the error message is unwarranted. The folks from SolidWorks tell me that the Boundary surface is more exacting in its tolerances of what it considers to be a tangent connection than either the Fill or Loft features, and so the feature will fail with this incompatibility warning more often, even when it theoretically shouldn't. In situations like this, you can choose one of two workarounds: Either back off the end condition to Tangent, or use a Loft or Fill feature. Figure 6.5 shows an example of this situation when the error is valid.

FIGURE 6.5

An example of the Incompatible Tangency warning

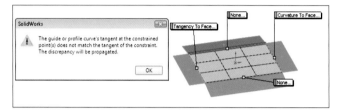

In Figure 6.5, I am creating the Boundary surface between four simple surface bodies, but the long bodies are not co-planar with the shorter ones — they are angled down by 10 degrees. This means that in the corners between the bodies, tangency in one direction does not match tangency in the other direction, which is what the warning message intends to say. Figure 6.5 shows a situation where this message is valid, but other situations exist when you will see a similar message that is not valid — for example, if instead of four separate surface bodies, the boundary was formed by four edges of a rectangular hole in a single continuously smooth surface, as shown in Figure 6.6.

FIGURE 6.6

A warning message when conditions are ideal

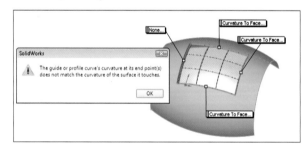

If you get a warning of this sort and it causes the feature to simply not work, then your remaining options are either using tangency, or using the Loft or Fill feature. If you need curvature continuity all the way around the surface, choose the Fill feature. If you can live with continuity in one direction and tangency in the other, then the Loft feature will work. In the academic example shown in Figure 6.6, the Delete Hole or Untrim functions will also work.

Figure 6.7 shows a similar error with the Fill surface, but the difference between the results is that the fill will loosen the constraints around the corner to make the feature work, even if it is not 100 percent accurate at the corner. You decide what you need, and use the tools at your disposal (Deviation Analysis, Zebra Stripes) to check the quality of the results.

FIGURE 6.7

A tangent consistency warning on a fill

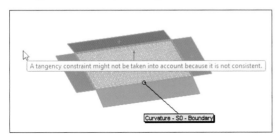

Figure 6.8 compares the actual results of making the Boundary and Fill features with bounding tangencies that don't match. The Fill feature is obviously more tolerant of some discrepancy.

FIGURE 6.8

A fill (left) and boundary (right) with a 10-degree tangency discrepancy

Selecting the Fill surface

I frequently call the Fill surface the "magic wand" in SolidWorks, because I am often amazed at the types of situations in which it works that you could not do any other way. Before SolidWorks formally introduced the Fill surface in released software, they internally called it the "N-sided patch." I think this name better characterizes the main intent and unique functionality of this feature. If you have a gap in a surface model that you need to patch, and especially if the gap is not a nice and clean four-sided gap, and the Delete Hole or Untrim features are not valid options, the Fill surface should be your first choice. The Fill feature fills in gaps with any number of sides, including circular or randomly shaped gaps, and can use edge, 2D/3D sketch, or curve geometry as the boundary of the gap. In recent releases, you can even leave sides of the gap open with the Fix Up Boundary option. The Fill feature is most useful when the boundary is made of edges of surfaces or solid faces.

CROSS-REF The Delete Hole and Untrim features are covered in depth in Chapter 11 with other non-parametric editing features.

I frequently use the Fill surface in gaps that I create intentionally. This typically happens when I need an area smoothed over. In this situation, I usually call the technique a blend. Another common use for the Fill feature is to replace degenerate three-sided patches caused by fillets on three intersecting edges on a simple prismatic part. One of the most common failures on imported geometry is this type of spherical corner. Figure 6.9 shows the before and after shots of the U-V face curves using a fill to replace the corner.

FIGURE 6.9

Replacing a degenerate corner with a Fill surface

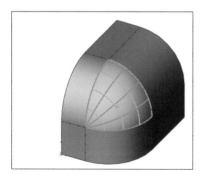 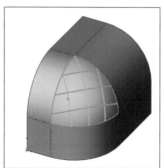

Another example of using the Fill feature in conjunction with fillets is the very powerful blend referred to as the "atomic bomb" fillet by Keith Pedersen of the New England reseller CAP. Figure 6.10 shows (from left to right) the original unfilleted part, the part with natural fillets, and the part with an atomic bomb blend at the intersection of the six edges.

The main underlying advantage of the Fill surface is that it typically does not create degenerate points on a face. The Fill feature overbuilds surfaces and trims them back to fit the gap, regardless of the shape. A Fill surface can make use of three edge conditions: Contact, Tangent, and Curvature.

The interface for the Fill feature is generally very easy to use, and you can select edges very quickly if all of the edges are on the same body. Edge selection can use any of the loop selection options from the RMB (right mouse button) menu, such as Select Loop, Select Open Loop, Select Tangency, and Select Partial Loop. Because all of the edges go into a single box rather than being separated into Directions 1 and 2, or profiles and guide curves, the interface is greatly simplified. The Fill feature does not make use of the SelectionManager.

Using a Fill surface to blend a complex intersection of fillets — the "atomic bomb" fillet

  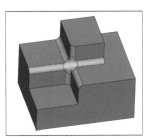

The one awkward part of the fill interface is in assigning conditions to each selected edge. Sometimes, when making a change (such as turning on the Apply To All option) that doesn't change the selection, the preview rebuilds. The only way to avoid this is to turn off the preview. Also, selecting edges from the list when there are enough edges to activate the scroll bars can be clumsy, and SolidWorks could easily improve upon the existing interface.

In early versions of SolidWorks 2007, Fill features that had Tangency or Curvature set for selected edges with sharp corners between them were often flagged with yellow exclamation marks in the FeatureManager. SolidWorks Corporation said this was due to the same condition described in the Boundary feature, where the tangency in the two directions was not compatible at the corner. In later versions, the tolerance must have been relaxed, because for the same models, the warning flags disappeared. In SolidWorks 2008, when the software detects this condition, it displays a message on the screen, as shown in Figure 6.7 instead of applying the yellow exclamation mark flag to the feature.

Recent versions of SolidWorks have brought exciting new functionality for complex shape modelers, particularly in the form of the Fill and Boundary surfaces. All of the primary shape creation features have particular strengths. However, not every tool is perfect, and knowing the weaknesses without having to discover them for yourself is a big advantage.

The rest of this chapter focuses on the actual usage of each feature, and how each option works. For model walk-throughs that cover all of the features in this chapter, look ahead to the chapters of Part 4.

Using Sweeps

Understanding the rules upon which features are built helps you understand what the features were intended to do, and enables you to push the limits of what each feature can do. Understanding the available options often opens new possibilities.

A sweep requires the following:

- **Profile.** The profile is a sketch that may be an open or closed loop for a surface, or only a closed loop for a solid. Both solid and surface sweeps may have nested loops (concentric circles). A surface sweep may even have multiple open profiles (concentric open arcs). You may also use the SelectionManager with sweep profile selection, which enables you to select only a portion of a given sketch, or select entities from multiple sketches, similar to the use of contours in Extrude and Revolve features.

- **Path.** The path does not need to touch the profile, and can extend past the profile plane. The path can be a 2D or 3D sketch, a curve feature or a model edge, or any combination of those when selected with the SelectionManager, and the elements touch end to end without gaps or overlaps. The path can contain sharp corners (when guide curves are not used), which produces picture-frame mitered corners. The path may also be either an open or closed loop.

Figure 6.11 shows several possibilities for simple sweeps involving just a profile and a path.

FIGURE 6.11

Simple profile and path sweeps

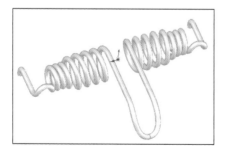

If the path is made of lines and arcs, the sweep may appear to be made of a series of extrudes and revolves (analytical geometry), with breaks between the faces. When the path is a spline, the sweep creates a single continuous face for any tangent profile sketch entities.

You can create all of the profiles and guide curves of a loft in a single 3D sketch, but you cannot make the profile and path of a sweep this way.

Orientation and Twist Type options

A simple sweep has a constant cross section. The cross section (profile) may twist, particularly if the path is a 3D path or a 2D path that has tight corners. Twist can be controlled (induced or eliminated) by using either settings or guide curves. You can find those settings in the Orientation/Twist Type section of the Options panel in the Sweep PropertyManager, shown in Figure 6.12.

FIGURE 6.12

The Sweep PropertyManager and the Orientation/Twist Type options

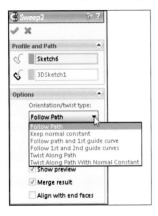

Follow Path

The Follow Path option maintains the original orientation of the profile with respect to the path throughout the sweep. That is to say that if the profile starts out at a 10-degree angle to the path, it will remain at a 10-degree angle throughout the sweep, although it may spin around the path.

Think about the profile as if it were an airplane traveling down the direction of the path. The pitch (angling up or down), yaw (angling side to side), and roll (spinning around the path) are the directions we are interested in controlling. Figure 6.13 shows this arrangement. The path controls pitch and yaw, because the profile always moves in a direction tangent to the path at any point. Roll is analogous to twist. The Follow Path option does not control twist (where the profile spins around the path); it only locks in the current pitch/yaw relationship between the profile and the path.

The official SolidWorks documentation never uses the pitch, yaw, and roll terminology, but it seems the clearest and most straightforward means of describing the possible rotations of the profile with respect to the path.

FIGURE 6.13

The pitch, yaw, and roll directions

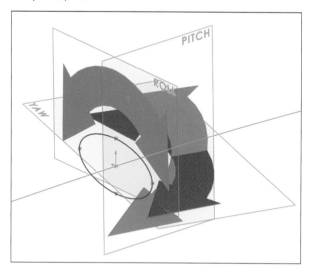

Path Alignment Type

The Path Alignment Type option is only available when using the Follow Path option. This is because it is the only option for which there is no other form of twist control. Path Alignment Type offers four options:

- **None.**
- **Minimum Twist.** This option is valid for 3D paths only, such as that shown in Figure 6.14, along with the Path Alignment Type in the Sweep PropertyManager. It prevents the sweep from becoming self-intersecting, although it may be somewhat arbitrary about how it actually accomplishes that. Minimum Twist is probably best left as a troubleshooting or "let's see what this does" type of option, because it does not create controllable, predictable, or intentional geometry.

FIGURE 6.14

Making use of the Path Alignment Type option

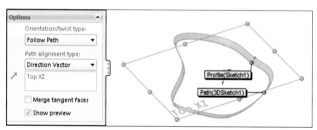

■ **Direction Vector.** The Direction Vector option requires the selection of a line, axis, or plane to establish a direction. SolidWorks then maintains the roll angle of the profile with respect to the axis. In this way, when using the Direction Vector, a swept surface often resembles a Ruled surface, and so if the sweep fails, you may be able to achieve identical or at least similar results with the Ruled Surface tool.

CROSS-REF Chapter 9 covers the Ruled Surface feature in depth.

■ **All Faces.** This option only applies when the sweep path is a set of edges that has one (for open surface edges) or two (for knit surface or solid edges) adjacent faces. The surface will be tangent to the adjacent surface.

Keep Normal Constant

The Keep Normal Constant setting maintains the original orientation of the profile, regardless of what the path does. I normally use this setting to assist in troubleshooting a sweep that I am having problems getting to work, and for sweeps where the path remains relatively close to a straight line. The reason for this is that keeping the profile in the same orientation (without changing pitch, yaw, or roll) reduces the possibility of a self-intersecting sweep. Figure 6.15 shows the difference between the Follow Path and the Keep Normal Constant settings.

FIGURE 6.15

Comparing the Follow Path setting to the Keep Normal Constant setting

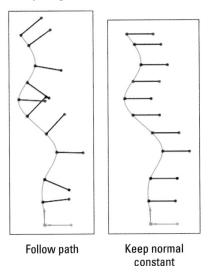

Follow path   Keep normal
                   constant

The lines in Figure 6.15 represent the orientation of intermediate profiles in a simple sweep. Notice that in one section of the Follow Path image, the profiles overlap with one another. SolidWorks refers to this condition as self-intersecting geometry. Using the Keep Normal Constant setting eliminates the overlap, and allows you to complete the Sweep feature so that you can fix the self-intersection problem.

The down side of the Keep Normal Constant option is that when the path deviates from a right angle from the original profile orientation, the sweep can seem smeared, or thinned out in an undesirable way.

Follow Path and 1st Guide Curve

The next section of this chapter covers the use of and rules governing guide curves in SolidWorks. I begin talking about guide curves here, though, because they are part of the twist control discussion.

Especially when working with guide curves, you must think of sweeps as dynamic features rather than static geometry. The sweep creates geometry as the profile moves down the path, or at least that is one way of visualizing it. What is actually happening is that SolidWorks is setting up a loft by solving the profile sketch at various locations along the path. Guide curves can actually change the size, shape, and orientation of the profile as it moves from one end of the path to the other.

Another way to visualize what is happening in a sweep with guide curves is to think of the path and guide curve as being roller coaster rails, and that the car is made of rubber, and deforms if the rails aren't parallel. Using two rails instead of one prevents the car from spinning.

The primary job of the path is to orient the profile plane in pitch and yaw as it travels through the sweep. You can also use it to locate the profile, although that is not mandatory. The primary job of guide curves is to control the roll orientation of the profile, and also to control points on the profile, and so indirectly to control the size or shape of the profile sketch.

Figure 6.16 shows a sweep in which a guide curve orients and resizes a profile, as well as orienting the plane the profile is on.

ON the WEB   The part used for the screen shots in Figure 6.16 is on the Web site for this book, in the folder for Chapter 6. You will be able to visualize what is going on much better if you open the part in SolidWorks. The part is called Chapter 6 – First Guide Curve.sldprt.

The path used in this case is a straight line, and the guide curve is a fit spline that is fit over a partial helix and two sketch segments. The profile is a rectangle. The path drives one corner of the profile, and the guide curve drives the other. As the guide curve twists around the path, it takes the profile with it. Also notice that it resizes the profile.

NOTE   It is often beneficial to remove extraneous sketch relations in sweep profile sketches. A Horizontal sketch relation may prevent a profile from rotating. It is best to use relations within the profile to the path and guide curve to establish the sketch orientation.

To best visualize what is happening with the sweep, expand the Guide Curves panel in the PropertyManager, and click the eyeglasses icon at the bottom; then use the spin arrows to show the intermediate profiles.

FIGURE 6.16

Using a guide curve to control the profile

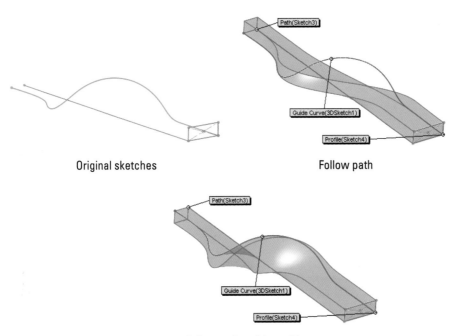

Original sketches   Follow path

Follow path and 1st guide curve

Follow 1st and 2nd Guide Curves

When using the Follow 1st and 2nd Guide Curves option, instead of determining the roll of the profile by the vector from the path to the first guide curve, SolidWorks determines the roll by the vector from the first guide curve to the second guide curve. If you have multiple guide curves, their order is important if you use either this or the previous setting. Other than that, the options function similarly.

NOTE   Sometimes it can be difficult to determine which curve should be the path and which should be the guide curve. In general, because the path orients the profile plane, it is best if the path is the entity that has the least amount of curvature, or deviates the least from a straight line. This can help you prevent self-intersection errors.

Another trick is to use a straight line as a path, which is really just the same as using the Keep Normal Constant setting.

Twist Along Path

The Twist Along Path setting is extremely valuable in a couple of situations. Primarily, it offers a means to control the twist of a sweep without the use of guide curves. Interestingly, one of its most valuable uses is to *prevent* twist rather than induce it. Figure 6.17 shows an example of a part that uses the setting to equalize the natural twist of a sweep that follows a 3D curve around a corner. You can use the setting in most situations when you are having problems with undesired twist.

FIGURE 6.17

Equalizing twist along a 3D path using the Twist Along Path setting

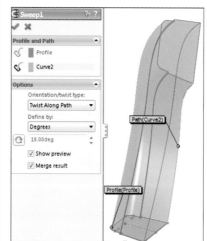

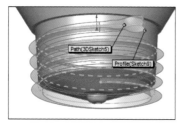
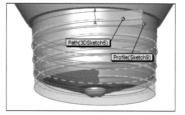

ON the WEB The models shown in Figure 6.17 are on the Web site for this book, labeled Chapter 6 – twist along path.sldprt, and Chapter 6 – twist along path 4.sldprt.

The image in the upper left of Figure 6.17 is of the part using only the Follow Path setting. In the top center image, the Twist Along Path setting is activated and left at the default value of zero degrees, and in the image to the upper right, the twist is set to 18 degrees. The complete transformation of the model from a useless, twisted wreckage to an intentionally designed solid model underscores the importance of understanding all of the settings and options, not just giving up if intuition or random button pushing does not produce the desired results.

NOTE In the lower set of images in Figure 6.17, if you examine the preview closely, you will notice that the preview for the cut (light bulb screw base) overlaps itself outside of the solid. This sweep would be difficult to accomplish if SolidWorks did not have some of this flexibility built into it.

Another use of the Twist Along Path option can produce either simple or very complex, twisted sweeps. What you would actually use this geometry for other than spiral telephone cords is up to you. I have used the twisted sweep along a straight line in place of creating a helix and sweeping along that. In the first example shown in Figure 6.18, I created the feature by drawing one straight line in each of two sketches, sweeping one line as a surface along the other, and then applying the Twist Along Path option. The figure shows models with and without the Twist Along Path setting activated.

The Twist Along Path option allows you to specify the twist in one of three ways: Degrees, Radians, or Turns.

FIGURE 6.18

More twisted sweeps

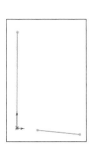
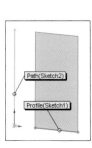
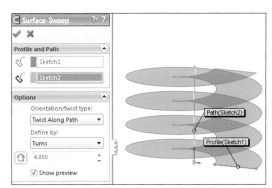
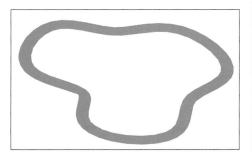
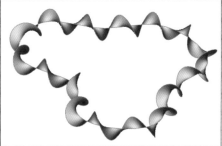

Twist Along Path With Normal Constant

This option is simply a combination of the two settings of the same names that are discussed previously. The profile plane remains parallel to its original orientation, and the entire profile sketch twists along the path.

Merge Tangent Faces

This function is mislabeled in the Help Index as Merge Smooth Faces. In theory, this setting would approximate any tangent sketch entities as a single spline, and then sweep that spline, thus removing any edges between tangent sketch entities. In reality, it appears to do nothing at all, and in fact this has been confirmed by SolidWorks tech support. I believe this is simply a relic of years past when it actually did function. New options and defaults in SolidWorks over the years have made it obsolete.

Show Preview

The Show Preview option enables a semi-transparent preview of the resulting body while the PropertyManager is still open. This preview can take time to create, but it can also help you diagnose self-intersecting situations. If you are already using Instant 3D or Move/Size Feature, you may not need feature previews.

Merge Result

Merge Result is only available for solid sweeps, and refers to merging the newly formed solid body into any intersecting solid bodies. The "merge" here is not the same as the mysterious Merge Tangent Faces, which would mean to remove edges between faces by approximating the profile (and possibly the path, as well) with a spline.

Align With End Faces

The Align With End Faces option either extends or trims both boss and cut sweeps to the next face where it can terminate gracefully. With a swept cut, this usually means that SolidWorks extends the cut smoothly, if possible, up to the next face or through all. It is similar in some ways to the Up To Next end condition for extrudes.

Figure 6.19 shows an example of a helical cut (yellow) and a helical boss (red) using the Align With End Faces setting.

Guide curves

When you get into guide curves, you leave the world of simple sweeps behind. Guide curves exist for two reasons: to prevent or to induce the twist of profiles, and to drive the position of points within the profiles. Guide curves can be actual curve features, 2D or 3D sketches, model edges, or a combination of any of those using the SelectionManager.

Sweep guide curves must not have any non-tangencies, and so they must be smooth. They must also touch the profile, and may extend beyond it. When the sweep is created, the sweep will end at whichever entity it gets to the end of first, whether it is the path or the guide curve.

FIGURE 6.19

Using the Align With End Faces option with both cut and boss sweeps

The order in which you select the guide curves also matters. You may remember the Follow Path and 1st Guide Curve option. The arrows to the left of the Guide Curves panel enable you to reorder the guide curves if necessary. Changing the order of the guide curves can change the orientation of the intermediate profiles, thus changing the shape of the finished feature. Sometimes the order of the guide curves can be the difference between a feature working or not working. Generally, the guide curve that is simplest, or has the least changes in curvature, should be listed first if other factors do not control order. Figure 6.20 shows the Sweep PropertyManager with the Guide Curves panel displayed.

The Guide Curves panel may be hidden if you have selected one of the Twist Along Path options. It will show up again if you select a different Orientation/Twist Type option.

FIGURE 6.20

The Sweep PropertyManager along with the Guide Curves panel

The Pierce constraint and feature order

In earlier versions, SolidWorks required that you create the profile last, with the path and guide curves coming first. The Sweep feature also used to require that you make pierce relations in the profile sketch between points in the profile and any guide curves.

For the last several versions, none of this is required. You can create a profile and then create the path and guide curves using the profile to locate them. This way is less constrictive, but you may notice that any models I have built tend to still use the old method. Most modeling in SolidWorks presents you with the option of an easy way, and a more reliable way. This is one of those cases. The new way doesn't have any advantage, other than being easier to create. I believe the older method is more robust especially in more complex sweep features. The choice as to which should come first, the profile or the path/guide curve, is more flexible now than it used to be, and it can be driven by the needs of the model rather than arbitrary rules of the software.

Consumed curves, rollback, and reuse

You may find several limitations when working, particularly with curve features and sweeps. These limitations are active as of this writing, which uses the latest available version, SolidWorks 2008 sp 2.0.

- **Cannot reuse curve features.** If you have used a curve feature as a guide curve in one sweep, you cannot reuse it as, say, a path in another feature of any type. Instead, SolidWorks displays the prompt, "Selected object is already owned by a feature." One workaround for this is to use a 3D sketch and convert the curve into a sketch spline, which can be reused by multiple features.

- **Cannot select absorbed curve feature from the graphics window.** This is a long-standing bug. After a curve has been used in a sweep, you cannot select it from the graphics window unless you are editing the feature that originally consumed it. This is particularly a problem with the old way of doing things mentioned earlier (path and guide curves first, profile last). An example would be that you make a curve, then make the profile and give it a Pierce relation, and then make a Sweep feature. Next, you change the curve in such a way that the Pierce relation goes dangling. To repair the dangling relation, you delete it and create a new one, but at this point you cannot select the curve from the graphics window; you can only select it from the FeatureManager. Selecting from the FeatureManager can also be a problem because the selection implies a location, which can be important if a curve pierces a sketch plane multiple times. When a situation like this backfires on you, all you can do is delete the feature and start again, or play tricks with replacing the existing curve with a new identical curve (and then submit an enhancement request).

- **Rolling back multiple levels of consumed features can be very tedious.** Say that a sweep uses a curve, but the curve is a composite curve, which is made of a helix and a projected curve. The projected curve is made of two sketches. So, you have three levels of consumed features: Composite, Projected, and Sketch. This is shown in Figure 6.21.

  If you wanted to roll back to just show the sketches, you would have to expand all of the levels under the sweep, roll back between the Sweep feature and the composite curve, and then answer Yes to the "This feature will be temporarily unabsorbed" prompt. You would then roll down to show the composite curve. You would have to go through the same procedure for the other two levels. This is tedious and wastes a lot of time but is the only way of doing it short of deleting the top-level feature.

FIGURE 6.21

Multiple levels of consumed features

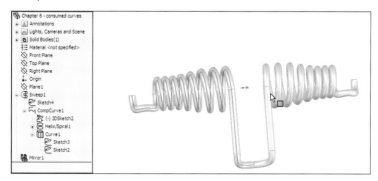

NOTE This might be a good time to suggest that you fill out the enhancement request form on the SolidWorks Web site. SolidWorks Corporation uses enhancement requests filed by users to prioritize functionality for new versions of the software. One of my favorite things to ask for is a straight history-based FeatureManager, without any consumed or indented features, in part to reduce the need for the tedious procedure outlined above.

Thin Features and Solid Sweep

Like the Extrude and Cut features, sweeps can be created as thin features. This simply means that instead of making a solid tube, you can sweep a hollow tube directly without the need for a swept cut or a Shell feature. It works just like an extruded or cut thin feature, in that all you specify is the thickness and the direction of the material. Other considerations, such as minimum radius issues, may cause the thin feature to fail, but these problems are not exclusive to this function.

Also remember that, although we have been mainly talking about either surface sweeps or solid sweeps, swept cuts exist as well. When you initiate a swept cut, it works just like any other type of sweep, except that you get the option to make either a Profile Sweep or a Solid Sweep. Please excuse the terminology here; in one case, "solid sweep" means creating a solid body rather than a surface body, but the meaning intended by this setting in the swept cut PropertyManager means that instead of sweeping a sketch profile, you can sweep an actual solid body. This is primarily applicable to simulating an end mill cutting material from a work piece. Figure 6.2 shows a part that has been cut with the Swept Cut Solid Sweep option.

The swept cut uses a separate solid body called the tool body, which you must make as a revolved feature. The sweep path must start on or within the tool body.

Figure 6.22 shows the PropertyManager along with the completed geometry for a Swept Cut Solid Sweep option.

FIGURE 6.22

Swept Cut with the Solid Sweep option

Start and end tangency

In my experience, it is not very common for a sweep to start at the end of existing geometry that it must be tangent to. It is even less common for a sweep to *end* at existing geometry that it must be tangent to. This is probably because a sweep profile must be a sketch — it cannot be a set of edges or a model face. Loft features can use edges and faces, and far more frequently require tangency to existing geometry on both ends or sides.

The available options for sweep end tangency are as follows:

- **None.** This is the default.

- **Path Tangent.** The start or end of the sweep is tangent to the tangency direction of the ends of the path.

- **Direction Vector.** If you need to specify the tangency direction at either end of the sweep, you can do it using this option with an edge, line, axis, or plane.
- **End Faces.** When the sweep begins or ends at a solid body, the existing faces can determine its tangency.

Using Lofts

If you get to the point where you are frequently modeling in complex shapes and surfaces, use of the loft will become second nature. A loft made between two profiles with tangency or curvature set at the ends is probably one of the most common types of features, although it is becoming more common for users to use the Boundary feature in place of the Loft feature. More complex lofts with more than, say, four profiles are less common. Lofts can be very simple features that take less than a minute to set up, or they can be complex and take several minutes to set up.

One of the reasons why the Loft feature is so prevalent is that it can make use of edges directly, rather than needing to make sketches for each profile. You will often see Loft features in the FeatureManager with no absorbed entities below them. Figure 6.23 shows the PropertyManager of the Loft feature.

FIGURE 6.23

The PropertyManager of the Loft feature

Using loft profiles

Loft profiles for surface features can use 2D or 3D sketches, sketch and reference points, edges, and curves. For solid features, the list includes 2D or 3D sketches, sketch and reference points, faces, and surface bodies. When a 3D sketch is used as a profile for a solid loft, the same kind of filling happens as when a 3D sketch is used for an Extrude feature.

The order of the selection of loft profiles is important. SolidWorks will try to loft in sequence from the first to the last. I have seen situations where the software automatically reordered profiles, and this may happen when it is not appropriate. Use the arrows on the left side of the Profiles selection box to move profiles up or down the order.

You can create all of the loft profiles and guide curves in a single 3D sketch. Doing things this way requires that you use the SelectionManager to select everything. I discuss the SelectionManager later in this chapter. Using a single 3D sketch also makes the Drag Sketch option available, which offers attractive options for making live edits to the sketch while watching the finished geometry update. This situation also holds true in the Boundary Surface feature, discussed later.

Using the Drag Sketch option

You can find Drag Sketch in the Sketch Tools panel of the Loft PropertyManager that appears when you have selected all of the profiles from a single 3D sketch. It is only activated when you edit a loft after it has been created; it does not activate as you build a loft. The Drag Sketch option enables you to dynamically drag sketch entities within the 3D sketch. The loft preview updates when you drop the entity you are dragging.

NOTE   While the Drag Sketch option sounds very attractive, other functionality in SolidWorks also allows dynamic editing, without the need for everything to be in a single 3D sketch. Prior to SolidWorks 2008, the Move/Size Features tool enabled you to do exactly the same thing without editing the feature. In SolidWorks 2008, SolidWorks has roughly replaced the Move/Size Features tool with Instant3D, which works the same way as Move/Resize Features, but requires a rebuild after dragging the sketch. This is probably a bug that may be fixed by the time you read this.

Of course, the upside to putting all of the profiles and guide curves into a single sketch is the immediate convenience and instant gratification of watching a complex loft update as you drag profiles and guide curves. However, the downside is that 3D sketches can be much more difficult to work with than 2D sketches. Also, to get the profiles set up correctly in most situations requires planes, and you may remember some difficulties described with the reliability of 3D sketch planes in Chapter 4. You will need to decide for yourself if the limitations are too great for the way you work, or if the benefits of the Drag Sketch option are worth your time.

Using Add Loft Section

Again, SolidWorks trips over terminology consistency. It is easy to confuse "profiles" with "sections," and hard to be consistent with the terms when SolidWorks is not. In any case, once you have created a loft, and then decide that you need an additional profile to help control the shape, you can just right-click a face of the Loft feature, and select Add Loft Section from the RMB menu, as shown in Figure 6.24.

FIGURE 6.24

Using the Add Loft Section feature

  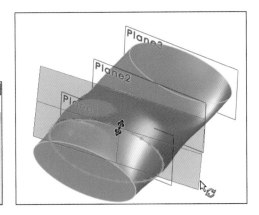

You can position the section by dragging the arrows along the loft. You can rotate the shaded profile plane by putting the cursor at the edge of the plane. Figure 6.24 shows the cursor changing to indicate that you can now pivot the plane. You can also select an existing plane using the list box in the PropertyManager. Just make sure that the plane comes before the Loft feature in the FeatureManager.

By right-clicking again, you can select the Edit Loft Section option to edit the sketch before finishing the command. The software automatically puts the new profile into the correct order in the list of profiles.

NOTE All of this can also be done manually, by rolling back the loft, creating the new profile, editing the loft to add the profile to the list, and then using the arrows to move it to the correct place in the order.

Using the SelectionManager

The SelectionManager, shown in Figure 6.25, is a means to create composite selections from sketch, edge, and curve data. It enables you to select multiple entities, which are then used as a single profile for Sweep, Loft, and Boundary features. The SelectionManager can automatically select open loops or closed loops, or allow you to manually select entities that SolidWorks uses in the feature selection. Figure 6.25 shows a selection, and how SolidWorks represents it in the PropertyManager.

FIGURE 6.25

The SelectionManager

 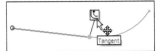

If a problem arises with a selection group listed in the PropertyManager, it shows an error, and you can fix or edit selection groups by right-clicking them in the PropertyManager selection list box and selecting Edit Selection. Other options available on the RMB menu are Clear Selections and Delete.

The buttons on the top row of the SelectionManager toolbar are OK, Cancel, and Clear Selections. On the bottom row are Select Closed Group, Select Open Group, Select Group, Select Region, and Standard Selection. You cannot use the RMB selection options with the SelectionManager, such as the loop selection options, but you can use the Propagate To Tangent icon shown in Figure 6.25.

> **NOTE**   While the SelectionManager is active, it disables the use or display of Loft and Boundary surface connectors. Closing the SelectionManager enables you to work with connectors again. Connectors are discussed in more detail later in this chapter.

A bug is also confirmed in SolidWorks 2008 sp 1.1 that prevents you from adding connectors to a loft if you have used the SelectionManager to select profiles.

Start and end constraints

Start and end constraints only affect the first and last profiles selected in the selection box, respectively. The available options are None, Direction Vector, Tangency to Face, and Curvature to Face. These options should now all be familiar to you.

Guide curves

Guide curves in Loft features are somewhat more forgiving than guide curves in sweeps. In lofts, the guide curve can extend past the profiles on both ends. While each guide curve must still touch each profile, there is no requirement for a Pierce relation. Guide curves must also not have any sharp corners.

In the same way that the first and last loft profiles enable you to specify end constraints, you can also specify tangency across the guide curve side of a loft. The options here are only None, Direction Vector, and Tangency to Face. You do not have an option for Curvature to Face for loft guide curves. To be able to specify Curvature across all four sides, use either Fill or Boundary. Figure 6.26 shows the panel for guide curves in the Loft PropertyManager.

In earlier versions of SolidWorks, the order of the guide curves of a loft mattered only inasmuch as it mattered which one was first. The first guide curve influenced the overall flow of the U-V mesh more than any other guide curve. In recent versions, the Guide Curves Influence drop-down list removes the significance of which guide curve is first, although the reordering arrows remain, as late as SolidWorks 2008 sp 2.0.

The Guide Curves Influence drop-down list has four options:

- To Next Guide
- To Next Sharp
- To Next Edge
- Global

FIGURE 6.26

The Guide Curves panel in the Loft PropertyManager

These options describe how far each guide curve affects the resulting feature shape. Not all of the conditions apply all the time, so you may find that some of the options appear to produce the same shape.

Notice that SolidWorks handles the edge tangency interface differently from the start and end condition. The start and end condition has a separate box for the start and end, but the edge tangency has only a single box from which you must set the two individual edges. This is a minor point, but I find the second situation, two settings controlled from a single box, to be tedious to work with, with a lot of extra clicking and mouse travel. This type of interface carries over into the Boundary surface feature and is somewhat different for the Fill feature.

NOTE I have it from a good authority within SolidWorks Corporation that loft guide curves are not as accurate as you might hope. The surface may not follow them exactly, and you should "think of them more as guidelines than rules".

Using the centerline parameters

A centerline loft is similar in some ways to a sweep, with the centerline taking on the role of the sweep path. Centerline lofts can make use of guide curves, but I usually use a centerline instead of guide curves because I believe the centerline gives a more natural-looking shape, with better control of the axial contour; this is because it does not rely on the placement of the profiles so much as the contour of the centerline. Figure 6.27 shows a practical application of this tool in a medical device.

The Centerline Parameters panel of the Loft PropertyManager, in addition to the centerline selection box, has a slider to select how many intermediate sections you want to create, and a button with eyeglasses, which enables you to toggle through all of the intermediate sections, primarily for troubleshooting. The intermediate sections functionality of the centerline loft is another sweep-like characteristic of the feature.

Practical application of a centerline loft

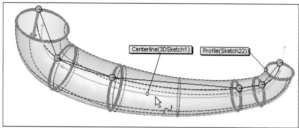

Model courtesy of Daniel Cook, MD, of Cookgas, LLC

Options

Like the Sweep feature, the Loft feature has a set of general options at the bottom of the PropertyManager.

Merge Tangent Faces

Unlike the same setting for the Sweep feature, this one actually works. If you are lofting, say, a line with a tangent arc in one profile to another line with a tangent arc in a second profile, turning this option on results in a single face, and turning it off results in a break between the face between the lines and the face between the arcs. The same is true even in the presence of guide curves.

Regardless of how you set it up, profiles that have non-tangent entities cannot make smooth finished faces. To most users this should sound obvious, but people expect strange things from the software sometimes.

Close Loft

If you want to make a closed-loop loft, where the loft ends at the same profile from which it begins, use the Close Loft option. In a sweep, you draw a closed-loop path. In order to make a closed-loop loft, you must have at least three profiles in the loft.

Preview

Preview is usually used to confirm that your loft is going to work the way you are expecting it to, or to troubleshoot a loft that is not working. It can cause performance slowdowns for complex lofts, but I generally keep it on because it is so useful.

Right Mouse Button menu options

Several options for lofts are only available through the RMB menu, which is shown in Figure 6.28.

FIGURE 6.28

The RMB menu for the Lofted Surface feature

> **NOTE** Where possible I am showing the RMB menus without the broken out icon bar at the top (known as the Context Toolbar) to simplify and clarify the names of the functions. The setting for showing the Context Toolbar or integrating its commands back into the normal RMB menu is found at Tools ⇨ Customize on the Toolbars tab in the upper right side.

Connectors

Connectors play a vital role in both the Loft and Boundary features. Connectors act as ad hoc guide curves that you do not sketch or make from curves, but place while the PropertyManager is open. Connectors can often rescue a loft with ripples or kinks by more evenly distributing the U-V mesh, and keep you from needing to make more drastic changes such as adjusting the position of profiles or guide curves. Figure 6.29 shows a part that makes extensive use of connectors to direct the U-V mesh.

> **ON the WEB** The part used in Figure 6.29 is on the Web site for this book, and is called Chapter 6 – connectors.sldprt.

> **NOTE** As noted earlier, if you do not have the option to show connectors, it could be that the SelectionManager is open, which for some reason interferes with connectors. Also, remember that there is a bug that prevents you from adding connectors in loft features where you have used the SelectionManager to select regardless if it is open or not.

To add a connector, right-click the edge the connector would start from and select Add Connector. You can also hide or delete connectors from the RMB menu, or you can reset them all back to the original defaults.

FIGURE 6.29

Using connectors to redirect the U-V flow of a loft

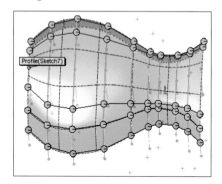

Mesh preview

The mesh preview is simply showing the underlying U-V mesh of the faces that the feature will create. This is very useful in troubleshooting feature failures or irregularities in the surface, such as kinks or ripples. Either setting or clearing any of these options in the RMB menu operates on not just the current feature being edited, but also on all features of this type that you work on with the same computer until the setting is changed. This also includes the Zebra Stripe Preview and the Opaque and Transparent Preview options that follow.

Zebra Stripe Preview

This setting causes SolidWorks to apply zebra stripes to the loft preview. The Zebra Stripes feature is covered in more detail in Chapter 14. You would primarily use zebra stripes for the analysis of tangency or curvature continuity of two faces across an edge, and within a single face, they are useful to help you find ripples, kinks, or areas of tight curvature. I generally do not use this option.

Opaque and Transparent Preview

This option toggles back and forth between the two settings. The default setting is for Transparent to be active, and so the menu will show the Opaque option. I like to see the preview as transparent, as it conveys to me that the form shown is still in progress.

Using the Boundary Surface Feature

You may want to choose the Boundary Surface feature for the bulk of primary faces in surface modeling situations when using SolidWorks 2007 or later. It is far more flexible than the Loft surface, and the surface resulting from the Boundary Surface feature is superior in most situations in which I have compared them.

You still need the Loft feature for lofting solids, because the Boundary Surface feature has no solid feature equivalent. The Loft feature is also useful for those times when you just can't get the Boundary Surface feature to work. Figure 6.30 shows the PropertyManager of the Boundary Surface feature.

Using the Curve Selection boxes

The Direction 1 and Direction 2 boxes are exactly the same. This setup is to stress that with the Boundary surface, unlike with the Loft surface, the two directions are treated exactly the same, and so there is no difference between selecting curves in either Direction 1 or 2. With the Loft feature, the results of the feature can be different, depending on which curves are used as profiles, and which are used as guide curves.

FIGURE 6.30

The Boundary PropertyManager

A Boundary surface can be created completely from selections in only one direction; it does not require selections in both directions. A minimum of two selections are required, either both in the same direction or one in each. If you choose curves in different directions, all of the curves in any direction must intersect all of the curves in the other direction.

You can use the SelectionManager to select curves for the Boundary Surface feature. The SelectionManager here works the same as it does for a sweep or loft.

Figure 6.31 shows the complete roadster model and the rear deck surface in progress. All of the main complex surfaces shown on the model are made using the Boundary surface. I have used lofts only on the underside of the car, where speed was more important than nice-looking surfaces.

FIGURE 6.31

Examples of Boundary surfaces

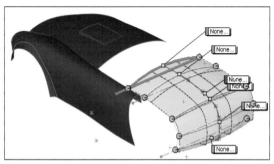

Using connectors

Connectors in Boundary surfaces are similar to connectors in lofts. If a Boundary surface preview is either twisted or doesn't work, you can try to manipulate the connectors to *synchronize*, or line up, the selections. You can easily flip the connectors on a selected curve by right-clicking the curve in the selection box in the PropertyManager and selecting Flip Connectors.

You can also add connectors manually by right-clicking a curve in the graphics window where you would like to place the connector and selecting Add Connector. You can add connectors in either direction, but they may only exist between selected curves. Just as with lofts, Boundary surface connectors manipulate the U-V mesh directly.

You can also use the connectors on selected curves to trim back a selection in a very freehand sort of way. As long as the SelectionManager is not active, the connector handles should appear and allow you to pull the handle back along the curve. This very handy functionality can eliminate editing on curve elements.

NOTE   **In early versions of SolidWorks 2008, a crash exists when manipulating connectors in Boundary surfaces. SolidWorks has identified the problem and claims that it will be fixed in SolidWorks 2008 sp 4.0.**

Curves Influence Type

The Curves Influence Type drop-down list only becomes available after you select at least one curve in each direction. With only one curve selected, the only choice in the drop-down list is Global. If you add a second selected curve to Direction 2, then more choices are added to the Curves Influence Type drop-down list for Direction 1, and vice versa. In this case, the choices for the single curve in Direction 1 include the following:

- Global
- To Next Edge
- To Next Sharp
- Linear

When there is only one curve, Global and Linear are essentially the same option. Global uses the curve to influence the shape of the entire feature. Linear interpolates the influence of two curves, so that if the first curve was a straight line and the second an arc, between the curves, the faces would gradually flatten out, even if there were multiple sharp corners.

Options and preview

The options available here are the same as for the loft, except for the Trim By Direction 1 option. This trims the resulting surface by the last curve in Direction 1, so that if the curves in Direction 2 overhang Direction 1, they are trimmed off at the curve. Depending on the curves you have selected, you could also see a Trim By Direction 2. For example, if the selected curves formed a shape like a number sign (#) you would have options to trim by both directions. An arrangement like an F would only allow you to trim in one direction (defined by whatever direction the top and middle lines of the F represented).

Display

The Display panel of the Boundary PropertyManager manages several display options. The Mesh Density can be helpful if you find localized problems in a Boundary feature, and need to refine the preview mesh to see in more detail what is causing it.

Zebra Stripes is also a function that is familiar from the Loft feature and is generally best used across edges.

The Curvature Combs setting displays curvature combs on all of the mesh curves created by the mesh preview. With large surfaces or dense meshes, especially with surfaces that have tight curvature in places, you can imagine that this fills the display with pink and purple comb lines. This option is usually the first setting I turn off when initiating a Boundary surface. Once it is turned off for a single surface feature, it remains off for that feature, and also for new Boundary surfaces in that session of SolidWorks, but when you exit and restart SolidWorks, it is turned on again in each new feature.

Using the Fill Surface Feature

The Fill surface has been around for a few more releases than the Boundary surface, and so it has fewer quirks, and is more understandable in most situations. The Fill Surface feature works best when filling in an enclosed patch in a surface or solid body, although you can use it earlier in the modeling process as well. The Fill Surface feature has some very useful options that other areas of the software could benefit from if SolidWorks implemented them throughout the software. I call it the "magic wand" because of the range of situations in which it works well.

Figure 6.32 shows the Fill PropertyManager for a model in which Fill surfaces have made all of the faces, except for a fillet. I used some construction surfaces, and I used some other surface-editing tools, but the Fill Surface feature is responsible for all of the major faces.

The Fill Surface feature works best when surfaces fully surround an open gap between the faces. In this situation, select all of the edges that surround the gap, and the Fill Surface feature creates an oversized rectangular patch and trims it to fit in the gap. Having faces around the gap and using their edges to define the gap boundary makes it possible to assign tangency or curvature conditions to the edges, to keep the patch smooth with the existing geometry.

The boundary around the gap can also be composed of curves or sketches, and there can even be openings in the gap boundary by using the Fix Up Boundary option, but I do not recommend doing this. When you leave an opening in the boundary, SolidWorks decides what to do in that area, and it usually bulges the surface out instead of just closing up the gap naturally, the way you might hope it would.

FIGURE 6.32

The Fill PropertyManager and an example part

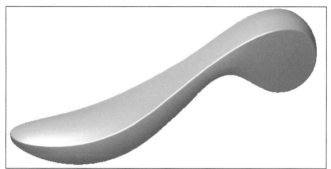

As an alternative, you can use the Curve Through Reference Points feature to select two points quickly and make a curve entity between them, and then you can use the curve to close the boundary. It is still rather arbitrary, but at least it gives you better control than allowing the software to make its own decisions.

A very common use for the Fill Surface feature is to blend over a bad transition. The chapters in Part 4 show several examples of this, but the roadster model has an interesting one.

In Figure 6.33 on the left, you see an awkward area between the grill and the headlight. I remedied this by trimming out the area and patching over it with a Fill surface.

I have found that patches without sharp corners tend to work better than trimming out rectangular patches and trying to fill them. The sharp corners frequently cause problems with the tangency settings on either side of the corner. For this reason, I tend to use circular, or in this case irregular shaped, trimmed-out areas.

FIGURE 6.33

Fill surface patching over an awkward area

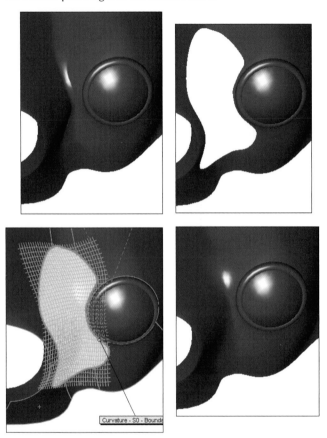

A well placed individual at SolidWorks Corporation has told me that it doesn't matter if the U-V lines of the Fill patch match the U-V lines of the surrounding surfaces. Getting these to line up would take a lot of effort, which would have little if any benefit.

When selecting the edges around the gap, I like to use the RMB menu options, such as Select Open Loop. This only works if the surfaces around the gap are all part of a single surface body. Select Partial Loop is a useful RMB selection option if you do not have a closed loop.

Edge settings

The Edge settings give you three possible choices: Contact, Tangent, and Curvature. You may sometimes find situations where the Curvature setting will not work, but the Tangent setting will. In these situations, you have to make a judgment call, whether Tangent is "good enough" or whether you have to pursue a different solution to the problem.

Alternate Face

The Alternate Face button toggles the face used for the Tangency or Curvature directions. When you select edges that are not open surface edges — for example, when making a patch over a hole in a solid, or over a set of other faces in a surface body — the tangency has the option of two faces to be tangent to, and sometimes the default guess is wrong. This button enables you to set it right manually if necessary.

Apply To All Edges

The Apply To All Edges option applies the currently selected Edge Setting to all of the edges in the Patch Boundary selection box. If any sketches are in the selection box, they are set to Contact, because that is the only setting a sketch can use. Other features enable you to use the Normal To Profile option, but for the Fill Surface feature, this choice is not available. The workaround is to use the sketch to create a small, extruded surface, then select the edge of the surface and assign the Tangent edge setting for that edge.

Optimize Surface

The Optimize Surface option generally only works on four-sided patches. It tries to fit a surface into the gap without overbuilding and trimming back. This is usually not helpful. Usually, the overbuilt surface gives a smoother transition between surfaces.

Some special cases do exist. The lever shown in Figure 6.32 has a Fill surface that only works if the Optimize Surface option is turned on, and then it makes a degenerate point at each end of a two-sided gap. The geometry is good, but the degeneracy is usually undesirable. Oddly enough, Fill surfaces are usually used to eliminate degeneracies, by trimming away an area around the singularity and patching over it.

Preview options

I usually keep the Show Preview and Preview Mesh options turned on. I turn off the Preview Mesh option when working on a complex fill, and each selection causes the preview to rebuild. Sometimes I am too impatient for that, or I already know that the preview will fail until I get to a certain point. The same technique may be used when making many changes to the Edge Settings and they have to be set one by one.

Constraint curves

The lever model from Figure 6.32 uses constraint curves. The curves do not seem to affect the direction of the Fill surface U-V mesh (in fact, other than the Optimize Surface option, I can find nothing that affects it), and they are not analogous to either guide curves in Lofts or Direction 2 in Boundary. Constraint curves do not need to go all the way across the boundary; they can be short sketch segments or even sketch points. Sketch points are often used when a Fill surface caps off a part like the end of a handle.

125

Resolution Control

The Resolution Control determines the density of the mesh. SolidWorks regulates this internally, and so it only allows the mesh density to go to an internally determined level, and then for performance reasons caps it off. The default is for the density to be set low, which in most cases works best. Moving the slider to the right can drastically affect rebuild speed for this feature.

Options

The Fix Up Boundary option, as mentioned earlier, enables the Fill Surface feature to use an open boundary. Again, this is not something you will want to make extensive use of, but it is handy in some situations.

The Merge Result option is very useful. When the boundary edges selected are the open edges of a surface model, it knits together any surface bodies used to create the Fill feature. When the selected boundary edges are either edges of a solid body, or edges of a surface body shared by two faces, the merge acts as a Replace Face function instead, and integrates itself directly into the solid or surface body. This is really amazingly automated functionality, and works well.

When you activate Merge Result, the next option, Try To Make Solid, also becomes available. You can imagine that this can also be a big time saver, because the Knit and Thicken functions are both common parts of the surface modeling workflow. You may or may not want to use this option. If something goes wrong, it can be difficult to tell if it was the Fill surface, or the built-in Knit or Thicken functions that went awry. For this reason, I still often use separate Knit and Thicken features; even though it takes longer to make, and makes the feature tree longer, it is also far easier to troubleshoot later on.

Reverse Direction

You use the Reverse Direction option when the Merge option fails on a solid body. This is because it is trying to put the solid on the wrong side of the surface, and you need to reverse it. No indication exists to show you which side it is trying to make a solid from, so if it looks like it should work, but doesn't, try flipping the direction.

Summary

The Boundary Surface feature should be your first choice in most modeling situations. It is the most flexible, and in most cases offers the best results. Loft is a good back up, and the Centerline Loft can do things that Boundary Surface cannot. Fill is usually best for filling odd-shaped gaps surrounded by surfaces. Sweep candidates usually distinguish themselves with a constant cross section and a definable path.

Considerable overlap between the feature functionality means that you have options for alternative methods when things don't work exactly the way you planned the first time around. These tools are extremely powerful and complex. Develop some intuition about how the tools work, and be willing to experiment.

Chapter 7

Using Advanced Fillets

Although you do not use fillets to create the major faces in complex parts, they can either make or break the look of a part. Knowing where to place (or *not* place) a fillet can be important not just to the look, but also to the quality of the model for downstream applications such as machining, mold design, or stress analysis. Further, being able to visualize what you want a fillet to do at corners and intersections and then being able to translate that visualization into CAD geometry can be crucial to a particular part. Having the complete set of filleting tools at your disposal gives you many options to create the geometry you want.

I think that filleting is one of the underappreciated functions in SolidWorks. The filleting tools can deliver results in an amazing range of situations, and a well-placed fillet can at times rescue a troubled model. When fillets fail, there is usually a tangible reason that you can identify, and then either fix the situation or approach the problem in a different way.

Fillets are also capable of introducing modeling difficulties when you apply them haphazardly. For this reason, I have added a section to this chapter that talks about best practice suggestions that may help you to avoid common pitfalls of filleting.

Differentiating Fillet Functions

You often hear fillets referred to as fillets, rounds, or blends. Technically, each one of these types is different in specific ways, but for the purposes of this book, I will not use the word *rounds*, but treat rounds synonymously with fillets. Fillets simply round off sharp corners whether the corners are concave or convex.

127

The term *blend* is another issue. Usually a blend is a corner where several fillets come together. In this chapter, that is the way the term is used. In later chapters, a blend is defined as a complex set of features that create a smooth transition between multiple shapes. This has nothing to do with fillets, aside from the fact that it is a freeform transition. It can be used to smoothly intersect three or more tubes, or even simply transition from one shape to another.

Figure 7.1 shows a variable radius fillet on the upper edge and a double hold line fillet on the lower edge of the part. By taking sections with spaced planes and the Intersection Curve tool and placing the cursor over each curve, you can tell what type of geometry each feature is using. In the variable radius fillet, in the image to the left, you can see that the cursor is showing the cross section to be an arc. In the image to the right, the cursor shows the cross section to be a spline.

FIGURE 7.1

The difference between arc-based and spline-based fillets

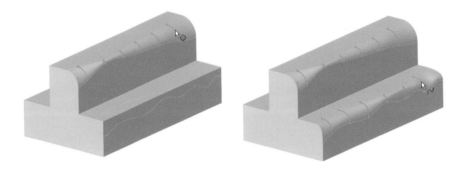

Arc-based fillets

Most of the time when you think about fillets, you are thinking about arc-based fillets. Arc-based fillets are tangent to faces on either side of an edge, and use a distinct radius in between. Even a variable radius fillet is arc-based, because if you take a cross section of the fillet at any point, the cross section is an arc.

Spline-based fillets

The alternatives to arc-based fillets are, of course, spline-based fillets. Spline-based fillets occur in a couple of situations, most notably any fillet that uses the curvature continuous setting, and any fillet that forces the boundaries of both sides of the fillet, such as a double hold line fillet. Both of these are described in detail in this chapter.

The importance of understanding the difference between arc-based and spline-based fillets is minimal, but it does help you understand why fillets might look the way they do or fail in certain situations.

Using Fillet Options

The Fillet tool has several separate functions, each of which you could consider to be separate features on their own:

- Constant Radius fillet
- Variable Radius fillet
- Face fillet
- Full Round fillet
- Setback fillet
- Hold Line fillet
- Curvature Continuous fillet
- Constant Width fillet

Some of these functions overlap somewhat. For example, the Setback fillet can be either Constant Radius or Variable Radius. Hold Line and Curvature Continuous fillets are both part of the Face fillet. This list is broken down according to the major functional fillet types, and how exactly you go about making each type is detailed in the following sections of this chapter.

Constant Radius fillet

The Constant Radius fillet is the default fillet type. Even though this seems like such a basic function, the Constant Radius fillet tool has several surprises in store for you. This book deals with advanced functionality, and so I do not want to spend too much time on a basic function, but this discussion warrants some attention.

Figure 7.2 shows some interesting filleting situations encountered with the Constant Radius fillet. The power of SolidWorks filleting is driven directly, for the most part, by the internal Parasolid geometry kernel that SolidWorks Corporation licenses from Parasolid/UGS/Siemens PLM. SolidWorks itself acts mostly as the user interface for the Parasolid engine functionality.

Figure 7.2 shows three situations in which the basic Constant Radius fillet can deliver unexpected results. Fortunately, this time, the unexpected results are a good thing. In the image to the left, the four original edges came together at the sharp corner, and the two edges that appear now to make a Y originally made a V. When edges that intersect at a shallow angle are both filleted, and the fillets collide, instead of the fillet failing or creating additional and probably inappropriate edges, the software instead merges the fillets into a single fillet for an edge that never existed.

The middle image in Figure 7.2 shows a situation where a non-tangency allows a fillet to run out in such a way that it creates an additional edge. Filleting that new edge would seem to create a completely different and incorrect fillet, but instead, the fillet is blended into the original in such a way that it looks like that was exactly what was intended.

FIGURE 7.2

Interesting filleting situations

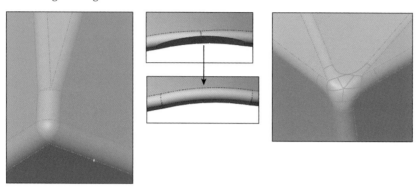

The image on the right of Figure 7.2 is possibly the most interesting of the three. In this situation, five edges are coming together at a single vertex. Some of the faces are at different angles to one another, but the same radius value is used for all of the edges; however, a standard spherical corner cannot be created because of the difference in angles. As the fillets approach the vertex along the edges, they begin to blend together in the same way that you will see the Setback fillet do. This is an unexpected, and I believe completely undocumented, behavior that probably saves the fillet from failing, and yet it is fundamentally different from a standard Constant Radius fillet.

When you see your fillets behaving in these ways, just be aware that the alternative was probably that the Fillet feature would fail unless it did something fancy. These are not bugs. If you want different results, you may try to fillet the edges one at a time, or trim out the corner using surface techniques, adding the fillets, and then using a Fill feature to blend the corner in the way you want.

Multiple Radius fillet

The Multiple Radius Fillet option is directly below the Items To Fillet selection box. It simply enables you to use a single Fillet feature, but apply different radii to different edges. I would not recommend this as simply a way to get as many edges as possible into a single Fillet feature, but it can be effective if you group your fillets into functional groups that may all be suppressed for FEA, or have been added for a rendering, or are all considered cosmetic fillets.

You may hear people recommend making as many fillets as you can in a single feature to help SolidWorks run faster. This is one of those misleading best practice recommendations. It is true that multiple fillets in a single feature is faster than multiple fillet features, but if a single fillet within the large group of fillets fails, the entire feature fails, and this can be difficult to troubleshoot. My recommendation is to group fillets together by function.

Figure 7.3 shows the Multiple Radius fillet interface, and how the different radius values are presented in the PropertyManager and the graphics window.

FIGURE 7.3

Multiple Radius fillet interface

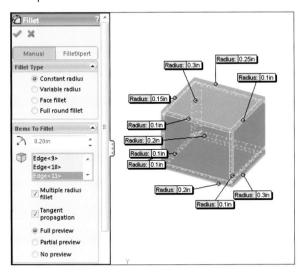

You can also use the Multiple Radius Fillet option with the Setback fillet, which is described next.

Setback fillet

Setback fillets are all about blending several filleted edges at a corner vertex. You must select every edge that intersects at the selected vertex, and you can select as many vertices as you care to in a single Setback fillet feature. You select the vertex in the Setback Vertices selection box in the Setback Parameters panel, shown in Figure 7.4. The special fillet type is the namesake of the setback distance from the selected vertex at which the blend starts to happen. You can set a different setback distance for every edge.

NOTE　When cycling through the edges to add setback distances, a pink arrow is displayed, pointing along that edge. If you have selected multiple vertices, there is a bug in the software such that the arrow often has nothing to do with the edge selected. For this reason, it might be most intuitive to use the callouts in the graphics window rather than the selection boxes in the PropertyManager.

This type of fillet can be the most time-consuming feature to set up, depending on the scope of the feature. On the other hand, there is nothing quite like the Setback fillet for providing a nicely blended and controllable intersection between fillets from three or more edges.

The Setback fillet interface

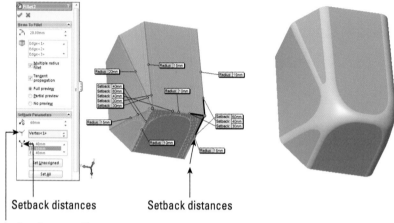

Setback distances   Setback distances

Select vertex or vertices

Selection options

You can select edges, loops, faces, and features in the selection box. A loop is just a loop of edges around a face, and is defined by the selection of a face and an edge on the face, or by using one of the right mouse button (RMB) selection options. Loops are particularly useful for inside loops, where all of the edges are inside the boundary of the face. Selecting a face directly selects all loops on the face.

The RMB selection options are very useful, particularly Select Tangency, Select Loop, and Select Partial Loop. Many users are not familiar with these options.

In addition, an option exists in the Fillet Options panel called Select Through Faces. This option allows you to select hidden edges, even when in Shaded mode. This setting is fine for less complex parts, but if you have a complex part with a lot of hidden edges in the background, getting the cursor stuck on edges you cannot see can be frustrating.

NOTE   The Select Through Faces setting in the Fillet PropertyManager overrides the setting at Tools ➪ Options ➪ Selection that enables you to select hidden edges in the HLR and Shaded modes.

Variable Radius fillet

The Variable Radius fillet enables you to assign different radius values along the length of a filleted edge, and allows you to select multiple edges to be filleted, even if they do not touch other selections. Variable Radius fillets propagate along tangent edges just like Constant Radius fillets, using the last value of the fillet at that end. Figure 7.5 shows the Variable Radius fillet PropertyManager in action.

FIGURE 7.5

The Variable Radius fillet PropertyManager

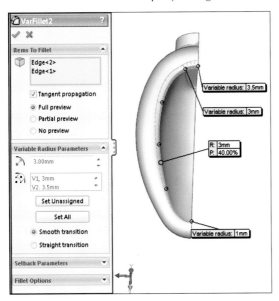

Variable Radius fillets also have two interesting properties that make them even more useful. The first is that you can specify one end of the fillet to have a zero radius. This is useful when you need to control how a fillet tapers off, or if you need to make a simple transition from a smooth to a sharp edge.

CAUTION When Variable Radius fillets use a zero radius end, this creates degeneracy. This can cause problems for downstream applications such as additional fillets over that point, shelled solids, offset surfaces, FEA, and CAM.

The second interesting property of the Variable Radius fillet is that it will sometimes work in situations when a Constant Radius fillet will not, even if all of the radius values are set to the same number. This is because the Variable Radius fillet uses different routines than the Constant Radius fillet.

Other types of fillets exist that create fillets with variable radius, but SolidWorks does not call them Variable Radius fillets. The Full Round fillet, Face fillet with two hold lines, and Face fillet with constant width all make fillets with variable radii. These fillet types are covered later in this chapter.

Face fillet

The Face fillet tends to get the reputation as that kind of fillet that you can never get to work. For one thing, often when another type of fillet fails, the error message suggests that you might try a Face fillet instead. So you try it, and inevitably, it fails.

The truth is that the Face fillet really does excel in situations that stymie other types of fillets. When a Face fillet fails, it is often because the fillet radius is *too small*, while other fillet types tend to fail when the radius is too large. Face fillets also work well in situations where the edge between the filleted faces is broken up or even nonexistent.

The reason Face fillets work in these situations is that when you use a default fillet, you select an edge. Two faces always bound any edge of a solid body, one on each side. In this situation, the fillet can easily select the faces it needs to be tangent to. However, some situations are not so clean and neat. A Face fillet works by the user manually selecting the two faces, either because the edge that you would normally use is not available, or because SolidWorks is having difficulty selecting the faces automatically from the selection of the edge.

Figure 7.6 shows an example of a fillet that any other fillet type would not be able to do, but the Face fillet works perfectly. Notice that the faces joined by the fillet never actually intersect.

A Face fillet works where other fillets would fail

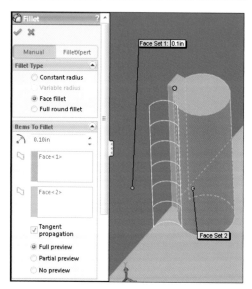

Notice also that there is a blue dot selected in the image. This is an example of a Help Point. The Face fillet can only create a single fillet at a time, unlike many of the other fillet types. In this case, there are two locations that you could fillet: the front of the boss, as shown, and the back of the boss. In this case, it defaulted to the back, and the Help Point just forces it to the front. You can specify the Help Point in the Fillet Options panel in the PropertyManager. If you ever wondered what the Help Point does, well, now you know.

The Face fillet also has some drawbacks. I have already mentioned the fact that you cannot use it to create disconnected fillets. Another limitation is that you can select as many faces as you want in each selection set, but only the last selection matters. It seems odd to have a large selection box when only a single face in each box is actually used.

Curvature Continuous fillet

From the discussion in Chapter 3 on splines and curvature, you should have some idea of what happens with the Curvature Continuous option of the Face fillet. This is a spline-based fillet. The difference between the Curvature Continuous and the Constant Radius option may be visually subtle, as Figure 7.7 shows, but it is mainly about appearance. Notice how the constant radius jumps suddenly from one color to the other in the Curvature plot shown, but the curvature continuous display changes more gradually.

FIGURE 7.7

A comparison between a Curvature Continuous fillet and a Constant Radius fillet

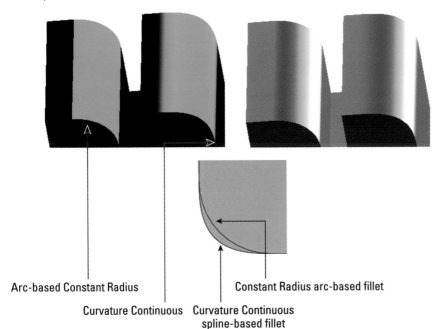

Arc-based Constant Radius

Constant Radius arc-based fillet

Curvature Continuous   Curvature Continuous
spline-based fillet

You may hear from some sources that the Curvature Continuous fillet uses less material or is stronger than a Constant Radius fillet. Neither of these statements is valid. For the material usage, it would depend on whether the fillet is concave or convex, and also whether the part is shelled or solid. The volumetric difference between the two fillet types is also far less than the difference between the model before and after the fillet. As for the strength, Curvature Continuous fillets always have a portion of the fillet with a tighter curvature than a Constant Radius fillet of the same size, and tighter curvature means a stress concentration. I have heard these assertions frequently enough to warrant comment.

Another thing you may want to be aware of is that because of the curvature-matching nature of the Curvature Continuous fillet, especially when filleting between flat faces, the fillet starts relatively flat on the ends and has to compensate with a section of tight curvature in the middle, when compared to a constant radius arc. The image in Figure 7.7 on the right shows this. Because of the flats and the area of tight curvature, a Curvature Continuous fillet, in order to look approximately the same size as a Constant Radius fillet, must use a radius value that is about 20 percent larger.

Of course, the radius value of a Curvature Continuous fillet is not exactly accurate, because splines have curvature that is constantly changing along the length of the spline, but the Curvature Continuous fillet is simply fit into the same size as a Constant Radius fillet.

Constant Width fillet

The Constant Width fillet is a relative newcomer to the SolidWorks filleting toolbox. Instead of specifying a radius, this fillet enables you to specify a width between edges of the fillet. For a standard 90 degree angle corner, the width is roughly the same as the radius. The Constant Width fillet is particularly useful in situations when you have a changing angle between the faces being filleted. Figure 7.8 shows a comparison between a Constant Radius and a Constant Width fillet.

The Constant Width setting is only available with Face fillets, and you can access this setting in the Fillet Options panel of the Face fillet PropertyManager.

FIGURE 7.8

A comparison between a Constant Radius and a Constant Width fillet

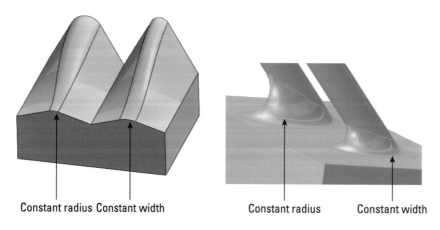

Constant radius   Constant width   Constant radius   Constant width

Hold Line fillet

When I use the Hold Line fillet, it almost feels like cheating! It is rare when I get to use this fillet option, but it is so cool that I try to invent situations to use it. It is a nice alternative to the Variable Radius fillet because by creating a smooth split line, you can create a fillet with a variable radius that does not have any of the random wobbliness of a typical Variable Radius fillet. You can create fillets with one or two hold lines. The hold line drives the fillet edge, and so it is forcing the fillet to a specific size. If you use a single hold line, you get an arc-based fillet. If you use two hold lines, one to drive the edge on each side of the fillet, then you get a spline-based fillet.

Figure 7.9 shows the Face fillet PropertyManager with the Fillet Options panel expanded and a couple of hold lines selected, as well as an example of two Hold Line fillets.

Users frequently use model edges as hold lines, which makes it easy to make a fillet go right up to the corner of a part — a "half round" fillet, as it were.

FIGURE 7.9

Hold Line fillet options and results

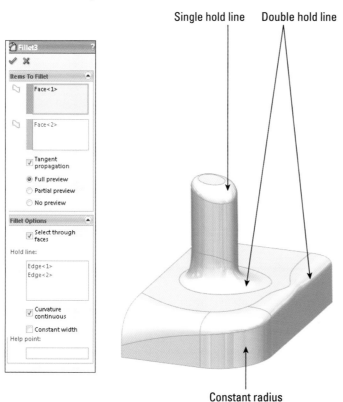

Single hold line   Double hold line

Constant radius

Sometimes, if you try to push the double hold line fillet too hard, it will fail. By this, I mean making too big of a difference between the distance of the hold line from the intersection edge of each of the two fillet faces. Unfortunately, you cannot control the profile of the spline used to create the fillet. If you find yourself in a situation like this and cannot get the fillet to work, it may be just as easy to use Delete Face to remove the faces that would be removed by the fillet, and to use the Loft or Boundary features to make the shape instead. This gives you much more control over profiles and shapes, but is also far more tedious than a Hold Line fillet.

This situation is a case where I would find a fillet with a user-definable section to be very helpful. I have often wished for an elliptical section, and had to create it with a sweep instead. This may be a good time to suggest an enhancement request.

Full Round fillet

Even the Full Round fillets in SolidWorks have some surprises! You may have thought this fillet type was predictable enough. Figure 7.10 shows two types of functionality you can get from the Full Round fillet. The big, full round on the end of the tombstone shape is the predictable result, but you can also see that the lofted shape on top can make use of the Full Round fillet as well.

FIGURE 7.10

The Full Round fillet interface and results

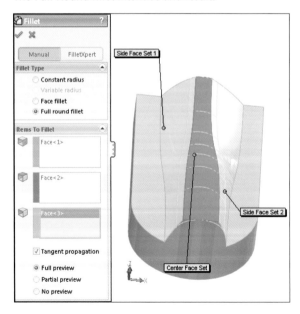

Navigating the interface of the Full Round fillet is a little clunky, with the need to select each selection box before selecting a face to go into it. You may wonder why it doesn't just automatically toggle from the first to the second to the third, like the Sweep Profile and Path selection boxes. Anyway, I have a feeling that SolidWorks will address this interface gaff before too long.

FilletXpert

Prior to SolidWorks 2008, the FilletXpert was used primarily to help beginning users by automatically figuring out feature order for large numbers of selected edges to be filleted.

In 2008, SolidWorks added a tool to help you quickly select large numbers of edges in a model. This part of it looks more enticing for experienced users. In some cases, it seems to have some value, but even in some simple situations, it complicates the process. When you cannot trust automated tools to work reliably and predictably, they are best left alone.

In a situation such as that shown in Figure 7.11, the selection tool is useful. To activate the tool, you must have a Fillet feature open, and click the FilletXpert button at the top of the PropertyManager.

NOTE In order to access the FilletXpert, the FeatureXpert must be activated in Tools ⇨ Options ⇨ General.

FIGURE 7.11

Using the FilletXpert

With the FilletXpert activated, clicking an edge brings up the shortcut toolbar shown in Figure 7.11. There are several different conditions represented by the icons on the toolbar, and frankly, neither the icons nor the tooltip names are descriptive enough to be called intuitive. The best option with this function is to simply move your mouse over all of the conditions and see which selection set best suits your needs. It seems to work best if all of the edges intersect a common face, or they are part of a common feature.

The selection set does not become a parametric selection; the edges are listed in the selection box individually. That is to say that if you added a rib to the part, the selection set would not automatically update to include the new edges; you would have to select the new edges on your own.

In less idealized situations than that shown in Figure 7.11, it might be best to use the Select Through Faces option along with a box selection technique to mass-select edges.

Another part of the functionality is the CornerXpert. These names do not seem to be applied consistently between the SolidWorks Help, the 2008 What's New documentation, and the actual interface. Activating the Corner tab on the FilletXpert PropertyManager enables you to select a three-sided face at the intersection of three edges of differing convexity (two convex and a concave or two concave and a convex), and to click the Show Alternatives button. Figure 7.12 shows the CornerXpert interface and alternatives.

Again, my experience with the CornerXpert showed the feature to be less than useful. On most corners where I tested it, it simply gave the message that it could not analyze the corner, or it displayed only a single alternative.

The FilletXpert is a function meant to simplify tasks mainly for beginning users. The only functionality that might be vaguely attractive to advanced users is the edge selection, and that may take some additional development to become sufficiently useful.

FIGURE 7.12

CornerXpert and alternative corners

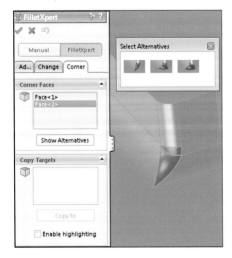

Fillet Best Practice Recommendations

Best practice suggestions are typically a set of contradictory bits of advice that never work in all situations. No one can sit down and write a formula or a set of rules that define exactly when to use what kind of fillet, or authoritatively lay down the law about what you must absolutely do all the time. If you think you have rules that are good enough to be that rigid, I'm afraid you may be kidding yourself.

Having said that, here is my list of favorite best practices. Take them with more than a grain of salt. These suggestions do not absolve you of thinking for yourself and using your own good judgment. The suggestions may at times directly contradict one another, but the idea is that when they do, they imply a value judgment that you have to make. For example, do you value rebuild speed or robustness of your model through changes? Do you value appearance or just getting the job done quickly? Do you value named features so that someone else can pick up the model and understand it, or as compact a FeatureManager as possible? Each one of these options might be valid in certain situations, and I cannot make the decision for you.

Try some of these suggestions, and make your own list. Many of these suggestions can also apply to chamfers.

- Create large structural fillets first and small cosmetic ones last.
- Cosmetic fillets should be the last features in the tree.
- Don't create sketch or feature relationships to edges, faces, or vertices created or modified by fillets. If the fillet fails, so will your dependent features.
- Don't mate parts in assemblies using faces or edges of fillets.
- Don't use fillets in the place of primary shape-creation features. If you find yourself trying to sculpt with fillets, you might try a different approach.
- Draft, Fillets, and Shell are like Rock, Paper, and Scissors in that getting two of the three to work together is easy, but working in the third feature can be challenging.
- Fillets larger than the shell thickness should come before the shell. Smaller fillets should come after.
- Avoid making fillets in the sketch. They are impossible to turn off separately from the rest of the sketch, and if they fail, the whole feature fails.
- Creating fillets together in a single feature rebuilds faster than using individual Fillet features.
- Collect fillets together into folders. You can reorder folders as a single item.
- If you add features after you have added all of your fillets, do it with the fillets rolled back.
- Don't apply fillets before draft. This has the potential to get very tricky because draft in some situations comes before the shell and in others after. Thus the Rock/Paper/Scissors conundrum.

As a part of the best practice suggestions, I would also like to add a list of troubleshooting tips that you can use when you can't create a new feature, when an existing feature fails, or in general when things do not work as expected. These suggestions are not offered in any particular order.

- Try turning off Tangent Propagation, and instead, explicitly select all of the edges you want to fillet. Remember that fillets will "trail off" if they are not propagated.

- Try using a Face fillet.

- Try using a smaller or larger radius value.

- Try using a Variable Radius fillet with all of the same values.

- Try using a Constant Width fillet if you are dealing with faces with sharp angles between them.

- If you are placing a large fillet over a small fillet, try to find another solution by reordering features in the tree.

- Fillet as much of an edge as you can, even turning off Tangent Propagation if that is the only way to get it to work, and then come back with a second feature and filleting up to the end of the first fillet. Often a fillet will heal itself and merge into the previous fillet faces.

- Try to use the FilletXpert to sort through large numbers of fillets.

- Eliminate unnecessary small faces from the model when you can. Fillets don't like edges that are broken up.

- Try to use the Heal Edges command (Insert ➪ Face ➪ Heal Edges) to merge several short edges.

- Try to imagine how you would visualize a particular fillet working, and then see if something is preventing it from working as you envisioned.

- Use Tools ➪ Check to check the model for invalid faces, short edges, and tight curvature.

- Make sure that a fillet that is removing material is not breaking though into an interior wall, for example, through a shell.

- Be careful about filleting at corners where several edges intersect.

- Manual filleting using sweep, loft fill, or boundary is laborious, but it can be effective when other methods are not.

Tutorial

For this tutorial, I have chosen a contrived part that walks you through several fillet types. Rarely would you get all of these fillet types in a single part.

1. Open the part from the Web site called Chapter 7 – Tutorialstart.sldprt.

2. Apply a Full Round fillet to the end with a small boss sticking out of it. The order of the selection of the faces matters, and although the boxes are big, you only need to select one face in each box.

> **NOTE** Notice that the Fillet Options pane is not available for Full Round fillets. This means that options such as Keep Features are not available. Step 3 is a workaround for this limitation.

3. Select Sketch 2 and extrude it Up To Next, up to the solid part.

4. Initiate a Fillet feature, and change the type to Face fillet. Then expand the Fillet Options panel and select Constant Width. Select the face of the boss from Step 3 and the face of the fillet from Step 2 in the appropriate boxes. Assign a width value of 0.2 inch (in the same box that you would normally use to assign a radius value). Figure 7.13 shows the PropertyManager with these settings, and the fillet preview. Click the green check mark to accept the fillet when you are satisfied.

> **NOTE** If you create a fillet, and then go back and edit it, the PropertyManager does not have the same options it had when you originally created it. Figure 7.13 shows the PropertyManager as the feature is being created. The ability to change the fillet type as a part of normal editing would be a welcome addition to the software. This is another enhancement request that I suggest making.

FIGURE 7.13

Setting up the Constant Width fillet

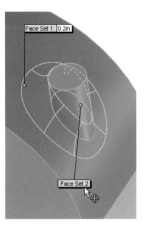

5. Next will be a Variable Radius Setback fillet. This takes a couple of steps to set up. Start by initiating the Fillet feature, changing to the Variable Radius type, and selecting the edges, as shown in Figure 7.14.

6. Assign radius values, as shown in the callouts in Figure 7.14.

Beginning the setup for a Variable Radius Setback fillet

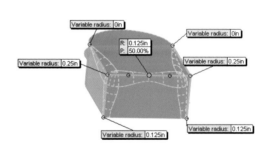

7. In the PropertyManager, scroll down to the Setback Parameters panel, and in the Setback Vertices box, select both of the vertices where the filleted edges intersect.

8. In the Distance box, type **0.5** and click the Set All button. This leads to a somewhat confused mess on the screen, but it allows you to see which setback distance is being applied to which edge. As a general rule of thumb, setback distances should be bigger than the surrounding fillets. For example, if you have a 1-inch fillet radius, and a 0.5-inch setback, the setback is swallowed up by the fillet.

9. With the preview of the Variable Radius Setback fillet showing, click the green check mark to accept the feature.

10. Create a Shell feature with a thickness of 0.05 inch, and remove the unfilleted large face of the part, as well as the small face of the boss created in Step 3. Notice how the zero-radius fillet is treated on the inside of the shell.

11. A fillet is needed on the edge created by the Full Round fillet, and that fillet needs to come before the Shell feature. Drag the rollback bar before the Shell feature, and try to create a 0.2-inch Constant Radius fillet on the edge, as indicated in Figure 7.15.

FIGURE 7.15

Applying a fillet onto the edge created by the Full Round fillet

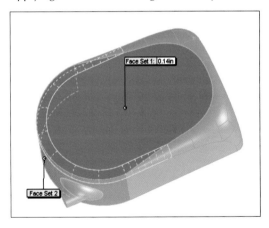

12. Notice that the fillet doesn't work as specified. Change the type to a Face fillet, and select the flat face and the full round face in appropriate boxes. This time it does work, and it integrates itself into the Variable Radius fillet.

13. Roll the FeatureManager back to the end of the tree and save the part.

Summary

Fillets in SolidWorks are surprisingly flexible, robust, and powerful. It does take a little bit of knowing how they work to evoke the most power from them. Still, you might be excused for wanting the ability to switch between fillet types after the fillet has been made, the ability to automatically find the largest fillet that will work in a given situation, and a fillet with a user-definable section.

The FilletXpert turns out to be mainly for beginners and users with a lot of patience and time on their hands. The idea of what SolidWorks was trying to achieve with this tool was admirable, but the execution leaves much to the imagination.

Chapter 8

Shelling

S helling is simply the use of the Shell feature to hollow out a solid model and make a thin-walled part. Shelling on its own is not a complex shape creation function, but many, if not most, complex shapes are used in plastic parts, which generally are shelled. In addition, when shelling complex shapes, you are more likely to run into difficulties than when shelling prismatic parts.

Shelling is an inherently *solid* function. You cannot use the Shell feature on a surface body. Sometimes, however, surfaces are used to manually shell a solid as a workaround when the Shell feature simply won't do the job for whatever reason. Manual shelling is generally not something you want to undertake except as a last resort, but sometimes it is the only way. When the automated tools can't handle the task, it is nice to know that you are not completely stuck.

The Shell feature has many mundane uses, but in this chapter, I discuss more advanced functions and describe several techniques for using the Shell feature that may or may not be new to you. I can't take credit for inventing any of these techniques; they are the product of many individuals experimenting with many different parametric design tools over the course of decades.

Thinking about the Manufacturing Process

The Shell feature is most frequently associated with modeling injection-molded parts. However, techniques exist that make it easy to create models for the thermoform and vacuum form processes as well. You might think of these models as lending themselves more to surfacing techniques because they are formed from constant-thickness thin-sheet material, but solid-only modeling techniques such as Indent can save you a lot of time when you are modeling something such as a shipping or handling tray for a part for which you already have a solid model.

A modeling process that is in many ways the direct opposite of Shell is Thicken. With the Thicken feature, you take an infinitely thin surface body and offset it, perpendicular to the face of the part, to create a thickness. With the Shell feature, you take a solid body, and remove material more than a given amount from the outer skin. Each tool has its appropriate uses.

The Shell feature can be used in unconventional ways to create conformal parts such as overmolds, dipped or sprayed parts, or vacuum-captured parts. You can also consider shelling a solid whenever you might otherwise consider making a surface and thickening it.

A thickened surface is a perfect modeling process for formed sheet metal parts because the thickness face of the sheet metal material is always perpendicular to the main face of the part, just the way a Thicken Surface feature works. You don't shear sheet metal at an angle.

Molded parts depend more on the direction of draw for the shape of the thickness faces, and this can be modeled by making faces that are perpendicular to the line of draw, which are removed by the Shell feature. Figure 8.1 shows the primary difference between how a surface reacts to a Thicken feature, and how a solid reacts to a Shell feature.

FIGURE 8.1

Thickening a surface compared to shelling a solid

Revolved surface sphere

Revolved surface sphere thickened

Revolved solid shape

Shelled solid shape

Many releases ago, SolidWorks enabled users to shell a part hollow without leaving an open side in order to better represent the rotational molding process. Prior to that change, we used to revolve a spherical cutout inside the part, and use Select Other to select the face of the cut as the face to remove. Granted, this was a crazy workaround, but it worked, and was necessary to get volume and weight calculations for closed hollow bodies, as well as FEA on this type of part frequently used for large outdoor equipment and children's toys.

While the person doing the modeling work is not always directly responsible for the product's manufacturability, it is wise to use modeling methods that are compatible with the manufacturing method. You rarely have the opportunity to model just strict geometry. From a product development and manufacturing point of view, geometry always has a context.

Using Shelling Options

Under most conditions, users typically use the default options for the Shell feature. However, like many features in SolidWorks, the Shell feature has some little-known or long-forgotten options that add useful functionality to an already powerful tool. In addition, you can use the Shell feature with certain techniques to produce parts that are otherwise much more difficult to create.

Removing faces

The Shell feature works by offsetting the outer faces of a part, either to the inside or to the outside, in order to hollow out a solid body to a consistent wall thickness. The Shell feature enables you to select faces where you want the shell to be open.

You can remove multiple faces or no faces at all. A shelled model with no faces removed is hollow like an eggshell, with no openings. You would use this technique for modeling parts manufactured using the rotational molding process. Figure 8.2 shows the Shell PropertyManager in action.

Removing faces that are tangent to other faces that are not removed did not work in early releases of the SolidWorks software, but in the past several releases, this is greatly improved. You are more likely to run into trouble when removing one face that is *almost* tangent or at a shallow angle from an adjacent face.

The Shell feature in SolidWorks is robust and reliable. In rare cases, I have seen it create unpredictable results, but when that happens, it is usually due to existing problems with the model geometry that you should probably repair for reasons including more than just the Shell feature. I discuss diagnosing problems with the Shell feature later in this chapter.

For example, in the part shown in Figure 8.2, the solid block was easy to create using Cut, Pattern, and Fillet features. This would have been more difficult to create with surface features. However, the resulting muffin tray shape would seem to be easier to simply thicken. In order to make this part using a Shell feature, you can remove the four sides, the four corner fillets, and the bottom, as shown in Figure 8.2.

149

FIGURE 8.2

The Shell PropertyManager in use

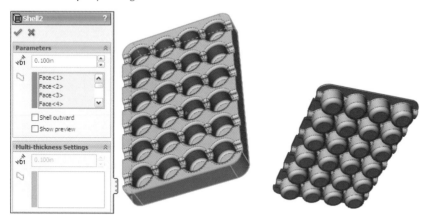

Figure 8.3 shows the process to create the part in Figure 8.2. With this interesting technique, you can use two Shell features to create features such as this wraparound lip. In this case, the second Shell feature removes all of the faces on one side of the tray.

Multiple Shell features can also be useful when combined with multi-body parts. Figure 8.4 shows a simple example of this. Sometimes you cannot get the correct wall thickness where you need it. Users who are new to SolidWorks frequently ask if they can limit the Shell feature to only a portion of the part. Of course, the answer is that you cannot do it directly. You must first break the part into separate bodies, shell the bodies as appropriate, and then join the bodies back together again.

In the part shown in Figure 8.4, the part is broken into three bodies, shown on the right, in blue, red, and blue. These bodies are then shelled individually and then brought back together to form a single body.

Using multiple Shell features in a single part

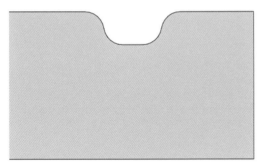

Original solid

Original solid shelled to a
thickness larger than needed

Fillets added to shelled solid

Re-shelled to the material thickness removing
all of the faces from one side of the model

Using multiple bodies to constrain the shell to an area

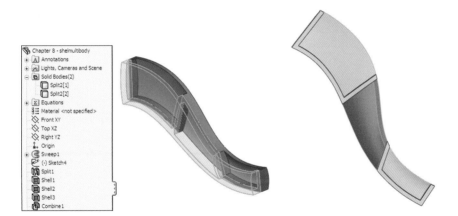

Multi-thickness shell

A Multi-thickness shell is a shell feature that allows for walls of different thicknesses. This option is enabled by selecting faces in the Multi-thickness Faces selection box. The Thickness setting in the spin box at the top of the PropertyManager sets the default face thickness, and then any face selected in the Multi-thickness Faces box can have a different thickness associated with it.

One limitation of the Multi-thickness setting is that all tangent faces must have the same thickness. Another way to say this is that if you want two neighboring faces to have different thicknesses, they must not be tangent, and the closer to perpendicular they are, the less likely the feature is to fail. The reason for this is that the software doesn't have any way to tell a face to have one thickness at the boundary edge with one face and a different thickness on another boundary edge. The software cannot do this with a simple offset, which is essentially what a Shell feature is.

A good example of an application for a multi-thickness shell is a blow-molded bottle. The neck and the base of the bottle must be thicker than the body of the bottle to support the stress of the threads and the weight of the contents. Figure 8.5 shows an example of a model of a detergent bottle created in this way and the Shell PropertyManager. The outside face of the neck of the bottle is selected in the Multi-thickness Settings selection box.

FIGURE 8.5

Using the Multi-thickness shell settings

To achieve a multi-thickness result between faces that must be tangent, you can apply the fillets after the Shell feature in the history tree. You may also be able to get away with a Move Face feature to thicken selected faces of the bottle, or even a combination of knitting a surface, extending its boundary, and then thickening it.

With blow-molded bottles, the interior faces are far less important than the outer faces, because other than in the neck area, the interior faces do not require tooling. You might be required to model the interior faces accurately in order to get the drawing correct, or to acquire finished plastic part weight or bottle contents volume measurement.

Shell Outward

The Shell Outward option is highly useful in certain situations. It adds material thickness to the outside of the solid body and removes the interior of the solid. It is as if you modeled frozen milk inside of a milk jug and then used Shell Outward to create the actual jug. You can combine the Shell Outward option with all of the other techniques and settings used for inward shells, including multi-thickness and face removal selection.

Diagnosing Shell Problems

Diagnosing shell problems is not as difficult as you may think. Most shell failures are typically caused by a handful of conditions that you can easily find.

 You can find more information on model evaluation techniques in Chapter 14.

Error Diagnostics

When a shell error occurs, SolidWorks shows a long error message in a tooltip balloon and adds an additional panel to the Shell PropertyManager called Error Diagnostics. Most users simply click through the error message as quickly as they can, rather than examining it to see if it might contain a clue to figuring out how to deal with the error. Figure 8.6 shows a sample error message and the Error Diagnostics panel.

FIGURE 8.6

A shell error message and the Error Diagnostics panel

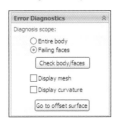

> **NOTE** You may notice that sometimes the Go To Offset Surface option appears on the Error Diagnostics panel, and sometimes it does not. It is not clear whether the omission is intentional or if it means or doesn't mean something in particular.

The error message that appears has four basic suggestions for where to start looking for the cause of the shell failure. The first is that faces of the part when offset are running into one another. Another way you could look at this message is to say that the wall of the shell might be too thick, or that the part is too narrow in one particular area to be shelled at the thickness setting you are using.

The second suggestion is that you may need to eliminate a small face that the software is unable to offset and merge into the offset faces accurately. Small faces and small edges cause problems with many other features as well, and so I always offer best practice recommendations to eliminate them when possible. If a Shell feature fails, this is certainly one place to look.

The third suggestion is to look at the radius of curvature of the model faces. Offsets and shells fail if the offset distance is greater than the minimum *inside* radius. So, if the minimum radius is 0.080 inch and you are using a shell thickness of 0.100 inch, the shell may fail. You will find times when SolidWorks can actually shell at a greater thickness than the minimum radius; this function of the software seems to have improved greatly in recent releases. I personally would not count on the software's magic for functions like this, but would manually correct the model to be sure that it is going to shell properly.

> **NOTE** When a shell greater than the minimum radius works, you should examine the results, because faces in the area of the small curvature may have errors or other blemishes.

The fourth suggestion is to use the link from the tooltip bubble to the SolidWorks Help, which has even more suggestions of things to look for, including small edges caused by creating a lofted or swept feature line-on-line with existing solid geometry, looking for degenerate faces which may not be able to offset.

I would suggest not wasting much time trying to get the tools on the Error Diagnostics panel to actually do anything. I have seen too frequently when they don't do anything at all. Better tools exist in other places, particularly under Tools ➪ Check.

The Check tool

Tools ➪ Check now has its own toolbar button! So, I suppose I should quit calling it Tools ➪ Check and just call it Check. If you often work with complex shapes and plastic parts, you will be spending a lot of time with the Check tool. The Check tool enables you to find some important troubleshooting information quickly:

- Find the minimum radius of the model faces
- Identify any short edges (you can define what "short" means)
- Find any geometry errors in the model

This is all key information when it comes to troubleshooting Shell features. The Check tool provides the same functionality that the Error Diagnostics panel provides, but with the advantage that it actually works.

Repairing the model

With the troubleshooting tips and the Check tool, you are prepared to find the problems causing your shell to fail, but once you have found the cause, how do you actually go about repairing it? Small faces and edges can be difficult. The Heal Edges tool can help merge short edges, and it is found at the unlikely home of Insert ⇨ Face ⇨ Heal Edges.

Small faces can be tough to overcome. Generally, you learn to do this with a lot of practice. Fillets have the tendency to split into faces every time they encounter a new edge. Sometimes you can get around this by replacing several fillet faces with the Delete Face tool to get rid of the original faces, and using a Fill surface to patch it all back up as a single face.

You can fix curvature that is too tight in a couple of ways. It generally depends on how you created it, but one method that works, regardless of how it was created, is to use Delete Face, Trim, or Cut to remove the section of the model with the tight curvature, and then use the Fill surface to fill it back in. This is particularly true of degenerate points. Degenerate points tend to have very tight curvature because of all the isoparameter curves converging to a single point. When the curvature spikes in an area like this, you cannot shell or offset the face.

Shelling Manually

If you get to the point where you are considering manual shelling, the situation must be serious. For anything except the most basic of models, you don't want to have to do this. Manual shelling involves offsetting surfaces, trimming, knitting, more trimming and knitting, and finally converting the surfaces to a solid or using the surfaces to cut a solid.

Sometimes you may not want the inside of a model to be an exact offset of the outside of the model. This is another case when manual shelling is a necessary option. Manually modeling both the outside *and* the inside of a complex part is anything but fun, but sometimes it is necessary to make a correct part.

On the other hand, if the alternative is remodeling a part to eliminate the problem area, or compromising on the desired shape just to get it to work, manual shelling does work; it's just tedious and could be subject to problems of its own.

Manual shelling can be particularly useful when you have corners (fillets or blends) between major model faces that will not shell at all. In these cases, just offset the major model faces independently, and then model the blends between them manually. Figure 8.7 shows a simple example of a model where I have done this. Interestingly, the part shells at 0.200 inch by simply squaring off the corners where the complex fillet is, but it does not shell at 0.100 inch. The model is shown partially transparent for clarity.

FIGURE 8.7

An example of basic steps for manual shelling

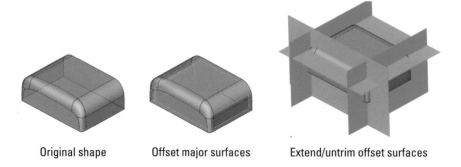

Original shape   Offset major surfaces   Extend/untrim offset surfaces

Trim surfaces   Fillet/blend to taste   Cut with surface

Tutorial

This tutorial gives you experience with some situations you will encounter in real-world modeling. It does not represent the entire range of situations you will find, but is representative of some common elements of shelling.

Tutorial: Troubleshooting and manual shelling

Follow these steps to gain some experience with problematic shell diagnosis and manual shelling. Some of the features used in this tutorial are explained more fully in Chapter 14.

1. Open the model from the Web site called Chapter 8 – Tutorial8.1start.sldprt.

2. Initiate the Shell feature, and select the four sides and bottom faces to be removed. Set the shell thickness to 0.05 inch. Click the green check mark to accept the feature.

3. The feature fails. In the Error Diagnostics panel that appears, click the Entire Body option. It returns the minimum radius and the reason for the failure. The minimum radius is greater than the thickness that you are trying to achieve.

4. Change the shell value to 0.03 inch and click the green check mark.

5. The feature works, but it has not shelled out under the Boundary surface. You must proceed by manual shelling.

6. Delete the shell that you just created. Even though the shell feature would be useful, it is a flawed feature and may cause problems later on.

7. Offset the main face only (created by a sweep originally) by 0.05 inch to the side of the material. Do not offset the Boundary surface shape.

8. Hide the solid body by right-clicking it in the graphics window and selecting Hide from the Body section of the menu.

9. Select the offset surface body and, through the menus, select Insert ⇨ Surface ⇨ Untrim. This removes the notch created by the Boundary surface.

10. Through the menus again, select Insert ⇨ Surface ⇨ Extend, and select the three edges that were not touched by the Boundary surface notch (do not select the edge closest to the origin). Use an Extend distance of about 1 inch. The selection and Extend feature settings are shown in Figure 8.8.

FIGURE 8.8

Selection for the Extend feature in Step 10

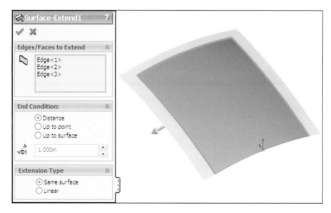

> **NOTE** Notice that although the Same Surface option was used, two of the three extended sides left edges, and one did not. This is probably a problem in the software, but represents the real-world types of issues you will face.

11. In the Filter at the top of the FeatureManager, type **Nose**. Show the NoseProfile sketch. Click the X on the right side of the filter when you are done, and the FeatureManager will reappear.

12. Open a sketch on the Right plane, and offset the spline shown in the NoseProfile toward the origin by 0.1 inch. Exit the sketch, and hide the NoseProfile.

13. Show the solid body by right-clicking the Extrude1 feature and selecting Show. Open a sketch on the Front plane, and use the Intersection Curve to create a spline at the intersection of the Boundary surface feature and the sketch plane. Create a second intersection curve at the intersection of the offset and extended surface and the sketch plane. Hide the solid body again when you are done.

14. Offset the first intersection curve to the inside, and turn both intersection curves to construction geometry. If you look closely, you can see that the offset spline does not intersect the offset surface. You need to extend the offset intersection curve at least as far as the second intersection curve.

15. The Extend sketch tool will not work to extend the offset spline to the intersection curve. You could proceed in several ways at this point, but just go ahead and draw a short line segment, tangent from the end of the offset spline, to go past the second intersection spline. Your screen at this point looks like Figure 8.9.

FIGURE 8.9

The state of the model as of Step 15

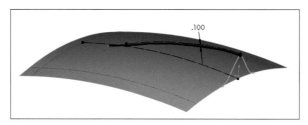

16. Exit the sketch and create a surface sweep from the menus at Insert ➪ Surface ➪ Sweep. Select the offset NoseProfile as the sweep profile and the offset intersection curve as the path using all default options.

17. Use the Trim feature to trim the surfaces, through the menus at Insert ➪ Surface ➪ Trim. Select the Mutual Trim option, select both bodies in the selection box, and then select the appropriate areas of the surfaces that you need to keep. Notice that the Mutual Trim option does not work in this case, displaying the error message, "Trimmed pieces cannot be sewn together." Although the terminology is not standard to SolidWorks, it is safe to assume that they meant, "...cannot be *knit* together." Don't despair. Sometimes when SolidWorks displays these error messages, they are just testing you.

18. Change the Trim option from Mutual to Standard. Select the large main surface as the Trim tool, and select the top side of the newly created sweep as the portion to keep. Accept the feature when complete.

19. Repeat the previous step, but this time use the trimmed swept surface to trim the large main surface, and keep the main outer portion of the main surface.

20. Now, knit together the two trimmed surfaces. Notice that you have just completed a workaround within another workaround. This kind of workflow is reasonably common when working with complex shapes and advanced features.

21. Show the solid again and make a cut with the surface, using Insert ➪ Cut ➪ With Surface.

22. Finally, hide the surface body. The finished model looks like Figure 8.10.

FIGURE 8.10

The finished model

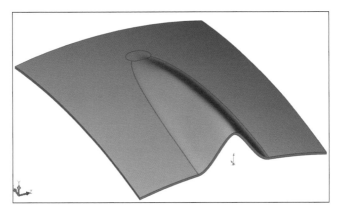

Summary

Shelling is a very powerful function in SolidWorks; however, there are still times when you will need to troubleshoot features that fail. Having all of the tools at your disposal can mean the difference between getting the job done correctly and hacking it together just to cover your bases.

Remember to match your modeling technique to your manufacturing methods if possible. This will help you design better parts for a particular process and make your drawing documentation more realistic and complete.

Part III

Using Secondary, Management, and Evaluation Tools

Chapter 9

Using Secondary Shape Creation Features

SolidWorks Corporation does not distinguish between primary and secondary features in any of its documentation or training materials. I have done so in this book mainly to assist you in assigning work-flow issues. One of the most commonly asked questions I get from users is, "Where do I start?" Classifying some features as primary and others as secondary helps in that determination. For example, you would never start a model with a Dome feature, mainly because it requires existing geometry to be applied to it. On the other hand, you might routinely start a model with a Loft or a Boundary surface because those features create 3D shapes from sketches or edges.

Some of the tools that you might expect to find in this chapter on secondary shape creation you will instead find in Chapters 10 or 12, with the discussions of hybrid tools and direct editing, respectively. I define these terms in more detail in those chapters. There is certainly overlap between the topics of all of the chapters in Part 3, but I have limited this chapter to those topics that do not fit into any of the more specialized topics.

The tools I discuss in this chapter I call secondary for a reason. They usually play a supporting role in the structure of a complex part, and while you can certainly use them for important features of your model, they tend to be built dependent upon other more primary features, and do not necessarily drive the overall shape of the part as much as the Fill, Boundary, Loft, and Sweep features do.

Some of these features are solids only and some are surfaces only.

Using the Dome and Shape Features

Dome and Shape features accomplish very similar results: Both of them essentially bulge a face in or out. The best way to think of these features is as a shortcut that you can only use on solid bodies for more involved, and often more satisfactory, results of the primary shape creation features. The good news is that if these techniques do not accomplish what you are looking for, there is always another way to accomplish it.

You may also find that the Dome, Shape, and Freeform features have icons that are very similar, and are positioned right next to one another in the Insert ➪ Features menu.

I do not recommend relying too heavily on the Dome and Shape features outside of the limited cases where they work best. They have a specific task that they perform, and they do not give great results outside of that area. These features are probably most useful for that little concave arch on the bottom of blow-molded bottles, or the arch on the top of plastic buttons for electronic devices. Still, these shapes are more controllable when made through other methods.

Figure 9.1 shows a comparison between the Dome and Shape features used with various conditions and settings.

FIGURE 9.1

Dome and Shape features used in various conditions

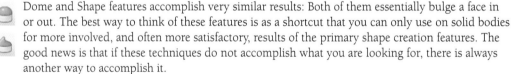

The numbers in Table 9.1 correspond to the numbers of the features in Figure 9.1.

TABLE 9.1

Dome and Shape Features

	Shape Type	Dome	Shape
1	Circular Boss	Default settings	Maintain Boundary Tangent off
2	Circular Boss	Elliptical Dome	Maintain Boundary Tangent on
3	Rectangular Boss	Default settings	Maintain Boundary Tangent off
4	Hexagonal Boss	Continuous Dome off	Maintain Boundary Tangent off (feature fails)

164

	Shape Type	Dome	Shape
5	Hexagonal Boss	Continuous Dome on	Maintain Boundary Tangent on
6	Closed Spline Boss	Continuous Dome off (fails if on)	Maintain Boundary Tangent off
7	Circular Boss with Non-planar Top	Default settings	Maintain Boundary Tangent on
8	Rectangular Boss with Non-planar Top	Default settings	Maintain Boundary Tangent off
9	Rectangular Boss with Fillets and Draft	Continuous Dome off	Constraint sketch used, Maintain Boundary Tangent on
10	Rectangular Boss with Fillets	Flipped direction, all other default settings	Negative pressure applied, Maintain Boundary Tangent on

Similarities between the Dome and Shape features

The Dome and Shape features have a lot of things in common — in fact, it is sometimes difficult to understand why they are two different features. When you are making a decision between the two types of features, it helps to know what the similarities and differences are.

- Both features can create concave or convex bulges.
- Both features work exclusively on solids, not on surfaces.
- Both features allow the use of a constraint sketch to help determine the shape.
- Both features can work on flat or curved faces.
- Both features are limited to adding shape to a single face at a time; they cannot span multiple faces.
- Neither feature can create geometry tangent to surrounding faces.

Differences between the Dome and Shape features

The differences between these features are probably more important than the similarities.

- Dome can be used on multiple faces in a single feature, while Shape cannot.
- The Elliptical Dome setting enables the Dome face to be perpendicular to the selected face, while Shape can only be tangent or at a default orientation to the selected face.
- Shape uses sliders to control the shape, as if you were applying positive or negative air pressure behind a rubber diaphragm, with another slider varying the stiffness of the rubber material.

Dome

The simplest and most straightforward of the two tools is the Dome feature. The Dome feature is best used on circular or elliptical faces that do not have drafted side walls. Dome has several characteristics that may make it attractive in certain situations:

- You can apply a dome to several faces in a single feature. This can be interpreted in multiple ways. Multiple individual domes can be made using a single Dome feature. Another way to read it is that you can create a single dome over multiple selected faces.

- You can apply a dome to curved surfaces.

- You can make a convex or concave dome that can either add or remove material.

- The Elliptical Dome setting creates a smooth shape that rises perpendicularly from the original selected face and is only available when doming circular and elliptical faces.

- You can establish a direction for the dome; it doesn't have to be perpendicular from the selected face.

Figure 9.2 shows the PropertyManager of a Dome feature in use. The bottle bottom is one of the classic uses of the Dome feature. The figure shows a case where a split line has been created around the bottom of the part, and then the dome is created. The shape on the bottom of the bottle exists to stiffen the bottom and also to prevent the bottle from rocking on a bottom that bulges outward.

The Dome feature in this case is not a very attractive shape, but it is on the bottom of the bottle, meets the functional requirements, and is easy to create. For a feature like this, where it is not a major aesthetic surface, the Dome feature is "good enough."

FIGURE 9.2

The PropertyManager of the Dome feature, with a sample application

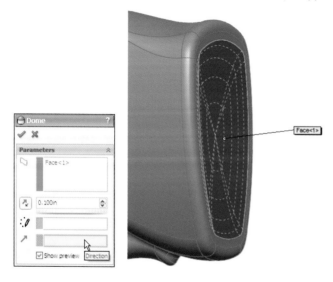

One drawback of using the Dome feature is that you cannot control the shape precisely; you are at the mercy of how the feature interprets the surrounding shape. Looking back at Figure 9.1 should emphasize that the Dome feature works best on closed tangent loops that do not change convexity, such as circles and ellipses.

Another important factor to keep in mind when working with domes, especially on plastic parts, is that there is no way to control the tangency direction of the sides of the dome other than by using the Elliptical Dome setting, which makes the sides of the dome perpendicular to the selected face. One critical implication of this limitation is that you cannot control the draft angle on the sides of a dome. The best you can do is to put big fillets around the edges of the dome. If that is not good enough, then your next best option is a Fill surface, over which you can exercise more control.

Shape

At first appearance, the Shape feature looks to be more sophisticated than the Dome feature simply because it has more controls and the interface looks more complex. Unfortunately, the repertoire of shapes that the Shape feature can produce is rather limited. Here are some of the distinguishing characteristics of the Shape feature:

- The boundary conditions of the faces of the Shape feature give you two options: either unconstrained, pivoting at the edges of the selected face, or tangent to the selected face starting at the bounding edges.

- An implication of the first characteristic is that you cannot make Shape features tangent to the side faces of existing geometry or a specific draft angle.

- You can use a constraint sketch to define the height of the Shape feature. A sketch point is the most frequently used entity type.

- As mentioned earlier, the Pressure and Stretch/Bend controls enable you to control the shape as if it were a balloon. Figure 9.3 shows the PropertyManager interface for the Shape feature.

FIGURE 9.3

The Shape Feature PropertyManager interface

I have never personally used the Shape feature for any production part. This is not to say that it is useless, just that I haven't found a use for it yet. SolidWorks Corporation originally intended that this feature would be used by industrial designers to add shapes to models, but in the end, it is my belief that the range of shapes it can create is far too limited to be either useful or, more importantly, intentional.

Using the Indent Feature

 The Indent feature is a difficult one for many people to accept as a regular part of their modeling toolbox. You can think of the Indent feature as pushing out a section of an injection- or blow-molded part, maintaining a wall thickness. It is a great way to make a plastic housing conform around a set of components, such as a motor or a circuit board, that act as a forming tool. You can specify a wall thickness and a gap between the tool and the actual part. This is a feature that works exclusively on solids, and preferably thin-shelled solids. Probably the best way to describe this feature is to show it in action.

Figure 9.4 shows part of a project that I worked on for a point-of-purchase display. I created the initial models, and then the customer came back and wanted changes that would be difficult within the framework of the "design intent" that I had initially established. The easiest thing to do was to make the change using the Indent feature, which took only a couple of minutes, as opposed to, say, 45 minutes if I had to reconstruct the design intent and repair a lot of sketch relations and feature references.

FIGURE 9.4

Original, tool, and finished models using the Indent feature

The image on the left is a section view of the original model. In the middle is the original model with a tool body directing the change. On the right is the section view of the finished part. It took only two features to create the change, and I didn't have to roll anything back or edit any sketches.

Of course, I would typically consider it bad practice to make changes that work around the design intent. Sometimes, however, the difference is between getting the job done on time and getting it done correctly, and speed can be a deciding factor. Additionally, this technique works on imported parts as well as native SolidWorks data.

The concept in use here is that you create a separate solid body that you can use as a tool body to indent the part. Imagine that the tool is hot and melts the plastic and then reforms it in a new shape and location. Figure 9.5 shows the PropertyManager for the Indent feature, with the feature shown in progress.

FIGURE 9.5

The Indent PropertyManager with the feature preview

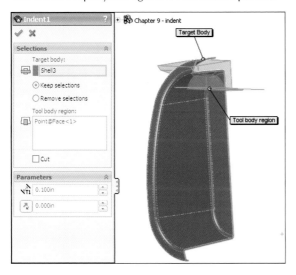

The target body is the main plastic part. The tool body is the yellow body shown. The gray sketch is the sketch for the tool body extrusion. It may be difficult to see in the figure, but there is a preview of the material being pushed into the part. The secret to the Indent feature is that the main plastic part has to dissect the tool body, and you select the region of the tool body that you want to push the plastic. It works almost like a forming tool for sheet metal, except that it can also create a gap between the tool and the part. If I had selected the outside region of the tool body, the plastic instead would have gone around the tool body the other way, encapsulating the tool body in a way that would be unmoldable.

Part of what made this change so easy was that I didn't have to be concerned about how the feature affected the geometry of the rim around the outside of the part; even though the tool body touches the part, only the selected region has any effect.

If you remain on the alert for possible applications for the Indent tool, I'm sure you can find more nice applications. It may not be easy to visualize how to use this tool in many situations, but think of it when you need to change a shape but maintain a wall thickness. Also remember its unique ability to create a gap between the tool and the part. Another situation in which the Indent feature would be very useful would be when you need to apply a Combine, Subtract, or Cavity feature in which there is a small offset between the part making the cavity and the cavity itself. With a little experience with the tool, I'm sure you will come to appreciate the Indent feature as much as I do.

Using the Radiate Surface

The Radiate surface is a surface type that the Ruled surface has largely superceded. (The Ruled surface is discussed next in this chapter.) Radiate creates a surface that is parallel to a reference plane and perpendicular from a selected edge. It has a couple of niche applications, although users sometimes find it difficult to visualize how it works.

The best example of a Radiate surface is a mold parting line that goes around a plastic part. If the parting line is planar and perpendicular to the direction of pull, the Radiate surface is planar. If the parting line is not planar, the Radiate surface is not planar. You can think of it as a flat skirt that sticks straight out of the part, perpendicular to the direction of pull of the mold. Not surprisingly, users who model parts with draft and by mold, as well as casting designers, most commonly use Radiate. Radiate often has problems around sharp corners and fillets.

Figure 9.6 shows the Radiate PropertyManager along with an example of a Radiate surface.

FIGURE 9.6

The Radiate PropertyManager with an example

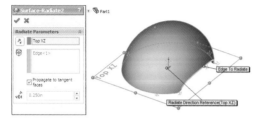

The orange arrows shown in Figure 9.6 indicate which side of the selected edge the Radiate will go to. You need to keep an eye on these arrows and make sure they are all pointing to the same side for a given Radiate feature. You can flip the side using the Flip Radiation Direction arrows next to the plane selection box.

Several workarounds exist for those times when a Radiate feature does not work the way you expect it to. Probably the most common workaround is to use the Ruled surface instead. Another option is to only create part of the Radiate in a single feature and then create the rest of the surface using another Radiate or another feature type altogether. You can also try to either add or remove fillets, and turn tangency propagation on or off.

The Knit feature has a special use that is unique to the Radiate feature. This use is particularly adapted to the creation of mold cavities, and can be an important time saver. When you have a Radiate surface that makes an entire closed loop around a part, and you use the Knit feature to select the Radiate surface, a new selection box is added to the Knit PropertyManager. Figure 9.7 shows this new selection box.

The Seed Face selection box added to the Knit PropertyManager when a Radiate surface is selected

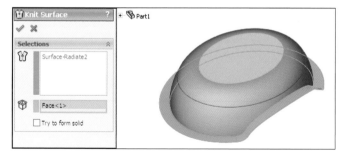

If you select the Radiate surface and designate a Seed face, SolidWorks automatically selects all of the faces on the same side of the Radiate surface. This function does not work if the part has any through holes in it that connect the two sides of the part. You may be able to visualize why this could be such an important function in modeling mold parts.

For example, in the Knit feature shown in Figure 9.7, the yellow surface is the Radiate surface. The blue faces are faces of the part. The pink face is the Seed face. The two blue faces showing will be selected automatically using the arrangement shown. This type of functionality does not exist for Ruled, Planar, Sweep, or any other type of surfaces, except for the Radiate surface. This function alone may make it worthwhile trying to make the Radiate surface work in situations where you want to use mold type functionality.

Using the Ruled Surface

The Ruled surface is a relatively new surface feature type, having been added at some time during the last five releases. A Ruled surface is a standard surface type where the face curves in either the U or the V direction are straight lines. The other direction can be anything, including splines. Sometimes they are defined somewhat more generally by saying that at any point on a Ruled surface, you can place a straight line through the point.

Ruled surfaces have many uses. Mold designers or plastic part designers frequently use them when trying to establish drafted faces around complex curves. You may find Ruled surfaces to be used often as reference or construction surfaces, with a major use being to establish a draft direction from which to build a Loft or Boundary surface. In these cases, the Ruled surface does not actually form any model faces, but only establishes something to be tangent to.

SolidWorks enables you to make Ruled surfaces in five different ways:

- **Tangent To Surface** — This option suffices in many cases as a workaround for an Extend Surface feature using the Linear option. If it is not an exact replacement, it is very close.
- **Normal to Surface** — Self-explanatory.
- **Tapered To Vector** — A plane normal establishes the vector, and the taper is an angle in a dialog box.
- **Perpendicular To Vector** — This type is most similar to the Radiate surface.
- **Sweep** — This might be better described as Parallel to Vector.

Here I would substitute the word Face for the word used by SolidWorks, which was Surface. This is because the Ruled surface works on surface and solid edges, and I hate to give the wrong impression of the functions just for the sake of correctness in copying SolidWorks naming missteps.

One of the odd limitations of the Ruled surface is that it requires that some 3D solid or surface geometry already exist within the model. You can only make a Ruled surface from edges, not from sketches or curves. Split Lines work because they are edges, but Projected Curves do not. This limitation is particularly aggravating because Ruled surfaces are frequently used as reference geometry from which to create other surfaces.

Further, the Help documentation on the Ruled surface function, as of this writing, is not only inadequate, but also inaccurate. In particular, the Help documentation says that the SolidWorks Draft feature does not work on imported parts, and it tells you to use a Ruled surface, but it doesn't describe how you would go about doing this. I'm here to tell you that the SolidWorks Draft feature works perfectly well on native and imported geometry. When fillets cause difficulties, you can use FeatureWorks or the Delete Face feature to remove the fillets.

Figure 9.8 shows the five options for creating Ruled surfaces.

FIGURE 9.8

Five options for creating Ruled surfaces and the Ruled Surface PropertyManager

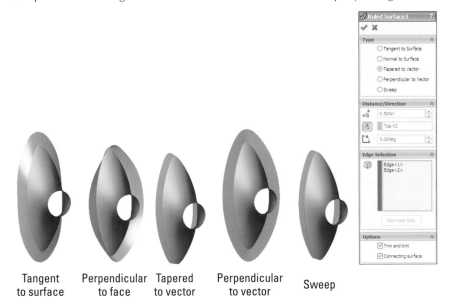

Tangent to surface   Perpendicular to face   Tapered to vector   Perpendicular to vector   Sweep

To get a better look at the part, open the file called Chapter 9 – ruled.sldprt from the downloaded example files. It has separate configurations for each type of Ruled surface so that you can see how I made each of them.

While the Ruled surface is handy, it is not very accurate. Figure 9.9 shows a deviation analysis run on the Tangent To Surface example. The maximum deviation is over six degrees, which is not acceptable in most situations.

FIGURE 9.9

Deviation analysis on a Ruled surface

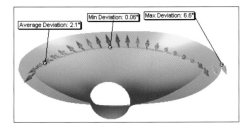

Tutorial

In a typical surface modeling exercise, a lot of things can go wrong, or at least have the potential to not work the way you think they should. Some people will find this tutorial frustrating because it presents a lot of potential real-world problems, and sometimes, real problems have messy workarounds. Maybe you think this is not the kind of example that should be put into a book on surfacing, but I disagree. In real-world surfacing with SolidWorks, you will run into things like this in every project; in fact, you may find situations where you have to come up with workarounds that are multiple levels deep to get where you want to go. I do not intend this tutorial to show all of the shortcomings of the tools, but as I was here anyway, and the shortcomings presented themselves, I don't see any reason to avoid them.

Follow the steps of this tutorial to learn more about using the features discussed in this chapter and how to get around some common shortcomings you may find with these tools.

1. Open the file from the downloaded material called Chapter 9 – tutorialstart.sldprt. This is an incomplete surface model that you will add to, solidify, and complete.

2. Initiate a Planar surface feature, and select the three open circular edges, two small and one larger. Notice that a Planar surface can create multiple bodies in a single feature, and they do not need to be co-planar. Accept the feature when you are done. At this point, you have six surface bodies.

3. Initiate a Fillet feature, use the Face Fillet option, and select one of the extruded surface bodies as one face, and the main lofted body as the second face. Set the Constant Width option, and the width/radius value to 0.20 inch. Make sure that the Trim and Attach option is set at the bottom of the Fillet Options panel of the PropertyManager. Figure 9.10 shows the PropertyManager settings, as well as the preview of the feature.

   Make sure that the arrows in the face selection box are both pointing to the outside of the part; otherwise, you may get a fillet that goes inside the part.

4. Create a similar fillet using the second extruded surface. Notice that when you have completed both fillets, you have only four surface bodies instead of six. The fillets have knitted together the surface bodies.

5. Try to initiate a Dome feature. Notice that it is either grayed out or not available (depending on where you try to access it). At this point, the model is still a surface model, and the Dome feature only works on solid models. Instead, you need to work on making this into a solid model, in the following steps.

6. Initiate the Ruled surface. Select the Tapered From Vector option, and select the edges around the bottom of the part. Set the angle to 5 degrees, and use the Top plane to establish the vector. Make sure that the Ruled surface goes toward the bottom and the outside by using a combination of the arrow in the Distance/Direction panel of the PropertyManager, as well as the Alternate Side button in the Edge Selection panel.

   Figure 9.11 shows the selections in the PropertyManager and the model preview.

FIGURE 9.10

The PropertyManager and preview for Step 3

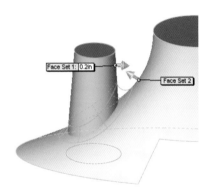

Accept the feature when the settings are complete. Notice that in the corners of the Ruled surface, the surface is slightly curved in a way in which it should not be. The effect may be subtle, but it is there. This needs to be corrected.

7. Edit the newly created Ruled surface feature, and at the bottom of the PropertyManager, turn off the Trim and Knit option, as well as the Connecting Surface option. Notice that this causes gaps at the convex corners and overlaps at the concave corners. Click the green check mark to accept the changes when they are complete.

8. Use the Extend Surface feature to extend the edges of the four surfaces at the two convex corners. Use an extension distance of 0.1 inch. You need to do this using three separate Extend Surface features because you can only extend one surface body at a time. One of the bodies has two edges that need to be extended. Figure 9.12 shows the finished extended corners.

FIGURE 9.11

Settings and preview for Step 6

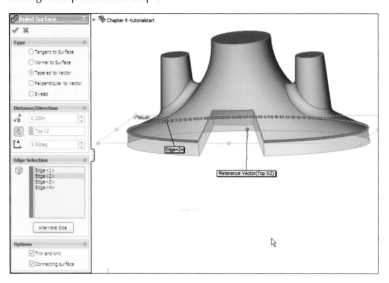

FIGURE 9.12

The extended corners

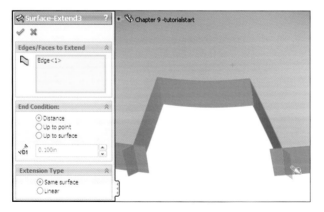

9. Use the Trim feature to do a Mutual Trim and keep the appropriate sections of the surfaces.

10. Notice that two of the surfaces do not match up with the rest. Use a Spline On Surface (Tools ➪ Sketch Entities ➪ Spline On Surface) to draw a spline from one vertex to another within a single 3D sketch, and then use the Trim feature to trim off the small slices at the bottoms of both sides. Figure 9.13 shows this step.

FIGURE 9.13

Trimming off the extra

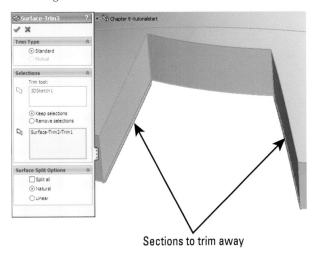

Sections to trim away

11. Knit together the three planar surface bodies, the ruled surface, and the lofted body.

12. Use the Thicken feature to give the surface body 0.1 inch of thickness to the inside of the body.

    Notice that when you do this, SolidWorks creates some faces on the inside of the part that you don't want, which are shown in Figure 9.14 as red and yellow faces.

FIGURE 9.14

Extra faces made by the Thicken feature

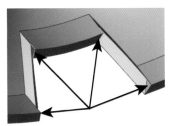

Extra faces created by the Thicken feature

13. To get rid of the extra faces, just use the Delete Face feature on the pair of symmetric faces indicated in yellow in Figure 9.14. Use the default option (Delete and Patch).

14. The Delete Face feature does not work for the red faces in Figure 9.14 because the surrounding faces cannot be extended to fill in. For this, you will need to be more direct. Loft a surface between the inside edges of the red faces, using the other edge indicated in Figure 9.15 as a guide curve.

FIGURE 9.15

Setting up a surface loft

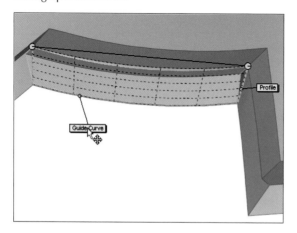

15. With the lofted surface created in the previous step, create a Cut With Surface feature, cutting off the small part of material. When you are done, hide the lofted surface.

    If the Cut With Surface feature does not work for you, use Extend to extend the lofted surface and then use Replace Face to replace the two red faces and the blue face between them.

    This finishes the work on the extra faces created by the Thicken feature.

16. Now begin work on using the Dome feature to cap off the flat end faces. Remember that the Dome feature can be used on multiple faces at once. Initiate the Dome feature, and then select the large flat face in the middle. Make sure that you select the face rather than the edge. Make the dome stick out instead of in, set the distance to 0.4 inch, turn off the Continuous Dome option, and turn on the Show Preview option. Figure 9.16 shows the state of the PropertyManager and the model preview at this point. Do not finish the Dome feature yet.

17. With the Dome feature still active, select one of the smaller flat circular faces. Notice that the Continuous Dome option goes away, and the shape of the preview on the big circle goes from short and squat to rather tall and pointy.

    Although you can use the Dome feature with multiple selections, when you use multiple selections, you don't get all of the options that you get with a single selection. To finish this feature, delete the small face from the selection, and apply the Dome feature only to the large face. Accept the feature when you are done.

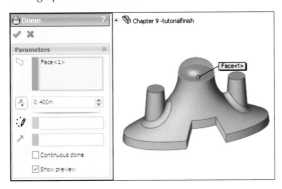

FIGURE 9.16

Setting up a Dome feature

18. Initiate the Dome feature again, and select one of the smaller faces. Notice that the choices this time are different. This is because of the difference between the edge of the lofted face used in the previous step, and the edge of an extruded face, which is used in this step.

   Turn on the Elliptical Dome option and set the distance to 0.2 inch.

   Try to select the second small flat face, but notice that this causes the Elliptical Dome option to go away and the preview of the smaller dome to change shape. As a result, you need to do these one by one. Eliminate the second face, and complete the feature.

19. Ctrl-drag the second dome onto the remaining flat face. You can originate the Ctrl-drag from either the graphics window or the FeatureManager.

20. Select the Front reference plane from the FeatureManager and activate the Section view. Notice that the Dome features did not affect the inside of the thickened solid.

NOTE   Turn on the Tangent Edges As Phantom setting in the View ⇨ Display menu. Look at the difference between the edges created by the first and second domes that Figure 9.17 shows. The first dome has a phantom line, meaning that it is tangent. The second and third domes have a solid line, indicating that they are not tangent. Both the elliptical dome and the default (non-continuous dome) settings make the dome tangent to the vertical. The end of the loft also happens to be tangent to the vertical, but the extruded faces are extruded at a 5-degree angle. Dome options cannot control the tangency of the dome to external faces; in this case, it was just coincidence that one of the faces was also tangent to vertical.

21. With the section view still active, apply concave domes (with the direction reversed so they remove material rather than add it) to the inside flat faces. Use the same distance values, with 0.2 inch for the smaller flat faces and 0.4 inch for the larger face.

   Figure 9.19 shows the finished part. Save and close the part before moving on to the next chapter.

FIGURE 9.17

Showing under the domes and the tangent lines

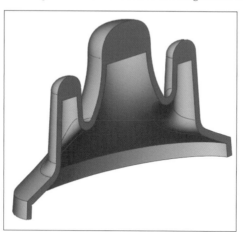

22. The last step is to use the Indent feature. Indent requires a solid body to use as a tool. Use the Insert ⇨ Part menu command to insert the part from the downloaded file, called Chapter 9 – tutorialtool.sldprt.

    Accept the defaults, without clicking in the graphics window. Clicking in the graphics window places the part where you click. You should line up the inserted part origin with the tutorial part origin.

NOTE I recommend changing the color of the inserted body to make sure it is easily differentiated from the main part body.

23. Initiate the Indent feature from the Insert ⇨ Features menu. Select the body of the part you have been working on as the Target Body. Flip the part over so you can see inside it, and click the portion of the inserted part that you can see inside the main part body. The PropertyManager settings are shown in Figure 9.18.

24. Use a 0.1-inch wall thickness with a 0.05-inch gap. The gap is between the inserted body and the main part body.

NOTE You will find more information on the handling of solid and surface bodies in Chapter 13.

25. When you have made the settings, accept the feature. Use the Section View tool to check the results. If everything is correct, use either Hide Body or Delete Body to remove the imported part from view.

26. Apply fillets to complete the part. Save and close the part. Figure 9.19 shows the finished part.

FIGURE 9.18

Setting up the Indent feature

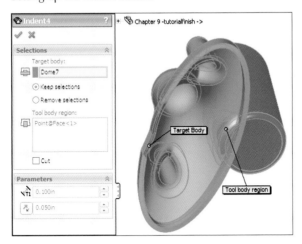

FIGURE 9.19

The finished part

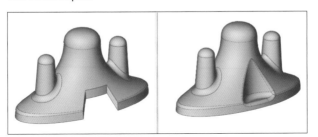

Summary

Secondary shape creation features work well for niche applications. The Dome and Shape features are not well suited to general shape creation, and of the two, the Dome feature is certainly the more useful one. It is best suited to capping ends of rectangular parts, rounding tops of buttons, and scalloping the bottoms of blow-molded bottles.

Indent is a wonderful little tool if you have an application for it. Don't be afraid to experiment with it a little. It is typically used on injection-molded parts, or any part with a consistent wall thickness. (Other than sheet metal, the Forming Tool functionality is the sheet metal equivalent of the Indent tool.)

On the surface feature side of things, you will find Radiate and Ruled surfaces are typically used with mold design, with the addition of draft, and as construction geometry. Ruled surfaces have made Radiated surfaces largely obsolete for most applications.

Chapter 10

Working with Hybrid Features

SolidWorks Corporation doesn't use the term "hybrid" in much of their documentation. You can find it in some of their training manuals, some Web-based demos, and a few SolidWorks World presentations, but these are relatively recent developments, and usually driven by a few specific people, me being one of them. Some folks dispute that the term "hybrid" has any meaning at all when used in reference to modeling in SolidWorks, their argument being that any surface modeling eventually evolves into a solid, and all solid modeling involves surfaces behind the scenes.

Beyond quibbling about words, hybrid modeling is all about the inter-changeability between solids and surfaces, and particularly about working with both at the same time. Certainly you can use methods that are strictly solid or strictly surface, but most of the complex modeling that you do will be some combination, some *hybrid* of the two. Hybrid modeling doesn't nec-essarily have anything at all to do with complex shapes; in fact, it is often touted as a way for machine design professionals to expand their toolsets by learning some surface commands.

Replacing faces of a solid with faces of a surface, using a surface to cut a solid, or extruding a solid up to a surface are all examples of using solids and sur-faces in the same feature. In these cases, you can think of the surfaces as act-ing as reference or construction geometry.

The more you work with solids and surfaces together, the less you tend to think about the differences between them. However, for people who don't work with them all the time, the difference at first seems important. That is to say, don't get too hung up on the hybrid terminology, because in truth it isn't that important. The important thing is that you are fluent enough in both solid and surface methods to move between them with confidence.

Moving Between Solids and Surfaces

Building a complex CAD model has some things in common with building a house. For example, both require a plan. You start a house by using stakes to sketch out the foundation. The CAD equivalent is the use of sketch pictures, layout sketches, or scanned data to lay out references for the part. You can't build the roof of a house before the foundation, and you can't (or shouldn't) create cosmetic fillets before structural elements of a model.

To carry the analogy a little further and connect it with the hybrid-modeling topic of this chapter, think of starting to install the drywall, carpets, cabinets, and interior fixtures before the house is fully enclosed. Those things require the house to be sealed off from the elements before they are installed. Also, once the house is closed in, you don't take out a wall to bring in a jacuzzi. This kind of work requires planning so that you only perform tasks once.

The connection with hybrid modeling is that you don't (or again, shouldn't) go back and forth between states. Of course, this falls into that vague morass of "best practice," which means different things to different people, and can never be pinned down to a single hard-and-fast rule, but it is something you need to be conscious of. Part of the whole point of this chapter is that you can move back and forth between solid and surface states and even use both at the same time. Complex modeling often turns out to be highly multi-body, which tends to confuse things even more.

To boil it down for you a little, if you start a model in surfaces and then progress to a solid, that is the ideal surface modeling workflow. If you start a model as a solid, then convert the solid to a surface and eventually back to a solid, that is also acceptable. It is also acceptable to have several solid and surface bodies simultaneously at any one point in the history of the part. What I am trying to steer you clear of in this section is flip-flopping back and forth, taking the same body from solid to surface to solid to surface, and so on. You need to plan your modeling so that you have a clear line in the FeatureManager after which you are working with a solid.

The three faces of hybrid modeling

You can define hybrid modeling in three ways:

- A modeling practice that uses solids and surfaces sequentially (changes from surface to solid and solid to surface).
- A modeling practice that uses solids and surfaces simultaneously (surfaces modify solids).
- Features that can be used on either solids or surfaces.

The terms *sequential* and *simultaneous* hybrid modeling are not SolidWorks terms, nor are they even industry standard terms. They simply serve to identify two distinct workflows and a set of tools within combined surface/solid modeling practice. Identifying them this way helps pin down techniques that you can use freely, and techniques that you have to plan for. The sequential techniques are the ones that you need to plan for because they can potentially cause performance and other types of problems by popping back and forth across that solid/surface line. When using the sequential tools, you need to make sure you have planned your approach carefully. You can use the simultaneous tools at any point along the history of a part without much forethought.

Fortunately, I wasn't able to come up with a catchy descriptive name for features that can be used on either solids or surfaces, so I'll just refer to them as hybrid features.

Identifying sequential hybrid modeling tools

The tools involved in sequential hybrid modeling convert bodies from solid to surface or from surface to solid:

 ■ **Thicken** (when used with an enclosed surface body)

 ■ **Delete Face** (with the Delete option)

 ■ **Knit** (with the Try To Make Solid option)

 ■ **Fill** (with both the Merge Result and Try To Make Solid options)

Notice that each of these tools is qualified with certain conditions. These are the tools that change a given body from solid to surface or from surface to solid. Tools like Offset and Knit (without the Try To Make Solid option) are not included because they work by essentially copying faces of a solid to a surface body.

Notice also that there is no option to simply convert a solid to a surface without either copying it or removing a face from it. This may be a somewhat esoteric point, but I have come across situations where it would have been useful to convert a solid directly to a surface without removing faces or copying. Maybe we can all pay a visit to that enhancement request Web site.

Identifying simultaneous hybrid modeling tools

The following are tools that enable you to use solids and surfaces simultaneously:

 ■ **Cut With Surface**

 ■ **Replace Face**

 ■ **Fill** (with the Merge Result option)

 ■ **Thicken** (to a specific thickness using open surface body)

 ■ **Split** (using a surface as a cutting tool)

 ■ **Extrude** (with surfaces as end conditions)

In order to use any of the above listed tools (except Fill), you first need to have a surface body created by some other means.

Identifying hybrid features

Other parts of this book identify features that only create or modify either solid or surface bodies. These include features like Rib, Dome, and Indent for solids, and Fill, Boundary, and Trim among others for surface features.

Another set of features exists that you can use interchangeably on either solid or surface geometry. This includes features such as the following:

 ■ Fillet

 ■ Draft

 ■ Wrap

 ■ Deform

 ■ Freeform

 ■ Move Face

 ■ Move/Copy Bodies

 ■ Delete Bodies

The Fillet and Draft features were not always hybrid features. It wasn't that many releases ago when users could only use those features on solid bodies.

Modeling efficiency

One of the arguments I commonly make in support of a hybrid modeling approach is to appeal to users' sense of efficiency. You can measure efficiency in many ways, but it is most often shown as a ratio, such as miles per gallon. In this case, it has to do with comparing rebuild speed to how long it takes to set up a feature in the first place.

I wish that I only had to create models once and could then move on to what is next, but if you've spent any time working in product development, you know this usually isn't the case. If you are anything like me, you wind up building a part once, and then modifying it many times. For this reason, efficiency is an important measure. How quickly you can do something the first time is important, but it is also important how quickly the software gets through it every time you have to edit the model. Every time you modify something high up in the FeatureManager, the rest of the tree has to rebuild.

It may be counterproductive to be extremely particular when it comes to rebuild speed, as one second here or there isn't going to put your project behind schedule. However, products are made of many individual parts, and individual parts are made of many features, and so if you pay that rebuild penalty for every feature in every part, every time you rebuild, it can really add up.

In the following examples, the Feature Statistics tool measures the rebuild times. The time measured by this tool is not the same as the total amount of time until SolidWorks releases control of the interface back to you. After the rebuild finishes, the software is busy with calculating display data, mass properties, and other types of data to be saved with the part. Still, Feature Statistics is a good way to measure for comparison, because even if it does not represent exactly the amount of time the software spends working, it is at least consistent in this respect.

In order to take a rational look at which features are going to cost you and which ones are going to save you time, I will use a couple of models that I have used in SolidWorks World presentations to look at a couple of typical hybrid techniques.

Sketch elements = solid faces

Part of the efficiency analysis in this section has to do with what is going on behind the scenes. While I don't expect you to fully analyze every modeling situation, I do want to expose you to at least one analysis so that you can understand why some types of modeling are better than others, from an efficiency point of view.

The first idea is that every time you use a non-construction sketch element to make a solid feature, that sketch element represents a solid face (or possibly more if you are using Thin Features) that SolidWorks has to create. Even if you never actually see the face, SolidWorks creates it.

Let's look at a simple example. Figure 10.1 shows a block with a corner cut out of it. To cut the corner, you might draw a rectangle, and then extrude a cut to a depth.

FIGURE 10.1

Cutting a corner from a solid block

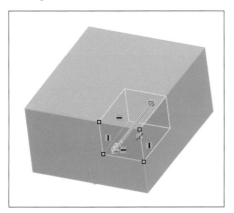

When you make this cut, SolidWorks is actually creating the cut as a solid block first, and then removing it from the larger block using a Boolean function. The preview shows the solid body that it creates. The Parasolid modeling kernel performs this, as it does most other modeling functions. This makes it doubly behind the scenes, first behind the SolidWorks interface, and then within SolidWorks, behind the Parasolid interface. Most of the actual geometry creation that happens in SolidWorks is handled by the Parasolid kernel or other third-party licensed components. SolidWorks itself is really just an interface that allows users to drive the kernel and other components and visualize the results.

Getting back to cutting the corner out of the block, the solid block has six faces, but the cut out corner only has three. That means that SolidWorks/Parasolid wasted half of the effort it put into making this cut, and you have drawn two lines more than you needed to.

From a purely theoretical point of view, a more efficient approach is to extrude the two sides of the finished cut as a surface, and then make a planar end cap. This method only models exactly the faces that are needed. Figure 10.2 shows the FeatureManager of this part, with the surfaces shown in a different color.

FIGURE 10.2

Cutting the corner with surfaces

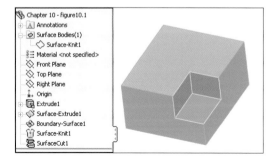

After you build the surfaces and knit them together, you have to use a Cut With Surface feature to make the cut.

NOTE   Generally speaking, most users consider it best practice to have the edges of a cutting surface extend past the boundaries of the solid. This is of most importance on complex shapes where edge tolerances can easily cause the software to think that a surface does not actually cut through the solid.

Theory and practice do not always mesh, and this is one time when they don't. In theory, the surface modeling approach shown in Figure 10.2 should rebuild faster, but in practice it doesn't. Using Feature Statistics, the solid method shown in Figure 10.1 rebuilds in 0.03 second and the method shown in Figure 10.2 rebuilds in 0.05 second. Again, these numbers are miniscule for consideration on their own, but you rarely make single features on their own.

A more popular way of measuring modeling efficiency is to count the number of features that it takes to make a particular part or shape. It usually takes more surface features to make a given shape than solid features. This is because you are making the shape face by face. Solids build everything all at once. In this case, the more popular measure turned out to be accurate. Still, I do not put much faith in the feature-counting method for measuring efficiency. It is probably best suited for contests and showing off to your coworkers than for serious modeling analysis.

Best-practice recommendations usually suggest that you make more features rather than fewer if you are looking for editability, ease of troubleshooting, the ability to remove features for FEA or add features for rendering, and so on. While it is true that if you put all of the fillets of a part into a limited number of actual features in the tree, which helps rebuild time, it is also true that edits to those mega features go much more slowly, and it is more difficult to troubleshoot when the entire feature fails.

A third measure is to examine how much time it takes you to create each feature. Surface features generally take less time to set up than solids, primarily due to the fact that the sketch is simpler because you are not trying to do everything at once. One reason I often elect to use surfaces over solids is that the sketches are easier to create, and because they are simpler with fewer entities, they are also less likely to fail later on. Complex sketches are very error-prone.

Regardless of the outcome in this particular situation, the rest of this chapter looks at modeling by comparing different techniques, and trying to understand which process best meets the current need. How many faces does a solid need, and how many for a surface? How long does it take the solid to rebuild, and how long for the surface? How long does it take to create the solid, and how long for the surface? Best practice is a bit of a balancing act. Every benefit in one area of the model comes at the cost of some other property. An example of this conundrum is that robustness through change requires a lot of extra initial modeling time. Fast rebuild time may also require some research.

Comparing four methods

Figure 10.3 shows the first model that I will use to compare solid and surface techniques. Although it is simple, it is also tricky because you cannot make the sides of the hole and the bottom of the hole in a single feature. It is also tricky because the hole is deeper than the shell feature. It gets trickier yet due to a geometrical difficulty that may be difficult to visualize, and is explained later in this chapter. The example gets around each of these issues in multiple ways, and I evaluate each method as I present it. The goal of this section is not so much to present as fact methods that are "the best," but rather to offer an excuse to talk about the various tools and their comparative merits, and to exhibit modeling techniques and possibly most importantly evaluation methods.

Consider the Feature Statistics values that are shown to be the baseline for this example. I obtained these results with the Verification On Rebuild option turned on. The main import of that setting in this case is that it has a larger effect on features that create more faces, which is to say that it tends to slightly exaggerate the results against solid features, and in favor of surface features.

FIGURE 10.3

The part used for the first set of examples

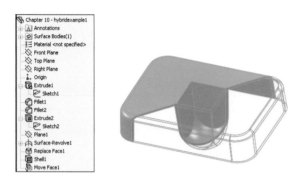

Because the resolution of the time measurement is so large (0.01 second) compared to the time measurement itself (typically 0.02 second), and because the rebuild time of the individual features as well as the overall part varies sometimes drastically from one rebuild to the next, Feature Statistics is not an ideal tool to measure the performance of individual features. Still, it is the only even vaguely analytical tool available to establish the relative rebuild speeds of features. Please keep in mind that the results are not perfect by any means; they should be understood in the context in which they are presented, and I am only using them for comparison.

NOTE   Notice that the Feature Statistics window is non-modal, meaning that you can leave it open and rebuild the model by pressing Ctrl+Q. When you do this, the feature order and the rebuild times can change, especially on simpler models like this one. For this reason, it may be a good idea to rebuild several times and use an average value.

In fact, with the Feature Statistics window being non-modal, you can continue to work with it open, and it will update as you add new features. While the window is non-modal when working within a single part, that does not carry over to allowing it to function between parts. If you change from one part window to another, you need to close and restart the Feature Statistics box.

These alternatives will be compared against a baseline model from the Web site called Chapter 10 – figure 10.1.sldprt.

Alternative method #1 — Solids

The first alternative method I will try is to make this part using all solid features. Figure 10.4 shows the feature tree and the Feature Statistics box. The purpose of this method is to show the most basic way to create this part using typical solid features. I suggest that you open the parts called Chapter 10 – figure 10.1-6.sldprt to examine along with this section.

The main differences here are that I created the hole with an extruded cut, and then partially filled it in with a revolve. Notice that of the five sketch elements of the revolve, only one of them makes any faces in the resulting solid. These non-construction sketch elements that don't create any solid geometry indicate that you may want to consider a different approach. The need for the extra sketch entities comes from the requirements of solids.

The final cut feature to move the wall up is another nested loop, this time two rectangles. In this feature, no sketch entities actually create any faces of the solid model. In addition, the rebuild time is about 30 percent slower for the solid version than for the baseline.

FIGURE 10.4

Alternative method #1 — Solids

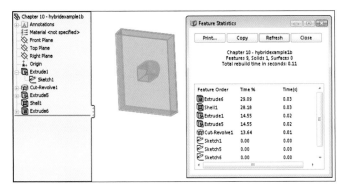

Alternative method #2 — Up To Surface

This is an example of simultaneous hybrid modeling. Although the Up To Surface techniques are discussed later in this chapter, I wanted to include them in the analysis here as a potential method. Figure 10.5 shows the finished part, along with a surface that is used to extrude up to.

FIGURE 10.5

Alternative method #2 — Up To Surface

  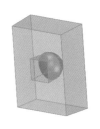 

Revolved surface   Extruded cut up
to revolved surface

Notice that the total rebuild time for this model is the same as the baseline. The only real difference between method #2 and the baseline is the difference between Up To Surface and Replace Face. To me, it seems that the Up To Surface method should be faster simply because it doesn't have the intermediate step of first creating a face that you don't want, and then replacing it with a face that you do want, but this turns out not to be the case.

Alternative method #3 — Cut With Surface

This is another example of simultaneous hybrid modeling. Another technique that this chapter discusses later on is the Cut With Surface method. Using this technique, I create the revolved surface, then extrude a surface to create the drafted sides of the hole, trim the revolved and the drafted faces using Mutual Trim, and then use the trimmed surface to cut the solid. This takes more features, and takes almost twice as long to rebuild. Figure 10.6 shows the FeatureManager and Feature Statistics for this alternative method.

FIGURE 10.6

Alternative method #3 — Cut With Surface

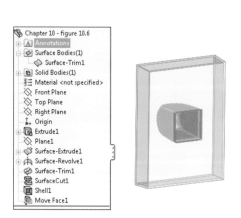
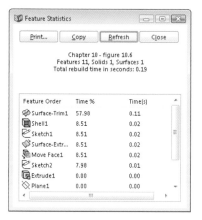

So what is the message you should be taking from these examples up to this point? Looking at the results, I would surmise that hybrid methods are the most efficient in terms of rebuild time. Strict surfacing is the least efficient both because of rebuild time and because of the number of features you are required to build. Still, you need to remember that you can't always model for maximum efficiency; sometimes, you just need to use surface modeling to get the added control, and you will have to accept the extra modeling time in addition to the extra rebuild time.

Alternative method #4 — Indent

This is a strictly solid-based technique. All of these techniques are very different from one another, and the Indent method is probably the most different of them all. Indent basically enables you to create a positive shape as a separate tool body that forms the negative shape into the plastic part. Figure 10.7 illustrates how this works.

FIGURE 10.7

Alternative method #4 — Indent

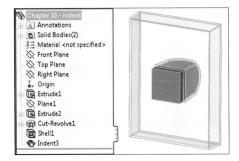

This technique can be very attractive in some situations. It is not a hybrid tool at all — it is 100 percent solid — but I show it here because it is a clever way of producing geometry that you might otherwise need a surface to create. Never discount options simply on the basis of whether they use surfaces or solids, or both.

NOTE The Indent feature falls victim to the same type of error that shows up in the rest of the methods used in this example. When offsetting the four flat faces, the corners are extended to remain in contact, and so they are actually offset by more than the offset distance. I have been able to gloss over this error in the other methods by using the Shell To Outside option. The offset/shell works when reducing the size of the hole geometry, but not when increasing it. Figure 10.8 shows this geometrical problem.

Notice that the distance from the corner of the original hole faces to the corner of the offset hole faces is 0.1412 inch, which is the offset distance, 0.1 inch, times the square root of 2 (the length of the hypotenuse of a right isosceles triangle with legs of 0.1 inch). Anyway, it is geometrically impossible to do what I have asked of the software, which is a reasonable excuse for it to fail. To make it work, the sphere would need to be offset by 0.141 inch instead of 0.1 inch. Instead of doing that, I simply made the sphere bigger than it would be if it were tangent, which avoids the problem and allows a constant wall thickness.

FIGURE 10.8

The offset problem

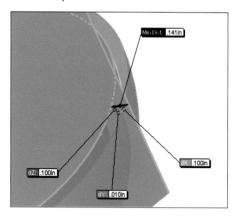

Comparing methods to shorten the wall

Starting from the baseline model, I used two different techniques to shorten the wall around the outside of the part. One way was the Move Face method, and the other was a nested loop cut. Of these, the Move Face is the more sophisticated method, with the nested loop cut being brute force, and also pretty ugly. Am I a modeling snob for saying that? Possibly. Let's compare a few methods and see which is the fastest and easiest.

CROSS-REF Chapter 12 covers the Move Face tool in more depth, along with other tools that enable you to directly edit model geometry, regardless of the feature history.

The following are methods to evaluate for shortening the wall:

- Nested loop cut
- Cut from side Up To Next
- Nested loop Cut With Surface
- Replace Face
- Move Face

Figure 10.9 shows the sketches and transparent surface features used to create models for each of these techniques.

All of these methods create the same geometry in the end, and each probably has one particular type of situation in which it is the best, or even the only, way to accomplish a particular goal. In complex modeling, it is important to have alternatives because the software is imperfect, and does not always work the way you envision that it should.

Comparing methods to shorten the wall

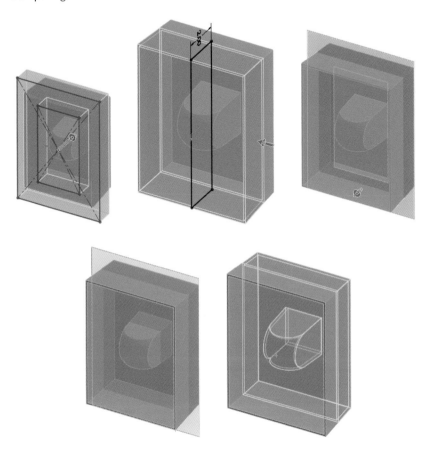

I recommend that you open the files from the downloaded data to follow along with the techniques I am using for these models. Using Feature Statistics on each of these parts shows that they all rebuild in approximately the same amount of time (0.02 second), except for the Up To Next cut feature which takes 0.03 second. Again, due to the fact that the measurement increment is about 50 percent of the measurement itself, these numbers are almost meaningless. It is actually more meaningful when time values like these are measured on a slower computer.

Nested loop cut

As mentioned earlier, this is the brute force, least-sophisticated approach of the five shown. It involves drawing two rectangles, one inside the other. It doesn't really matter if the rectangles are dimensioned because the sketch entities don't actually create any geometry; however, you want the size of the rectangles to change along with the size of the part if it happens to change. Dimensions seem to be a waste here, but at the same time they are necessary.

Up To Next cut

The Up To Next cut is probably the most unexpected of these techniques. In this case, the sketch remains on one of the default planes, and the start condition is offset to one side, and then extruded Up To Next. Interestingly, it avoids cutting the pocket around the hole that protrudes down. I'm not sure what rule or condition you could apply that would predict this kind of behavior, and I'm not sure exactly why I tried to do it this way, but it does work.

Cut With Surface

The Cut With Surface technique has some of the same drawbacks as the nested loop because it uses a nested loop sketch to create a surface feature that doesn't touch the pocket around the hole. This option is interesting, but in this case probably not much better than the nested loop solid cut. This functionality is explained in more detail later in this chapter.

Replace Face

Replace Face is a function that you need to become familiar with if you aren't already. It is extremely handy because it is one of the few tools that can actually add and remove material in a single feature. You can use it on solid or surface bodies, but the new face must be a surface body. The interface and limitations of this feature appear in a more detailed description later in this chapter.

Move Face

Many users have discovered the Move Face feature, and find it to be a simply amazing tool. It is covered in more detail in Chapter 12, which covers Direct Editing.

Move Face can be seen as a non-parametric tool because it enables you to make changes to part geometry directly, without worrying about features, history, dependencies, or anything else. The Direct Modeling concept is one that is gaining a lot of momentum in the CAD market right now, and SolidWorks is trying to include non-parametric tools so that it is not left behind by its competitors.

Extruding to Surfaces

One of the most commonly used and most powerful of the hybrid tools available to users in SolidWorks is using surfaces for extruded feature end conditions. This functionality enables you to extrude up to planes, faces of solids or surfaces, or even solid or surface bodies. As of SolidWorks 2008, this pertains only to the Extrude feature, but you can use a surface as both the starting face and the end face of an extrude. There are currently no options to revolve features from or up to surfaces, but I have heard this requested many times.

Figure 10.10 shows a sketch and two surface bodies, and some of the PropertyManager options for working with this type of geometry.

FIGURE 10.10

Using surfaces for Extrude end conditions

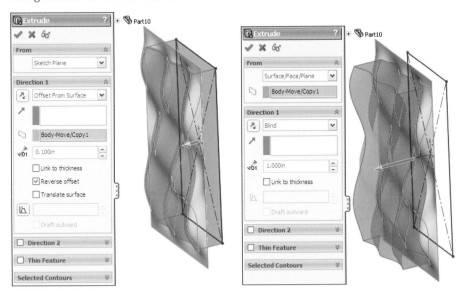

The available end conditions for using surfaces with the Extrude feature are as follows:

- **From Surface**
- **Up to Body**
- **Up to Surface**
- **Offset from Surface**
- **Offset from Surface with reverse offset**

The "from" and "to" end conditions can be combined in a single feature or used independently.

The From Surface start condition, when combined with the Blind end condition, results in a solid similar to the Thicken feature, but the side walls are parallel to the direction of the extrude instead of perpendicular to the surface thickness. Figure 10.10 shows this in the image on the right.

The Offset From Surface end condition stops short of the surface, and the Reverse Offset option goes past the surface by the same distance.

NOTE   Please note the difference between a true offset, which performs a radial offset always in the direction perpendicular to the surface, and the "translate" type of offset, which simply copies the entire surface at a fixed linear distance. True offsets distort curvature; "translate" offsets do not.

The Up To Body condition can be a big timesaver. Sometimes in the selection box, the Up To Surface condition only picks up a *face*. You may be familiar with the error message that says, "The end face cannot terminate the extruded feature," shown in Figure 10.11.

FIGURE 10.11

The error message stating that the end face cannot terminate the extruded feature

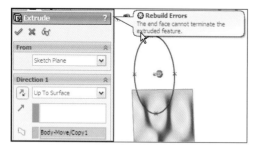

This error is caused when the sketch being extruded does not fully project onto the face that you have selected as the Up To face. In other words, the sketch hangs off the end of the face. This is all right for some types of faces, like analytical faces where the software can extend them indefinitely very easily. However, it does not work for complex NURBS faces that cannot be extended easily.

The Up To Body condition can come in handy in situations where you see this error message. Instead of selecting only a face, you can select an entire body. That body can be either a solid or surface body. It's not as picky as the Up To Surface condition. Also, if you need to, you can use a Knit or Offset tool to join several faces together into a single surface body, and rather than selecting a single face to extrude up to, you can select an entire body.

The Up To Body condition can be even more useful in situations where you pattern a feature that is extruded with an Up To Body condition. The entire pattern will work with the intelligence of the end condition.

You can even extrude surfaces up to surfaces, although there is less reason to do that than to extrude solids. In general, the fewer inter-body references you can make, the better off you are when it comes to making repairs after changes.

Lofting Between Surfaces

Many users do not realize that you can loft a solid using surfaces as profiles. Yes, it sounds odd. Yes, it's a thing you don't use frequently. But yes, it is also a technique that I have had to rely on at times to get things done. Typically, lofting between surfaces is done as a workaround when a thicken or any other function meant to create constant-thickness solid geometry doesn't work as expected.

One way of using this type of loft is to use offset surface bodies to create geometry similar to a shell or a thicken feature. Figure 10.12 shows the results of this method. Using offset surfaces can be a risk in some situations because the offset will fail if a portion of the parent surface has a section of curvature less than the offset distance.

FIGURE 10.12

Lofting between surface bodies

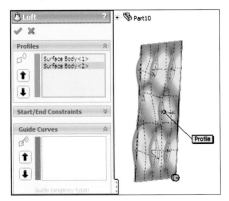

In the image on the right, Figure 10.13 shows a second method you can use when lofting between surface bodies, which is to use faces that you have copied and moved using the Move/Copy Bodies feature. This method is preferable when the distance between the surfaces is much less than the curvature of the faces. It is tough to identify situations when you would want to use each of these methods, but if you keep them in your toolbox of available tricks, opportunities will present themselves.

Be aware that the side faces created by the first method will be perpendicular to the face at the edge, and the side faces created by the second method will be parallel to the direction in which the copied face was moved. Also, you should be careful if you choose the second method and any of the copied faces have a significant angle between the copy direction and a vector normal to the face, as the thickness at that point will appear to be reduced. Figure 10.13 demonstrates this difference between a true offset and a simple translate.

Also remember that you can create a lofted cut between surface body profiles. This is the equivalent of a thicken cut. You can also use both methods discussed above with a lofted cut.

FIGURE 10.13

A potential problem when copying instead of offsetting surfaces for the loft

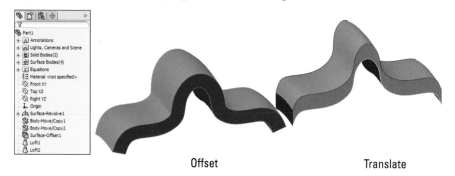

Offset   Translate

Using Thicken for Bosses and Cuts

The Thicken feature is one that I have tended to avoid. Nothing is inherently wrong with the Thicken feature, but it does have the potential to give low-quality results. The main cause of bad results with Thicken is that the thickness faces are always normal to the main face. If you have a main face with a lot of curvature changes, this may lead to a situation where the thickness faces are wavy or simply go in the wrong direction. Often, I find that extruded faces, or more commonly ruled surfaces, are better to use because they are cleaner, more predictable, and maybe most importantly, more controllable.

Another potential source of problems with the Thicken feature is that when you have face-to-face contact between bodies, and then add thickness to one of the faces and try to merge the bodies as solids, you can run into small tolerance errors that cause tiny gaps between the bodies. In addition to this kind of result adding significantly to rebuild time while SolidWorks tries to figure it all out, it is similar to the warnings you hear frequently about line-to-line contact when creating sweeps or lofts. Theoretically perfect contact between entities does not work well with interpolated geometry, which is not theoretically exact.

Alternatives to using the Thicken feature for adding or removing material can include the following:

- Offset or move a surface body, and then extrude Up To Surface
- Offset surface, and then use extruded, ruled, or radiated surfaces around the edges of the offset body
- Thicken in both directions (into and out of the part) to avoid the face-to-face contact
- Enclose a solid body and then shell (this primarily avoids some of the problems with irregular thickness faces)

After all of that, Thicken is still sometimes the best way to go. Figure 10.14 shows two applications of the Thicken feature on a single part.

Two applications of the Thicken feature on a single part

The first image shows the base part shape using the Thicken feature to create a solid from the open surface. On this part, the thickness faces are relatively well controlled, and a fillet is added to them later to minimize any undesirable effects. Notice that I built the surface as the inside face, and then thickened the part to the outside of the face. You could use this method for a couple of reasons. First, on this part, the dimensional constraints are on the inside, where it mates with a matching part, and also need to accommodate an item that goes inside of it. Second, if you have trouble controlling curvature, the Thicken feature does not thicken to the inside of the surface if the minimum inside radius is less than the thickness. I just mention this to remind you that you don't have to get stuck in the frame of mind that says you always have to model the outside face of an object directly.

The second image shows the finger grip area being thickened from a trimmed surface. To accomplish this without the errors mentioned earlier, I thicken using the Thicken Both Sides option. This makes sure that when the software tries to merge the newly thickened body with the existing body, there are no face-to-face contact errors.

Removing an edge between faces

It is not exactly related to hybrid modeling, but what follows is a great tip that I can't pass by without mentioning. This tip involves using the Delete Face feature to remove an edge between faces. The image on the left of Figure 10.15 shows the intersection of the thickened finger grip area with the thickness face of the original Thicken feature, and I have added a fillet to the corner. The fillet has to have an end face, and to make that end face, it has to extend a neighboring face, either the thickness face from the first or second Thicken feature. Solidworks makes that decision without your input, and might do something different on the mirrored end of the feature.

The intersection between two Thicken features

Trying to roll subsequent fillets over this intersection of faces can be messy. In fact, I couldn't get it to produce the results I was looking for. Fillet features seemed to fail for no reason, until I realized what was going on.

In some situations you can get away with using Delete Face to remove an edge, and I was just lucky to come across one situation where I could demonstrate all of these techniques in a single area of the model. Delete Face feature causes SolidWorks to extend a neighboring face to fill the gap caused by removing an existing face. The image on the right in Figure 10.15 shows how nicely you can smooth this area over. Notice also that the fillet takes care of any draft issues that existed in that area. If you choose not to use such a large fillet, you would need to use a Draft feature to correct the undercut around the finger grip area. The draft in this area is the type of geometry that you could also handle by using extrudes or the ruled surface mentioned earlier.

Using sub-surfaces to thicken small areas

Each of the individual bars of the finger grip area in the part shown in Figure 10.15 is made by a separate Thicken feature, and each has to originate from separate surface bodies. Often the way users do this is to use a Split Line on a solid face, and then use Offset Surface on the split face. Split Line does terrible things to parent/child relations in SolidWorks, and so my preferred method — and the one used on this example part — is to roll back to a place in the FeatureManager where the face to be used is clean and whole, offset that face, and then trim it to leave the surface bodies you need to make the Thicken feature from. This works much better than the Split Line on solids approach.

Thickening corners

Remember the problem shown in Figure 10.8 where offsetting the flat faces and offsetting a spherical face by the same distance do not result in compatible geometry? This has to do with what happens when you thicken surfaces around a corner, and the surfaces are not knit together.

Figure 10.16 shows two conditions. On the left is the condition where flat surfaces that intersect at a corner are not knit, but are thickened, leaving a notch open at the intersection. On the right is the case where the surfaces are knit, causing the corner to be filled.

FIGURE 10.16

Thickening surfaces that form a corner

Leaving a notch out of a thickened corner is not just a problem on right-angle corners, but it can also be a problem in any situation where adjacent surfaces that are not knit together are thickened, including slight non-tangencies. The same sort of thing can happen when offsetting sketch entities where the endpoints of the sketch entities are not merged into a single point.

Thickened cuts

Thicken features have several uses. They are a great starting point for overmolded material, or a mating part that is inset into a larger part to offer a color or material break. You can also use thickened cuts for areas for logos or stickers.

Figure 10.17 shows a part with a thickened cut around a grip on a plastic device. More detail is required to make this area ready for an overmold, but the hard part has been done — getting the thickened cut set up appropriately.

FIGURE 10.17

An inset for an overmold

This geometry is created by copying two faces of the handle, then using the Untrim feature to fill in the holes caused by the grooves, trimming the shape with a spline, and then creating the thickened cut.

The one problem that arises from a situation like this is the draft around the inset. The Thickened Cut feature does not provide a way to implement draft along with the feature, and the regular Parting Line draft doesn't work well in these situations where the edge being used as the Parting Line turns parallel or nearly parallel to the direction of pull for even a short distance. You have to add this type of draft manually, and it may not be a straightforward method to create it, depending on the needs of your particular situation. For one approach on how to do it, open the SolidWorks part from the downloaded materials called Chapter 10 – thickencut.sldprt, and examine the ruled surface features.

Using Replace Face

You can use Replace Face in many situations where you have a solid, and you have a surface that represents the shape you want to work into the solid. The lofted surface feature above the handle in the part shown in Figure 10.17 uses a Replace Face feature to integrate the surface shape into the solid part. Figure 10.18 shows the PropertyManager interface for this feature.

The Replace Face feature

I can never keep the terminology straight for the Replace Face feature. The top selection box is labeled Target Faces For Replacement, and the lower selection box is labeled Replacement Surfaces. I just remember that the top box is to select the old faces, and the bottom is for the new faces. The interface would be so much simpler if they could use simple intuitive words like old and new. Anyway, the old faces can be part of a solid or surface body, but the new faces must be from a surface body.

Also recall the use of the Replace Face feature in the example part in the first part of this chapter, shown in Figure 10.5. The rectangular flat-bottomed hole was created in a block, and then a spherical surface was used to replace the flat bottom. SolidWorks trims or extends the side faces as needed to make the surface fit, if it is possible. Remember too that the replacement surface can add or remove material from the part, or it can even do both at the same time.

Replace Face is another tool that enables you to get around some of the pitfalls of parametric editing and design intent. It works on native and imported data.

Replace Face can be touchy about the selected geometry. You must select all of the faces that you want to remove, and all of the new faces. For example, open the part that Figure 10.18 shows. The first time I tried that Replace Face feature, I didn't select the second face. The second face is a planar face that fills a gap, and I wasn't sure that it would be necessary, hoping that the flat face at the symmetry plane would extend. This didn't work the way I imagined, though, and so I made the planar face and then it worked.

Replace Face can also use over-built surfaces to replace exact-fitting faces, although this does not always work. If you try it and it doesn't work, trim the surface back to fit exactly, and you may find that it works.

An alternative method when Replace Face doesn't work is to use Delete Face with the Delete option to remove the faces you want to replace, and then use the Knit or Trim tool to add the new face into the body.

Using Advanced Options of the Fill Surface

I have covered the Fill surface in Chapter 6, but saved a few choice tidbits for this chapter, such as the Merge Result option. Fill is truly a magical tool. As you spend more time with the software, you will come to appreciate this tool more and more. Certainly there are times when it falls short of expectations, but most of the time, it really can perform amazing feats of fitting a smooth surface into an open gap.

Merge Result

The reason I have saved some aspects of the Fill feature for use in this hybrid chapter is because, even though it predictably produces surfaces, it also has options that can directly knit adjacent surfaces and convert to a solid body, or Fill can also be integrated immediately into a solid body. The example file used to create Figure 10.19 is included in the downloaded files.

FIGURE 10.19

Integrating a Fill feature directly into a solid body

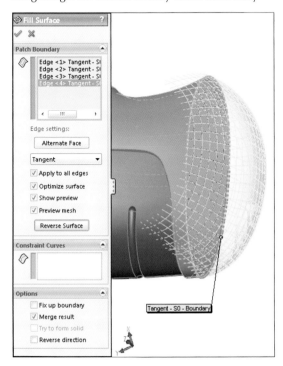

Figure 10.19 shows a Fill surface being created from the edges of a solid body; then, using the Merge Result, the Fill is immediately integrated into the solid. The integration happens exactly in the same way as if you had used the Replace Face tool, except that you can do it all in a single feature.

> **NOTE**   **Notice in Figure 10.19 that the part of the Fill surface adjacent to the finger grips does not maintain the tangency setting. This is a relatively common problem with the Fill surface, and one that you have to watch out for.**

Merge Result and Try To Form Solid

The second advanced option of the Fill surface is the combination of the Merge Result and Try To Form Solid options. The name of the second option has always made me chuckle a little bit. You have to love SolidWorks Corporation's optimism: they aren't sure if they can make the solid or not, but they will surely give it a try. The Try To Form Solid option only becomes available when the Merge Result option is checked and only edges of surface bodies are involved.

Do not expect the Merge Result option to allow you to select any surface body in the part; it does not do that. It only knits together bodies that are touched by the newly created Fill feature.

SolidWorks usually reserves the "merge" term for solids, and prefers "knit" for surfaces, but in this case, "merge" is used for both solids and surfaces. Either way, whether you start with a solid or a surface, you can use Fill to complete the model and turn it into a solid body.

Fill and Delete Face

SolidWorks has added the Fill feature functionality to the Delete Face feature PropertyManager. One of the Delete Face options is Delete and Fill, and when that option is activated, another option called Tangent Fill becomes available. This uses the Fill feature in the background. When I intend to use Fill, I will tend to use it directly rather than indirectly. Direct options give you more control, for example with the Curvature option rather than simply the Tangent option.

Using the Wrap Feature

The Wrap feature has unique functionality within its limitations. That is to say that it is a useful feature that does things no other feature in SolidWorks will do, but it will always leave you wanting more because it has some significant limitations. The main limitation is that you can only apply a wrap to flat, cylindrical, or conical faces.

To use the Wrap feature, you must draw a sketch on a plane that is parallel to a plane that is tangent to the conical or cylindrical face. To say it another way, you don't have to sketch directly on a tangent plane, just on a plane parallel to the tangent.

The image in Figure 10.20 shows a part with a commonly requested shape. I created this part by first drawing the line-arc-arc-line sketch, using a bi-directional offset with capped ends, and then using the Wrap with the Deboss (remove material) option.

FIGURE 10.20

FIGURE 10.20

The Wrap feature

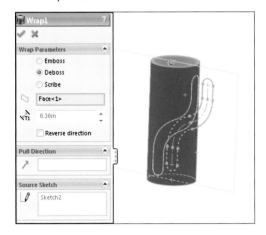

Wrap options

The Emboss and Deboss options only work on solids, adding and removing material, respectively. The Scribe option works for solids or surfaces, and basically creates a split line. The part in Figure 10.20 used a Deboss option with a distance greater than the thickness of the tube material to make a through slot.

Using Pull Direction

When wrapping onto a plastic part, you need to be conscious of the direction of pull for the mold. The Wrap feature enables you to account for this, as Figure 10.21 illustrates.

FIGURE 10.21

Wrapping with the Pull Direction option

I exaggerated the geometry in Figure 10.21 to make it easy to see. You can apply the Pull Direction option to either Emboss or Deboss features, but if you look at the Wrap PropertyManager, you may notice that there is no way to specify draft angle. Applying draft to a feature like the one shown is going to be a lot of work, because there is no way to mass select everything that you need to draft; you will have to select each of the edges individually.

NOTE For reference, the part shown in Figure 10.21 uses sketch text wrapped and embossed onto a conical surface with the Pull Direction option. If you are interested in any of those specific methods, you might want to examine the part from the downloaded file called Chapter 10 – wrap2.sldprt.

You may be able to use the Wrap feature as a workaround for times when you want to create multiple loop split lines. Keep in mind that as counter-intuitive as is may be, you can wrap a flat sketch onto a flat model face. Another workaround for this need is to extrude a set of surface bodies from a single sketch and use the Intersection option in a Split Line feature.

Using Scribe with surfaces

You cannot pattern the actual Wrap feature, but you can pattern bodies that result from it. For that reason, sometimes it is useful to wrap a Scribe onto a surface, delete part of the surface, and then use the Thicken feature to emboss or deboss as necessary. This is a technique frequently used in jewelry design. Figure 10.22 shows a pattern of surface bodies that resulted from wrapping a sketch with two shapes onto a surface with the Scribe option, and then using the Delete Face option to get rid of the unwanted portion.

FIGURE 10.22

Scribing a surface body

Wrap limitations

The Wrap feature also offers plenty of opportunities for things to not work the way you expect them to. A common question from users is how to use an open sketch profile to essentially wrap a curve onto a face. Wrap cannot use open contours. It wraps single and multiple closed loop sketches and nested loops.

Another common problem comes when users try to wrap all the way around an object. If your wrap overlaps, you can see unexpected results. The wrap can go around as many times as you have space for, if you want to wrap at an angle to the axis, as Figure 10.23 illustrates.

FIGURE 10.23

Wrapping all the way around an object

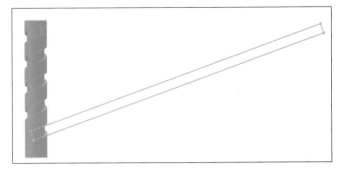

I have also heard many users ask if they can wrap non-sketch geometry, such as existing solid, surface, or even curve geometry. You can twist solids and surface bodies with the Deform and Flex tools, which I discuss in Chapter 12, but the Wrap feature only wraps sketches. You cannot use it to alter curve geometry.

Tutorials

These tutorials give you a small sampling of several different hybrid techniques.

Tutorial 10.1: Plastic clip

Follow these steps to get some hands-on practice.

1. From the downloaded files, open Chapter 10 – tutorial1start.sldprt. This is a partially finished plastic clip, built completely in simple solids. Figure 10.24 shows the part in its original state.

2. One thing you generally want to avoid on your parts, even when they are as simple as this one, is unnecessary breaks in the faces. Breaking up faces with edges causes problems with draft, fillets, and other types of features. The modeling technique used to create the starting part is not necessarily optimal, and it leaves some edges that this tutorial will help you get rid of. Start by creating a zero distance offset of the larger of the red faces shown in Figure 10.24.

FIGURE 10.24

The starting point of the first tutorial

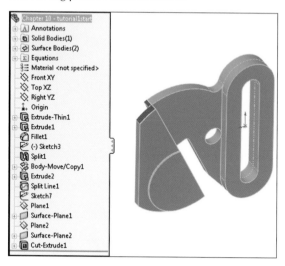

3. Use the offset surface with the Replace Face feature to replace the smaller of the red surfaces. This step removes the edges between the two red faces of the solid. Hide or delete the offset surface body when complete so that the faces merge into a single face. (Don't delete the Offset feature; rather, use the Delete Body option to delete the surface body.)

4. Use Delete Face with the Delete and Patch option to delete the combined face that you just used Replace Face on. This combines all three faces into a single face, which makes everything much smoother.

 You can only combine adjacent faces when they are the same type of analytical face with the same parameters or if they were originally a single complex face that has been split.

5. Click Surface-Plane1 and Surface-Plane2 and show both of them. You will have difficulty visualizing what is going on unless you turn both surfaces transparent.

6. Notice that the surfaces are slightly angled from one another. When this clip is in use, it uses two identical pieces that are rotated 180 degrees from one another, and fit together. In this step you will use the Replace Face feature to make the faces flow into one another when the two parts are assembled. Initiate a Replace Face feature, and select the face of the solid indicated in Figure 10.25 as the old selection (the dark blue face), and Surface-Plane1 (from the FeatureManager) as the new selection.

FIGURE 10.25

FIGURE 10.25

The first Replace Face feature

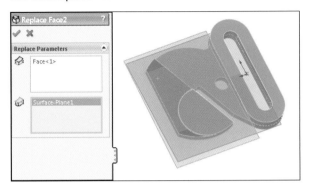

7. Initiate a second Replace Face feature, and this time select the semi-circular face adjacent to the solid face from Step 6 as the old selection, and Surface-Plane2 as the new selection. Figure 10.26 shows the finished result with draft and fillets, with two identical parts assembled.

FIGURE 10.26

The finished assembly

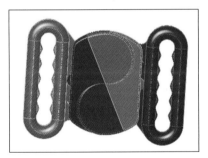

Tutorial 10.2: Finial

This tutorial walks you through creating a couple of Fill features that integrate themselves directly into a solid body. To complete this model, work through the following steps:

1. Open the part Chapter 10 – tutorial2start.sldprt from the downloaded file for Chapter 10. It looks like the image in Figure 10.27.

FIGURE 10.27

The start model for tutorial 2

2. Use Sketch 26 to create a Split Line feature on the face of the red feature on the part.

3. Initiate a Fill feature, and select the split line created in the previous step.

4. Use the sketch point in 3D Sketch 5 as the Constraint Curve, and set the edge condition to Tangent.

5. In the Options panel of the Fill PropertyManager, select the Merge Result option, and click the green check mark to accept the feature.

> **NOTE** If the feature fails or gives a warning message, you may have to use the Reverse Direction option at the bottom of the panel.

6. Use Sketch 27 to make a second Split Line on the red feature similar to the previous one.

7. Use Delete Face with the Delete option to delete the face inside the split line. After you accept the feature, notice that the main body of the part is now a surface body. Check the Surface Bodies folder to verify this.

8. Create another Fill surface using the Tangent edge condition and the 3D Sketch 6 as a Constraint Curve. Again, use the Merge Result option, but this time, also use the Try To Form Solid option along with it.

9. Create the final lobe of the floral pattern using Sketch 28 and 3D Sketch 7, using a method of your choosing to create similar results as the steps above.

10. With Step 9 complete, use the Delete Face with the Delete and Patch option to remove the Fill surface and the split line you just created.

> **NOTE** There is no reason to do this, other than to demonstrate the technique, which doesn't make much sense on native parts, but is a big benefit on imported parts.

11. Show the existing Surface-Extrude1 surface body. (Click and select the tool that looks like eyeglasses.)

12. Use Cut With Surface to cut away the biggest part of the model.

13. Using Mirror and Circular Pattern, finish the part, shown in Figure 10.28.

The completed finial with Real View

Summary

In some ways, hybrid modeling is just another CAD buzzword, but in many respects, it represents an entire way of working that respects the advantages of both solid and surface techniques. This chapter uses three different definitions for hybrid modeling: sequential surface to solid, simultaneous surface and solid, and hybrid tools that are surface or solid. For some features, one method may be required or may not be available, and you will have to make due with another. In any case, it is important to have multiple ways to approach each modeling task because of minor differences in the results of each method, and because you may need to work around bugs in the software or geometrical difficulties in the part.

Performance considerations are important, but they often conflict with other equally important considerations such as modeling time, design intent, and robustness through change. You need to decide for yourself which of these is most important for each situation. I also recommend avoiding changing back and forth between solid and surface more than necessary, simply as a matter of best practice and performance.

Chapter 11

Managing Surfaces

W hile solids and surfaces in SolidWorks hold much functionality in common, there are also some significant differences. This chapter is dedicated to all of the tools used to manage surface bodies, in particular, those tools that are unique to surfaces. I mentioned earlier that if you are going to work with surfaces in SolidWorks, you need to become comfortable with the concepts and terminology around multiple bodies. Both solids and surfaces can use bodies, but the difference is that with solids, multiple bodies are the exception, while with surfaces, they are the norm.

Some of the tools introduced in this chapter have solid equivalents, and some do not. It is all part of the vocabulary of advanced SolidWorks functionality.

IN THIS CHAPTER

Copying, merging, and moving

Changing boundaries

Tutorial

Copying, Merging, and Moving

Offset, Knit, and Move/Copy are commonly used surface body management tools. To some extent, these tools have overlapping capabilities, although their main purposes may seem widely different. These features are sometimes used interchangeably to copy surfaces in place. Knit and Offset (with a zero distance) are used to copy solid faces to create surface bodies. The zero distance Offset in particular is favored when the situation in which Knit does not work for this purpose arises, which is when you want to copy a single face of a surface body which only has a single face and Knit complains that you cannot knit a body to itself.

Offset/Copy Surface

The Offset Surface feature is probably most frequently used, not as an offset at all, but as a copy function. When you use an offset distance of zero, the name at the top of the PropertyManager changes from Offset Surface to Copy Surface, as shown in Figure 11.1. I frequently use this function to create surface bodies from solid bodies by simply copying faces of the solid.

FIGURE 11.1

Offset changes to Copy with an offset distance of zero

 The Knit feature can do exactly the same thing: copy a selection of faces of a solid or surface body into a new surface body. However, there is one situation in which a zero distance Offset/Copy works when a Knit does not; this is when you want to copy a surface body that is made from a single face. In this situation, Knit tells you that it cannot knit a body to itself. For this reason, I tend to only use the zero distance Offset for copying and use the Knit only for joining multiple surface bodies.

Knit

Because of the discussion in the Offset/Copy Surface section, I prefer to use the Knit feature only to join surface bodies together, rather than using it to copy surface bodies or create surface bodies. The Knit PropertyManager is shown in Figure 11.2.

FIGURE 11.2

The Knit PropertyManager

Knit is analogous in some ways to the Combine feature, which joins solid bodies. The main difference between joining solids and joining surfaces is that solids require face-to-face contact, or interference of the solid bodies to be joined, and does not work with edge-to-edge contact. Knit, on the other hand, requires edge-to-edge contact and does not work with any other type of contact or intersection.

Knit also has other functionality. In the Knit PropertyManager is an option to Try To Form Solid. This option is always available, regardless of whether or not the selection is valid for making into a solid. The main problem with using this option is that if it fails to knit the selection into a solid, the Knit feature may still work, but the Try To Form Solid option is turned off and the user is not warned. The only way to know if the Knit has succeeded in making a solid is to look for a solid in the Solid Bodies folder. If the Try To Form Solid option has failed, the option check box is automatically cleared.

 For this reason, I usually prefer to use a separate Thicken feature to make an enclosed surface body into a solid body. Two advantages come with using separate features. One is that troubleshooting failure is easier when separate operations are segmented into separate features in the tree. The second is that if solidification fails, the Thicken feature gets a red X on it, instead of simply no notice at all on the Knit.

Move/Copy

SolidWorks calls the Move/Copy feature "Move/Copy" in the menus (both Features and Surfaces menus), "Move/Copy Bodies" when used on a toolbar, and simply "Move/Copy Body" at the top of the PropertyManager. You can use Move/Copy with either solids or surfaces. You can use Move/Copy to translate, rotate, or position bodies by mates or by delta values; however, you cannot translate and rotate at the same time unless you use mates.

You can specify translation and rotation using numbers in the spin boxes or by dragging the arrows attached to the body in the graphics area. Dragging the rings around the body rotates it in that plane. Figure 11.3 shows the Move/Copy Body PropertyManager and the drag handles for translation and rotation.

You can use the Copy option at the bottom of the Bodies To Move panel, regardless of whether you have specified a new location with a distance, angle, or mates. If you use the Copy option without a new location, after you click the green check mark, a warning tells you that you didn't specify a new location and asks if you really want to proceed.

To switch to the Mate interface, use the Constraints button at the bottom of the PropertyManager. This enables you to apply mates between bodies in the same way that you would apply mates between parts in an assembly; however, you will find a couple of significant differences. Primarily, mated bodies within a part cannot move with Dynamic Assembly Motion, like parts in an assembly. Secondly, as Figure 11.3 shows, it allows you to specify which body moves to meet the other body.

Finally, remember that Move/Copy Bodies is a *history-based feature*, meaning that it is applied at a certain point in the timeline along the FeatureManager. If you move a body, SolidWorks only considers it moved after a certain point in the tree. This can be a little disorienting if you need to work with models rolled back, and you have to roll back before the Move/Copy Bodies feature.

FIGURE 11.3

The Move/Copy Body PropertyManager

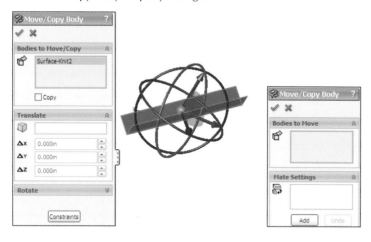

Changing Boundaries

 Most faces in SolidWorks, whether solid or surface, begin life as a four-sided patch and are automatically trimmed by the software to fit the present need. The concept of the underlying four-sided patch with a trimmed boundary is one that comes up again and again, particularly in surface modeling, and when solid models have to call on the underlying b-rep (boundary representation) data to extend faces.

Most of this trimming and extending happens automatically behind the scenes, but you can also do it manually when the situation requires.

CROSS-REF If you are interested in changing the overall shape of an existing surface, you might want to consider the Flex, Deform, or Freeform tools. These are all described in detail in Chapter 12.

Trim

The Trim surface feature is analogous to the solid Cut feature, but the Trim surface feature only works on surface bodies. The word *trim* comes from standard CAD terminology.

Solids cannot be trimmed; they can only be cut by surfaces, planes, or sketches. You can trim surfaces with other surfaces, planes, or sketches.

You can either use one surface to trim another (standard trim) or you can use both surfaces to trim each other (mutual trim). You must perform Trim between separate surface bodies; a single body cannot trim itself. A surface body used to trim another surface body must touch or cross the other body. The minimum contact is that the edge of the body doing the trimming must touch the face of the body being trimmed.

When trimming with sketches, the sketches are projected an infinite distance in a direction perpendicular to the sketch plane. You can use open or closed loop, multiple closed loop, nested closed loop, and even sketch text to trim. You can also mix types, such as using a line crossing a circle, similar to the way that contour selection works for extrudes.

Another type of trim that is relatively new in SolidWorks allows you to trim with a Spline on Surface. If you sketch the spline directly on a surface of a model, whether curved or flat, you can use the Intersection option in the Trim feature to trim along the spline, as long as the spline is either a closed loop or both ends touch the surface boundary.

Trim and Split Line features are similar in some ways, although Split Line splits faces into multiple faces rather than eliminating them altogether. Sometimes Split Line is used to isolate a section of a face, followed by Delete Face to eliminate the face.

Still, the features are not one-to-one equivalent. Trim is far more flexible when it comes to the types of sketches that it can use. Split Lines cannot use the contour selection or multiple loops or sketch text.

 Mutual Trim features can become very difficult to visualize, especially when you have more than two surfaces involved. The Trim tool allows you to choose if you want to select the parts of the surface you want to keep or the parts you want to get rid of. This is because sometimes you cannot see the parts you want to keep because other faces are in the way. Figure 11.4 shows a relatively simple example of a Mutual Trim.

FIGURE 11.4

Trim Surface PropertyManager along with a moderately difficult trim visualization

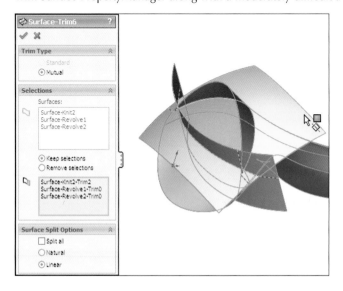

Untrim

The Untrim feature in SolidWorks comes as a revelation for many people who are not familiar with it. Untrim takes a surface and restores its original four-sided default boundary. This is important in many kinds of modeling, but is probably the most dramatic when done with imported geometry. Because I always think of imported geometry as being "dumb" — that is, without any history — many CAD users in general believe that in parametric modelers, you cannot change imported solids or surfaces.

Untrim can be used on selections of edges or on the entire surface. You can use it on interior trims or trims at the boundary. If you are untrimming a single whole face, you can also extend it using a percentage. This can be useful to avoid using an Extend feature.

CROSS-REF For a simple example of using Untrim, have a look at the part used for the Chapter 8 tutorial.

When Untrim is used on a closed loop interior trim, it works the same as the Delete Hole feature.

Delete Hole

The Delete Hole feature is a bit of an anomaly. There is neither a menu selection nor a toolbar button for it. Delete Hole has recently appeared in the Help documentation, and so at least it is documented, although you probably would not find it unless you knew to look for it.

Delete Hole exposes the underlying surface geometry where a hole has been trimmed into a surface. It works only for closed loop interior trims on a surface. If the edge touches the boundary of the surface, you will have to use Untrim. Like Untrim, Delete Hole works on native as well as imported geometry.

To activate Delete Hole, select the edge of a hole in a surface, and press the Delete key. SolidWorks prompts you to choose whether you are trying to delete the selected feature or the hole. A Delete Hole feature appears in the FeatureManager. Figure 11.5 shows an example of the Delete Hole feature at work.

Extend

You can use the Extend feature in SolidWorks to extend surfaces even beyond their original underlying boundaries. You have two choices when extending surface boundaries: Linear (tangent from the existing edge) and Same Surface (the software attempts to extrapolate how the curvature of the surface will change). The Linear option usually creates edge breaks from the original edge of the surface.

The main advantage of the Same Surface option is that there are no edge breaks, but the disadvantage of using it is that, especially with non-analytical surfaces, it becomes unpredictable as it gets farther from the original edge. The main advantage of the Linear option is that it is more likely to simply work. For most applications it is usually considered a distant second choice.

For analytical and ruled type surfaces, extending the surface is easy and predictable, because circles, ellipses, and straight lines have well-defined shapes that the software can extend easily. Figure 11.6 compares original surfaces to Linear and Same Surface extensions.

Delete Hole at work

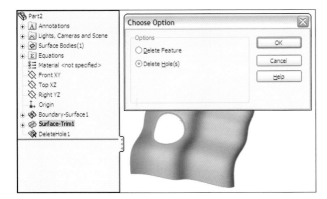

A comparison of original surfaces to Linear and Same Surface extensions

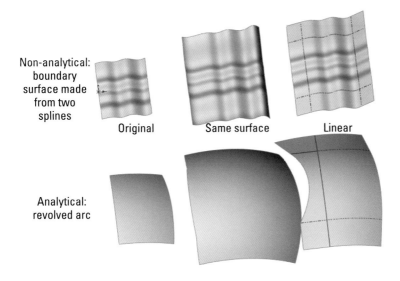

Non-analytical: boundary surface made from two splines

Original   Same surface   Linear

Analytical: revolved arc

Notice that in the case shown, the arc surface shows the most difficulty extending with the Linear option. Typically, it is best practice not to rely on the Extend feature to extend surfaces more than, say, a few percent of their original size.

If Extend has any comparable feature in solids, it might be the Move Face feature. Move Face does the same sort of extension of a solid through extrapolation. It is not a very good analogy, because if you are not familiar with Extend, it is likely that you are also not familiar with Move Face.

Extend is typically used to make surfaces slightly bigger than they need to be. For example, if a surface is going to be used to cut a solid, but the surface edges are exactly on the faces of the solid, you may have some difficulty getting the cut to work. If the surface edges extend out of the solid, however, there is less chance of a problem. Also, when trimming surfaces, if the surfaces extend past one another, it is easier to get a clean trim edge. The Extend options include extending a specified distance, up to a point or up to a surface.

Tutorial

This tutorial employs simplified versions of the type of tasks you will find in real-life modeling situations. Real-life modeling is rarely as clean and tidy as the example you see in this tutorial, and real-life modeling is far more time consuming, but the basic skills are the same.

1. Open the file named Chapter 11 – Tutorialstart.igs from the Web site. This is an imported IGES file. If it asks you to run an Import Diagnosis on it as soon as it opens up, answer No, and continue.

2. With this part, your task is to reverse the angle of the top face and rebuild the part as a solid without the hole or the missing fillets. You do this using only the tools described in this chapter and a simple Axis.

3. The first task is to reverse the angle of the top of the part. Initially, the face slopes down in the positive Y direction, and you change it to slope down in the negative Y direction. Start by making an Axis that goes through the center of the hole in the top. To do this, open a sketch on the Top plane, and convert the edge of the hole as a sketch. Notice that this comes in as a pair of splines instead of as an ellipse, as you might guess.

4. Draw a construction line between the endpoints of the converted splines.

5. Add a sketch point at the midpoint of the construction line.

6. Create an Axis perpendicular to the Top plane through the sketch point. (The Axis tool is located at Insert ➭ Reference Geometry ➭ Axis.)

7. Open the Move/Copy Bodies tool through the menus at Insert ➭ Features ➭ Move/Copy. Select the top surface in the Bodies To Move selection box. Change to the Rotate panel, and in the selection box select the Axis. Type in **180** for the angle. Figure 11.7 shows the preview of the feature. Accept the feature when it looks right.

FIGURE 11.7

A preview of the Move/Copy Bodies feature in Step 7

8. Click one edge of the hole in the top face, and press the Delete key. Answer Delete Hole to the prompt, and press Enter to accept.

9. Activate the Untrim feature (Insert ➪ Surface ➪ Untrim), and select the face of the body that was rotated in Step 7. Notice that the preview is a rectangular patch. Accept the feature.

10. Notice now that two edges of the top surface are too long for the part and two of them are too short for the part. Activate the Extend feature (Insert ➪ Surface ➪ Extend), and select the two edges that do not extend far enough. Set the distance to 1.5 inches, and accept the feature.

11. The Up To Surface and Up To Point options do not work because the side faces of the part are in places taller than, and in other places shorter than, the surface you want to go up to. In the Faces To Extend box, right-click one of the side faces of the part and choose Select Tangency from the menu. Then drag the arrow up so that the distance is at least 1.2 inches and the side faces extend past the top face.

12. Now both the top and side faces should be too big. Too big is good. Activate the Trim feature (Insert ➪ Surface ➪ Trim), and use the Mutual option. Select both bodies in the Surfaces box at the top, and then select the Pieces To Keep box below. Activate either Keep Selections or Remove Selections, depending on your preference as to which set is easier to select. After you make the selections, click the green check mark to accept the result.

NOTE Notice that the Mutual Trim option knits together the resulting bodies. Standard Trim does not do this. This is another reason why the Mutual Trim option is often a better choice to make the workflow faster and more fluid.

13. To solidify the part, use the Thicken feature, which is found at Insert ⇨ Boss/Base ⇨ Thicken. After you select the enclosed surface body that you want to convert into a solid, the Thicken interface should add the option to the bottom to Create Solid from Enclosed Volume. Make sure this is selected, and click the green check mark to accept the feature.

14. Make sure the surface body converts to a solid body. Add a fillet around the top face of 0.060 inch.

> **TIP** If you cannot find a Solid Bodies folder in the FeatureManager, it may be that it is turned off in the System Options. Starting with SolidWorks 2008, many items of the FeatureManager can be either disabled or made to show or hide automatically, which has a tendency not to work properly. You can find the settings at Tools ⇨ Options ⇨ FeatureManager. Make sure the options are set to Show rather than either Hide or Automatic.

Summary

Many, but not all, surface management tools have solid equivalents. Sometimes the comparisons between the surface and solid functions are not exact or complete. Learning to work in surfaces becomes less intimidating if you can relate the functions to things you are already familiar with.

Some of the surface management tools have functionality that is not immediately obvious, but may be useful all the same. Remember that advanced modeling in SolidWorks tends to involve knowing three workarounds for every one thing you try, because the first couple of tries may not work as you expect.

Chapter 12

Using Direct Editing Tools

Direct editing tools (sometimes also called direct modelers or non-parametric modelers) enable you to edit 3D geometry directly, instead of indirectly through a set of parameters. This means that you can move a face directly instead of editing it indirectly through a dimension on a sketch. The most important implication of direct editing is that you do not have to worry about how something was created — it removes the process-based part of working with CAD data. It is a polar opposite to parametric modeling in many respects.

Using direct editing, you might work this way: "Move this face 1.5 inches in that direction," whereas in parametric modeling you would work this way: "Decrease the length of this sketch element by 1.5 inches." With direct editing you are concerned only with the resulting geometry, while with parametrics you are concerned primarily with the process of how you make the geometry.

The CAD industry as a whole is starting to emphasize direct editing more and more as a tool for non-specialists, and as a way to circumvent complex parametric modeling schemes. I do not believe that direct editing will ever completely replace parametric modeling, simply because the benefits of parametrics are real and have been demonstrated many times. Still, not everyone needs the "design intent" capabilities of parametric modelers. For some users who make simple or occasional changes, a direct editor may be a better fit.

Examples of direct modelers are McNeel's Rhinoceros (also called Rhino), Kubotek's KeyCreator (formerly CADKEY), PTC's CoCreate OneSpace (formerly HP Solid Designer, and even further back, known as HP-30), and SpaceClaim. Of these, only Rhino is well suited to working with complex surface geometry. Rhino enables you to tug and pull on surface control points to edit the shape directly, much like the intention of the Freeform feature in SolidWorks.

SolidWorks has several tools that function as direct editing tools, even though SolidWorks as a whole is a decidedly parametric system. These tools enable you to make changes to existing geometry without rolling back, to change values in a PropertyManager, or to edit sketches. SolidWorks does this by adding a feature to the tree representing the non-parametric change. Mixing parametric and non-parametric features in one software package seems more than a little odd, but it does have advantages over using either system independently.

This chapter shows ways in which you can make good use of the non-parametric direct editing tools available in SolidWorks, and it also raises the question about how to manage best practice with these tools.

CAUTION **Because the tools do not follow the parametric scheme of things, other users making changes to parts modeled with a combination of techniques might become confused, especially if they are not familiar with these tools — and honestly, not many users are familiar with them. You will have to decide your own best practice recommendations. I feel I must warn you, however, because some of these tools are so effective and simple that they can be extremely addictive alternatives to using parametric relationships and feature history.**

One of the criteria I used for putting features into this chapter is whether the feature can operate on imported geometry without creating new geometry, but only editing the existing geometry. This is how direct modeling tools work. They have some rudimentary way of creating the initial geometry, and then more sophisticated ways to enable you to edit that geometry directly without regard to how it was created. In fact, one of the benefits that most direct modeler vendors tout is that all geometry is native geometry.

For years, imported geometry in SolidWorks has been called "dumb solids" because there was nothing you could do with it. Although some of these tools have been around for several releases, many people do not know anything about them, or that they can be used to manipulate imported models to some extent.

Between surface modeling b-rep capabilities and SolidWorks direct editing tools, you have a small toolbox to edit imported data without rebuilding models.

Using Move Face

 The most representative example of direct editing in SolidWorks is the Move Face feature. Chapter 10, the hybrid-modeling chapter, mentions the Move Face feature briefly because it works on both solid and surface bodies. It is both a hybrid and a direct editing feature, but because it is most representative of direct editing, it is presented here in more depth.

Move Face enables the user to offset, translate, or rotate existing model faces within the confines of the surrounding faces' boundary representation. This means that neighboring faces may have to be extended or trimmed back to accommodate the move. Extending faces works by using the underlying geometry of the faces. If an adjacent face cannot be extended in the direction of movement, the feature will fail. For example, if you have a block and one face is surrounded by fillets, you cannot move that face to enlarge the block. You could, however, move the face to shorten the block, but it would also mean that the fillets are no longer tangent, and that they are no longer 90 degrees. On the other hand, if you move the face and all the fillet faces, it would work, as long as the side faces are straight with no draft.

Part of the beauty of this feature is that you can use it on native as well as imported geometry. Some of the best practice concerns come into play when using Move Face on native data, because a face could wind up with two features that control it: the original feature and the Move Face feature. This situation can cause confusion, even for the user who created the model. When you work with imported data, Move Face is definitely the way to go. Figure 12.1 illustrates the situation that I have just described by moving the faces of a simple block.

FIGURE 12.1

The Move Face PropertyManager

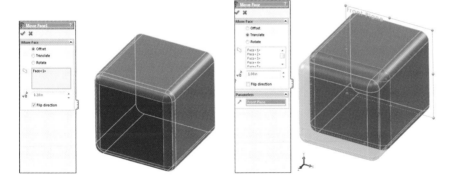

Notice also the difference between the Offset and the Translate options. Offset is quicker to set up when you are working with a single flat face being moved in a direction normal to the face itself. Translate requires that you establish a direction with a plane, edge, sketch, or axis.

When working with multiple faces, Offset works as long as all the faces tangent to the selected face are also selected. Offset also defaults to the same value every time instead of remembering the value you used last time.

The Rotate option also requires an axis of rotation that can be a sketch, edge, or axis. Be aware that there may be an easier way to accomplish the same thing that a Rotate Move Face accomplishes. The Draft feature in most situations does either exactly or approximately the same sort of thing, and may be easier to set up.

Figure 12.2 shows the Move Face feature at work on a more difficult part, extending the vents on a baseball helmet.

FIGURE 12.2

Move Face works on complex geometry

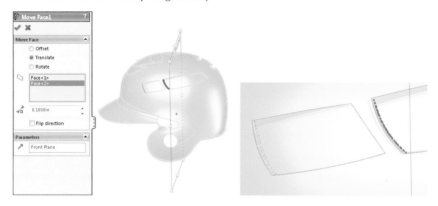

With complex geometry, Move Face becomes much more likely to fail, particularly when you ask it to extend faces. This is because analytical geometry can be extended indefinitely, but complex NURBS faces in SolidWorks must extrapolate because the underlying surface data is limited in size. When adjacent faces are both complex and must be extended, the possibility of the feature failing is even greater.

Once you start to use Move Face, you may be tempted to use it more frequently, as it will seem like the perfect solution to more and more problems. It is certainly a useful and effective tool, but you need to make the determination if you want to use it as a part of your normal production modeling workflow. It is addictive and can become a crutch or bad habit.

Using Delete Face

 The Delete Face feature is another tool for which I must confess a weakness. Like Move Face, it is another quick-fix tool that you might be tempted to overuse because of its simplicity and effectiveness. Delete Face has three options that enable it to do three very different functions.

Delete and Patch option

Figure 12.3 shows the Delete Face feature in action, along with its PropertyManager. In this image, Delete Face is being used to remove a thin ledge. Because the Delete and Patch option is selected, the face to the right of the blue selected face will be extended until it intersects the face to the left of the blue face, completely eliminating any trace of the blue face.

FIGURE 12.3

The Delete Face feature and its PropertyManager

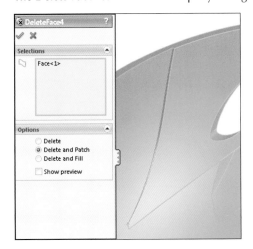

The Delete and Patch option uses the underlying b-rep to extend faces, and so if the extended portion of the face ever actually existed but was trimmed away, it is easy to extend the face. If the required geometry never existed, then extending the face becomes more difficult. If you use Delete Face on a solid body, it maintains the solid. You can also use it on a surface body. The best thing about the results of using the Delete and Patch option is that it leaves no trace of the removed geometry.

For example, Figure 12.4 shows a portion of an imported part with a blended protrusion coming through it. For whatever use this part is now intended, you need to remove the blended protrusion. Regardless of whether the large face is analytical or NURBS, the underlying b-rep face contains the patch that lies under the protrusion, and so the Delete and Patch option will replace the geometry and the fillet with the underlying whole patch. Notice that even with the edge display turned on, the face where the bump was is now a single smooth patch.

FIGURE 12.4

Delete Face removes geometry without a trace.

Delete and Patch is the default option every time you use the Delete Face feature. Depending on how you work, that setting may or may not be a good starting point. For my purposes, it works well enough. I probably use Delete and Patch about the same amount as Delete, and so the default works for me. I rarely use the Delete and Fill option.

Delete option

The Delete option simply removes a face and does nothing to replace it. If the model was a solid body before the command, it will become an open surface body after the command. (It makes a manifold body non-manifold, to use the jargon.) Keep a close eye on the body folders in the FeatureManager to keep track of changes like this.

Delete and Fill option

The Delete and Fill option combines the Delete option with the Fill feature to maintain a closed body if that is what you started with. I don't typically use this option, instead preferring to be more manual about it. When using the Fill feature, I like to have access to all of the settings, but this feature is too automatic, and prone to failure.

To accomplish the same results as the Delete and Fill option is supposed to produce, you would first apply the Delete Face feature with the Delete option, then use a Fill feature to fill the gap created by the Delete Face, and finally use Knit to knit the Fill back into the rest of the body. You could shorten the process somewhat by using the Merge Result and Try To Make Solid options in the Fill feature, as demonstrated in Chapter 10.

I prefer the more manual approach for three reasons. First, by creating the Fill feature separately, you have the option of using any edge conditions you need to use. Second, the Delete and Fill option only allows you to use either Contact or Tangent for all of the edges. Third, if you do not want to use the Fill feature at all, but prefer a Loft or Boundary, those options are open to you as well. Figure 12.5 shows the additional settings that become available in the Delete Face PropertyManager when you activate the Delete and Fill option.

Figure 12.5 also shows the result of the Delete and Fill option, which leaves a little hump on the model that does not look very natural. Also, the Deviation Analysis graphic that accompanies it does not show very encouraging results.

The Delete and Fill option is something you might use when you are modeling quickly and you know that the b-rep is not going to suffice for the patch you are trying to create — for example, if you need to fill in a patch where multiple faces come together, and it was modeled in such a way that there never existed any geometry under the face or faces you want to eliminate.

To sum it up, the Delete and Patch option is addictively effective, and you may be tempted to go out of your way to find uses for it. When it works, it's a beautiful thing. You will usually use the Delete option to go from a solid to a surface, and then patch the hole manually. Delete and Fill should probably be used sparingly, because it is not as effective as the Delete and Patch option, although it does automate a few tasks that would otherwise have to be accomplished manually.

FIGURE 12.5

Options available with the Delete and Fill option of Delete Face

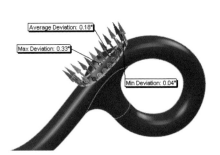

Using the Freeform Feature

Freeform enables the user to tug and pull points on a face to shape the face by manipulating it directly rather than indirectly through sketches, dimensions, and dialog box parameters. It is the closest thing to Rhino- or Alias-type freeform surface modeling that you are going to get in SolidWorks.

The Freeform feature in SolidWorks is one of those features that you want to be stunning. You want it to be an amazingly artful tool that enables you to do things that you could simply never do before. You want it to be the answer to your prayers, a dream come true, too good for words. You want it, in effect, to make SolidWorks as good at organic shape development as Rhino is. However, in the end, it's not any of those. It is a merely adequate feature that provides some interesting, but hardly stunning, effects.

Still being a rather new feature, only available at this writing for two releases, there is not a large body of work from users showing examples of this tool. With patience and the willingness to experiment, one could develop some interesting shapes with it. I envision some organic facial features that would be much more difficult through traditional parametric design methods—eyes, noses, lips, this sort of thing.

However, with the way the interface and feature process has worked out, I think this kind of shape development will be more difficult than it needs to be. Specifically, the requirement to use curves, as you will shortly see, limits the workflow, as you feel like all of the control points are not available all at once. The curve requirement seems to me like an unnecessary limitation on the process.

Part of the reason that my hopes for this tool were so outrageous is that I was involved to some extent in convincing a product definition employee at SolidWorks Corporation to include this in the development schedule. I feel responsible only for a few dusty corners in the SolidWorks software. It isn't as fulfilling as you might think. When someone who cannot read your mind translates your imagination into reality, sometimes the result is difficult to recognize.

First, the name "Freeform" is a bit overblown. The major limitation of the Freeform feature is that it is limited to a single, continuous four-sided patch. Humbug. A four-sided patch is hardly a very free form, and yet that is where you must start. You must have an existing four-sided face, either surface or solid, to start using the Freeform feature; the Freeform feature does not create the face for you. True to its direct editing roots, Freeform only edits existing model faces.

The next bit of unfortunate news is that the Freeform icon is almost unidentifiably different from the Dome and Shape feature icons, and they all sit right next to one another in the Insert ➪ Feature menu. Further, the Freeform icon looks misleadingly like it is resting on a circular base, rather than on a four-sided base.

The imported part from the Delete Face section will serve as a simple example from which to start. I want to create a thumb rest on the handle, such that your index finger would go through the loop, your thumb would go on top, and the flat end would be a handle attached to something, possibly a candlestick. Figure 12.6 shows the preview of the thumb rest, along with the Freeform feature PropertyManager.

Setting up the Freeform feature

Ironically, the most difficult part of the Freeform feature is learning the process. I know, I said that direct editing is really about leaving the process behind, and a feature called Freeform should allow you great freedom in how you make changes. In general, all of that is still true, but because you are trying to do process-free modeling inside a highly process-dependent CAD program, things don't always work out the way you might think.

For anyone who has used Rhino, the intuitive workflow for the Freeform feature might be something like this:

1. Activate Freeform feature.
2. Select four-sided patch.
3. Show surface control points.
4. Tug and pull control points to shape the surface directly.

FIGURE 12.6

The Freeform feature

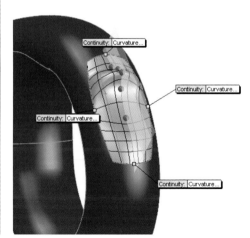

If you thought that this was what the workflow would look like, you would be almost right. However, there is a bit of a process you have to go through to create the surface control points yourself. Here is the entire process:

1. Activate Freeform feature.

2. Select four-sided patch.

3. Identify directional symmetry, if any. In Figure 12.6, I use symmetry in one direction.

4. In the Control Curves panel, identify the type of control, whether Through Points or Control Polygon. (This works similar to spline manipulation options.)

5. Add curves. The U-V mesh lines that are shown by default on the face are not enough; you have to add your own curves to which you will next add points, and you will only be able to move the surface at the points. To flip the direction of curves you want to place, use the Tab key.

6. Place control points. I recommend turning off the Snap To Geometry option, because it seems to add points randomly, not where you click. Remember that the parameterization placement of the point along the curve cannot change; that is, if a point is placed at 65 percent of the way along the curve, it will always remain at 65 percent, and just deform the U-V grid if you pull it toward one end or the other. You can delete and re-create points, but you cannot edit their placement along the curve.

7. Turn off the Add Points button, and begin moving points.

As you can see, there is a bit of a process to it.

Moving the points

When you move the points in a Freeform feature, it is similar to moving points on a spline in 3D space. The teeter-totter effect is a problem in splines, and is equally a problem with surface manipulation. Also, because the points are free to move in 3D space, you may find it advantageous to move the points in a controlled manner.

Avoiding teeter tottering

Do you remember the term "teeter tottering" from the splines chapter, Chapter 3? This is the effect caused when you move a spline point on one side of a fixed spline point; the curve on the far side of the stationary point moves in the opposite direction, much like a teeter totter pivoting about the fixed spline point. The teeter-totter effect on a surface is just like on a spline, but it happens in two directions instead of only one. Three ways of minimizing teeter tottering exist:

1. Use only one curve and only one control point, and there will be nothing for the teeter totter to pivot about. This method doesn't leave much room for making interesting shape changes.

2. For any point you want to move, use five points to help define the deformation. The outer two should be stationary, the middle one moves to the height you want, and the two about the center move to some intermediate distance. The part shown in Figure 12.6 employs this method. You may want to extend this scenario to the curves as well as the points, using five curves, with two to anchor, one to shape, and two to compensate.

3. Use the Control Polygon option in the Control Curves panel of the Freeform PropertyManager. Because you are not controlling the surface directly, the teeter-totter effect along the length of the curve is not as pronounced as it is when you use the Through Points method. It does still cause teeter tottering in the direction perpendicular to the active curve.

Many beginning users do not consider the control polygon to be highly intuitive, because the points of the polygon do not actually lie on the surface; however, many advanced users I have spoken with about the topic claim that it is easier to get a smoother shape when using the polygon, both with splines and with surfaces.

Moving points with control

By default, unconstrained points in 3D space move in a plane parallel to the view in which you see them. The Freeform feature enables you to select controls on a triad with wings between the axes. Pulling an axis moves the point in the direction of the axis. A wing is a plane defined by two axes, and dragging it drags the point in that plane. Figure 12.7 shows the section of the Freeform PropertyManager in which you specify whether the triad should be aligned to the global origin for the part, to the surface normal, or to the curve.

FIGURE 12.7

Using a triad to move points

 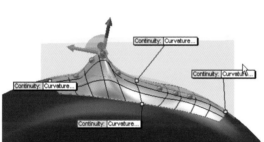

Another way to move the points with some degree of precision is to use the spin boxes in the PropertyManager. The arrows on the spin boxes use the increment set in Tools ➪ Options ➪ Spin Box Increments. Also remember that using the scroll wheels while you hold down Alt divides the increment by 10, and if you hold down Ctrl, the increment is multiplied by 10. Very useful stuff, and a great example of a good interface.

CAUTION I do not recommend using the Surface or Curve Triad orientation settings in combination with the scroll wheels or spin arrows, because it may be impossible to get the point back to its original location. The point will go up in one direction, but come down in a different direction. When possible, I recommend using the Global setting, if for no other reason than to use a familiar direction orientation.

To me, one of the most useful options with this feature is the ability to set symmetry. This functionality is conspicuously absent when working with lofts and boundary surface connectors. The symmetry options become available if the selected face is symmetrical in either direction.

Be aware also of the edge conditions that you can set around the edges of the Freeform. At edges where the adjacent face is roughly perpendicular, you can get some interesting effects because the side face gets extended.

Using Flex

 I think that the Flex feature is one of the most misunderstood features in SolidWorks. Some users compare it to the global shape modeling available from other CAD tools. This comparison may have some validity, but I would prefer to look at it simply for what it is, without comparison. The Flex feature in SolidWorks enables you to do the following:

- Bend
- Twist
- Taper
- Stretch

You can perform these operations using the Flex feature on any body in the part, including solid and surface bodies. In general terms, you establish a pair of Trim Planes between which the flex takes place, and then, using settings or drag handles on the screen, you specify how much bend, twist, or whatever you would like to put on the part.

Remember that this feature is completely independent of the way the part was originally created. You can also use it regardless of the shape or complexity of the original body. The model still has to pass the normal self-intersection checks, which can cause problems with some parts.

This is a feature I would avoid getting too carried away with. I suggest that you limit using this feature to creating pictorial representations of parts in various elastic states, but I would not count on the Flex feature to create manufacturable data. The transitions between flexed and unflexed geometry are too abrupt, the resulting geometry is not as smooth as I would like it to be, and it can often be uncontrollable or give results that are not purely intentional. My suggestion is that if you want a part with flexed geometry, model it that way intentionally using more direct methods. Yes, the direct methods may be more difficult, but they will also give better results.

I use the Flex feature to show rubber parts in alternate flexed states, or vacuum-formed clamshells such as clear plastic salad containers, or injection-molded parts with living hinges, in a flexed position. In each of these cases, the alternate position would be used in some sort of image, or as reference on a drawing, but never as manufacturing data. I just don't trust it. I'm not trying to say that this is an invalid tool, but I do think you need to be careful about your intentions with it.

To get on with an example, Figure 12.8 shows a basic rubber toilet valve flapper. This part is manufactured flat but is used flexed. Figure 12.8 shows the PropertyManager and the feature in preview.

FIGURE 12.8

A flat part flexed using the Bending option

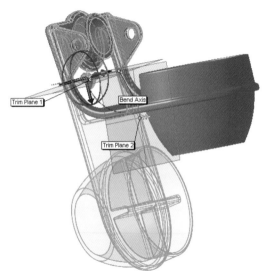

The workflow for using the Flex feature is this:

1. Initiate the Flex feature.

2. Select a body to flex.

3. Drag or use the spin boxes to place the two Trim Planes. Trim Planes denote the limits of the affected area.

4. Position the bend axis by moving the triad or positioning it in the Triad panel of the PropertyManager. This determines which part of the model stays fixed relative to the original position of the part. You may also constrain the Trim Planes with sketch geometry.

5. Specify the bend angle or radius in the Flex Input panel. You can also drag the edges of the Trim Planes to create the bend angle, or change the bend direction.

If you drag the handles on the screen, some of the numbers appear to be able to change randomly or without warning. This is one reason why I have found this feature difficult to use. If you try to figure out the interface on your own, it seems even more difficult to use.

When the Hard Edges option is enabled, SolidWorks splits the faces right at the Trim Planes. Sometimes the feature fails with Hard Edges disabled. Enabling it makes it easier for SolidWorks to create the necessary faces. Models are obviously preferable without the extra edges.

The same type of workflow works for all of the Flex options. The Trim Planes limit the action of the feature, and you can drag the edges of the Trim Planes or input values for Twist, Taper, or Stretch.

Using Deform

Deform is a trickier feature than the others. It has three top-level options. By far the most useful of the three is the Curve To Curve deform, which enables you to deform one body to match another using a start and a finish curve. A second Deform option is the Point deform, which enables you to grab a point on a model and globally deform the entire model, based on how you move that one point. A third Deform option is the Surface Push, which vaguely works like the Indent feature, but completely lacks all precision.

Deform first requires some experimentation to figure out what it can do, and then it requires some imagination to see what you would do with it. I personally only see a real applicable use for the Curve To Curve option.

Deforming Curve To Curve

Figure 12.9 shows a sample application of creating a vent in a surfaced baseball helmet. In this case, reusing the faces of the helmet itself to create the inside of the vents makes the shape fit more naturally into the shape of the helmet.

In this sample, I cut the vent holes, and then moved the inside face of the vent inward. I then used Deform to match one edge of the cutout to one edge of the helmet itself, while keeping another edge of the cutout stationary. This does not create any new surface bodies, but it does deform an existing one. Deform works in a hybrid environment (it works on solids and surfaces) and is a direct editing feature.

The Curve To Curve Deform option is commonly used to create finger grips in handles or generally to add shape to parts. While you can use 3D curves to deform 3D edges, a more common practice is probably to use 2D sketches to deform 2D edges. It is probably also a better idea to use a deform early on in a part, rather than after other features have been added. For example, if you were deforming the edges of a handheld computer case, it would be best to do so before button holes, reveal grooves, or any engineering features such as bosses or holes have been added. This is because you would not want the engineered features to be deformed. Holes need to remain round, and you cannot guarantee this if the holes exist when the part is deformed.

The Deform Curve To Curve PropertyManager and a sample use

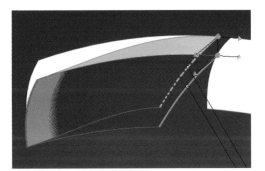

Deforming using a point

Point Deform requires that you select a point on the model; then, based on settings within the PropertyManager for the feature, the model either bulges or contracts from that point. Figure 12.10 uses the helmet from the Curve To Curve example.

The top number in the Deform Region panel is a radius value that represents the size of the area around the selected point that is pulled or pushed. The small icons in the Shape Options panel may be an odd way of specifying the deformation distribution, but the slider the icons are associated with works much like the weighting handles in a spline. The accuracy slider under these icons controls the mesh density of the resulting surface, and also controls how well the resulting surface matches the original surface.

FIGURE 12.10

The Deform Point option

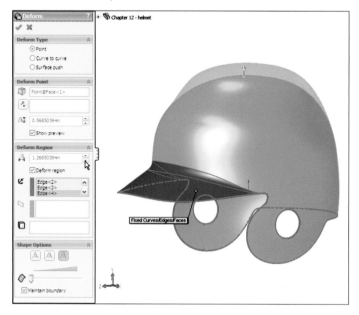

Deforming with Surface Push

The Surface Push Deform option is probably the least useful of the three types. With Surface Push, you use a tool body to push the target body, which sounds exactly like the Indent feature. Unfortunately, the result doesn't look anything like Indent. It usually works out that the tool body actually sticks all the way through the target. It is difficult to see what the developers of this feature had in mind when they created it. I don't believe that you can get any results from this feature that are even remotely intentional. Figure 12.11 shows the result of using the Surface Push option again on the helmet model.

The image on the left in Figure 12.11 shows the red target body and the yellow tool body. The image on the right shows the finished feature. The resulting star is a vague facsimile of the tool body. The secret to getting nearly usable results from this feature is to use as low a Deform Deviation value as you can use without either crashing or hindering rebuild speed beyond usefulness. The Deform Deviation value is the last spin box in the Deform Region panel. The larger the deviation value, the more vague the resemblance between the result and the tool body.

I do not find this Deform option very useful, although your opinion may vary. I prefer to model more precisely, and this tool is, at best, approximate and vague.

FIGURE 12.11

A Surface Push tool body and the result

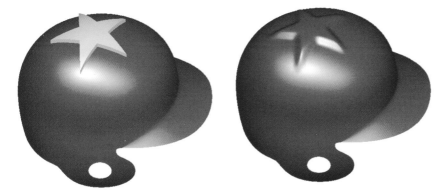

Tutorial

This tutorial gives you some experience with using the features and tools discussed in this chapter. I recommend following the tutorial steps closely once, and then going back through the exercise and trying it on your own or experimenting a little with the options. This tutorial is somewhat contrived in order to allow all of the features to be used. You would probably not see all of these features used in a single part in real-world modeling.

1. Start by opening the SolidWorks part from the downloaded file for Chapter 12 called Chapter 12 – tutorialstart.sldprt. This part is just a simple solid half-cylinder. Notice also that the part is imported.

2. On the flat, semi-circular face on the opposite end of the part from the part origin, open a sketch, and draw a vertical centerline on the end of the arc. It doesn't matter how long the construction line is. Exit the sketch.

3. Use the Move Face feature, and select the face that you just sketched on. Select the Rotate option, with the construction line as the axis, and the angle being 35 degrees, which should add material rather than remove it. Accept the feature when you are satisfied with it. Figure 12.12 shows the model as of Step 3.

4. Use the Delete Face feature to delete the two semi-circular ends and the long flat face, using the Delete option. This turns the solid into a surface body with only a single cylindrical face.

5. Activate the Freeform feature, and select the cylindrical face. Click the Add Curves button, and place a curve down the middle of the part. Then click the Add Points button and place seven points, as shown in Figure 12.13. When you are finished adding points, you need to click the Add Points button again to turn it off.

FIGURE 12.12

FIGURE 12.12

The tutorial part as of Step 3

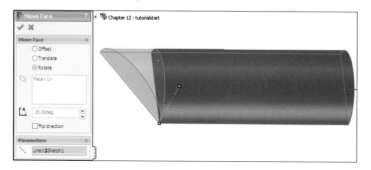

FIGURE 12.13

Setting up the Freeform feature

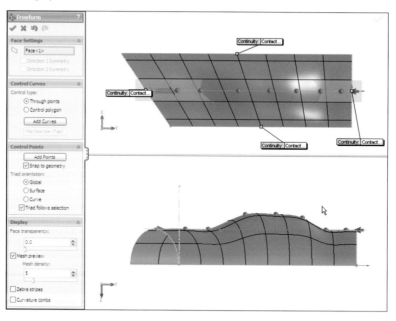

6. Set the triad to follow the Global orientation, and use the triad to pull the three middle points up to about the same height, to produce a bulge in the cylinder. Try to use the next-to-last points on each end to compensate for any teeter tottering. Teeter tottering causes the ends of the surface to look concave from a side view. Accept the feature when it looks good to you.

NOTE The screen was split vertically for the image in Figure 12.13, which helps to visualize the part from two angles at once.

7. Activate the Flex feature, set it to the Bending option, and select the surface from the graphics window. You may have to select the surface body from the Bodies folder in the flyout FeatureManager instead. Don't panic if you see a warning or error message.

8. For whatever odd reason, SolidWorks usually puts the Flex triad in the part at some minute angle. In this case, because the part is asymmetrical, SolidWorks puts the triad in at an obviously wrong angle. You have to correct this manually. Use the Triad panel of the Flex PropertyManager to change the X, Y, and Z angles to the nearest 90-degree values — in this case, 270, 0, and 180 degrees, respectively. Figure 12.14 shows the starting point of the triad angles when the feature is initiated.

FIGURE 12.14

The original triad angles

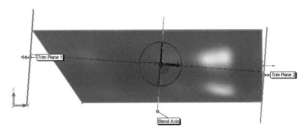

9. Make sure the Trim Planes are outside the part. The software should automatically place them at the ends of the part.

10. By default, in this part, the Bend Axis is parallel to the X axis, but you want it parallel to Z. To accomplish this, change the Z angle value to 270.

11. To finish off the Flex feature, change the Angle value in the Flex Input panel to 35 degrees. Figure 12.15 shows the model with the preview of the Flex feature. Accept the feature when you are done.

FIGURE 12.15

The state of the model in Step 11

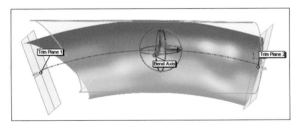

12. Make a Split Line feature using the Silhouette setting and the Right reference plane.

13. Create a sketch on the Front reference plane that looks like Figure 12.16. I sketched both of these splines in the same sketch. When you are satisfied with the sketch, close it.

FIGURE 12.16

Creating a sketch for the Deform feature

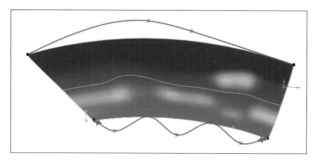

14. Initiate the Deform feature. Set it to the Curve To Curve option. In the box for the Initial Curves, select the surface edge near the finger grip sketch (concave side of Flex). In the Target curves, select the wavy spline. Think of Initial as Old and Target as New.

    Next, select the edge created by the Split Line in the Fixed Curves box (the one with the anchor). Adjust the accuracy slider (the top slider in the Shape Options panel) all the way to the right. Adjust the Moving/Fixed slider to the left to prevent too much movement from causing undercuts in the finger grip area. Accept the feature when it looks right.

15. Do the same thing with the edge and sketch on the convex side of the Flex bend. The only difference with this second feature should be that the Fixed/Moving slider should be adjusted to the right to create more bulge. Accept the feature when it looks good to you.

16. Save and close the part when you are done. Figure 12.17 shows the finished part.

FIGURE 12.17

The finished tutorial part

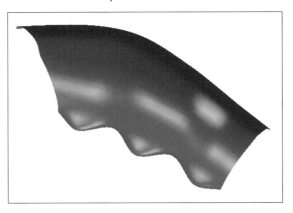

Summary

Direct editing tools are simultaneously a boon and a bane when used inside the parametric modeling scheme in SolidWorks. Process-free tools are out of place among history-based, process-dependent features. They are a boon because they enable you to work with imported geometry, shortcutting what could otherwise become a lengthy rebuild project. They are a bane because they tend to shortcut best practice, and can lead to sloppy modeling techniques and long rebuild times.

Sometimes the shortcut is the best way, and sometimes it is the only way. I don't like to encourage sloppy modeling, but I do want you to have the tools at your disposal to accomplish what you want to do. Add these tools to your toolbox, and use them when you need to. In the same way that a steady diet of chocolate is probably not the best choice, there is also such a thing as over-using direct editing tools in SolidWorks.

Chapter 13

Managing Bodies

S olids and surfaces alike make use of bodies in SolidWorks. With solids,
bodies are an option, but with surfaces, they are almost unavoidable.
Most new surface features that you create will create a new body rather
than adding to an existing one. Body management techniques are important
with solids, but doubly so when working with surfaces.

While bodies in parts are in some ways analogous to components in an
assembly, available body management techniques are not as sophisticated
as component management techniques in assemblies.

In addition to the questions about how you should handle bodies, there
are some best-practice concerns, especially when it comes to working with
multi-body solids. These can mostly be summed up by saying that multi-
body solid modeling is not a replacement for assemblies.

Further, some features are hyper-sensitive to changes in the numbers of solid
bodies, for example, the Rib feature. If a part has a single solid body, and
a rib is made on the part, and then the part is rolled back and altered such
that at the time of the Rib feature there are now two solid bodies, then the
Rib feature will fail.

Organizing Bodies

Both solid and surface bodies are listed in the Bodies folders at the top of
the FeatureManager. Prior to SolidWorks 2008, the Solid Bodies and Surface
Bodies folders would appear or disappear as that type of body became available in the part. Even if you were rolling back through the history of the

part, the folders would appear and disappear according to need. Starting with SolidWorks 2008, the behavior of the Bodies folders can be set to Automatic, Hide, and Show.

Using body folders

Figure 13.1 shows the settings for these folders, found at Tools ➪ Options ➪ FeatureManager. These settings enable you to control which folders show up in the FeatureManager window. The settings are not document-specific; they apply to all documents across the board. My experience with these settings is that the Automatic option is not completely reliable. The way the folders worked prior to SolidWorks 2008 was theoretically the same as the current Automatic setting. Folder visibility used to work perfectly, and now the folders do not always display when they contain something. For this reason, I recommend simply using the Show option for critical folder types, such as bodies and equations.

FIGURE 13.1

The settings for FeatureManager folders and other items

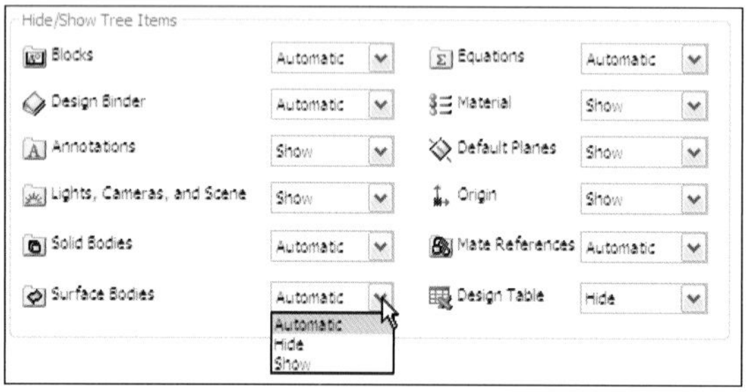

The folders display the bodies in the order in which they were created, with the newly created bodies being at the bottom of the list, and the oldest bodies at the top. Bodies cannot be reordered within the folders. When an existing body is modified by a new feature, the body is renamed using the name of the feature, and is moved to the bottom of the list.

If a single feature creates or affects multiple bodies — for example, extruding multiple disjoint sketches or a Split feature that makes many bodies from a single body — SolidWorks gives all of the bodies the same name, with a number in square brackets after the name.

You will also find some odd inconsistencies. For example, you cannot manually add folders within the Surface Bodies folder, although you can manually add them to the Solid Bodies folder. Inevitably, this inconsistency leads to a tortured explanation that makes sense to no one except people at SolidWorks Corporation as to why they intentionally left the software that way, and why it is beneficial to users.

Naming bodies

Another frustrating oddity that exists before SolidWorks 2008, but appears to be fixed in this version, is body naming. You can rename bodies, but in versions prior to 2008, any renaming you do is undone by any feature that makes a change to the renamed body. This means that your name only remains as long as no new features touch that body.

If you have a large number of solid bodies that you need to keep organized while working on other bodies, you can create folders within the main Solid Bodies folder.

NOTE The SolidWorks Mold Tools create special folders within the Surface Bodies folders for special functions. This is the only time that SolidWorks creates folders automatically. Figure 13.2 shows custom folders two levels deep in the Solid Bodies folder and the automatically created Mold Tools folders within the Surface Body folder.

FIGURE 13.2

Folder arrangements in the Bodies folders

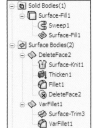

Body folder functionality that is underused is the Show Feature History option, located on the right mouse button (RMB) menu. Using this option, you can show the features that have contributed to the geometry of any body. You can access this option by right-clicking the solid or surface folder itself. The image to the right in Figure 13.2 shows the expanded bodies with their parent features indented underneath.

Visualizing Bodies

When working with multiple bodies, the ability to control visualization is the key to working efficiently. I find myself using visualization techniques frequently, especially in combination with rollback functionality. Some of the newer functionality, such as Isolate, is certainly a welcome addition. Body visualization techniques are not as sophisticated as assembly component visualization techniques. You may find several situations in which multi-bodies are inconsistent and frustrating.

Hide and Show bodies

Hiding and showing bodies are probably the most commonly used body visualization tools. You can access these tools through the right mouse button menus on the body shown in the graphics window, in the FeatureManager, on the body listed in the Bodies folder, or on the folder itself. You can multi-select bodies from the Bodies folders, or, using the Selection Filter, you can select them from the graphics window.

SolidWorks treats solid bodies and surface bodies somewhat differently, especially when it comes to hide-and-show functionality from the FeatureManager. When dealing with solid bodies, you can hide or show a solid body by right-clicking any feature affecting a particular solid, and selecting Hide or Show from the menu. To hide or show surface bodies, you can only right-click the last feature that affects that body. This is certainly frustrating.

You can easily hide bodies from the graphics window, but there is no equivalent for showing bodies. That must be done from the FeatureManager, either in the list of features, or by using the body folders.

Isolate

The Isolate function in multi-body parts works very similarly to how it works for assemblies. The main differences are that multi-body has no wireframe display option, and that you cannot create a display state in a multi-body part. Aside from that, you can make all of the bodies except the isolated ones transparent or hidden. Figure 13.3 shows how the Isolate interface works in multi-body parts.

When selecting bodies to use with Isolate, you can select faces (from the graphics window) but not features (from the FeatureManager). Using the Selection Filter set to select bodies is also a useful technique.

FIGURE 13.3

Using Isolate with a multi-body part

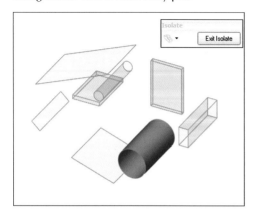

Using colors and appearances

Colors and materials seem to be areas that are constantly in flux. Rarely a release goes by without touching this functionality somehow, and so you seem to be always relearning how this area of SolidWorks works. Even the way in which SolidWorks colors are used in PhotoWorks has changed, and needs to be accounted for when using colors or RealView appearances. For SolidWorks 2008, there have been sweeping changes to the RealView functionality; the old "materials" are now called "appearances," and now you can apply the appearances to individual bodies, not just at the part level.

Using RealView in SolidWorks 2008 also interferes with your ability to apply traditional colors to parts, features, bodies, and faces. When you apply colors and appearances to bodies within a part, the best way to keep track of this is to use the display panel that flies out from the right-hand side of the FeatureManager. Figure 13.4 shows the grid that displays visibility, edge display mode, colors, textures, appearances, and transparency. Interestingly, the icons for visibility (hide and show) and transparency are nearly the same, and there is no way to change the edge display mode for bodies within a single SolidWorks part.

FIGURE 13.4

Using the display panel to reveal color, texture, and appearance settings for bodies

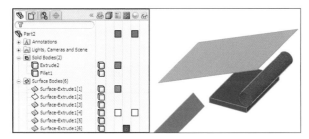

You can apply RealView appearances to bodies by dragging the appearance icon from the RealView panel on the Task Pane, and dropping it onto the body in the Bodies folders in the FeatureManager. Check the display panel to make sure you have applied the appearance correctly.

Combining and Moving Bodies

Although this book covers these topics elsewhere, no chapter on managing bodies would be complete without a discussion of combining and moving bodies.

Combining solid bodies

To combine solid bodies, they must either interfere or have face-to-face contact. If contact involves only an edge or a point, this results in a "zero thickness" error.

 The use of the Combine feature with the Add option is probably the most common way to do this, although others also exist.

To combine solid bodies without using a Combine feature, you can use an Extrude feature, or any other solid feature that automatically merges with any touching body, such as Revolve, Loft, or Sweep.

You can also combine multiple solid bodies into a single solid body using surface techniques. An example of this would include knitting the faces of the solid bodies to create a single body, or deleting faces of the solids to create surface bodies, then using Mutual Trim to trim the bodies, and then knitting them back together into a single solid body again.

The Combine feature has three options: Add, Subtract, and Common. Each of these functions results in a single solid body, and so the input bodies are all consumed. For example, when you use the Subtract option, you might frequently want to subtract Body1 from Body2, and still keep a copy of Body1. This feature does not have an option to do that, and so what you need to do is to first use the Move/Copy feature (described later in this chapter) to make a copy without moving the body, and then use one of the copies in the Combine feature. To make this seem even more like a clunky workaround, the Move/Copy feature gives you a warning when you copy a body without also moving it.

Combining surface bodies

 Surface bodies are more limited in the ways that you can combine them. Surface bodies can only be combined when they intersect, outside edge to outside edge. There are three ways to accomplish this. The Knit feature is by far the most direct way to combine surface bodies. The Knit feature can simultaneously join surface bodies and convert an enclosed volume to a solid body.

A second technique is to use the Mutual Trim, which uses multiple surface bodies to trim one another, and then knits together all of the resulting bodies. This is not always appropriate, however.

A third method is to use a Face fillet. Under most circumstances, fillet features do not work on multiple bodies, but a Face fillet can be applied between surface bodies. The fillet trims off any of the surface beyond the fillet, and knits the two bodies together. This can be used if the bodies cross one another in, say, a V, T, or an X shape, or even if they do not quite touch one another, but the fillet needs to be large enough to bridge the gap between faces.

252

Moving bodies

I maintain the belief that users should not use multi-body parts in the place of assemblies. This becomes a more and more difficult assertion to maintain when the functionality of assemblies keeps finding itself being copied over in the multi-body part environment. Still, I believe that the reasons to avoid making assemblies as parts (data organization) outweigh the reasons in favor of it (laziness).

CROSS-REF **Chapter 11 also addresses multi-body topics.**

Several pieces of important assembly functionality are still lacking from multi-body parts:

- Bill of Materials
- Individual centers of gravity
- Dynamic assembly motion
- Interference detection
- Custom Properties for individual bodies

Other reasons why you may want to keep the concepts of multi-body parts and assemblies separate include the following:

- You will want to avoid a single FeatureManager with all of the features to all of the parts being solved as a single part for reasons of speed, data organization, ease of editing, and troubleshooting.
- Making drawings of each body in a multi-body part is more involved than if you have completely separate parts.
- Reusing parts becomes much more difficult (read impossible).

I'm sure you can think of other reasons to be careful about keeping your assemblies as assemblies, and to avoid the temptation to combine them into a single multi-body part. It is a question of best practice, and when people try to get away with it, I find it looks a lot like "robbing Peter to pay Paul" — meaning that in the end you are not ahead of where you were, you just have a different set of limitations to live with. If you are prepared to deal with the downside of it (and I will never have to work with your data), knock yourself out.

Translating and rotating by the numbers

 When you have a multi-body part, and need to move some of the bodies around, use the Move/Copy Bodies feature. You can use this feature by keying in specific numbers to either translate or rotate the body. If you need to simultaneously translate and rotate, you need to use two separate features to accomplish this. Figure 13.5 shows the interface for the Move/Copy Bodies feature.

FIGURE 13.5

Translating and rotating bodies by the numbers

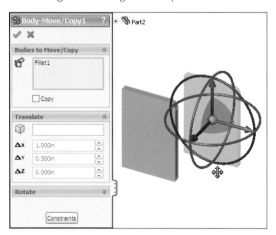

Instead of using the spin box interface, you could use the arrows to drag a translation in a specific direction, or use one of the wings between arrows to drag the body within a plane. If you drag a ring, you can rotate the body. (Note the difference between *wings* and *rings*. Regardless of which method you choose, you cannot use both translation and rotation within a single Move/Copy Bodies feature.

Positioning bodies using mates

In Figure 13.5, at the bottom of the Move/Copy PropertyManager is a button called Constraints. Clicking this button causes the Move/Copy PropertyManager interface to change to look more like the assembly Mate interface that you can see in Figure 13.6.

When you apply the Move/Copy Constraints, the bodies do not animate from one location to the other as parts do in assemblies; they just snap into position. As you see in Figure 13.6, the mates display indented underneath the Move/Copy feature in the FeatureManager.

When positioning using the numbers, you cannot both translate and rotate at the same time, but with the Constraints options, this limitation does not exist.

Regardless of whether you use the position-by-the-numbers or the mate constraints option, the Move/Copy feature is a history-based parametric feature, and so it has only been executed after a certain point in the history tree of the model. There is no such equivalent in SolidWorks parts as a non-parametric move similar to what you get in an assembly by simply dragging an underdefined part in the assembly with your cursor.

FIGURE 13.6

The Move/Copy Constraints PropertyManager

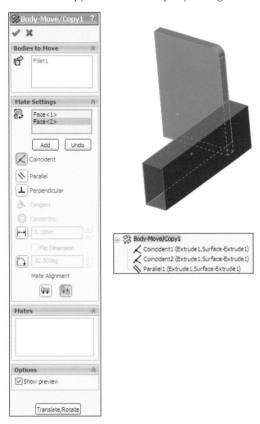

Copying bodies

In the Move/Copy PropertyManager is a small option box labeled Copy. This is meant to be used when moving or copying a body; you can turn the feature into a pattern by leaving the original where it is, and creating a new body at the translate or rotate position specified.

If you do not specify any translation or rotation movement, but you still have the Copy option box checked, upon clicking the green check mark, SolidWorks prompts you to confirm that you really want to copy the body without specifying a translation or rotation value.

Copying bodies can be particularly useful when using a feature that consumes bodies, such as the Combine with the Subtract option, or a Mutual Trim feature.

Insert Part

The Insert Part PropertyManager also has an interface for positioning inserted bodies. This interface is called Locate Body, but works just the same as the Move/Copy feature; in fact, it creates a Move/Copy feature that is displayed indented under the Insert Part feature in the FeatureManager.

Deleting Bodies

The term "deleting" bodies is a bit of a misnomer. Although it appears that you are actually deleting something, nothing is deleted at all. What is really happening is that any bodies that are "deleted" in fact still remain, but they are no longer accessible to the user through the interface.

You can delete bodies in a couple of different ways. The Surfaces toolbar has a Delete Body feature on it, or you can select a body from the Bodies folders and press the Delete key. The Delete Body feature is also available from the RMB menu.

The reason for the fact that the Delete Body feature doesn't actually delete anything is that Delete Body is a time-dependent, history-based feature. This means that if you move the rollback bar back before the Delete Body feature, the body is still there; the body data is not deleted from the file. The only difference is that the body is no longer accessible to the user, even though it still exists in the part file. In what situation is it beneficial to have something exist, but not be accessible?

Some people use the Delete Body feature for housekeeping of sorts. Some have suggested that their employees are not sophisticated enough to avoid getting terminally confused by the presence of multiple bodies in a single model (yes, at least one SolidWorks user has actually used that as a justification for using Delete Body — it seems he has a rather low opinion of his employees).

When I create a body for a specific purpose, and it performs that service — for example, as reference geometry from which to establish tangency for a Fill feature — I will sometimes use Delete Body to remove the body from the body folder. If you fill the body folder with a lot of junk, navigating the bodies can become tedious to find the body you need.

On the other hand, if you re-create a body because you didn't realize that it already existed, this causes a significant inefficiency. It is easy enough to run your cursor over the bodies in a body folder to get a preview that keeping extra bodies should not cause any problems, especially seeing that there is little benefit to getting rid of the extra bodies.

The setting used to allow moving your cursor over bodies in the body folder to display a bounding box preview of the body in the graphics window is at Tools ➪ Options ➪ FeatureManager ➪ Dynamic Highlight.

Tutorial

This tutorial gives you some practical experience with using some of the body management tools available in SolidWorks, and along the way, it puts the tools in the context of functions that require multiple bodies in order to work properly. Follow these steps to learn more about body management techniques.

1. Open the file from the Web site folder for Chapter 13 called Chapter 13 – housing.sldprt. Check your settings to make sure that both the Solid Bodies and Surface Bodies folders are always shown. Go to Tools ➪ Options ➪ FeatureManager, and set options for both folders to Show.

2. Use Insert ➪ Part to insert the part called Chapter 13 – motorbody.sldprt as a separate body. It is tempting to click in the graphics window to place the new body, but clicking will end the command and not give you an opportunity to precisely position the part.

3. With the Insert Part PropertyManager still active, select the options as shown in Figure 13.7, paying particular attention to the Launch Move Dialog option at the bottom.

FIGURE 13.7

The Insert Part PropertyManager

4. Click the green check mark in the Insert Part PropertyManager and use mates to position the motorbody part so that the mounting plate is inside the housing, lined up with the mounting holes, and with the long motor housing extending outside the housing. This will take one coincident mate and two concentric mates.

5. Click the green check mark to accept the position of the body. Right-click the body from the Solid Bodies folder to display the Appearance fly-out menu, then select the color option and assign it a color to make it contrast with the housing box. Also assign a transparency value of 0.50.

6. Activate the Indent feature through the menus at Insert ➪ Features ➪ Indent.

7. Select the housing as the Target Body. Select the portion of the motorbody that is outside the housing in the Tool Body Region box. Set the Thickness value in the Parameters panel to 0.050 inch. Click the green check mark to accept the feature.

8. In the Bodies folders, hide the motorbody body that was brought in and used to create the well for the motor by right-clicking the body in the Solid Bodies folder in the FeatureManager.

9. Expand the Surface Bodies folder, select the Offset surface body, press Delete, and accept the feature. Immediately use the rollback bar to verify that if you roll back the Delete Body feature, the body again shows up in the folder, and can be shown on the screen.

10. Save the part to a new name, and close it.

Summary

Body management in SolidWorks is not up to the sophistication level of component management techniques used in assemblies, yet body management tools are necessary to make the most of the bodies data in your part documents. To make up for this, you have to be extra careful when working with bodies, especially solid bodies.

You and your organization will do well to establish and follow a set of well-thought-out best practice suggestions covering the topic of bodies. Multi-body solid modeling is somewhat different from surface modeling, which by its very nature is almost required to use multiple bodies.

Chapter 14

Evaluating Geometry

W hen you are modeling complex geometry with the intent to manufacture through any process that requires expensive hard tooling, you have to do some evaluation and analysis. Evaluation tools are also indispensable in situations where you are having trouble getting features to complete properly. Fortunately, SolidWorks has some nice tools to help you evaluate models, find errors, analyze draft and thickness, and look for undercuts and typical design for manufacturing mistakes.

Some of the evaluation tools are subjective, offering only visual cues about the results, and some are objective, offering actual numbers. Many times the subjective results are all that you need, because any changes that you make are only going to be subjective changes anyway. For example, Zebra Stripes is a visual evaluation tool, and helps you see curvature and changes in curvature in a different way, making it easier to spot small disturbances in smooth surfaces. In this case, numbers would not help you to adjust a spline or tangency weighting on a loft.

Using Model Quality Evaluation Methods

It is always important to make sure that the model you are building does not have geometric flaws that the normal geometry checking tools of SolidWorks may have overlooked. Geometry problems can be the source of additional downstream errors for anyone who uses your data, such as drafters, FEA, CNC, mold designers, animators, renderers, and other people reusing your data. Even you might come up against some difficulties with adding features if your geometry contains errors.

SolidWorks software has built-in error checking, but depending on your settings, it may not be doing as thorough a job as it could.

Verification On Rebuild

By default, the Verification On Rebuild setting is turned off. You can find this setting at Tools ➪ Options ➪ Performance, at the top of the page.

Without this setting, SolidWorks checks every face of the model against every adjacent face to make sure that one face does not penetrate the other. When you turn on Verification On Rebuild, SolidWorks checks every face in the model against every other face in the model to make sure there are no inappropriate face intersections.

Before talking more about why this setting affects you so much, let me discuss exactly how it affects you. Have a look at the part in Figure 14.1, which is a simple shelled box with a fillet on four sides, shown in section view.

FIGURE 14.1

Shelled box with a fillet

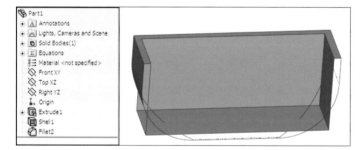

Do you notice something strange about the display of the part? The fillet is so large and the shell is so small that the shell is breaking through the wall of the fillet. This is strange, mainly because it is not causing an error. The reason it is not causing an error is that Verification On Rebuild is turned off, and the faces that are intersecting one another are not adjacent faces; other model faces separate them.

If you turn on Verification On Rebuild and rebuild the model, the fillet feature fails. Turn it back off and rebuild, and the fillet "works" again.

If you assume that every face is surrounded by four others, the number of default checks equals the number of faces times four. With Verification On Rebuild turned on, the number of checks becomes the number of faces times the number of faces minus two ($X*[X-2]$). For example, for a model with 10 faces, this means the difference between 40 checks (without verification) and

80 checks (with verification turned on). That's a ratio of 1:2. Who makes models with just 10 faces, though? For a model with 100 faces, the difference is between 400 checks and 9,800 checks, or a ratio of 1:24.5. For 1,000 faces, the difference becomes 4,000 and 998,000 checks, or a ratio of about 1:250.

Some users have reported that filleted models tend to run more slowly with verification turned on than unfilleted models. I would attribute this to the increased number of faces created by the fillets.

This discussion all sounds very esoteric, but it has a very concrete application to your everyday life, especially if you make complex models, or assemblies with a lot of parts in them. All face checks equate to rebuild time. For example, using the SolidWorks roadster model as a test bed, the rebuild time measured by Feature Statistics after a Ctrl+Q without Verification On Rebuild is 73 seconds on the computer I am using to write this book (HP tc4400 tablet PC, Core 2 Duo T7200, 2.0 GHz with 3 GB RAM and Intel GMA 950 integrated video). With verification turned on, the Feature Statistics time is 126 seconds. The roadster model has 508 faces.

Verification On Rebuild is a necessary tool. SolidWorks added it to the Performance page of the Options so that you can speed up very lengthy rebuilds. Use this tool wisely. You don't need to have it turned on all the time. With simple models, it probably doesn't matter whether it is on or off, but with more complex models, you can see that it matters.

On the other hand, missing out on knowing about problem faces can be frustrating. Not every error is as obvious as the shell breaking through the fillet. I recommend that you leave this setting off, and turn it on to check the model when you have problems you can't explain, or when you are ready to release a finished model. Some people do recommend turning the setting on all the time, but they must be working with models that don't have a lot of faces.

As a bit of conjecture, I am willing to bet that multi-body parts are less prone to slowdowns because the faces are distributed across separate bodies. It doesn't matter if faces of separate bodies intersect one another, and I am willing to guess that the programming ignores checks between bodies. That is to say that a multi-body part with verification turned on will rebuild faster than an equivalent single-body part.

The Check tool

Figure 14.2 shows the interface for the Check tool (known in earlier versions of the software as Tools ➪ Check). Now there is a toolbar button so that you can get to it directly. I also use a hotkey for even more direct access.

Check helps with many things. It can help find short edges, open edges of a surface, the minimum radius of a curved face, and errors in native or imported geometry, including face faults and invalid edges. You can check either the entire model or only a specific selection.

A new option in the last few releases is the Stringent Solid/Surface Check, which I am taking to mean that it overrides the Verification On Rebuild option.

FIGURE 14.2

The Check tool interface

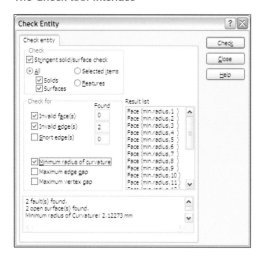

If you are having difficulty placing a fillet, or making a shell, or creating any other feature that should work but doesn't, the Check tool is a great place to start looking. Of course, Check only finds the geometry error; it doesn't fix it for you. After reading this book, you should have a good intuition about what kinds of geometry are considered risky and error prone, and a few tips on how to model around those situations without falling prey to common traps.

Feature Statistics

I mentioned Feature Statistics while discussing one of the previous tools, but I think it deserves a little section on its own. Feature Statistics shows a detailed list of the features in the model, listed in the order of rebuild time per feature. The total rebuild time for the entire model is given, in addition to the time and percentage for each individual feature.

While this function is useful, don't put too much weight on the results it gives you. Other users have pointed out that the rebuild time is not the complete story. From the time a rebuild starts to the time you regain control of your computer, is a period usually 20 to 50 percent longer than the rebuild time itself. Presumably this extra time goes toward saving data or creating previews, or some internal housekeeping.

Feature Statistics is probably best used as a comparison of rebuild times on the same computer, or when rebuilding the same part on different computers. It can serve as a bit of a hardware benchmark to compare one computer with another.

CROSS-REF Chapter 10 makes extensive use of the Feature Statistics tool.

Using Shape and Continuity Evaluation Methods

SolidWorks offers many ways to evaluate model shape and continuity. The tools alone do not fix your models for you, and they don't even automatically point to problem areas, but they do help you visualize certain properties of the geometry. With a newly trained eye, you will be able to identify these properties as problems, and armed with a new toolbox of knowledge, you will be able to figure out a way to work around them.

Curvature Combs

I have discussed the importance of curvature combs in the Splines chapter, Chapter 3. In this chapter they are put to work as a visual representation of local curvature, and matching combs across transitions between splines can help you interpret face smoothness across the edge.

Curvature combs are usually used on splines drawn as a part of creating a feature, but this chapter is really talking about evaluating finished 3D geometry. Curvature combs can still be helpful with this task. When combined with Intersection Curves, curvature combs can be highly useful in evaluating existing geometry. Figure 14.3 shows the SolidWorks roadster model again, this time with several planes created across the hood of the car, Intersection Curves taken, and Curvature Combs shown to evaluate the transitions.

FIGURE 14.3

Curvature Combs used with Intersection Curves to evaluate the SolidWorks roadster

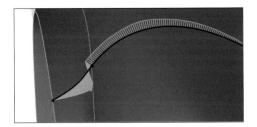

Combs here make it easy to see that the fender flares do a good job of matching the curvature of the fender itself. You can make sketches like this across the model in both directions to evaluate the quality of the surfaces and the transitions between surfaces.

Curvature combs can also be used, with less beneficial effect in my view, on features like Boundary surfaces. To me, curvature combs within a single face are not particularly useful. They are most useful when showing transitions between faces. I'm sure that point could be argued either way, but the most questionable areas of a model are typically the edges between faces rather than areas within the face itself. You could apply this same argument to the Zebra Stripes that can be applied to the preview of Loft or Boundary features.

Curvature display

The Curvature display tool is a qualitative look at instantaneous curvature all over the model, all at once. This tool displays the range of curvature as a continuum of colors. You can put your mouse over the model to get actual radius and curvature values at any point. Curvature display is best used as a way to visualize if curvature changes abruptly, or if you have surprise areas of small curvature in the middle of a face. In some respects, this is much better than the curvature combs applied to splines because you can easily interpret the Curvature display in 3D space. Constant radius areas are easy to spot because the color does not fade. Abrupt changes in curvature are also easy to spot because the color forms a sharp edge rather than fading gradually from one color to the next.

Figure 14.4 shows the SolidWorks roadster model when Curvature is applied to it.

FIGURE 14.4

The SolidWorks roadster model with and without Curvature applied

Curvature display has a toolbar button that you can place on the View toolbar, or you can access the command from the View ➪ Display ➪ Curvature menu. The menu and toolbar apply the display to the entire model. You can also apply it only to selected faces, either for effect or for performance reasons. To apply Curvature only to a selected face, right-click the face and select Curvature from the menu. You cannot apply Curvature to more than one face at a time, but you can apply Curvature to a face that you have already applied Zebra Stripes to. This gives a bizarre effect, superimposing the existing Zebra Stripes pattern with the Curvature display, and I can't imagine that it is particularly useful, but the capability exists.

Deviation Analysis

Deviation Analysis is one of my favorite evaluation tools. It is the one tool that can really give you some insight into which features produce the best results, and it gives you a way to actually quantify how good the feature is. Figure 14.5 shows the Deviation Analysis interface and results. You cannot save the results, and they disappear when the interface is closed down.

FIGURE 14.5

Deviation Analysis interface and results

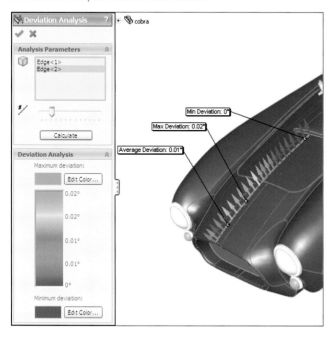

Deviation Analysis is really measuring how far (in degrees) two surfaces are from being tangent to one another along the length of an edge shared by adjacent faces. It doesn't have anything to do with curvature continuity, although if the faces aren't tangent or aren't very tangent, there isn't much chance of curvature continuity meaning much.

The one concept that the Deviation Analysis conveys if you use it enough is that there are a lot of intermediate states. Just because you make a Loft feature, and tell one end to be C2 to the adjacent face doesn't mean that it is really going to be C2, or even tangent. You are probably used to thinking of geometry as either being tangent or non-tangent, but with the Deviation Analysis tool, you may consider 0.05 degrees to be tangent enough, and then again, you might not. If you are on a quest for all of your smooth model edges to be exactly tangent, you will likely be very disappointed.

The controls on the Deviation Analysis interface include the density of the arrows and the color range of the deviation.

Zebra Stripes

Zebra Stripes is another tool that takes some skill to interpret. The purpose of Zebra Stripes is to give you a visual analysis of how closely the curvature on either side of an edge matches. It does this by applying a reflective pattern to the surfaces. Imagine that your part is completely reflective, and that it is in a room that is either spherical or a cube where the walls have been painted with black and white lines.

The concept at work here is that curved surfaces are very difficult to see on their own. To see the curvature, you either have to move the geometry around so that it reflects light from various angles, or make it reflective so that it distorts whatever it is reflecting. This is why curvaceous products have a tendency to be shiny rather than having a matte finish — to show off the curvature. Cars are curvaceous and shiny. This is not a coincidence.

With that in mind, imagine a single straight line is painted on the ceiling of the room that holds a reflective part. The part reflects that single straight line. You expect the straight line on the ceiling to look like a smooth curve on the part as long as the surface of the part is smooth. The reflected line should be smooth as long as the changes in curvature on the part remain smooth.

However, if the curvature remains tangent but makes a sudden jump, say, due to a fillet, the reflected line is no longer smooth. It changes directions sharply, but the reflection immediately on either side of the edge of the location of the reflected line is still lined up.

If there is a hard edge in the part, the reflection of the line on one side of the edge may not match the location of the reflection on the other side of the edge.

The sharp edge is the condition called *contact*, because the only thing you can really say with confidence about the faces on the opposite sides of the edge is that they contact one another at the edge.

All of this is part of the reason why it is so easy to spot a dent in the door of a car. On a gray and rainy day, it is hard to spot the dents in a car, but on a bright sunny day with a lot of things around to reflect (such as trees, buildings, and spotty clouds in the sky), it is much easier.

Figure 14.6 shows the Zebra Stripes PropertyManager and the result of the tool. Zebra Stripes remain on the model until you turn them off.

FIGURE 14.6

Controlling Zebra Stripes

You can control the width, spacing, and coloring of the stripes. The difference between the spherical and cube maps is mainly in the way the lines are displayed at the corners of the cube or at the poles of the sphere. Both cases have these singularities where all of the lines converge into a point, but the sphere only has two of them, while the cube has 8 points and 12 edges.

When you click the green check mark, you exit the Zebra Stripes PropertyManager, and you can go about all of your normal SolidWorks modeling operations with the Zebra Stripes active. To edit the Zebra Stripes settings, go to View ➪ Modify ➪ Zebra Stripes.

You can also apply Zebra Stripes to the Loft feature preview by right-clicking in the graphics window while the Loft PropertyManager is active. Once this setting is on, it is on for all subsequent Loft features, not just the current one.

Reflectivity/Specularity/RealView

Using any of the visual properties of a part to evaluate curvature or edge transitions, fillets, or anything at all is valid; it is also very similar to using Zebra Stripes, except that it is more intuitive, and it is less difficult to look at.

Specifically, if your computer is equipped to display RealView materials, which are any sort of shiny material with a background that reflects (such as the kitchen or industrial backgrounds available), then this combination works almost as well for curvature detection as Zebra Stripes, and is easier to look at for long periods of time than the psychedelic Zebra Stripes arrangement.

If your computer lacks the ability to use reflective RealView materials, you may find that applying several spot or point lights and turning up the specularity on your part may work almost as well. The specularity is also a type of reflection, but it is simply reflecting a bright light rather than a background image.

Tangent Edge display

Tangent Edge display shows any edge that SolidWorks judges to be tangent as a phantom line type. You can set up Tangent Edge display in Tools ➪ Options ➪ Display/Selection ➪ Part/Assembly Tangent Edge Display.

It is highly gratifying when it works, but it turns out that it doesn't always work the way you want it to. The reason for this is the same as the reason for the Deviation Analysis showing intermediate states rather than clear-cut on or off tangency. Tangent Edge display does not display edges as tangent unless they are dead-on tangent. Fillet features tend to create edges that are displayed properly by this setting, but many of the more complex feature types do not do so reliably. SolidWorks Corporation claims this is a tolerance problem and that it is looking into relaxing the tolerance of the tangent edge display so that it works in a wider range of situations.

The available options are As Visible, Removed, and As Phantom. As Visible is the default option, and it does not differentiate tangent edges from any other kind of edges. The Removed option makes the part look strange if there are a lot of tangent edges. If every edge on a model is filleted and you use the Removed option, the part appears in silhouette. To me, the best option is the As Phantom option. This makes it clear that a tangency exists, but the edge is not as heavy as a hard edge.

Figure 14.7 shows a model using the As Phantom option. Notice that not all edges that should be tangent are displayed as tangent.

FIGURE 14.7

Tangent edges shown as phantom edges

Face Curves

Face Curves are not so much tools to evaluate curvature as tools to help you visualize the underlying U-V mesh of a face. You can find the Face Curves tool on the Sketch toolbar or through the menus at Tools ➪ Sketch Tools ➪ Face Curves.

You can only apply Face Curves to a single face at a time, and if you click the green check mark to accept the function, Face Curves creates a separate 3D sketch for each curve. For this reason, I typically use only the preview to query the U-V mesh, and then cancel out of the function.

Using Plastics and Machining Evaluation Methods

Several evaluation techniques exist that are aimed exclusively at molded product analysis. Some of these tools are useful and flexible. You may find others difficult to interpret. These analysis tools are not directly aimed at complex shapes, but many times complex shapes are involved in general plastic or cast parts, and these types of analysis are certainly well used for plastic and cast parts. Also, while this book is not specifically aimed at mold designers, mold designers are usually heavy surfacing users.

Draft Analysis

The Draft Analysis tool is probably the best known and the most useful of this suite of plastics analysis tools. When you specify a direction of mold pull and a minimum amount of draft, SolidWorks can represent each face of the model in different ways to show the draft on the face. Figure 14.8 shows the Draft Analysis PropertyManager along with the results on a fully developed plastic part.

The Draft Analysis tool

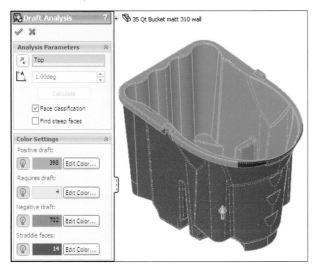

My favorite way to run Draft Analysis is using the Face Classification option, as Figure 14.8 shows. Face Classification enables the software to count the faces in each classification, and it also allows you to turn off groups of faces by clicking the light bulbs.

If you don't use Face Classification, SolidWorks uses a different type of shading that enables colors to blend on a single face, showing a change in draft across the face. This is further accentuated if you use the Gradual Transition option. Also in this mode, the faces for each type of draft are not counted. With Face Classification turned on, SolidWorks uses regular Open GL shading for a constant color on each face.

The Requires Draft face classification identifies faces with between zero and the minimum draft angle.

The Find Steep Faces option, when used with the Face Classification option, identifies faces that have draft that varies between more and less than the minimum draft angle. This condition would happen if you were analyzing the draft on a sphere; the draft at the parting line is exactly zero, and then at some point, it transitions past the minimum draft angle into positive draft territory.

Thickness Analysis

In plastic parts, it is important to keep the thickness of the part consistent. Sections that are too thick can cause sink marks and warping. Areas that are too thin can cause the flow to freeze off or not fill properly. Thickness is not always easy to visualize, particularly where items intersect with the main plastic wall, such as ribs, bosses, or corners.

Thickness Analysis is part of the SolidWorks Utilities, and so it is only available with SolidWorks Office and higher, and not available with the base SolidWorks package. To activate it, go to Tools ➪ Add-ins, and click next to SolidWorks Utilities. Then in the SolidWorks menus, select Utilities ➪ Thickness Analysis. Figure 14.9 shows the Thickness Analysis PropertyManager and a sample result.

FIGURE 14.9

The Thickness Analysis PropertyManager and a sample result

You can run Thickness Analysis with two different goals in mind: looking for areas that are too thick, and looking for areas that are too thin. This tool does not display the thicknesses very accurately, but it does give you a sense of what is going on with the part, and helps to identify areas that require additional attention. The resolution slider at the bottom of the PropertyManager allows for some adjustment in the display accuracy.

When using the Show Thin Regions option, you have to determine how thin is too thin. The model is colored to represent which faces are close to the nominal target thickness, and then scaled to show thicknesses of less than that amount.

When using the Show Thick Regions option, you have to specify the maximum thickness that you consider acceptable. Color coding starts from the nominal target thickness, and then starts indicating areas above the Thick Region Limit value that you specify.

Undercut Analysis

It is difficult to get useful results from the Undercut Analysis tool. I have found only two situations in which it gives reliable results every time, and those are an undercut with no draft and occluded undercuts. Other than those conditions, the Undercut Analysis tool is 100 percent wrong 100 percent of the time. This sounds pretty drastic, but, this has been the case since the feature was first released, up to and including SolidWorks 2008 sp 2.1.

Figure 14.10 shows a part that I know does not have any undercuts in it, yet according to the Undercut Analysis, all but four of the 1118 faces on the part are undercut. In fact, the four faces that it reports as not undercut are not drafted faces. If you add proper draft to the faces that are shown as not undercut, then those faces would also become undercut, according to the Undercut Analysis.

This error has been reported to SolidWorks several times, but this tool is apparently a very low-priority fix, because SolidWorks Corporation has done nothing about it.

What is happening is that the people who designed the Undercut Analysis tool consider any face that is drafted in Direction 1 to be undercut from Direction 2. Of course, this is academically correct, but it is totally irrelevant and not a valid way of presenting the information. It is completely backwards. This seems to me to be a huge embarrassment in the software, but apparently they do not agree, because it has been like this for at least four years. However, there is no way to get things fixed quite as effectively as putting known gaffes in print. Let's hope this works and that the fix to the software precedes the second edition of this book.

FIGURE 14.10

Undercut Detection interface

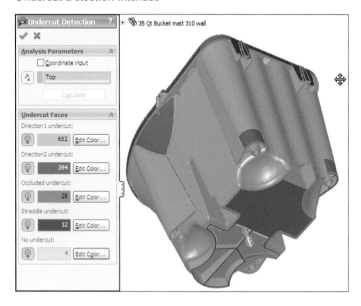

DFM Analysis

The DFMXpress tool is aimed at machined parts rather than molded parts. (DFM stands for Design for Manufacturing). It helps you identify features like sharp inside corners, rounded outside corners, deep small-diameter holes, holes on non-flat surfaces, and other similar types. DFMXpress is provided for free by a third-party partner company to extend the functionality in the SolidWorks software. It is also intended as a bit of an introduction to a more full-featured paid version of the software.

You can access DFMXpress through the Tools menu. The results show up in the Task pane. Figure 14.11 shows the results panel for a sample part.

Following the recommendations in the DFM analysis can help you to decrease machining costs for components. Although the DFMXpress tool is intended for beginning users, it is included here as an evaluation tool, and also because it is relatively new to the software and many users may not be familiar with it.

FIGURE 14.11

The DFMXpress results in the Task pane

Tutorial

This tutorial does not walk you through all of the tools described in this chapter, but it does allow you to get some hands-on time with a few of the more popular ones.

1. Open the part from the Web site called Chapter 14 – tutorialstart.sldprt.

2. Open the Draft Analysis tool from the Tools menu. Set the Direction Of Pull to be the Top plane, the Draft Angle to be 1 degree, and turn on Face Classification. Click Calculate.

3. Notice that some of the Negative Draft faces exist in the finger grip area, as shown in Figure 14.12. Technically, these are undercuts, and need to be resolved by adding draft to the part.

FIGURE 14.12

Results of Draft Analysis on the tutorial part

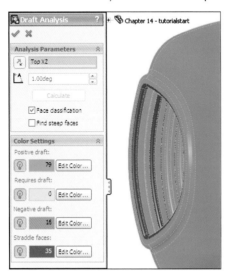

4. Isolate the red faces by clicking the light bulbs of all of the other colors, leaving only the red color light bulb active. Notice that two of the red faces are not connected to anything else. This indicates that they are pulling the wrong direction from the wrong side of the part.

5. Turn the other light bulbs back on. Click the green check mark, and answer Yes to the prompt to save the colors.

6. Initiate the Undercut Analysis through the Tools menu, click the Top plane as the Direction of Pull, and click Calculate.

7. Isolate the Occluded Undercut faces by turning off light bulbs. Although you could not count on this result being correct without verifying it with personal experience, in this case, it actually is correct. However, the No Undercut box says that there are no faces of the model that are not undercut; in other words, all the faces of the model are undercut, which is obviously incorrect.

8. With some of the faces remaining hidden, click the green check mark, and answer Yes to the prompt to keep face colors. Notice that it now looks like a surface model, with some faces hidden.

9. To get faces back to their original display state, click the name of the file at the top of the FeatureManager, and then click the Edit Color toolbar icon from the Standard toolbar. Then click the Remove All Colors button below the selection box. Click the green check mark to dismiss the Edit Color PropertyManager.

10. Initiate the Check tool from the Tools menu. Click the Minimum Radius Of Curvature option, and then click the Check button in the upper-right corner. Figure 14.13 shows the results. Clicking one of the minimum radius values in the list displays an arrow pointing to the geometry on the screen.

FIGURE 14.13

Using the Check tool

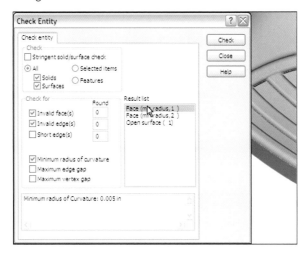

11. Next, check the rebuild times of features. To do this, start with a Ctrl+Q, and then record the total rebuild time as reported by Feature Statistics. Then go to Tools ➪ Options ➪ Performance, turn on Verification On Rebuild, exit the Options dialog box, press Ctrl+Q again, and again record the total rebuild time reported by Feature Statistics. When you are done with this step, go back to Tools ➪ Options and turn off Verification On Rebuild.

12. Next, if you have the SolidWorks Office package or higher, go to Tools ➪ Add-ins and activate the SolidWorks Utilities. Then in the Utilities menu, initiate the Thickness Analysis.

13. Set it to Show Thick Regions, and use 0.10 inch as the thickness and 0.15 inch as the Thick Region Limit. If you get these numbers right, you can predict sink marks on your part. Also make sure the Treat Corner As Zero Thickness option is turned on. If this is not on, most of the thickness faces see the part length as a thickness.

14. Run the cursor over the part and observe that it returns a thickness value where it points.

15. Close the part.

Summary

Analysis tools in SolidWorks have matured over the years, and in some cases are very effective, answering questions about your models and finding problems. In general, however, they seem to be somewhat less easy to use, less sophisticated, and less robust than the geometry creation features. Some of the results from the most sophisticated tools (like Deviation Analysis) bring into question some of the general assumptions about what it means to make a tangent feature.

If you are having difficulty with a mode, these analysis and interrogation tools are a great place to start. Use the tools to help develop an intuition for conditions that cause problems in the software.

Part IV

Using Specialized Techniques

Chapter 15

Modeling a Ladle

Nothing quite matches seeing the tools in actual operation. Each of the chapters of Part 4 walks you through building a model. This is not the highly structured step-by-step instructions of previous tutorials, but rather a conceptual walkthrough. You should have enough knowledge of each of the specific features to use this chapter, along with the provided part, as a guide to rebuilding a similar or identical model.

The previous parts of this book are useful from a reference point of view, but the chapters of Part 4 give you the feel of looking over my shoulder while I build the part, and talk my way through each example. In the real world, things are rarely perfect the first time, and so these chapters reflect that fact. You may need to change your initial modeling approach: Some approaches will turn out to be dead ends, and sometimes you may just want to compare another way of doing things.

Everything that you do in SolidWorks you can probably achieve in multiple ways. This is an important concept. Moreover, it is important to keep a toolbox full of techniques for doing all sorts of things in different ways. The truth is that not all functions work perfectly the way you imagine that they should all of the time. It might turn out to be the fault of the software or the user. Don't be too quick to pass judgment on the software, because as soon as you say, "it can't be done," someone else will find a way.

To be successful with modeling complex shapes in SolidWorks, above all, you need patience to work through problems that may or may not be software- or computer-related. You also need both creative and analytical approaches to problem solving, an eye for geometry, and an intuition for the software. It never hurts to be a little curious, asking the question, "I wonder what this does?"

Getting Started with a Complex Model

If complex modeling is all about anything, it's about shapes. This whole book is all about shapes. The big question is this: Mechanically, how do you take your set of tools and create a particular shape? I'd suggest that you don't worry immediately about faces; just try to understand the shape goal, and then identify the tools that you will use to get there. From that decision, the rest of the arrangement of faces is simply a by-product.

Chapters 2 and 6 talk about how to get started with a complex model in a theoretical way, but in this chapter I want to address the issue using a practical, hands-on approach. In this chapter, I will guide you through how I built a 3D parametric SolidWorks model of a plastic ladle that you might find in your own kitchen or any kitchen store. Figure 15.1 shows an image of the part I am working with.

The physical part that is modeled in this chapter

It's important to first define the task. For example, is this project supposed to result in a model that is accurate to +/– 0.005 inch? 0.050 inch? 0.500 inch? Understanding the purpose of the model is the most important first step. You wouldn't want to spend two weeks on a rough concept that should take you a few hours; likewise, budgeting a couple hours to create a complex production model may also not be realistic. For reference, it took me about 3.25 hours in a hotel room to build this model from the photographs.

It is also important to know what kind of data you have to start with, and how closely you need to stick to it. Are you building a part from your own imagination or hand sketches, and have only conceptual guidelines for it? Are you trying to rebuild a Pro/Engineer part exactly? Are you making a "looks like" model from a couple of digital pictures? Are you trying to precisely reverse engineer a component that you have in your hand? Do you need to use scanned data to reverse model a part? Before you do anything on the computer, you have to make sure you know where you're going, and possibly more important, where you are starting from.

Mapping major shapes to features

You may hear another SolidWorks user say, "it's all about faces" or "don't even think about features." Although I've heard each of these comments more than once, neither comment has ever made much sense to me. How do I know where the faces break up? What if I break something into a face that I cannot model using any existing feature? You have to think about features; in fact, you must consider features before faces. Faces are a by-product of features.

To me, the sensible and practical approach is to first think about shapes. Identify functional shapes that you can build with prismatic solid features such as bosses, ribs, and holes. Identify complex shapes that you can build with identifiable features. Faces are just a result of that process, not the driving motive. Shapes drive features, and features drive faces. If it's all about anything, it's all about shapes.

In that spirit, break up the part shown in Figure 15.1 into shapes that you can make with features. When I look at this part, I see four areas, described in Figure 15.2.

FIGURE 15.2

Identifying shapes in the model

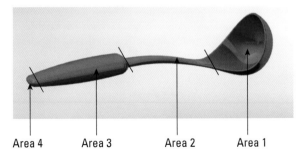

Area 4   Area 3   Area 2   Area 1

As identified in Figure 15.2, Area 1 is a constant thickness bowl. You can make the face with a Loft, Fill, or Boundary feature, and the thickness with a Shell or Thicken feature. Area 2 is a transition, and best made with a Loft or Boundary feature. You could do Area 3, the grip, in almost any way, including solids or surfaces, sweep, loft, or boundary. Area 4 is a frequently encountered case that I call a cap-off. In this case, I use a fill with a constraint curve to smoothly cap off the end of the handle.

Preparing the layout

I do not intend the steps that follow to be a detailed step-by-step tutorial; you could consider it more of a walk-through. You should already have a decent understanding of each of the individual tasks you need to accomplish to finish the whole project. My purpose here is to string the little tasks together into larger modeling strategies. It will be most useful to read through these steps while rolling back the FeatureManager of the finished part on the Web site once, to get a feel for how I constructed the part. Then read through them a second time and try to build the part on your own.

CROSS-REF If you are a little uncertain about any of the individual tasks, you may want to reference the features in earlier chapters of this book or in the current edition of the *SolidWorks Bible*.

The first step in working on a complex model is to collect some reference data and apply it to the SolidWorks part as appropriate. I start by drawing a reference line from the origin in the vertical direction, and dimensioning it to 12 inches to lay out the overall size of the spoon.

Next I added a Sketch Picture, using a JPEG file, provided on the Web site. The Sketch Picture comes into the sketch at scale of 1 pixel of the picture to 1 mm of the model. This usually means that you need to scale the Sketch Picture way down. Use the 12 inch sketched line made earlier to size the Sketch Pictures. Add Chap15Front.jpg on the Front plane, and Chap15Side.jpg on the Right plane. These pictures are included in the download materials from the Web site for the book. The Sketch Pictures need to be in separate sketches. These pictures are not perfect, but you can use them to trace over general shapes.

In some situations, selecting where to locate the origin can be more important than in other situations. In this case, the placement is not critical, but one location exists that will make the necessary tasks easier. Where the edge of the rim of the bowl crosses the plane of symmetry is where I have decided to locate the origin. In cases where you are working on plastic parts, your decision for the origin location may be driven by the direction of pull for the mold.

The pictures here, like most of the pictures you will probably have to work with, are less than ideal. They are not lined up perfectly, they have obvious perspective in them, they are not perfectly in focus, and the part color is too dark for an ideal sketch picture photograph. Still, the pictures will suffice because you only need to make a model that is recognizable as the one in the pictures, without out visibly identifiable differences.

In addition to errors in execution, there are also difficulties in concept. Real-world parts have a tendency to have rounded corners, while CAD models, particularly early on in the design process, tend to have a lot of sharp corners. Extrapolating the sharp corner from the geometry can range from being easy to very difficult. You need to make sure that your expectations of a process involving reverse modeling from photographs is in line with the actual limitations of the process. For example, I would not expect the results of this modeling exercise to produce anything closer than +/– ⅛ to ¼ inch from the original part, but it should be visually equivalent.

NOTE Starting in SolidWorks 2008, SolidWorks has included an add-in to the software called Autotrace. This tool traces sketch entities around the boundaries between high-contrast images. Autotrace is still in its infancy, and you could argue that SolidWorks might better have left it out of the initial release of the software. SolidWorks employees tell me that it works best on block art rather than line art. You can turn it on through the Add-ins interface, and it is then initiated as a small arrow on a blue circle on the top-right corner of the Sketch Picture PropertyManager.

Modeling from the Available Data

Some areas of this model lend themselves to thickening a single surface, while for others a front and back face will need to be created. Also, the edge of the bowl needs to be completely rounded. Tracing outlines is simple enough, but modeling a finished part does not always work nicely with the over-simplification sometimes employed in sketching outlines. Available data cannot always be interpreted literally.

Modeling Area 1: the bowl

I will continue by stepping you through how I model Area 1. I do not claim that this is the only or even the best way to model this geometry. Many possible methods exist, each of which has its own merits. This is just the way that I am doing it, regardless of various arguments for or against what is best.

This type of shape is a very common one. In essence, it is symmetrical, and has an edge curved in 3D space. Many types of products have similar shapes that you can model in a similar fashion. The basic mantra with this type of shape is to draw the symmetry line, draw the edge, and then create the surface shape between them with loft, fill, or boundary.

Figure 15.3 shows the shape at the symmetry plane and the edge around the bowl.

FIGURE 15.3

The shape at the plane of symmetry and the edge around the bowl

Edge around bowl

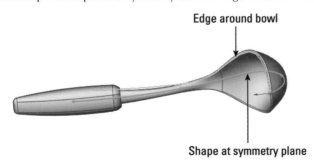

Shape at symmetry plane

Use the side view of the part to sketch the shape of the outside of the model at the plane of symmetry. Do this with a spline. Try to get as close to the digital image shape as possible, while using as few spline points as possible. Use the spline handles to give some direction at the ends of the spline.

Next, I create a Projected Curve to represent the rim of the bowl. The Projected Curve is made from a pair of sketches that I created by tracing the edges of the two Sketch Pictures from two different planes, such as the Front and the Right planes. When making these sketches, you should decide precisely what part of the edge the curve is going to represent. In reality there is no sharp edge across the thickness of the bowl, so you have to trace an imaginary edge. Is that on the inside, the outside, or at the midplane? Is it simply where the light reflects off of the curves? You need to have a consistent answer for each part. In this case, I placed the curve at the theoretical inside sharp of the bowl.

After the Projected Curve is made, you can use one of several methods to create the surface of the bowl. My first preference is to use the Fill surface, because the Fill surface will not create any sort of a degenerate point where the sketch and the Projected Curve intersect.

A Fill surface can only control tangency from the edge of a face, not from a direction normal to a sketch, like a loft. As a result, in order to use the fill, you have to create a surface from the sketch on the plane of symmetry. Simply extruding this sketch a short distance away from the Projected Curve gives you a surface to be tangent to. The Fill surface can be made between the edge of the extruded surface and the Projected Curve.

Unfortunately, the Fill surface idea does not work, and so I must try another method. Recently, I have become enamored with the Boundary feature because it generally gives very high-quality surfaces and it is very flexible in the surfaces it can make. However, this time the Boundary surface gives a very bad result, as Figure 15.4 shows.

FIGURE 15.4

A poor-quality Boundary surface

> **NOTE** Do not become discouraged when a method, even a really good method, doesn't work out. This happens very frequently in real-world modeling, and is part of the reason why SolidWorks has so many tools that overlap slightly, and why I find it so important to learn alternative methods.

It is possible that tweaking the Direction 2 curves across the width of the bowl might have resulted in a better shape, but instead of spending more time with it, I decide to try the loft instead. The loft works, using just the Normal To Sketch end condition for the sketch profile, and no end condition for the Projected Curve. The weighting of the tangency on the sketch side of the loft controls the shape of the bowl. Because of the degeneracy created at the front peak of the bowl, the loft method is not my primary choice, but the fact that it works when the other methods did not gives it a distinct advantage.

I have overbuilt the bowl section primarily because I am in the habit of building surfaces larger than I need them to be. The section toward the handle is too long. The overbuilt section of the surface needs to be trimmed away. Do you trim it from the side and get a straight cut, or do you trim it from the front and try to make the trim normal to the edges of the bowl? I know to ask this question now, but when originally modeling this part, I did it the first way. I trimmed it from the side, and so I was limited to a straight cut. Later, I realized that the cut has to match the curvature of the bowl, and it has to be curved, such that when I create the Area 2 transition feature, lofting tangent from the edge allows the new surface to flow naturally from the trimmed bowl.

This type of thinking is not always the kind you know to do up front, but is sometimes only diagnostic in nature — you do it after you realize that whatever else you did isn't working. Still, being aware of concerns like this always helps you to be a better modeler.

With the bowl area trimmed, I realize the difference between Area 1 (bowl) and Area 2 (transition) is that the bowl is a constant thickness, and the transition is not. In order to start Area 2, the trimmed section of Area 1 needs to provide both inside and outside of the bowl rather than just an infinitely thin skin that could be either. This means that I need to thicken the bowl surface, and so I thicken the bowl 0.100 inch to the outside.

Next, the edges of the bowl are not sharp, and in order to start the transition of Area 2, the edges of the bowl must be rounded. A Full Round fillet takes care of this nicely.

The next step that I take in building this model is not necessary, but I take it anyway. I convert the solid made by the Thicken feature into a surface body by deleting the two faces of the thickness of the part at the trim. You could still build the Area 2 feature from the edges of a solid. I did this more as an instinctive reaction to modeling in surfaces so early on in the process for a part rather than modeling in solids. Figure 15.5 shows the trimmed, thickened, and filleted bowl with the faces deleted to make it into a surface body.

FIGURE 15.5

The completed Area 1 modeling

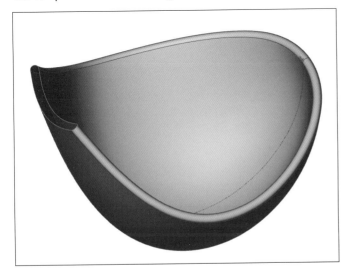

Modeling Area 2: transition

Modeling the transition area is a little trickier than the bowl, and requires a little more experimentation. The feature has to be either a Loft or a Boundary feature, because it forms a tubular closed loop. A Fill feature cannot do it unless created in multiple features, and the nature of the transition disqualifies use of a sweep.

Part of the difficulty here is that the trimmed edges of the bowl are not all one continuous, single entity, but the sketches used for the other profiles are elliptical. Usually, it is recommended that all of the loft or boundary profiles have the same number of elements. For example, if the first profile has four segments, then each of the other profiles should also have four segments, or that is the conventional wisdom, in any case. While you might call this a best-practice suggestion, it becomes less and less necessary with succeeding software releases.

The reason this is important is that SolidWorks is trying to match points on adjacent profiles. This is easy to do when each profile is just a single spline, or when each profile is four line segments, but when one profile has four segments and the next profile has only a single segment (like an ellipse), this becomes more difficult. In situations like this, it may be important to use the *connectors*, the lines between the blue dots that are available on both Loft and Boundary features and that assist in manually "synchronizing" sections. Synchronizing can be a very important tool for getting Loft and Boundary features to behave nicely. You can think of the connectors as ad hoc guide curves.

To get started with this feature, I re-use the symmetry plane sketch used for the first Loft feature. This sketch allows me to place planes perpendicular to the basic direction of the handle on which I place profiles. You should approach placing profiles for Loft or Boundary surfaces in a similar way to how you would approach placing or adding points to a spline. The first rule of thumb is that "less is more," meaning that it is better to use fewer profiles when possible. The second rule of thumb is that you need to place more profiles in areas of tight curvature.

Other concepts used in spline creation, such as teeter tottering, can also be useful in the creation of Loft and Boundary features, which, when it comes down to it, share many similarities with splines.

NOTE By *teeter tottering*, I'm referring to the effect that you get when you move a profile or spline point on one side of a fixed profile or point, and the spline or surface on the other side of the fixed point moves in the opposite direction. You can sometimes compensate for teeter tottering by moving the pivot point or by placing multiple points in close succession.

Getting back to the part, with three planes created along the length of the spline on the plane of symmetry, I draw an ellipse on one plane, dimension it appropriately, exit the sketch, and copy/ paste the sketch to the other planes. This is a simple step that saves a little time and work.

Figure 15.6 shows the preparation for the transition feature.

My first attempt at a feature such as this is usually the Boundary feature. This time, this instinct pays off. With some manipulation of the connectors and the tangency weighting, the feature works out nicely. I have placed the connectors along the plane of symmetry to keep the profiles aligned. You can see some teeter tottering from the loop of edges on the bowl across the first boundary profile, but you can compensate for this by moving or changing the size of the first sketch profile. You could also try to clamp this teeter tottering to some extent using additional profiles, although this can be very time consuming, and so other techniques are usually used.

FIGURE 15.6

Sketches preparing to create the transition feature

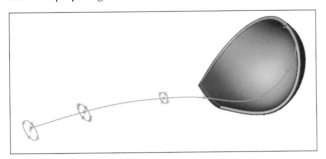

The SelectionManager is an essential tool when working with Loft and Boundary surfaces. The SelectionManager enables you to select profiles from among sketch, edge, and curve data, mixing and matching to suit. SolidWorks automatically activates the SelectionManager when the sketch you select is not appropriate to be used in its existing form, such as when you sketch the path and a guide curve for a sweep all in a single sketch because it seems more convenient than placing them in separate sketches. The SelectionManager can also automatically select and highlight closed loops and open loops, or enable you to manually select individual entities to build your own selection set.

Be careful when trying to access connectors while the SelectionManager is active. The SelectionManager disables connectors. I have also identified a bug which prevents you from adding connectors to a loft if the SelectionManager has been used to select profiles. This bug is active as of SolidWorks 2008 sp 2.1, but may be fixed in any release after that.

Figure 15.7 shows the Boundary feature PropertyManager and a preview of the feature. Notice that from this view, you can see the teeter tottering around the second profile from the bottom.

A detail must also be added to the transition area, a feature that cores out the back of the handle. This is an easy shape, but it has to fit with the character of the surrounding geometry. A sweep would work well, but in this case, I chose to show off some more of the functionality of the Boundary feature.

NOTE It is difficult to overemphasize the importance of the new Boundary feature for SolidWorks. The last major feature of this stature that was added to the software was the Fill surface. Freeform is also rather new, but I don't think it has the importance of the Boundary feature.

I may tend to overemphasize the Boundary feature in this book, but I am doing it consciously because there is an existing body of examples available in the broader SolidWorks community that show how the more familiar Loft, Sweep, and Fill features work, but Boundary is under-represented.

FIGURE 15.7

The Boundary feature set up for the Area 2 shape

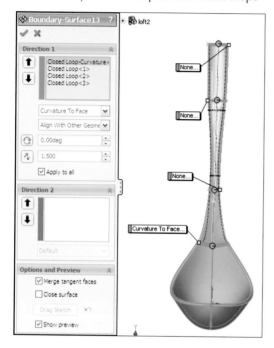

The sketches I use to create the Boundary surface are exactly the same sketches that could have driven a sweep of approximately the same geometry. The profile was simply an arc representing what the cross-sectional shape at that point looked like, and the path equivalent was a spline that followed the overall transition shape, but trailed out of it slowly.

With a sweep, you would have more control over the profile orientation using either the Follow Path or Keep Normal Constant settings. I had no good reason for using a boundary instead of a sweep, other than to demonstrate the similarities between the features.

Once the surface exists, I use the Mutual Trim to trim both the transition and the detail.

Next I add a fillet. Ideally I want a Constant Width fillet, but probably because of the sharp curvature of the edge between the two surfaces, the Constant Width fillet does not work, and so I approximate the effect of a Constant Width fillet with a Variable Radius fillet.

Modeling Area 3: handle

The handle geometry can be made in many different ways. Just to give a good range of examples, I create the handle with a solid sweep. I trace the silhouettes of the handle from both the front and side views from the sketch pictures used early on. I have traced both left and right profiles in a single sketch, mirrored them, and approximated the positions because the image is not placed exactly, in addition to not being photographed exactly.

Because the sketches I use for path and guide curves each contain multiple open loops, I need the SelectionManager to differentiate them. Figure 15.8 shows the Sweep PropertyManager and the feature preview.

From looking at Figure 15.8, you may have difficulty telling exactly what is going on, but if you open up the part, you can tell that one pair of arcs that are on the symmetry plane is exactly where the sketch geometry matches the 3D geometry. The second pair of arcs is placed on a more convenient plane. These arcs are used as guide curves, or more accurately, one of the arcs is used as a guide curve, and symmetry in the sketch drives the other side. Further, a construction line is used to help the guide curve actually drive the geometry. The arc pierces the endpoint of the construction line, and so as the sweep profile moves through the feature, the point where the arc touches the profile plane moves; this moves the construction line, which in turn moves the profile geometry. This scheme of a guide curve driving a sweep profile indirectly through construction geometry is possibly more complex than putting the guide curves exactly on the geometry, but in this case, the second set of guide curves would need to have curvature in two directions. This would make them projected curves rather than flat 2D arcs.

FIGURE 15.8

Creating the handle sweep

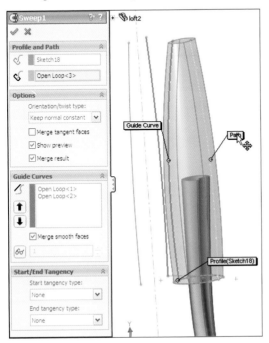

The technique that I have just outlined may be a little confusing, but it enables you to drive a shape using a 2D guide curve, rather than requiring you to make a 3D guide curve. I believe it is a technique worth learning. If anyone would like to suggest a name for this technique, please send me an e-mail. I have been calling it a *soft pierce* because the width of the ellipse is being driven indirectly by construction geometry piercing the out-of-plane guide curve. The logic may be fuzzy, but the technique works.

Modeling Area 4: the cap off

Many times when you have to model a handle, you also have to cap off one flat end of the handle. Solid features are especially prone to flat ends, and so capping off solids is probably the most popular form of this technique. Many methods exist by which you can create this type of geometry, but in this example, I make use of a stunningly simple, effective, and attractive cap-off technique using some of the more powerful options of the Fill feature.

To set this feature up, all I need is an arc placed where the capped-off edge of the handle will be; to create the arc, all I need is a plane. The plane is simple to create using a sketch on the flat end of the handle, locating the axis from round to round. Next, I make a plane at a 90-degree angle to the flat face through the sketch line.

The Fill surface is easy to set up, using just the edges around the flat face. Set the Curvature edge setting all the way around, and use the arc as a Control Curve. Figure 15.9 shows the PropertyManager settings and a preview of the feature.

One of the beautiful things about constraint curves is that they can just be partial curves — they do not have to extend all the way across the feature. The Fill surface does a great job of figuring out what goes in between.

Notice also that a couple of the seldom-used options are enabled here. The Merge Result option seems a little out of place. The Merge Result term is usually used when merging a new solid feature with an existing solid body. The Fill feature is a surface feature. Merge Result does indeed add the Fill surface to the existing solid body. If you had to do the same thing manually, it would require either the combination of a Knit feature and a Combine feature, or a single Replace Face feature. Notice that the Reverse Direction option is also used for this feature. This is not any kind of visible setting. Essentially, if the Merge Result option does not work, you should toggle the Reverse Direction option.

You may run into other methods for capping off flat faces like this, but rarely will you run into anything that works so nicely as the Fill feature.

The final portion of the handle is the cap that goes around the intersection of the handle and the transition shape. The final result shown is the product of trying several other methods. It is not as neat and clean as I would like, but it is one way to work around several limitations encountered while trying other more intuitive and simple methods.

FIGURE 15.9

The Fill feature PropertyManager settings and a preview of the finished feature

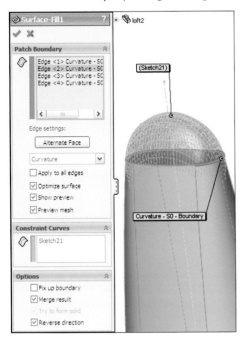

I choose to use a combination of a swept surface and a boundary surface. To start the swept surface, I create a plane perpendicular to one of the edges at the endpoint. For this, it doesn't matter which you select. Then, on that plane, I sketch a single arc that is not tangent to the surrounding geometry. I want the edge to be noticeably non-tangent. It is an advantage for you to open the part provided and follow along, starting with Surface-Sweep3.

The problems begin when trying to select the sweep path. The intuitive thing to do is to sweep around the entire closed loop path, but that results in a failed feature and some bizarre preview geometry. In the end, I settle for sweeping along three edges, and using a Boundary feature to close the loop. To select a sweep path using three edges, I use the SelectionManager. This is obviously not ideal, but it has the advantage of working while the closed loop sweep did not.

Using the SelectionManager

I want to go through using the SelectionManager at least once, rather than assuming that you can just figure it out.

SolidWorks automatically enables the SelectionManager only if you are trying to select a sketch element from a sketch that the software cannot use in its entirety due to multiple open profiles, or any of a number of other illegal sketch situations. Otherwise, you must enable the SelectionManager manually.

To enable the SelectionManager manually, right-click in a blank space and select SelectionManager from the top of the menu. The SelectionManager itself is a small toolbar with some selection options, including Select Closed Loop, Select Open Loop, Select Group (implies manually), Select Region, and Standard Selection (turns off the SelectionManager). I most frequently use the Select Closed Loop and Select Group options.

Once you have selected the sketch/curve/edge entities you want to use for the feature — in this case, a sweep path — click the green check mark. In this situation, select three consecutive edges, starting from the edge you created the sketch on, and click the green check mark.

Sweep the profile along the path. This should look like the image in Figure 15.10.

This leaves one side open, which I have closed by using the open ends of the swept surface created previously as the curves in Direction 1, and the remaining edge of the solid not used by the sweep as a curve in Direction 2.

FIGURE 15.10

Creating a second handle cap

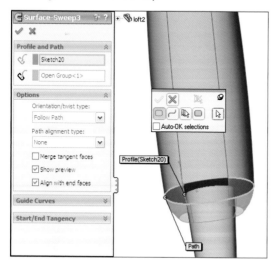

Tidying Up the Loose Ends

By looking at the Body folders at the top of the FeatureManager, at this point you are left with a solid body for the handle, a surface body for the transition and core-out detail, a second surface body for the bowl of the ladle, and two surface bodies for the second handle cap. All of this must be joined into a single solid body.

Starting with knitting the transition and bowl into a single solid, hide all of the other bodies. You can hide bodies by right-clicking them in the graphics window or in the Body folders in the FeatureManager.

With only the transition and bowl bodies shown, view the large open end of the transition. Right-click one of the edges, and choose Select Tangency from the menu; then pick the Planar Surface from the Surface toolbar, and click the green check mark to accept the feature.

Next, knit the new Planar surface, the transition body, and the bowl body together into a single solid body. You may want to use the Knit and Thicken combination rather than the Try to Make Solid option in Knit.

Show the handle, the sweep, and the boundary surfaces. Create another Planar surface to seal off the combination of Sweep and Boundary features. Knit together the new planar along with the sweep, boundary, and hidden end face of the handle. You need to use Select Other to select the hidden end face of the handle. Thicken this knit body, and use the Combine feature to merge the newly created solid with the handle solid and the transition-bowl solid.

At this point, the entire part should be one single, solid body, which is shown in Figure 15.11.

FIGURE 15.11

The finished part

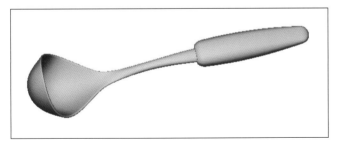

Summary

When working through a complex modeling project, workflow is as important as understanding what each of the individual options does. When you understand what to expect in a real-world modeling situation because you have watched someone else walk through it, that experience gives you more confidence, and a sense of "it's not just me." If all of the tools worked perfectly as you imagine they should all of the time, then anyone would be able to do this kind of work. As it is, I believe complex shapes and surfacing require more patience than other modeling tasks. I have presented many sessions on complex modeling where I show modeling as a series of workarounds for things that seem intuitively like they should work, but in real life don't actually work. To some people, it looks like I'm just being nit-picky or bashing the software, but people who have really tried this kind of work often come up to me afterward and thank me for showing them that "it isn't just me," that the complex modeling tools are really not as predictable as the prismatic modeling tools.

The one concept you need to take from this is that there is never a single solution to any problem. Complex modeling is not necessarily so much about shape creativity as it is about understanding the available processes for creating shapes. Laying out the shape is important because it helps you make choices about what feature to use to create each portion of the required shape.

Chapter 16

Modeling a Trowel

IN THIS CHAPTER

Modeling the handle

Modeling the scoop

T he part used in this chapter is a part that I had an industrial designer draw up for me. I wanted to show some examples of working from hand sketch data just to get a range of realistic data types. If you already do work like this, you are probably familiar with techniques for dealing with this kind of data. If you are new to this kind of work, working from hand sketches is somewhat less precise than using other types of initial data such as digitized 3D data, imported data, or dimensional data.

Some of the techniques on display in this chapter are layout sketches, sketch images, blending a sharp edge into a smooth face, capping off the end of a handle, and some hybrid modeling techniques.

In this example, I am not assessing the shape, manufacturability, process, or cost of the product; I am only concerned with interpreting the shape communicated in the sketches. You often cannot follow sketches like this exactly because they are drawn freehand and may not line up exactly when arranged next to one another. For this reason, I use the word *interpreted* when talking about tracing or otherwise copying the shapes rather than something more precise.

Figure 16.1 shows the sketches that I used to build this part.

This walk-through does not give all of the explicit steps needed to create the model. By this point in an advanced book, I am assuming you know a few things. One of the things you need to know, which I don't always state explicitly, is how to make a spline that when mirrored across a symmetry plane will be tangent to itself. I also assume you know how to manipulate sketch pictures, create reference planes, and use several other basic tools in the software. If you need a good reference book for basic functionality, please use the current edition of the *SolidWorks Bible*.

295

FIGURE 16.1

Sketches used to create the trowel part modeled in this chapter

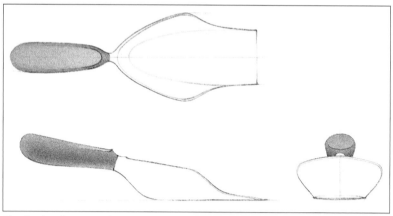

Sketches by Chris Kujawski (www.chriskujawski.com)

Modeling the Handle

You can use the following steps to guide you through the re-creation of the trowel, or you can just follow along. The text of this chapter alternates between structured and ordered tutorial steps and explanatory comments.

1. Create a new part from a template. I use inch dimensions in this example, so use an inch template.

2. Open a sketch on the Front reference plane of the part, and using the Sketch Picture sketch tool, insert the image called TrowelHandleFront.jpg from the data for Chapter 16, which you can download from the Web site.

3. Draw a circle as shown in Figure 16.2, and size it as shown. Resize the image so that it is approximately the relative size shown in the figure by dragging corners to make it smaller. In this case, the picture is resized to 4.09 inches in the Y dimension, as reported by the Sketch Picture PropertyManager.

NOTE When the Sketch Picture image comes in, it is at the scale of 1 pixel to 1 mm. Except for very large-scale items, this usually means the image must be scaled down significantly. To resize a Sketch Picture, double-click it and drag the handles. To get out of the Sketch Picture edit mode, click the green check mark in the Confirmation Corner.

FIGURE 16.2

Resize the Sketch Picture relative to the size of the circle

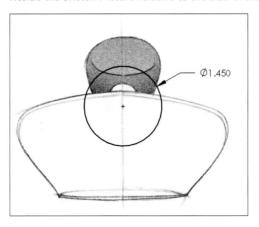

⌀1.450

4. Insert and resize the Side and Top Sketch Pictures as well. The Side picture should be 3.35 inches in Y, and the Top should be 4.33 inches in Y. When you have completed this, the aligned and sized images should look like Figure 16.3, and the FeatureManager will look as shown, with the Sketch Pictures displayed indented under the sketches. It is always a good idea to rename Sketch Pictures and layout sketches for later reference.

FIGURE 16.3

FeatureManager and alignment of Sketch Pictures

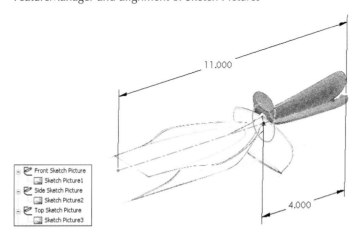

11.000

4.000

Front Sketch Picture
  Sketch Picture1
Side Sketch Picture
  Sketch Picture2
Top Sketch Picture
  Sketch Picture3

> **NOTE**
> When the background of a Sketch Picture has been set transparent, double-clicking the image to activate it shows the eyedropper by default. If you are not careful, it is possible to accidentally change the transparent color when in this mode. You need to be careful to turn off the eyedropper before selecting anything. This bug has lingered since the transparent background functionality was first introduced.
>
> Also, it is usually not advisable to put feature sketch geometry in the same sketch as the Sketch Picture. This is because when you use a sketch in a feature, SolidWorks reorders the sketch and indents it underneath the child feature. You will probably want to keep the Sketch Picture sketches at the top of the FeatureManager where you can access them easily.

5. You may use one of several methods for making handles, but generally speaking, the methods come in two varieties: making profiles that go around the circumference of the handle or making profiles that look like cross-sections of the handle along its length. These methods are illustrated in Figure 16.4.

    In this example, you will loft three profiles, Top, Side, and Bottom, to create only one-half of the handle initially, and then from that you will create the rest of the handle.

FIGURE 16.4

Two possible ways to loft the handle

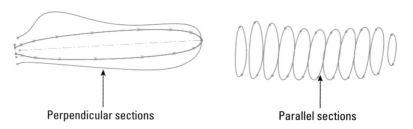

Perpendicular sections   Parallel sections

Each of these methods, parallel and perpendicular sections, has its strengths and weaknesses. Generally, the perpendicular sections are easier to create, but this method gives you less control over the cross-sectional shape of the part. Parallel sections give great control over cross-sectional shape, but sometimes the overall profile of the part suffers in ways for which you cannot compensate when using the Loft feature. The perpendicular sections, as shown, will automatically create the rounded end, while the parallel sections may require you to use a point as the final loft profile.

Both methods, lofting to a point and having a single point where all loft profiles intersect, cause a "singularity" or "degeneracy" in the model, where the U-V mesh converges at a single point. This often causes trouble with features like Offset, Shell, or Fillets. You can trim off the singularity and use another method to cap the end.

> **NOTE**
> The sections of the parallel sections method do not need to be actually parallel or evenly spaced as shown. In fact, just like spline points, it is often an advantage to not place sections evenly.

You can employ a hybrid method combining the Parallel and Perpendicular methods, which uses one set of sketches as profiles and the other set as guide curves. This is obviously more time-consuming and error-prone because of the number of sketches required and the intersections between the sketches.

The information given appears to be focusing on the side and top profiles of the part, and so you will create it using that data. This means that you must use the perpendicular sections to create the part. The handle of the part is slightly angled, and so you will create two of the four profiles on a plane angled to match the axis of the handle.

Before you can model the handle, you need to make another decision about how to proceed with the thumb rest area. Regardless of which method you choose, this shape cannot be created as a single feature with the rest of the handle, and so you will use a separate feature. You will probably need to first build the rest of the handle, then trim out the area where the thumb rest goes, and then build the thumb rest back into the part.

6. On the Right plane, sketch all the way around the outside of the handle as shown in Figure 16.5. Notice that I have sketched a large lump that is not in the original ID sketch. It is simply to get the correct tangency on the area in front of the thumb rest, and the rest of the bump I will later trim out and replace with another feature. The spline rejoins the outline of the handle at the point where the edge of the thumb rest has transitioned smoothly back into the rest of the handle.

Figure 16.5 shows the sketch from this step.

FIGURE 16.5

Creating the first handle sketch

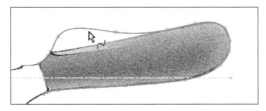

People who do surface modeling often "overbuild" surfaces, or make them larger than they need to be and later trim them back to the proper fit. Several reasons exist for using this approach, including setting up the right angles on the ends, or making sure the U-V mesh is clean first, and then trimming to make sure you have good edges.

Although the sketch shown in Figure 16.5 serves as both the top and the bottom profile, I show it as a single sketch for simplicity and smoothness. In a future step, the sketch is broken into two parts.

7. Open another new sketch on the Right plane, and sketch two construction lines as shown. There is no way to directly make a line perpendicular to a spline, so you will need to make the short spline tangent to the spline, and then make the longer line perpendicular to the short spline. The sketch relation symbols have been shown for clarity in Figure 16.6. The longer of the two lines will serve to define the second profile plane.

FIGURE 16.6

Construction geometry setting up the rest of the sketching for the handle loft

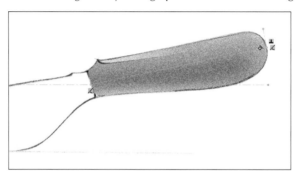

NOTE   You could have eliminated the need to create this plane by orienting the sketch pictures such that the axis of the handle was in the Horizontal direction, but then you would have needed to do something similar for the bottom of the trowel scoop.

8. Exit the sketch and rename it Angled Plane Sketch or something else that represents the function of the sketch.

9. Create a new plane using the existing Right plane and the long construction line from the previous step. The angle between the new plane and the Right plane should be 90 degrees. Click OK to accept the plane, and then rename it Angled Plane, or something indicative of its function.

To trace the top profile of the handle on the newly created Angled Plane, you may also want to put the sketch picture of the top view on this plane as well, in order to get a more accurate trace. On the other hand, the scanned image was drawn as a straight top view, and so putting it on this angle will distort it somewhat, and you may have to stretch its length. Regardless of how you resolve the issue, there is going to be some approximation involved. In the sample part provided with the downloaded data for this chapter, the image is on the Top plane, the sketch was made on the Angled Plane, the length was driven by the placement of the side profile sketch, and the profile estimated to make it look reasonably similar. Figure 16.7 illustrates the way I made the sketch in the sample, completed part.

FIGURE 16.7

Placement of the Sketch Picture and top view sketch

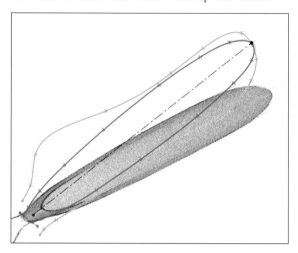

Figure 16.7 shows the entire top profile of the handle. If you look at the downloaded sample file, you may notice that the spline was set up such that each spline point has a symmetric sketch relation with another point. This type of work is time consuming, and in many cases unnecessary. For the purposes of following along with this tutorial, you can simply create one side of the spline.

10. To sketch one side of the handle as a spline, trace half of the profile from the top view, and assign a Pierce relation between the end point of the spline at the plane of symmetry and the side profile sketch, and a Horizontal relation on the tangency handle at the same end of the spline.

Exit the sketch when you are satisfied that it is complete.

11. Create a new sketch on the Right reference plane, select the Side Profile sketch, and use Convert Entities to copy it. Then use Split Entities to break it up into top and bottom profiles. The reason for doing this to a copy is because doing it to the original makes the original far more difficult to edit.

Notice that once you place the Split Entities point, it is blue and can be moved anywhere along the length of the spline. Add a coincident relation between the point and the endpoint of the construction line made in the previous step.

When you split a sketch entity into two entities with the Split Entities tool, you can later delete the split point to join the two parts back into the original single entity again. You can split open loop entities in one or multiple locations. For closed loop entities (such as circles, ellipses, and closed splines) you must place at least two split entities points. If you place only a single point on a closed loop, SolidWorks treats it like a sketch point, but when you add the second split point, both points become endpoints of individual segments.

In either the open or closed cases, you can delete the split points to return to the original single sketch element, except in the case of closed splines, where it doesn't work. I have reported this as a bug, and so this behavior may change at some point in the future, if SolidWorks fixes it.

12. With this sketch, you are preparing to loft three profiles to form half of the handle shape, and you will mirror the second half from the first.

As with most functions in SolidWorks, there are multiple ways to accomplish any stated goal, and the steps in this part of this tutorial are no exception. In the most "classic" usage of SolidWorks, each loft profile corresponds to an individual sketch. One loft profile equals one sketch feature. This is how earlier versions of SolidWorks required things to be set up for years.

In recent versions, however, the software allows other techniques that enable you to select individual profile contours from within a single sketch that contains multiple contours using the SelectionManager. These selections can be 2D or 3D, using sketches, edges, or curves. Lofts where you select all of the profiles and guide curves from a single 3D sketch do have some special advantages, such as enabling you to manipulate the contours while in the Loft PropertyManager. These techniques sometimes pose additional problems, however, such as any one of the numerous difficulties associated with 3D sketches, feature history, and editability issues.

SelectionManager takes the place of the older Smart Select tool used in Loft features prior to SolidWorks 2007. SelectionManager is far better in some respects, mainly in that it can select closed loops and regions automatically. It also has some of the same limitations as Smart Selection in that if the feature fails on initial creation, you cannot save your selection groups.

13. Initiate the Surface Loft feature, and using the SelectionManager (available from the RMB menu), set it to select open contours, as shown in Figure 16.8. Click the green check mark on the SelectionManager to accept the selection for each loft profile.

FIGURE 16.8

SelectionManager settings for Step 13

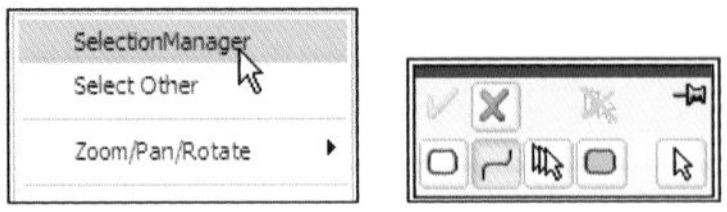

SolidWorks shows items selected using the SelectionManager in the PropertyManager as either open or closed groups in the PropertyManager selection windows. Figure 16.9 shows the selected groups as well as the end conditions used, and a preview of the lofted feature.

FIGURE 16.9

Loft settings and preview for Step 13

14. The next step is to trim out the area for the thumb rest, including the area for the smooth to edge transition. Open a new sketch on the Right plane and sketch along the edge of the thumb rest. Where the edge gradually blends into the smooth surface, end the spline and draw a line roughly perpendicular to the edge of the surface, as shown in Figure 16.10. You may want to turn on the Right sketch picture to trace the edge.

FIGURE 16.10

Creating the cutout for the thumb rest

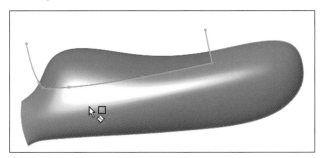

15. To make the new thumb rest geometry, draw a spline on the Right plane, spanning the gap created above by the trim feature. Make the end of the spline nearest the rounded end of the handle to have a Curvature sketch relation to the edge on the plane of symmetry.

    Extrude the spline a short distance away from the half-handle to be used as a reference surface.

16. Use a Fill feature to create the thumb rest. Use a curvature condition on the section of the trimmed surface created by the straight line, and a tangent condition to the extruded construction surface. The part at this point should look like Figure 16.11.

FIGURE 16.11

The handle as of Step 16

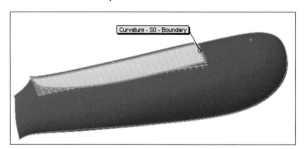

NOTE   It is often best to make sketch relations to other sketches rather than edges when possible, but on this particular part, the relation would have to be made to the middle of an underlying spline, which SolidWorks cannot do, and so it is most practical in this situation to make the relation to the edge of the trimmed loft.

The end of the spline nearest the thumb rest should not be tangent; in fact, it should have a slight concavity built into it using the spline tangency handle. In this case you do not want to overbuild the surface being created from this spline. You are actually creating a construction surface not used in the final part, but used to create another surface that will be in the finished part.

The edge around the thumb rest blends smoothly into the handle because of the differing use of the tangent and contact edge conditions of the Fill feature. Other methods exist that can help you create this kind of geometry, but the things they tend to have in common include trim out an area, and then use a primary face creation tool to transition from non-tangent to tangent geometry.

17. This step is an optional one. Often when users create a construction surface that is not likely to have another use, they may choose to delete that body from the model. The Delete Solid/Surface feature does not truly delete anything. It is a history-based feature that simply hides and makes a body inaccessible after this feature in the FeatureManager, but the geometry for the body is still saved inside the file. Thus, there is no display or calculation speed benefit to using Delete Solid/Surface (usually referred to as simply Delete Bodies). You would normally use Delete Bodies as an organizational aid, to keep extra bodies in the Bodies folders from cluttering up the display.

You can use the Delete Bodies function in two different ways: You can activate it from the toolbar or the menus (under Insert ⇨ Feature ⇨ Delete Body), or by selecting a body from the Bodies folders and pressing the Delete key. You can delete the extruded construction surface if you choose, or simply right-click it in the FeatureManager, graphics window, or Surface Bodies folder, and select Hide.

NOTE **Any feature associated with a solid body may be used to hide that solid body (through the RMB menu option Body ⇨ Hide), but only the last feature that affects a surface body may be used to hide the surface body.**

18. As you have modeled just half of the handle, it remains yet to mirror the other side. Initiate the Mirror feature, expand the Bodies to Mirror panel, and select both surface bodies from either the Surface Bodies folder or the graphics window. Use the Right plane as the Mirror plane.

When mirroring multiple bodies, the Knit Surfaces option does not knit the result of the mirror into a single surface body; all it does is (when possible) knit together each mirrored body with its original. So in the example shown here, because you have mirrored two bodies, the result using Knit Surfaces would be two surface bodies. If you want all of the bodies knit together, you must use a separate Knit feature.

19. Draw a line and do a mid-plane surface extrude to close off the end of the handle near the scoop. The hand sketches are not very explicit about this shape, so make it match the scanned drawings as well as possible. The main requirement is that the new surface cut all the way through the original and mirrored surfaces.

20. Use a mutual trim to close off the handle. Use a Thicken feature to make the handle into a solid.

21. Finally, add a couple of small fillets (~0.035 inch) to the sharp edges. You may want to put these fillets into a folder, and take special care when working on the scoop in the next section not to make relationships to the edges or faces of the fillets. When the scoop modeling is complete, you can reorder the entire folder with the fillets in it.

Modeling the Scoop

I have divided the modeling work for this part into two sections that are not dependent on one another. The handle that you just finished is not a prerequisite for modeling the scoop.

The handle of this part was a chunky solid, but the scoop incorporates both chunky solid and constant thickness sections. Although this chapter is not doing much in the line of modeling for specific manufacturing methods, the method of manufacture is something that is constantly on my mind when modeling parts. With a constant thickness section and a chunky solid section, this is probably a cast or forged part.

Follow along with the steps to build the scoop geometry.

1. Show the side sketch picture, then open up a new sketch on the Right plane, and trace the bottom of the trowel scoop and the top. When you trace the top, just make the top line and extend it to the end of the scoop. When you trace the bottom, use a straight line for the portion that is straight, and the curved section should be a spline with an Equal Curvature sketch relation to the straight line. Use Figure 16.12 as a guide.

Setting up the first sketch for the scoop

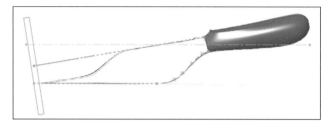

2. Use the Contour Selection to extrude as a surface only the bottom contour of the scoop sketch. Figure 16.13 shows this step. Extrude the surface using MidPlane, and make it at least 3 inches wide. Rename this feature Scoop Bottom.

Extruding the surface for Step 2

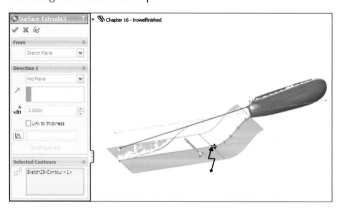

3. Make a new plane offset from the Front plane by 2.7 inches, in the direction of the scoop. Rename this plane as MidScoop Plane.

4. Open a new sketch on the Angled Plane you created while modeling the handle section, and show the Top sketch picture. Set the view Normal To the Angled Plane. Trace a spline over half of the scoop edge profile. Remember to use a horizontal or vertical relation to the handle on the symmetry plane end of the spline; it is usually best practice to extend the spline beyond where it needs to go.

   Figure 16.14 shows this arrangement. By making this spline, you are preparing to create a projected curve.

FIGURE 16.14

Setting up a projected curve

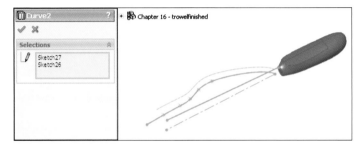

5. From the Right plane, copy (using Convert Entities) the straight line drawn in Step 1.

6. Create a projected curve using the spline from Step 4 and the straight line from Step 5.

7. Make a plane perpendicular to the end of the projected curve, and rename the plane Scoop End Plane.

8. Open a new sketch on the flat face of the Scoop Bottom extruded surface feature, and trace the bottom edge of the scoop with a spline (where the flat bottom face intersects the curved sides). Make sure this sketch stays inside the projected curve from Step 6 and is drawn so that it will be tangent across the symmetry plane. Rename this sketch as Bottom Inside Of Scoop. Figure 16.15 illustrates this.

9. Using the Scoop End plane and the MidScoop plane, as well as the Right plane (symmetry plane), draw loft profiles that are pierced on one end by the projected curve and on the other end by the Bottom Inside Of Scoop sketch from Step 8. Figure 16.16 shows all of these entities in their finished states. I have changed the sketch colors for clarity.

Tracing the bottom edge of the scoop

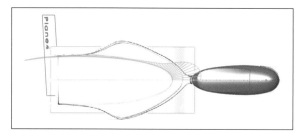

Setting up the scoop loft

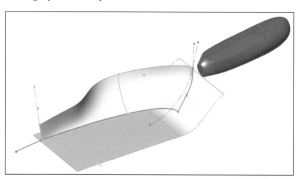

10. Initiate a Loft feature. Select the three short splines as profiles. Select the Bottom Inside Of Scoop sketch as the first guide curve, and the projected curve as the second guide curve. Assign Normal To Profile condition to the profile at the symmetry plane. Accept the feature when you are satisfied with it.

11. Mirror the newly created loft, using the Knit Surfaces option.

12. Create a Trim feature, using the Mutual Trim option, and trim the bottom and sides of the scoop faces with one another.

13. Open a sketch on the Right plane, and draw a set of lines as shown in Figure 16.17. Make the vertical line at the end of the sketch coincident with the end of the side faces so the end of the scoop is trimmed off square.

FIGURE 16.17

FIGURE 16.17

Trimming the end of the scoop

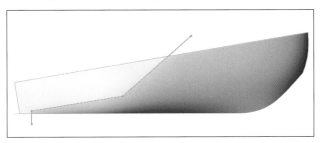

14. Make a variable radius fillet between the trimmed surfaces with values as shown in Figure 16.18.

FIGURE 16.18

Adding a variable radius fillet

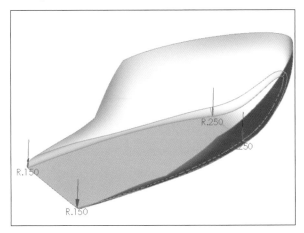

15. Use Delete Face with the Delete option to remove the three faces (two fillet faces and one created by the bottom face extrude) from the scoop surface body.

16. Use the Fill surface to fill in the gap. Right-click one of the open edges created by the Delete Face and choose Select Open Loop. Set all of the edges to Tangent. (Notice that if you use the more desirable Curvature setting, the face creates odd and asymmetrical bumps.) Figure 16.19 shows the Fill surface preview.

FIGURE 16.19

FIGURE 16.19

Filling deleted faces

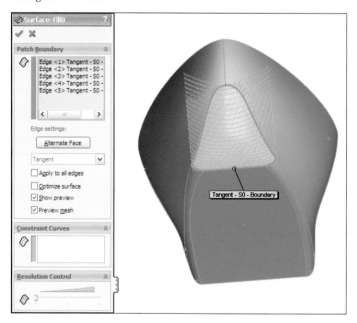

17. Use the Thicken feature to make a solid 0.08 inch thick. Add the thickness to the outside of the scoop.

18. With this step you will begin to model the handle-to-scoop transition area. Show the handle solid body if you have hidden it, and then open a new sketch on the Front plane. Offset the edges of the flat face to the outside by 0.15 inch.

NOTE Do this (offset the edges of the flat face) by selecting the face rather than the edges. By selecting a face, you automatically select a loop that updates parametrically if the edges around the face change by adding a fillet, a cut, or by some other means. Selecting edges makes the selection highly prone to losing references.

19. Use the sketch from Step 18 to create a Split Line on the two outside faces of the thickened scoop.

20. Use the Delete Face feature with the Delete option to remove the two faces inside the split line.

21. Open a new sketch on the flat end face of the handle. First select the flat face and offset the outside loop to the inside by 0.035 inch. Next draw a horizontal line 0.22 inch above the origin as shown in Figure 16.20. Then use the Trim sketch tool to trim the offset and the lines to form a clean, closed loop.

FIGURE 16.20

Creating a sketch for the handle-to-scoop transition

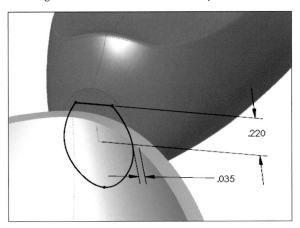

22. Start a Surface Loft feature to create the handle-to-scoop transition area. Activate the SelectionManager, and use the pushpin to keep it up. Select the two trimmed splines of the sketch and click the green check mark on the SelectionManager; then select the two corresponding edges created by the split line, and click the green check mark on the SelectionManager again.

NOTE   **If you notice the loft preview is twisted, you can straighten it out by dragging the light-blue handles of the connector. Unfortunately, connectors do not work when the SelectionManager is active, and so you will need to close it before manipulating connectors.**

23. Set the end conditions of the surface loft to be Normal To Profile for the sketch end, and Curvature To Face for the scoop end. Figure 16.21 illustrates this step.

FIGURE 16.21

A preview of the surface loft for the transition

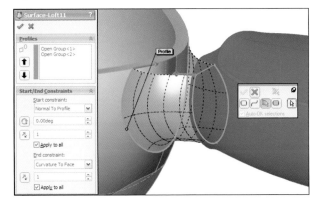

NOTE   Initially, I needed to create this transition as a surface instead of a solid because it simply does not work as a solid, and also because different parts of the scoop end profile need to be treated differently. With a solid, SolidWorks assigns the entire profile the same end condition, and cannot assign different portions of a single profile to have different conditions. On the scoop end profile, the surfaces that the edges are attached to are perpendicular to one another, and the software cannot create a single surface feature that is simultaneously tangent to mutually perpendicular surfaces. For this reason, I have chosen to create the top surface of the transition separately from the rest.

I could have chosen to do this several other ways that did not include turning the thickened scoop back into a surface. It is my personal preference to not get into the type of situation where I have to merge two solid bodies that share a complex face. Merging surfaces edge-to-edge works much more cleanly than merging solids, complex face to complex face.

You will later run into the same issue between the transition and the handle, but the surface between those is planar, not complex. Merging solids that share planar faces works well.

24. Use a Loft or Boundary surface to fill in the top-side of the transition. Do not use any end conditions.

25. Hide the handle body, and use a Fill feature to cap the handle end of the transition. Then knit all of the surface bodies comprising the scoop, and finally use the Thicken feature to make a solid of the enclosed surface.

26. Finally, use a Combine feature to join the scoop and handle solids, and add fillets as shown in Figure 16.22.

FIGURE 16.22

Completed trowel with fillet values

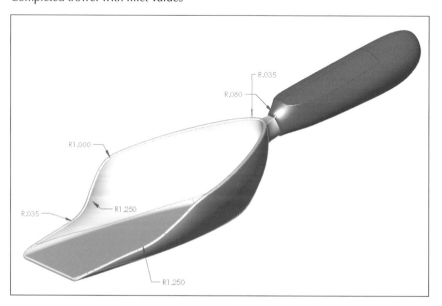

Summary

The key points of this modeling exercise are the sharp to smooth transition, capping off the end of a handle, and removing faces of solids or surfaces to be replaced with other geometry. Also, notice that the surface modeling is highly multi-body by nature.

Probably the most important thing to take from this exercise is that there is no single set way of doing any one thing. You can use multiple methods to create most types of geometry in SolidWorks. You want to be careful to try to pick the most robust option based on the types of changes that you expect to do.

Chapter 17

Modeling Blends

Many people think of blends as the simple equivalent of fillets. To me, blends are a type of geometry that you have to create intentionally and manually rather than automatically like SolidWorks fillets. Blends involve primary surface types being used to transition between bodies. One common example of a blend is the intersection of three or more frame elements, or the base cover for an office chair. You can adapt the blending techniques that this chapter demonstrates to a wide range of actual applications.

This chapter also shows some techniques that are not directly related to blending, but are used to solve problems that come up in this kind of modeling. Some unexpected modeling occurs as a result, showing both the failure of features to work in some situations and ugly hacks to work around software bugs.

Other techniques include patching over bad geometry to smooth over bumps, creases, or edge mismatches.

Modeling a Plastic Cover

In this exercise, I start from a partially completed model and walk you through blending together the legs of a plastic frame-type shape. This section deals with several less-than-ideal situations in a real-world way and helps you see what sort of challenges you will be up against when using SolidWorks for this type of modeling work, without any of the oversimplifications or idealized situations typical in tutorials, training books, and sales demos. I have not massaged the material to make things flow smoothly; I want to present the process realistically with all of its imperfections.

315

The part used in this section is a small injection-molded plastic cover. The part details are not complete; there are locating features, ribs, reveals, or fastening features missing from the model. The completed part included with the downloaded data for this chapter only includes the primary shape and features to make it solid.

The following steps start from the part file from the downloaded data, named Chapter 17 – plasticframestart.sldprt. I created this part from an unconstrained spline sketch that outlines the overall shape of the part, and so this sketch controls the shape of the part as viewed from the Right view. This layout sketch also controls the positions of loft planes using construction lines in the sketch. Modeling from a completely unconstrained sketch of splines is acceptable in concept modeling, but probably not for production modeling, particularly when matches to other parts are involved. For links to other parts, some sort of master model or skeleton should be used that is associatively linked to each part, either through in-context relations or by using associative sketch blocks, linked library features, inserted parts, or other methods that provide similar functionality.

Figure 17.1 shows this layout sketch. I have overbuilt the splines for a couple of reasons. The first reason is to make sure that the spline has the desired curvature at the point where it ends in the finished part. Default splines have curvature that tapers to zero at the ends, which is the same as giving them an Equal Curvature sketch relation to a straight line. You will usually want splines to have some curvature at the ends, and the two ways to address this are to overbuild the splines and trim them back, or to use the tangency weighting and direction handles at the ends of the splines. I have used both methods in this sketch.

The second reason for overbuilding the splines is so that I could place sketch planes to create lofts such that the loft profiles were at least approximately perpendicular to the splines.

FIGURE 17.1

The layout sketch for the plastic cover part

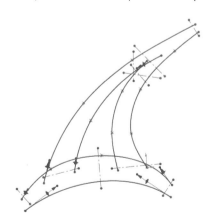 

One thing about this method of using a layout sketch to drive overall shape on a part that I wish worked differently is that the sketch is absorbed under the first and any subsequent feature that uses selections directly from the sketch (using Contour Selection or the SelectionManager, for example). One way to avoid this is to make new sketches with Convert Entities. I wish that the use of only selections from a layout sketch enabled the sketch to remain at the top of the tree where it was originally created.

Unfortunately, it doesn't work that way, and so users must use the Convert Entities, derived sketches, sketch blocks, or some other technique, such as the search filter at the top of the SolidWorks 2008 FeatureManager, to find a sketch with a particular name (such as "Layout").

Follow these steps for a directed tour of creating blends in SolidWorks:

1. Open the file from the downloaded materials for Chapter 17 called Chapter 17 – plasticframestart.sldprt. Notice that most of the features to create the shape are in a folder called Basic Shape. This exercise makes the blends between the legs of the frame so that it transitions smoothly.

    A finished part comes with the downloaded data. The finished part has the name Chapter 17 – plastic frame.sldprt. You may find it useful to have both files open along with this book to examine how I did things in the finished part.

Blending between the three legs shown in Figure 17.2 is a multi-feature process. The underlying concept is that you break the blend into several simple features that you can create easily with surface lofts, and in so doing, isolate a multi-sided patch. Then use a Fill feature to fill in the patch. Figure 17.2 shows the part in the state with the simple surface lofts (colored blue) in place.

FIGURE 17.2

Beginning the first blend with simple lofts

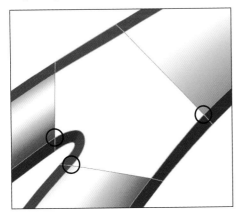

NOTE A cleaner way to model this is to create all of the side faces, meaning the heavily drafted faces around the perimeter of the frame as shown in Figure 17.1, as complete faces instead of making the two straight sections shown in Figure 17.2. This would produce a final part with fewer separate faces and edges, and probably a cleaner finished product.

Setting up these lofts is easy, but because each blend has three small lofts, and the part has three blends, this part has a fair amount of repetitive work. Each blend is subtly different, and requires a slightly different approach to get it to complete correctly. Each person likes to work differently and has different standards for how good is "good enough" and how much work is "too much." In SolidWorks, no magic formula exists for this kind of work, although the Fill surface feature certainly makes it easier.

If you just loft from one open surface edge to another open surface edge using Curvature To Face end conditions, the unconstrained edges of the loft do not follow the edges of the parent faces, but instead they come off of the open edge perpendicular to the edge. So unfortunately, that will not work for this application. For this part, it is important for the edges to be continuous and smooth. To make that happen, you will need to use guide curves to force the edges exactly where you want them to go.

2. Open a sketch on the Right plane, and use a 3-point spline to connect the edges as shown in Figure 17.3. Assign an Equal Curvature between each end of the spline and each edge. Shape the spline to make it look as natural as possible.

FIGURE 17.3

Setting up the first simple loft

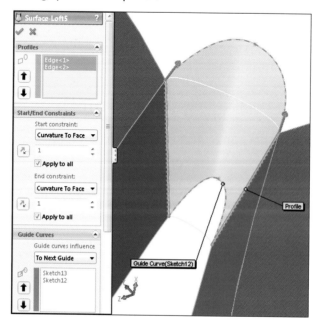

NOTE It would be better if you could use only a 2-point spline and control the shape using spline tangency weighting handles, but SolidWorks does not allow you to control the handles when they have Equal Curvature relations. The alternative is to use a 3-point spline. Remember that you can use the handle on the middle point to control the "pointy-ness" in the middle of the spline, and that Alt-drag enables you to drag the magnitude handle symmetrically.

3. Create a plane parallel to the Right plane, using three vertices at the ends of the curved edges, as indicated by the black circles in Figure 17.2. All of the vertices should be at the same distance from the Right plane.

4. On this new plane, sketch another spline similar in character to the one you sketched in Step 2, but attached to the edges farther from the Right plane.

NOTE Alternately, if you want to be more precise, you could create an angled plane such as Plane10 in the finished model, and a sketch such as Sketch11 in the finished model, to help align the middle point of the two guide curve splines. You could even use this control sketch as an additional loft profile.

5. Create the loft from one edge to another, and select the two splines as guide curves. You do not need the SelectionManager for this selection set. Figure 17.3 shows the preview of the Loft feature for this step. Accept the feature and move on to the next step when it looks good.

6. The other two outer faces are somewhat easier to create. You can reuse a SelectionManager selection from the original layout sketch as the lower guide curve for both of the outer lofts. To do this, type the word **Layout** in the filter at the top of the FeatureManager tree (in 2008 and later), and show the Layout sketch.

7. Start a 3D sketch, and draw a 2-point spline between the vertices of both of the outside patches, two non-intersecting 2-point splines in a single 3D sketch.

8. Create two lofts, lofting the open straight edges with the Curvature To Face end conditions, and using the SelectionManager to select the sketches as the guide curves. Figure 17.4 shows the arrangement for this step.

9. Do the same on the other side, so that now you have surrounded the gap in the middle by surfaces on all sides. Use the Knit feature to combine the three lofts and the three original surface bodies into a single surface body.

10. Hide any of the sketches shown from previous steps. Remember that with SolidWorks 2008, you can use the shortcut toolbar available when left-clicking items to hide things like sketches and bodies.

11. Right-click an open edge of the gap in the curved face of the part, and choose the Select Open Loop option. Now initiate the Fill surface. Make sure the Apply To All Edges option is Off.

12. The edge settings for each of the new lofted surface edges should be Contact, and for the curved edges of the surface bodies from the original part, the setting should be Curvature. The settings in the Fill selection box should alternate, for example, Curvature, Contact, Curvature, Contact, and so on. Use the Merge Result option to immediately knit the Fill into the rest of the surface body. Refer to Figure 17.5 for the arrangement at this point.

FIGURE 17.4

Arrangement for creating side lofts for the first blend

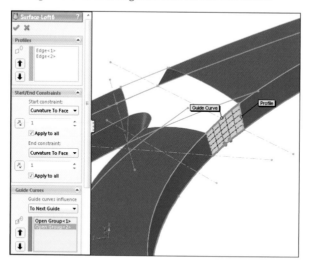

FIGURE 17.5

Settings and preview for the Fill surface

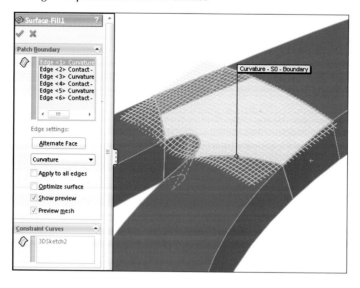

13. Open a new 3D sketch, and use Convert Entities to copy the edge shown in light blue in Figure 17.6. This sketch will be used as a guide curve in both remaining blends after the edge itself is trimmed away in the next step.

14. Trim the two lower intersections as shown in Figure 17.6. The main goal with this is to trim approximately the same distance back from the intersection of each leg. If you want to copy my results more closely, you can copy and paste Sketch14 and Sketch15 from the finished part to your part. Click the sketch in the FeatureManager and press Ctrl+C, then click the Right plane in your part and press Ctrl+V.

FIGURE 17.6

Trimming to start the two lower blends, and setting up loft guide curves

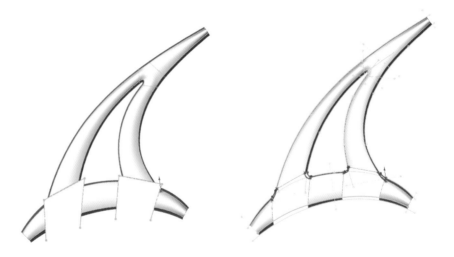

15. Using the same procedure as for the first blend, create the small lofts first, and then use Fill to span the gaps for both of the remaining blends.

NOTE When you are creating the small lofts, sometimes the Curvature To Face end condition may not work with the guide curves. In situations like this, when the guide curves have equal curvature already, this may not be as important as it first seems. If the Curvature To Face option causes an error, try to back off to Tangent, and if that still doesn't work, back off again to None. As always, when shapes are critical, it makes sense to analyze the results with Zebra Stripes and Deviation Analysis.

Tinkering with the Solid

Using the same part, with some minor geometrical changes, as the steps in the previous section, this exercise walks you through some common difficulties you may encounter when changing between surfaces and solids.

1. This exercise uses a different starting point. Open the file called Chapter 17 – tinkeringstart.sldprt from the downloaded data for Chapter 17. This is the part from the first exercise after all of the surfacing work has been completed.

2. Place a Fillet feature on the inside loop edge of the part using a constant radius fillet with a 0.05-inch radius.

3. Place fillets on the three outer edges of the part with a constant radius of 0.035 inch in a single feature.

4. Use a Thicken feature to thicken the surface body into a solid by 0.025 inch to the inside of the part. Although this chapter is not analyzing manufacturing methods, this is a bit thin for most injection-molded parts, and the part is rather small for vacuum form, but the application that this part is to be used for requires it, and the material selection allows it.

Take a moment to look at the three end faces of the part. Notice that because of the Thicken feature, these faces are not nice and clean, particularly if this is to be an injection-molded part. Also have a look at the thickness faces around the rest of the part and notice that the faces are not flat. Figure 17.7 points out the problem areas.

The Thicken feature created faces that are not cleanly flat or drafted for molding

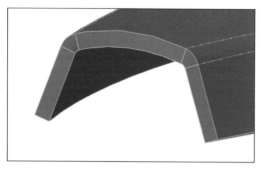

To fix these problems, follow these steps:

5. On the Right plane, open a sketch and create a rectangle of arbitrary size and position. Use the rectangle to make a Planar surface.

6. Initiate a Replace Face feature, and select the thickness faces of one of the three outer edges in the top selection box, and the planar surface in the bottom selection box. Figure 17.8 shows the faces to select for this feature highlighted in blue. Only select one connected set of faces for each Replace Face feature.

7. Repeat Step 6 for the other two sets of thickness faces of outer edges.

Faces to replace

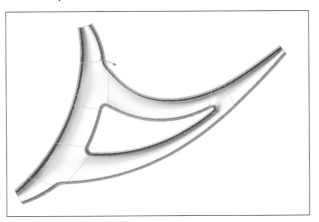

8. When the three Replace Face features are complete, repeat Step 6 Replace Face technique with the loop of thickness faces around the open center triangular window (the only thickness faces not highlighted in Figure 17.8).

NOTE I have done this example several times, and sometimes this Replace Face works in SolidWorks 2008 sp 2.0 and 2.1, and sometimes it does not. If Replace Face works for you, skip Step 9. If it does not, perform Step 9 and then move on.

9. If the Replace Face feature in Step 8 does not work for you, you will need to use a Cut With Surface feature and use the Right plane as the surface to cut away the portion of the part that crosses the Right plane. This Cut With Surface feature could be used in place of all of the Replace Face features. Part of the goal of this chapter, and indeed this entire book, is to expose you to a variety of methods, and let you make up your mind about which features you want to use.

10. For the next few steps, I will also offer alternative methods. Call this first method "steady as she goes" because it allows more control, but requires more setup.

    Press the Spacebar and click the Right view. Zoom into the upper narrow opening in the part (if the part looks like a shark fin with the shark swimming to the left, zoom to the top end of the fin). Open a sketch on the Right plane, and draw a straight line connecting the outside vertices of the end opening, as shown in the left image of Figure 17.9.

Extrude the line as a surface with five degrees of draft such that it leans back into the part. It doesn't need to extend all the way through the part.

11. Use Replace Face to replace the five solid faces with the one extruded surface. Notice that if the outer corners are used for the sketch, the Replace Face has to both add and remove material in a single feature. This is something that a Cut With Surface cannot do.

When the feature is complete, the end of the part turns into a single clean face with appropriate draft.

12. Try this as an alternative method to the "steady as she goes" method in Steps 10 and 11. It is faster but less accurate. Call it the "fast and loose" method. It is less accurate because the direction of the edge is not something that has been established intentionally, but happened pretty much as an accident involving the collision of several features. Select the lower-right opening (when viewed from the Right view). Because the bottom face of the part was either cut or replaced a few steps ago and is now parallel to the Right plane, the edge can be used for other purposes.

To initiate a Ruled surface, use the Tapered To Vector option with the Right plane as the vector, and select an edge as shown in the middle image of Figure 17.9; make it go the right direction with the correct draft (five degrees again, leaning toward the part). You may have to use the Alternate Side option as well as the Reverse Direction arrow to get the Ruled surface to lean the right way and go to the correct side of the Right plane.

13. Again use a Replace Face in the same way as in Step 11, using the Ruled surface instead of the Extruded surface.

FIGURE 17.9

Extruding a surface and making a Ruled surface

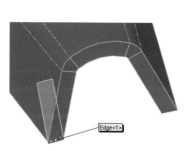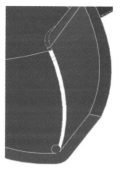

14. For the remaining open end faces, use the Ruled surface method. The Ruled surface creates an error in the part. The Extruded surface avoids the error, but the concept behind the method here is to show you how to cope with real-world modeling situations that may not be ideal. The image on the right of Figure 17.9 shows the error. A thickened fillet face has done something unexpected — namely disappeared and inverted an arc.

> **NOTE** This is a bug in the Parasolid command for the Thicken feature. I have an SPR (software problem report — bug) number for it from SolidWorks Corporation — it's not an operator error. Changing product geometry to accommodate a bug in your modeling software is never a pretty thing, and so I will not do it here. I will confront the bug geometry head on by stepping you through a method to repair the bad geometry.

15. Using the Delete Face with the Delete option activated, select the face that appears to be missing or transparent. This is a bug, and so things will seem strange and not well behaved. The three-quarter arc (that should be a one-quarter arc) should highlight around the edges.

16. The result is a surface body, but it does not necessarily look any better than the original.

Create a Boundary surface using the two long edges of the deleted fillet face, and the one short (correct) arc on the opposite end of the fillet edge from the incorrect arc.

17. Use a Trim feature with the Boundary surface as the Trim Tool to trim away the three-quarter arc face.

18. Knit the Boundary into the main body and make it solid.

19. Another way to tackle this issue is to start by trimming off the three-quarter arc with a Spline On Surface that creates the one-quarter arc edge. Then use an Intersection Trim and then a Fill surface to close the gap, knit, and solidify.

20. Save and close the part.

Why would someone write a book about bugs in the software? Why wouldn't they? Surfacing doesn't get as much attention as some other areas of the software, and so fewer bugs are reported and more remain. Bugs are a part of life when you make your living with surfacing in SolidWorks, and probably with any other software. Hopefully this section will help you be a little less afraid of bugs or unexpected problems in the software. You still have to get your job done, regardless of whether or not there are bugs in the software, and you can't count on the software developers to solve these problems for you on your schedule.

Modeling a Stool Concept

Figure 17.10 is sketch of a stool concept from an industrial designer. The part of the stool that is of interest for the purposes of this chapter is the bottom of the stool, and in particular, the way that the legs blend together. The previous plastic frame example was more of a 2D part, but this one is clearly 3D in the way that it all comes together. As you might expect, the blend technique is slightly different, but still uses a similar concept.

Artist concept of a stool

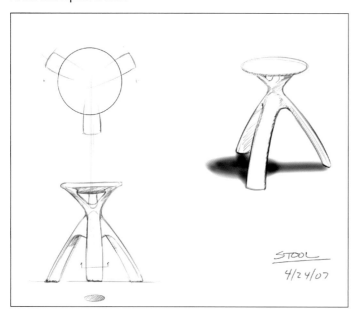

Follow these steps to create the base of a stool with three legs blending together smoothly:

1. From the material downloaded for Chapter 17, open the part called Chapter 17 – stoolstart.sldprt. This part has only a swept surface and a couple of layout sketches.

2. I made the leg of the stool larger than it needed to be intentionally. The sketch called TrimSketch is what you will use to trim the leg, but you need to make some modifications to it first. The end of the leg has to be left in a state similar to the Plastic Frame part, such that you can loft from one leg to the next to create a boundary of faces to completely enclose a gap.

   To do this, the trim line itself must be broken into pieces.

   Use the Split Entities tool (Tools ⇨ Sketch Tools ⇨ Split Entities) to do this. First, show the sweep path, then edit the TrimSketch and set the view to Normal To the Front plane. Then place two Split Entities points, one on either side of the sweep path, with about 0.85 inch between them.

3. Use TrimSketch to trim away the top portion of the sweep. Check the trimmed edge of the surface to make sure that it is broken into two long segments along the large radius, and two short segments along the smaller radius ends.

4. Make a circular pattern of the trimmed surface body. To do this, first create an Axis using the Front and Right planes, then set the instances to 3 and make sure that the Equal Spacing option is On. Activate the Bodies To Pattern panel and select the surface body.

5. Initiate a surface Loft feature, and loft from the short edge on the end of one leg to the neighboring short edge on the neighboring leg, as shown in Figure 17.11.

   Set the end constraints for both edges to Curvature To Face, and set both Tangent Length settings to 3.

FIGURE 17.11

Preview of one of the short edge boundary face lofts

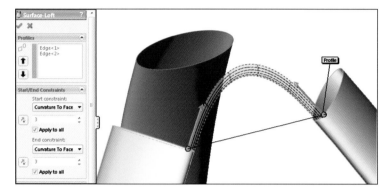

6. Create another Circular Pattern, and pattern the newly created lofted body, using the same axis and spacing.

7. Use the Knit feature to join together all six of the bodies into a single surface body.

8. Open a new 3D sketch, and place a sketch point in empty space, taking care not to pick up any unintentional relations. Then create a coincident relation between the point and the axis you created in Step 4. Finally, put a dimension between the point and the origin, and set the dimension to 12.5 inches. Exit the sketch when you are done.

9. Initiate a new Fill surface feature. With the edge selection box active, right-click any of the edges on the underside of the patterned lofted surfaces, and choose the Select Open Loop option.

10. Make sure that Apply To All Edges is on, and that the edge settings are set to Curvature.

11. Select the 3D sketch point made in Step 8 in the Constraint Curves panel of the Fill PropertyManager. The preview at this point is shown in Figure 17.12.

NOTE If the Fill surface is not smooth, but has bumps or spikes on it, you can try to adjust the width between the Split Entities points in Step 2.

12. Create another 3D sketch with another sketch point, this one constrained in the same way as the last, but this time using a dimension from the origin of 14.5 inches.

13. Follow the same procedure as you followed in Step 9 to put a cap on the top of the intersection of the legs.

14. Use the Section View tool, and notice that starting in SolidWorks 2008, Section View now works on surface bodies as well as solid bodies. Examine the peak area for reasonable uniformity of section.

FIGURE 17.12

Setting up a Fill surface under the peak of the intersection of legs

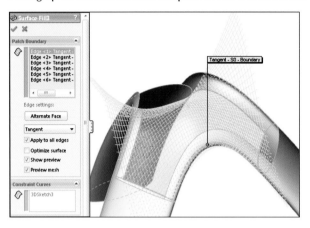

15. Apply planar surfaces to the bottoms of the legs and knit all of the surface bodies together into a solid. Remember that you can select multiple loops for multiple Planar surfaces in a single Planar surface feature.

16. Knit the surface bodies and make into a solid. Figure 17.13 shows the finished model.

FIGURE 17.13

Finished model demonstrating 3D blends between shaped legs

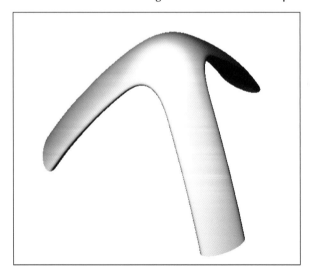

Patching Bad Geometry

Sometimes in the course of making a lot of good geometry, you also wind up creating some bad geometry. It is just inevitable. From time to time, it may be better to just cut out the bad geometry and patch it, rather than trying to fiddle around and get all of the good geometry without any bad geometry.

For example, in Figure 17.14, the front end of the SolidWorks roadster model displays exactly what I am talking about. Notice that the area around the grill looks nice, and the fender around the headlight looks nice, but the fillet that runs between them is hideous. After working with it for a while to try to correct it, I saw that the Fillet feature was simply the wrong tool for that part of the model, but it was the right tool as you go farther up the hood of the car.

There is only one way to fix this, and that is to cut out the bad geometry and remodel it with a different tool. That seems like such a bad practice in a parametric modeler, but sometimes it is the only way.

Follow along with these steps to replace the bad geometry in the SolidWorks roadster model with better geometry:

1. From the downloaded data for Chapter 17, open the part called Chapter 17 – cobra.sldprt.

2. Orient the model so that you are looking at it from the Front view. Make sure Perspective display is turned off (View ⇨ Display).

3. Open a sketch on the Front plane, and sketch the set of lines and a spline shown in Figure 17.14. The lines around the headlight need to go right up to the trim ring around the headlight.

4. Use a Split Line to split the faces that the lines project onto.

5. Use Delete Face with the Delete option to remove the faces inside the split line.

6. Use a Fill surface to fill the gap. Right-click an open edge and Select Open Loop. Make all of the edges Curvature except the edges of the headlight trim ring, which should be Contact.

FIGURE 17.14

Splitting out the bad geometry

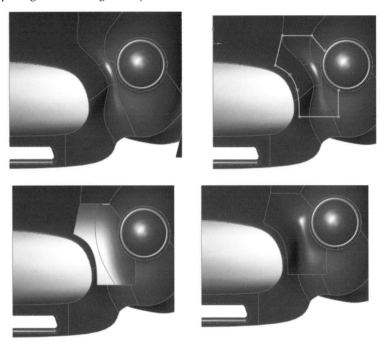

Summary

Blends are far more than just complex fillets; they are a complex set of features that work together to flow gracefully from one shape to another. Blends are often required between frame elements that may be simple circular cross-sections, or more complex.

Even with bugs in the software, it is sometimes amazing what you can do with SolidWorks. You can't let software problems get in the way of your work. You can almost always find a way around most functionality or geometry bugs in the software.

Chapter 18

Modeling a Plastic Bottle

I n this chapter, I walk you through modeling a plastic blow-molded bottle, starting from artist sketches. Modeling containers involves some special techniques that can also be applied to other types of modeling, including the Shell Outward option, multi-thickness shell, finding the volume of liquid a container can hold, draft on complex shapes, molded nonstandard threads, ruled surfaces for the application of paper labels, design for efficient packaging, locating the empty and filled center of gravity, and other considerations. While this chapter focuses on the modeling, I am not completely against mentioning tangential issues that have some relevance. You will get another chance at modeling a bottle in Chapter 21, which covers working with 3D digitized data.

Figure 18.1 shows the artist's drawing of the bottle. This chapter works from these views as Sketch Pictures, allowing us to trace over the hand-sketched data.

FIGURE 18.1

FIGURE 18.1

Artist's drawing of a bottle

Drawing by Stan Kujawski of Design Tech

Laying Out the Task

Most complex modeling tasks can benefit from some sort of plan, and this one is no exception. The data that I have to start from is a set of hand sketches, made from orthogonal views. Hand sketches are good at conveying sharp edges and silhouette profiles, but they aren't so good at conveying cross-sectional shape information, or 3D surface shape.

Starting point affects results

The type of data that you start with definitely affects the way that you build a model. With the hand sketch data available for this model, I usually tend to draw silhouette edges and to allow the process (surface loft) to interpolate the shape between the silhouettes. With hand sketches, I tend to avoid lofting from cross-sections, because I don't have that information; however, in this model, I use the silhouette data as guide curves and have guessed at some cross-sectional shapes, mainly to accommodate the shape around the handle.

The fact that the starting data affects your modeling process, and dictates the types of weaknesses your model may be susceptible to, is one you should keep in mind constantly as you build. When building from silhouette sketches, you need to be more careful about the cross-sectional shape of the resulting model, and you may need to check that shape more frequently to make sure that the software isn't doing something unexpected with the freedom you are giving it.

By the same token, if you model from a set of cross-sectional data, you need to be more careful about the silhouette shape of the model.

Modeling scenarios

When modeling complex shapes from reference data, you can proceed in one of two ways. One way is to model sharp edges or symmetry silhouettes as either sketches or curves, and then fill in the faces between the edges. Edges are much easier to identify from 2D source data, and in Projected Curves they can be very attractive if you have orthogonal views of the edges — views that show edges from, say, a front and a side view.

Another way to work is to make the faces independently as overbuilt surface bodies, and then trim the faces; the edges simply fall at the intersection of the edges. I would tend to work this way if starting from some 3D format, for example, modeling from point cloud data or making a parametric model from an imported solid. To me, modeling from faces is more difficult; edges are easier. I usually select modeling from edges, although there are exceptions. A single part can even mix methods.

For example, in the bottle used in this chapter, I built the overall shape using silhouette data, but I created some of the detail features by making faces and cutting them into the model to produce edges, and then going back and adjusting the faces to change the edge placement.

The reason for this is that visually edges are easier to identify than faces. If you get an edge wrong, it is more obvious than if you get the curvature on a face wrong. Allowing edges to fall in a haphazard way, wherever the face intersection makes them fall, puts a lot of confidence in the shape of the faces you have created. I prefer to be explicit about edges and fudge a face if fudging is required.

Modeling the unknown

Regardless of your starting point, and whether you model using faces or edges as reference, you will often run into shapes or details that you don't have enough information to model with confidence. I'm referring to things such as, for a given volume, how tall does this bottle need to be? In situations like this, I recommend starting with the information that you do know. You can put information like this into a layout sketch. For example, what diameter neck/cap do you want to put on the bottle? What size box does it need to fit into for shipping? What is the size of the handle grip? Some of these factors can be scaled with the bottle, and some will have to be a specific size, regardless of the size of the bottle. For example, to go from a 1-gallon to a 1-quart container, you can't just scale the 1-gallon container down by a certain percentage of its original dimensions, because you still need to accommodate adult hands on the small container. Also, the gallon container may need to be proportionately thicker in some areas, such as the handle, due to load-bearing requirements.

My suggestion with all of this is, as much as possible, to model what you know first. Often, the unknown figures itself out if you block in the things that you do know. This is part of the reason for the layout. The layout represents all of the information that you have to work with.

Building the Model

Enough talking about it; let's do some modeling! Follow along with these steps using the data provided in the downloaded files for Chapter 18 from the Web site, or build the part from scratch using the step-by-step instructions.

1. Open the file named Chapter 18 – bottlestart.sldprt from the downloaded data. I have inserted the sketch pictures into this start part for you. If you would rather get some practice inserting, positioning, and resizing sketch pictures, you can start from a blank part and use the *.jpg files that are also found in the downloaded data.

2. Figure 18.2 shows the cross-sectional sketches in red, as well as the silhouette sketches in blue. The origin for the part is at the center of the bottom of the bottle.

Cross-section and silhouette sketch information

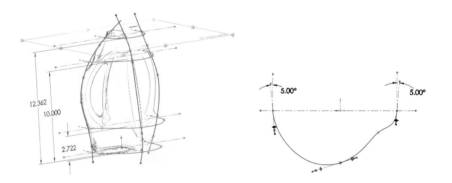

One way to create the cross-sectional sketches is to simply trace the bottom, and then make several offset planes and copy the bottom sketch to the new planes. Use Figure 18.2 to create the cross-section planes.

I used the silhouette profile sketches as guide curves to drive the width of the sections, and then I used the cross-sectional splines to slim down the sections in the area of the handle. It is necessary for the silhouette and section sketches to intersect one another where they cross.

I only sketched half of each section because the bottle is symmetrical. Notice the construction lines in the image to the right. The spline is tangent to the construction line that is angled at five degrees. The angle represents the draft at the parting line of the mold. I made each of the section sketches in the same way. This is the reason copying them is such a good idea, because setting up all of the construction geometry and sketch relations is a lot of work that you can avoid by copying sketches.

CAUTION When you copy sketches, external sketch relations (relations to things outside the sketch) do not get copied, so you will need to add relations to locate the sketch to the origin. It is also possible for a sketch to flip or rotate between a default plane and a reference plane. If this happens, repair the first sketch it happens to using Modify Sketch (with its capability to mirror and rotate entire sketches), and then copy the repaired sketch rather than the original for the rest of the instances.

NOTE I had to deviate somewhat from the artist drawing because the front view and top view do not seem to give corresponding information about the width of the bottle. I also needed to include an area of the bottle where it was limited to curvature in one direction, and would allow a paper label to be stuck there without puckering. This is best seen in Figure 18.2 in the image to the left. In reality, this is probably not "close enough" to one-directional curvature to satisfy requirements for a paper label.

3. When the sketches are prepared to your satisfaction, initiate a Lofted Surface feature. Select the section sketches in the Profiles box, and then use the SelectionManager to select the silhouette sketches in the guide curve box.

   Set the tangency for the two outer guide curves as Direction Vector, and for both of them make the Front plane the vector, set the angle to five degrees, and make the arrow point toward the center of the bottle. This setting just reinforces the draft angle established by the sketch construction geometry.

   Figure 18.3 illustrates these settings for the Loft feature.

4. Use a Trim feature and a sketch similar to that shown in Figure 18.4 to trim out the handle section of the bottle. I created two loops, one representing the actual through hole in the handle area; the larger one is the area of the original outer surface that needs to be trimmed to curve back smoothly to the through hole.

   Getting concentric spline loops to look right can be tricky. Turning on curvature combs may help to keep the shape from becoming too lumpy.

5. The next step is to create the inside of the handle area. I will outline a couple of things that I tried, and the results.

FIGURE 18.3

Settings and preview of the main bottle surface loft

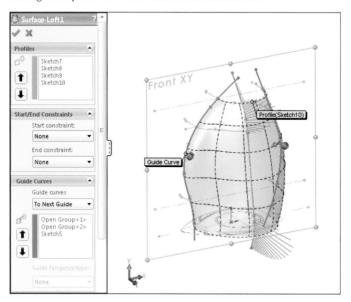

FIGURE 18.4

Trimming the handle hole

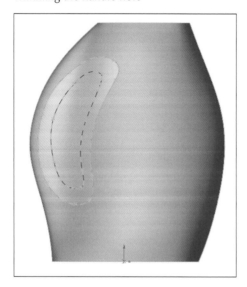

If you take the easy route, and simply do a loft from the trimmed edge of the lofted surface to the inside profile of the handle, the geometry works, but it creates ripples in the tight curvature of the ends of the grip area, and the loft does not allow you to add connectors to straighten out the U-V mesh. Because of the ripples, you have to trim out the corners and replace them with Fill surfaces. This works okay, but the problem with the connectors bothers me, and you can only specify a single value of the tangency weighting for the entire trimmed edge.

NOTE I found a bug in the software by working with this example: You cannot add connectors to lofts where you have used the SelectionManager to select profiles. An additional limitation exists in that lofts do not allow connectors in the second direction. Boundary surface connectors seem to overcome both the bug and the limitation, but as of SolidWorks 2008 sp 2.1, there is an intermittent crash bug when adding or adjusting connectors in the Boundary surface. Connectors, although highly useful, are a bit of a minefield. Save your data frequently.

My next attempt was to use a Boundary surface instead of a Loft. This solved the problem with the connectors, but still created ripples in the ends, and I therefore still needed to trim out the bad geometry and Fill. In addition, I could not assign multiple tangency weights along the perimeter.

The final attempt required that I just accept that Loft and Boundary will always produce ripples in the corners, and that these areas have to be modeled separately with Fill surfaces. With that in mind, I divided the handle area into four sections, two ends and the smoother midsections. I did this by using Split Entities to split the kidney-shaped trimming splines shown in Figure 18.4 into four sections, which corresponded to separate edges on the trimmed surface, similar to the technique in Chapter 17 for dividing edges to set up a blend. Figure 18.5 shows this process.

6. Divide both kidney-shaped handle splines into four sections using Split Entities points, isolating the high curvature ends.

7. Trim the handle area from the first loft surface.

8. Create Boundary surfaces from the two large radius areas of the handle area. Use Curvature setting at the edge, and Direction Vector at the sketch, with the Front plane as the vector, and an angle of two degrees. Also use connectors to make the U-V grid behave. The weighting for the sketch end should be about 4, and for the edge end should be about 0.9 for the boundary surface pictured with its PropertyManager in Figure 18.5.

   For the second boundary, use 0.6 at the edge and 0.3 at the sketch. For this feature, you need to be careful that the surface does not begin to create an undercut at the parting line. This is the reason for using comparatively low values for the tangency weighting.

9. Create small, extruded construction surfaces to enclose the end corner areas. To do this, you need to open a new sketch on the Front plane, and convert entities to copy the tight curvature ends into the new sketch, and then extrude with two degrees of draft.

10. Use Fill surfaces to fill in the two corners of the handle area, with the Curvature option on all edges for both features.

FIGURE 18.5

Steps to model the handle area

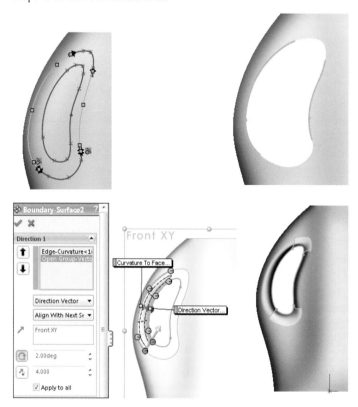

> **NOTE** I realize these steps are difficult and may lead to features that do not work for you on the first try, but this is the nature of working with complex models. Examine the steps I outline and the model provided with the downloaded data and use that information to try to understand what is going on with your model. Slight sketch differences between my data and your data can cause a completely different set of circumstances.

11. Use Delete Bodies to delete the two small construction surfaces.

12. The inset shape opposite the handle is a bit of a freeform shape, and is tough to model, maybe because it has no apparent function. I have created this using a face creation method, but it would be arguably better to use a curve-based technique instead. Using faces, it takes a fair number of guesses to get the faces to trim to an edge that looks roughly like what the artist intended.

Figure 18.6 shows sketches on the Front and Right planes respectively, between which I lofted a surface, and then trimmed it out of the main surface body.

FIGURE 18.6

Sketches for the inset shape loft

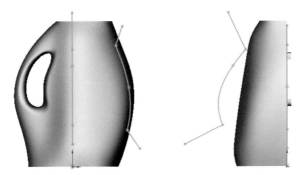

13. When you have made the sketches, loft a surface between them. Use the Normal To Profile setting for the sketch on the Front plane, and use the tangency weighting for that profile to control the shape of the feature.

14. With a Mutual Trim, use the new lofted surface to trim out a section of the main bottle surface.

15. Create a plane offset from the highest plane shown in Figure 18.2. The offset distance should be 0.70 inch in a direction away from the part origin.

16. On the new plane, draw a construction line between the open vertices in the bottle-neck area, as shown in Figure 18.7. Create an arc with the center at the midpoint of the construction line, and with a radius of 2.25 inches.

FIGURE 18.7

Beginning to build the neck of the bottle

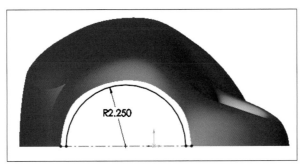

17. Create a lofted surface from the top loft profile of the first Loft feature and the newly sketched arc.

> **NOTE**   If you examine this loft closely, you may notice that where it transitions to the rest of the bottle, in some areas the transition is concave and in some it is very slightly convex. Because of this slight convexity, a fillet will not work here at all. To smooth the transition, you must first trim out a section, and then create another loft.

18. Open a new sketch on the Front plane, and sketch a rectangle, as shown in Figure 18.8. The ends of the rectangle must extend beyond the bottle faces.

FIGURE 18.8

Trimming out an area to blend

19. Loft between the trimmed edges using Curvature settings for both edges.

20. Open another sketch on the Front plane, and sketch an arc that cuts into the top of the handle area, as shown in Figure 18.9. Also draw a construction line to act as an axis to revolve a surface about. This scoops out a small area in the handle that will act as a thumb rest.

FIGURE 18.9

Preparing the thumb rest

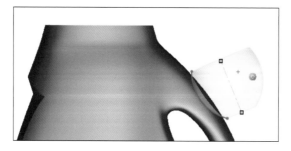

340

21. Revolve a surface through enough of an angle to cut through the main surface, but less than 360 degrees.

22. Use a Mutual Trim to trim out the scoop and remove the excess revolved surface.

23. Open a sketch on the Top plane, and use Convert Entities to copy the bottom edge of the first loft into the sketch. Then draw a straight line to connect the open endpoints.

24. Use the sketch to create a Planar surface on the bottom of the bottle.

25. Make a series of fillets according to the values shown in Figure 18.10. The two fillets in the notches of the inset feature are Variable Radius fillets, which is why they have two values for each fillet.

FIGURE 18.10

Fillets for the bottle

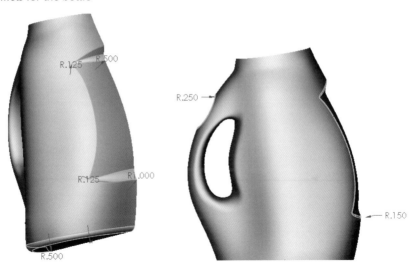

NOTE When filleting the bottom planar surface created in Step 24, remember that the planar surface is not yet merged into the rest of the bottle body, and the only way to fillet between bodies is by using a Face Fillet. Because you have to make a Face Fillet anyway, go ahead and use the Constant Width setting to make the edge of the fillet go straight across the bottle, rather than varying in height to accommodate a constant radius.

26. Group all of the fillets into a single folder, and rename the folder Fillets.

27. Mirror the bottle body about the Front plane, and use the Merge Result option.

28. Use another Planar surface to cap off the body, and then Knit and Thicken it into a solid.

29. Open a sketch on the Top plane, and select the bottom-most sketch of the first loft. Offset the spline by 0.75 inch to the inside. Then draw a construction line between the open endpoints and mirror the sketch.

30. Use the new sketch to create a Split Line on the bottom face of the bottle.

31. Create a Dome feature on the face inside the split line. The Dome should remove material, and be 0.375 inch deep, as shown in Figure 18.11.

FIGURE 18.11

Doming the bottom of the bottle

32. Apply a fillet with a 0.125-inch radius to the sharp edge of the Dome.

33. Open a sketch on the flat face where the neck of the bottle should be, and sketch a circle centered on the face with a diameter of 3.75 inches. Extrude the circle 1.0 inch with three degrees of draft.

34. Place a fillet with a 0.125-inch radius on the edge indicated in Figure 18.12.

FIGURE 18.12

Neck and fillet dimensions

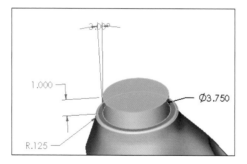

35. Finally, create a multi-thickness Shell feature, removing the face at the end of the neck. The overall Shell feature should have a 0.03-inch thickness, and the neck of the bottle should have a 0.10-inch thickness, selected in the Multi-Thickness Faces selection box at the bottom of the FeatureManager.

36. Save the part. You will use it again in the next sections of this chapter. If you have not built the part, but would still like to work through the next sections of this chapter, you can use the part from the downloaded data.

Creating a Thread

A very common help request from users modeling plastic parts has to do with modeling threads. Plastic threads in most respects are not as demanding as ground metal threads or lead screws. The most complex things about them is that you cannot just call them out on a drawing with a standard tap size and allow them to be created by a standard process with standard tooling, unless you work for a company that does enough of it to have developed standards. If you want threads on your plastic parts, you have to explicitly model them.

There are two methods for molding threads onto plastic parts. The simplest way is the method for external threads, where you can just cut the threads right into the mold steel. For every external thread (on the neck of a bottle, for example), you must also create an internal thread (on the cap), and internal plastic threads are more difficult to manufacture, requiring an unscrewing core.

NOTE Going slightly further into the topic than I need to for the purpose of this section of the chapter, unscrewing cores brings up an interesting modeling question to which I have not yet found an adequate answer. Draft Analysis in SolidWorks can help you find undercuts in a straight pull mold, places where plastic is trapped behind steel and cannot be pulled out of the mold. That is relatively easy and has been around for a while. The thing that doesn't exist at this point is any sort of unscrewing core undercut checker. If you design parts that require an unscrewing core, check your parts carefully to make sure they can actually be unscrewed.

Continuing on with making a thread on this bottle, I will assume that as an external thread, it can be pulled from a standard blow mold, where the threads are cut into the two sides of the mold, which pull straight away from the part.

Follow these steps to add a thread to the neck of the bottle you modeled in the first part of this chapter. If you did not model the part but would like to model along with these steps, use the finished part provided in the downloaded data for this chapter.

1. From the flat face that the neck extrusion sketch is made from, create an offset plane with an offset of 0.25 inch. To use better modeling practice, do not offset from the face, but instead from the plane used to create that face, from Step 15 in the Building the Model section.

2. On the new plane, open a sketch and use the Intersection Curve sketch tool to capture the diameter of the neck at that location. The result should be a circle.

3. Initiate a Helix feature, and use the settings shown in Figure 18.13 to create the curve. Remember that this face has three degrees of draft on it, and so you need to make sure that you use the Taper Helix option, and taper the helix in the same direction as the face.

FIGURE 18.13

Setting up the helix

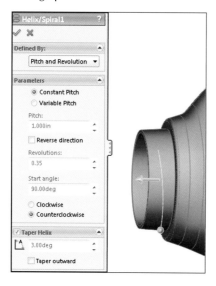

4. Open a 3D sketch, select the helix, and click Convert Entities.

NOTE   If you have to select the helix from the graphics window after it has already been used in a feature like the sweep, you will have problems. Curve features, for whatever reason, cannot be selected from the graphics window after they are consumed in a feature like a sweep. If you have to create a sketch relation like a Pierce or create a plane normal to curve — features that are affected by where you select the curve — selecting from the FeatureManager may not be good enough. You have a 50/50 chance of getting the correct solution. In cases like this, you may have to delete the sweep and re-create it.

Some workarounds exist to get around this bug without having to delete the feature, but the workarounds can arguably be more work than deleting the feature. One such workaround involves temporarily redefining the sweep with another path (which removes the helix from the sweep), redefining the relations or features that need it, and then replacing the helix back into the sweep.

Another workaround would be to create an identical helix, redefining items from the new helix, and then replacing the old helix with the new one in the Sweep feature.

This very frustrating bug has been in the software for several releases now. SolidWorks is definitely aware of the problem, but they have chosen not to do anything about it.

5. Switch to a Top view of the part, and draw a short (¼ to ⅜ inch) spline on each end that goes from the end of the converted helix toward the center of the bottle, without breaking through the wall. Assign Equal Curvature relations between the converted helix and the short splines. The 3D sketch from the top should look like the image on the left in Figure 18.14.

FIGURE 18.14

Extending the helix

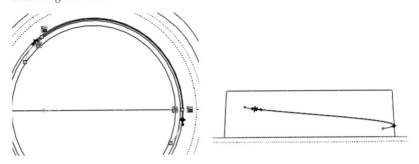

You cannot start or end the thread with square ends; the ends should taper down into the neck. Several methods exist by which you can do this, but the cleanest is to make the taper part of the sweep path. This is the function of these short splines.

6. Turn the model 90 degrees and make sure that the short spline segments flow smoothly out of the converted helix. Use the image on the right in Figure 18.14 for reference. The model is shown in wireframe for clarity. Exit the 3D sketch when you are satisfied.

7. Create a plane perpendicular to the free end of one of the short spline sections.

8. Open a sketch on the new plane, and draw a sketch as shown in the image on the left in Figure 18.15. The sketch relations are shown on the sketch to help you reconstruct it. The free end of the construction line has a Pierce relation to the splines created in Step 5. Make sure that the thread profile sticks out of the neck of the bottle, the 10-degree taper is on the bottom, and the 20-degree taper is on top.

9. Use Offset Surface (with a zero-distance offset) to make a copy of the conical face inside the neck of the bottle. The threads may stick through a little, and this surface body will make it easy to clean up later. You could also use Delete Face for this, but it requires the selection of four faces, one of which is hidden and requires you to use Select Other. These faces to be selected are patterned in three places, and you may need to repeat the selection for both ends of the sweep. So you could make one Cut With Surface feature or make up to 24 tiny face selections for a Delete Face feature — it's up to you.

10. Make a solid Sweep feature, using the thread profile as the Sweep profile, and the 3D spline sketch as the path. Set the Orientation/Twist Type to Follow Path, with the Alignment Type set to Direction Vector and use the Top plane as the vector.

FIGURE 18.15

The thread profile sketch

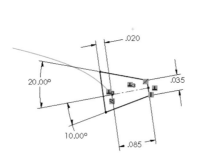

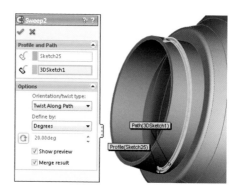

11. Turn on the display of Temporary Axes, and initiate a Circular Pattern feature, patterning the swept thread three times around the neck of the part.

12. Use the Offset Surface from Step 9 to make a Cut With Surface feature to cut away any small ends of the swept threads that poke through the neck of the bottle to the inside.

At this point, you should be done with modeling the bottle threads. You may find other ways of creating the threads, in particular, the taper of the thread into the neck.

Checking the Volume

Now that the model of the bottle is complete, you need to check the volume that it will hold. SolidWorks will give you the volume of the bottle, meaning the volume of material it takes to manufacture the bottle, but it does not tell you automatically how much liquid the bottle will hold. Calculating the volume of liquid the bottle will hold requires an additional modeling task.

To find the volume, you must model the liquid inside. This is not as difficult as it sounds, and there are a number of ways of doing it.

If all you are interested in is the volume of liquid the bottle will hold, you can do that using a multi-body part. If you also need to find the combined mass or center of gravity of the bottle and the liquid without doing any hand calculations, you must use an assembly. This is because multi-body parts cannot assign different densities to the plastic and the liquid.

Follow these steps to find the volume of liquid that the bottle you just modeled will hold:

1. Open the part you modeled in the first section of this chapter or open a finished part from the downloaded data for Chapter 18.

2. Open a sketch on the Top plane of the part. Set the view to the Top view, and sketch a rectangle that surrounds the bottle.

3. Extrude the rectangle up to the fill line. In this case, the fill line is at 13 inches. It is important to remember to turn off the Merge Result option for this extrude.

4. Use the Combine feature (Insert ⇨ Feature ⇨ Combine) with the Subtract option. Select the extruded block as the Main Body, and the bottle as the Bodies To Combine.

   Choose the Selected Bodies option on the Bodies To Keep dialog box shown in Figure 18.16. This dialog box is difficult to use: You cannot select bodies graphically, you have to use the check boxes to do it, and you cannot rotate the view when this box is up.

FIGURE 18.16

Using the Combine feature

> **NOTE** The result of the Combine feature with the Subtract option is that any bodies listed in the Bodies To Combine section are consumed, and so they will not be available after the Combine feature in the tree. If you want to see both the bottle and the contents after the Combine feature, you must use Move/Copy Bodies (Insert ⇨ Features ⇨ Move/Copy Bodies) to make a copy of the bottle body before the Combine.
>
> To use Move/Copy Bodies to copy a body, check the Copy option, select the body, and click the green check mark. SolidWorks gives you a warning message asking if you really want to copy without moving. Answer at your own discretion.

5. If you are left with just a body representing the liquid contents of the bottle, you can use the Mass Properties tool (Tools ⇨ Mass Properties) to find the volume. Be aware that any hidden solid bodies will be included in the volume result. If there are other solid bodies in the model, you can remove them by using the Delete Bodies feature, and then getting the mass properties data.

6. If you want to do this process in an assembly to find a center of gravity for the combination of bottle and contents, simply make the block in a separate part in the assembly. While editing the block part in the context of the assembly, use the Insert ⇨ Features ⇨ Cavity feature (without any shrink) to subtract the bottle from the block. Use Delete Bodies to remove the unwanted portion of the block.

Summary

Beginning a modeling project with a layout that includes given information is essential when building models that take more than a basic effort. Layout information can come in several forms, including pictures, imported data, point cloud, and sketch data.

This example shows how bugs or limitations in the software can have a big effect on how you model a part or a portion of a part. You can almost always find a workaround for any given problem in the process; you just need to exercise a little creative ingenuity and maybe most important, patience. Be aware that there are usually many different ways to do any single task in SolidWorks, and that the results of each technique can be subtly different.

Chapter 19

Modeling Decorative Features

Decorative techniques in SolidWorks can be extremely difficult and time consuming. Often the biggest difficulty comes from visualizing the finished shape and the steps that are required to create it. To be perfectly honest, SolidWorks is not really meant for this kind of work, and this kind of work is not really meant for parametrics, but nonetheless, we are still called upon to do it from time to time. Decorative work, when it needs to be done explicitly in 3D, is often done by hand sculpting. When done on the computer, it is often done in software like Rhino. It is not impossible with a history-based modeler, although it is not usually easy.

The range of potential shapes and techniques that you can run into is mind-boggling. The kinds of shapes I am talking about are not found in products as much today as, say, a hundred years ago, when shapes were created by hand sculpting and casting. Think about floral and leaf patterns in cast-iron lampposts, or cast-concrete birdbaths. Think about cast-iron fences, curtain rod finials, and decorative fireplace mantels. Think about decorative architectural details and indoor lighting fixtures. Think about garden decorations, decorative shelf brackets, and hand railing panels. Somebody designed these products, and they weren't all made in the 1800s.

Maybe the toughest thing about this kind of work is the fact that none of the features have any function whatsoever; they are purely decorative. Often, they do not even represent anything "real;" the shapes are just abstract, or have evolved to have some symbolic meaning over years, centuries, or even millennia. To some people, this chapter might seem a waste of time, but in some ways it is truly the culmination of all of your training, knowledge, and imagination.

I have had a few paying jobs modeling decorative objects. One was for a national interior-decorating manufacturer, another for a high-end specialty indoor lighting manufacturer, and I have done a fair amount of work for a volume jewelry manufacturer.

Parametric modeling is not a good fit for this type of work because any changes that you make are likely to violate your original design intent, and the parametric process becomes an obstacle to shape development. As mentioned earlier, non-parametric tools like Rhino are probably better suited to the kinds of shapes, changes, and processes involved in this type of work. Still, there are a lot of skills you can learn from this kind of work, and many techniques that might be useful in many kinds of modeling, not just decorative forms.

In this chapter, I will walk you through several models, or at least several aspects of several models. I will not explain the details of how to make each sketch or the particular settings for each feature, but rather, I will just give a conversational overview of the main aspects of each model, and point out the interesting tricks or special techniques used. First I will discuss an egg-and-dart pattern on a curved ring. Next, it will be a woven pattern in a shelf bracket. Then I will show a flower-like curtain rod finial, followed by a fleur-de-lis cap for an iron gate post. You will learn how to create a helical scroll detail on a cast-iron lantern. Finally, I will turn to a leaf pattern for some unusual kinds of special modeling techniques.

Each of these projects has unique challenges, and ideally, each would probably be a part of a bigger project; but in order to make each of these digestible, I have broken them down separately to limit the size of the task.

Modeling an Egg-and-Dart Pattern

Due to the complexity of the parts in this chapter, I am just going to give a brief overview of each feature involved in building these models, without explaining how to create every detail. For details such as sketch dimensions and feature settings, I strongly suggest that you follow along using the downloaded data. Figure 19.1 shows the finished egg-and-dart part.

FIGURE 19.1

The egg-and-dart model

The part for this section is called Chapter 19 – Egg And Dart.sldprt. The main features of this part are making a pattern on a curved surface, making a simple loft, and using construction geometry with the Fill surface. I strongly recommend that you follow along with the part rolled back and watch each step unfold.

The egg-and-dart model starts with a solid revolve, done using the MidPlane option to make sure the Front plane remained centered in the part.

Next, a plane perpendicular from the Front plane through a construction line in the sketch for the revolve is created to have a plane that is roughly parallel with the surface I will be working on. This plane is called the U Construction Plane because I will use it to construct the U shape of the egg.

The revolved surface is added as an end condition for extrudes and a projection surface for a projected curve. It was not made as an offset from the solid because the faces of the solid have an additional arc that I didn't want in this end condition surface. I wanted the revolved surface to ease back into the solid.

Modeling the egg border

Next is the U shape around the egg. The first thing that needs to be done is to create a projected curve, projecting a spline onto the Reference Surface. From Figure 19.2, you can see that I created the spline symmetrically about the centerline. This has to be done manually, because there is no automatic way to make a mirror with a single spline. The automatic way is to mirror one spline, which creates a second spline.

FIGURE 19.2

Sketching the U shape

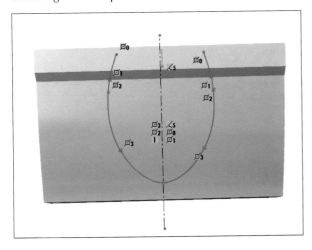

The profiles for the Loft feature are simple line and arc sketches, but the profiles on the end are the same. This is where I used a Derived sketch. To make a Derived sketch, click the sketch, Ctrl-click the plane you want the sketch on, and through the menus, select Insert ⇨ Derived Sketch. In this case, I had to mirror the Derived sketch, and I used the Modify Sketch tool for that purpose.

NOTE As of this writing, where SolidWorks 2008 sp 2.1 is being used, and throughout the 2008 beta period, a bug exists where the Modify Sketch origin symbol flashes on the screen, and then disappears. The only way around this is to turn the tool on and off, and try to find where the origin symbol should be. It still works if you can get your cursor where the symbol should be; you just can't see the symbol.

The middle lofted section was copied from the larger one and scaled down with dimensions. I rotated it slightly to provide a constant aspect to the viewer. I located the profile by using a Pierce constraint between one of the sketch corners and the projected curve. Figure 19.3 shows the preview of this Loft feature.

The loft is straightforward, without any settings or special manipulation. Using the projected curve as a guide curve is essential to get the correct shape. Next, I applied some Full Round fillets to give the U shape a less hard-edged look, and I also used Curvature Continuous Face fillets on the inside edges.

FIGURE 19.3

Creating the U loft

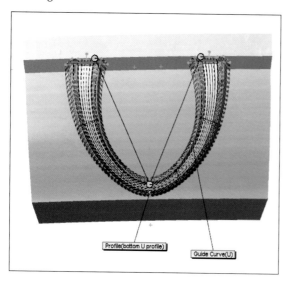

Modeling the egg

To create the actual egg, I started with a Ruled surface made from the inner edge of the U shape. The ruled surface has a taper to control the initial tangency direction of the egg.

To specify the upper edge of the egg, I opened a 3D sketch and used a Spline On Surface to connect the open ends of the Ruled surface, and I made a Coincident relationship between the middle point of the spline and the Front plane. You are not able to place a Symmetric relation on spline tangency handles in a 3D sketch, and so I estimated it, and declared it "close enough."

To prepare for when the egg shape would be finished, I used a Knit command to knit the face inside the U shape to the face immediately above the U shape, where the 3D sketch Spline On Surface was created. These faces are necessary, along with the egg, to create a solid body.

From here, I hid the main solid body, and created the Fill surface from the Ruled surface edge and the sketched 3D spline. Then I used the egg to trim the Knit surface body, and knit, solidified, and merged the result into the rest of the solid. Then I added a small fillet between the egg and the U shape.

Modeling the dart

Because the basic work surface is a curve, I had to make another plane tangent to the curve in about the middle of the Dart feature. This was accomplished first with a layout sketch specifying the angle, and then with a 3D sketch and some clever sketch relationships. From this, the Dart Plane was created.

The dart is a simple extrude that uses the Offset start condition and an Up To end condition. The inset face on the dart is just a cut Offset From Surface, with the Reverse offset option.

To make the patterning easy, the Dart was cut in half, mirrored to the other side, and then joined together with the rest of the solid, and patterned as a body. Figure 19.4 shows the result as a progression of working with bodies, mirrors, and patterns in different combinations.

FIGURE 19.4

Preparing to pattern the body

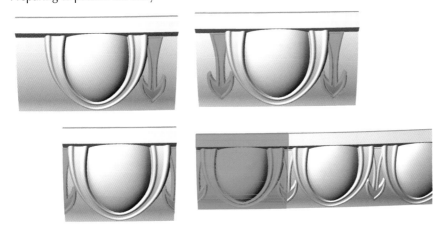

Comments on the construction

Some cleanup was necessary using the Delete Face with the Delete and Patch option. Delete Face is a useful tool for cleanup, but be careful not to overuse it, as it can cause rebuild times to increase significantly.

When modeling shapes on a curved surface, construction geometry is going to be very helpful. In this type of modeling, everything takes a little longer because you've got to set up each feature more carefully.

Modeling a Woven Pattern

Woven patterns are actually more common than you might think in all sorts of household products and even toys. Fortunately, this is not something we, as designers and engineers, have to do frequently, but rather than figuring it out from scratch next time, you can use this chapter as a reference. Figure 19.5 shows the finished product in this modeling exercise.

I invite you to open the part from the downloaded data for this chapter, and follow along using the rollback bar.

As simple as the techniques involved in this part are, I ran across an extraordinary number of bugs, even crash bugs during its construction, which was rather disconcerting.

FIGURE 19.5

The finished model

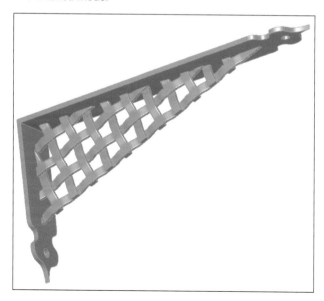

The initial bracket feature is straightforward, just a Thin Feature extrusion of two lines. The decorative shape at the end of the bracket was trickier because the second feature on the long end of the bracket used a Derived sketch. A Derived sketch is a valid and useful tool, but if you drag an endpoint in a Derived sketch and try to pick up an automatic sketch relation with it, SolidWorks will crash without a message, as of SolidWorks 2008 sp 2.1. You can make the relations manually, but avoid using the drag-and-drop technique with Derived sketches.

The real challenge here is, of course, the weave. The first step is to lay out the geometry in 2D with a sketch. Some space must exist between each element in the weave just to make the transition. Most brackets of this sort do not have a solid gusset between the arms of the bracket, and so I decided to allow a bit of air in the weave.

I am familiar with two basic ways to create a weave. The first and easiest method would be to sketch the weave from the side, and simply extrude each element of the weave. The second method is to model the overlapping sections from either side of the weave, and then loft between them. Between the two methods, in this part I chose to use the second (more difficult) type, but also the type that can be more easily applied to non-flat weaves. For example, if you had to wrap a weave onto the surface of a finial, you could do this with the second type of weave, but not the first. This is often the case with household products like curtain rods. Figure 19.6 shows an example of a part with this more complex type of weave using a similar scheme as the current part to create the weave.

The first order of business is to decide how thick the woven elements should be. I decided on 0.10 inch. Because I want to represent the element at the midplane rather than one side or the other, I made two planes offset from the Right plane, with a Link Value keeping the planes equidistant from the Right plane. The distance needs to be half of the thickness plus half of the thickness, and so a full element thickness, or 0.1. For reasons that you will see later, this number turns out to be not quite right, but with the Link Values in place, it is an easy change to make.

FIGURE 19.6

A more complex non-planar weave

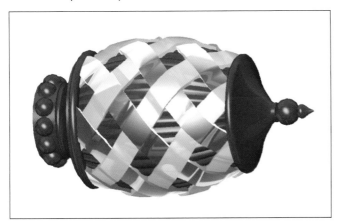

Starting the weave, I created little planar surface panels where the elements would overlap, on alternating sides of the center plane, as shown in the image to the left in Figure 19.7. Then I lofted between the panels, as shown in the image to the right in Figure 19.7.

FIGURE 19.7

Lofting between planar patches

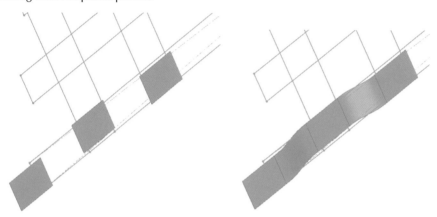

From there, I patterned the planar and lofted bodies into a long strip, the longest that would be used in the part. Then I knit the bodies together and thickened the knit into a solid. After thickening, I added a fillet to the edges of the part, which has an impact on manufacturability concerns for this part, as you will see later.

In this part, I made extensive use of both the Move/Copy Body feature and the Linear Pattern for bodies. It was not always clear to me which one to use. When I used Move/Copy to move a body, but used the Copy option, this suddenly began to look like a pattern. The next time I needed multiple instances at a distance, I went for Move/Copy again, only to realize that it doesn't work just like the pattern, or only works like a pattern if you only want one copy.

Once this first element of the weave was created, there was no need to create another one. All of the elements of the weave are identical, just positioned differently. The next step was to make a linear pattern of three bodies, and then use Move/Copy to flip the middle one. The flip was accomplished by drawing a centerline on the center plane, and using it as an axis for the Move/Copy feature. So the result looks like Figure 19.8, with the image on the left being just after the pattern, and the image on the right being just after the Move/Copy feature. In the image on the right, the sketch axis for the Move/Copy feature is orange.

356

FIGURE 19.8

Adding elements with a pattern and flipping one of the elements

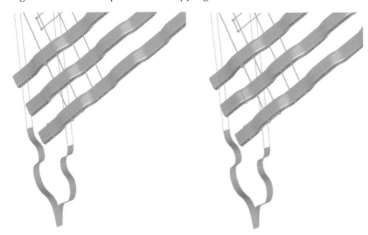

NOTE   The shaded sides of the cuts at the ends of the bracket are a display bug in the software that appears to be unavoidable in this case.

With the alternating element flipped, I made another pattern, this time patterning the flipped element to give me four weave elements, alternating in direction.

Following the same logic, I used Move/Copy again to rotate the first element so that it started the elements in the second direction of the weave. This also had to be flipped and moved, and then patterned to finish the weave. Figure 19.9 shows this process in progress.

FIGURE 19.9

Adding elements in the second direction

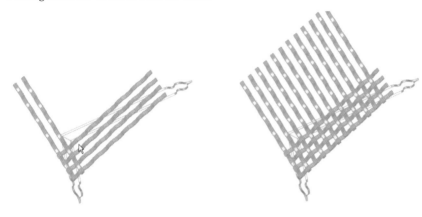

Finally, I used the original open sketch of the Thin Feature to cut away the unnecessary parts of the weave, leaving me with the triangular section of woven solids. Once I combined these, I realized that the fillets cause problems with undercuts, and the elements would have to interfere by the amount of the fillet radius. To do this, the offset planes had to be moved closer together by half of the radius distance.

Modeling a Flower-Trumpet Finial

This part started out as a challenge from a student in a surfacing class. It is a good example of what can be done, and what kinds of things you sometimes run into trouble with, when modeling in a free-form way with SolidWorks. Figure 19.10 shows the finished model.

FIGURE 19.10

The finished flower-trumpet shape

When modeling things that look complex, the first thing to look for is symmetry. The second thing to look for is patterns. This part has both. Recognizing that up front can help prevent a model like this from becoming a research project.

Notice that each patterned petal of the flower is symmetrical. So, instead of making 12 petals, you only need to make one, and instead of making the whole thing, you only need to make half. I always knew that laziness would eventually pay off if I worked at it hard enough.

So, to model just half, I drew a spline that represents the center ridge of the petal, revolved it enough for one petal, and then trimmed the ends to the pointed shape. Figure 19.11 shows this much of the model.

The revolved surface with trimmed ends

Each of the petals needed to have an interesting cross section, not just a straight thickness. So I started by offsetting the original revolved sketch, and then lofted between the original and the offset. This produced a planar mid-plane for the petal. Then, from the open edge of the new surface, I lofted to the outside edge of the revolved surface, creating a sharp edge. The small triangular open ends could then be closed with Fill surfaces and knit together into a solid, and then mirrored as a complete individual petal. You may have an easier time following this with the part open and rolled back. Figure 19.12 shows the model at this point.

The completed shape of the petal

Sometimes the simplest features look difficult until you know where to look. The petal needed a groove along the inside, and the groove needed to fade out before it got to the end of the petal. Part of the equation looked easy, because the groove is right along the original spline sketch of the petal, and a cut sweep would work nicely. All except for the fadeout, this idea works well.

What I did was to open a sketch on the same plane as the first spline was sketched on, use Convert Entities to bring the spline into the current sketch, delete the On Edge relation, and use the Simplify

Spline tool to add control points back to the spline. Then I just tweaked the last spline point to make the sweep trail off slightly. The rest of making the sketch plane, drawing the circle for the profile, and making a swept cut, I assume is trivial for someone who has read this far into this book. Figure 19.13 shows the finished feature with the two spline sketches.

Adding the groove to the petal

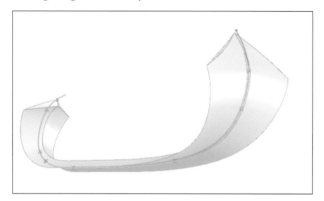

Without any reason for adding the feature, the student with the modeling challenge said that each petal needed to have a pattern of evenly spaced little spheres stuck along the centerline of the petal. The initial sphere was easy, but the pattern was not. So I opened a sketch on the plane that I had been using as the plane of symmetry, sketched a semicircle partially interfering with the existing solid, and revolved it.

Next, I started a Curve-driven pattern, and used the edge on the plane of symmetry as the direction, turned on Equal Spacing, set it for 60 instances as shown in Figure 19.14, and crossed my fingers. The preview looked correct, but when the feature completed, one of the spheres had fallen off, probably because it did not contact the main solid body. This is the situation that the Offset curve option was meant to deal with, but in the end, Offset did not work quite the way I expected it to. The Offset option requires you to select a face that the edge is on, and with that being an angled face, the offset pattern was skewed to one side. The Ruled surface trick didn't quite work out correctly, as you can see in the finished part.

Again, the rest of the features in this model are simple enough that you don't need a book to figure them out.

FIGURE 19.14

Setting up the Curve-driven pattern

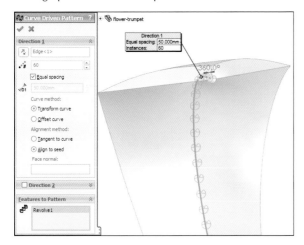

Modeling a Fleur-de-Lis Decorative Piece

Of all the parts in this chapter, this fleur-de-lis is the one that gave me the most trouble. The trouble spots are exactly where you would expect them to be: on the pointy ends of the lobes of the flower. I had at one point given up on it, but I decided that expressly because the piece was so difficult, I had to include it in this book. Figure 19.15 shows the finished part.

This model starts from a digital photo. That part of the process should be familiar to you by now, and so I will not go through it again. I traced splines over the photo, and used primarily Boundary surfaces to create most of the shapes in the flower portion.

I only had one digital photo of this part, and so I had to guess on the depth dimensions. I took some other liberties with the part, and designed my own base with some decorative features that I see frequently on lamp bases and other items.

In this model, I experimented a little with combining sketch elements for multiple features in a single sketch. This method does present some difficulties, but it also has some benefits. I will comment on both as we work through this model. So if you see extraneous sketch elements, now you know why they are there.

The finished fleur-de-lis decorative model

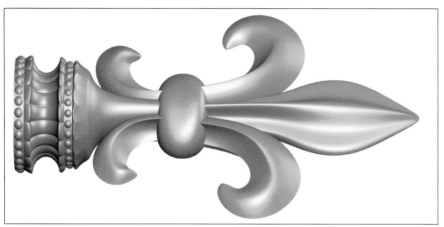

fleur-de-lis decorative piece model

This part is very 2D. The majority of the sketches for the part are on the same plane. Additionally, I have only created one truly 3D curve, which was a 3D sketch spline. For this particular curve, it would have been almost impossible to create the shape using a projected curve, and so I used a 3D spline. Three-dimensional splines can be difficult to visualize correctly, but with good techniques, they can be managed effectively.

Building the first lobe

The first surface feature that I created in the part is the vertical lobe of the flower. Seeing symmetry, I created only half of it. This is a Boundary surface, with two curves in each direction.

I would have preferred to get a more consistent ridge down the middle of this feature (meaning to the left of the feature as shown, modeled in half). I thought the two curves in Direction2 should have been enough, along with the tangent influence settings, but I was unable to get the shape to cooperate. In particular, the Normal To Profile settings, when combined with a Direction2 curve, seemed ineffective. I am sure this had something to do with the direction of the tangent weighing on the Direction2 spline handles. Boundary seems to be more sensitive to this kind of inaccuracy than Loft. (By inaccuracy, I mean that the Direction1 curve is set to Normal To Profile, while the initial direction of the Direction2 curve is a few degrees off of the normal direction). Possibly I would have had better results on this part had I used the more tolerant Loft rather than the more accurate but fussy Boundary.

Figure 19.16 shows the Boundary PropertyManager along with the feature preview.

Building the first surface feature in the part

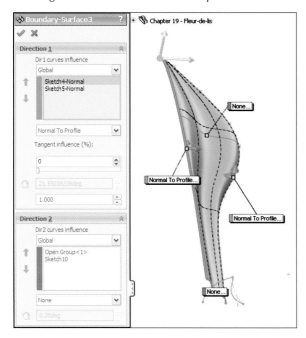

Building the second lobe

The second feature in the part was a curly lobe on the side. This was more challenging than the first. The main reason for the extra challenge was that the lobe curls through more than 180 degrees, and there is no way to use a simple 2D sketch to control the ridge along the height of the feature.

The inside surface of the curl looked like it wanted to be concave, while the outside face wanted to be convex. This suggested a pair of arcs, combined to look like a curling wave of water, so that this feature curls when looking at the Front plane, and also curls in cross section from the Top plane.

Controlling the U-V angles

Figure 19.17 shows the PropertyManager and the preview of the feature. The preview helps you to see what is happening with the U-V mesh of the part, which was part of the cause of the problems I was having.

FIGURE 19.17

Building the second surface feature in the part

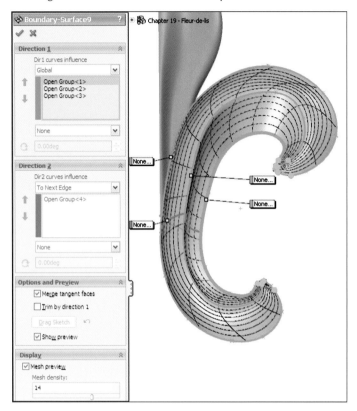

> **NOTE** When the U-V lines start to have a strong angle between them and with the edges of the part, you can have problems similar to trying to stretch fabric at an angle rather than straight on — you can get wrinkles, and the surface/fabric can curl up on you in unexpected ways.

You can control the angle between the U-V directions to some extent by using connectors. Remember the limitations of connectors when the SelectionManager is active. Also, connectors seem to tamper with the tangent influence settings for the Direction2 curves in this part. If you place a connector, the Direction2 curve has no influence past the connector.

The main problems with this feature predictably came at the pointed ends. As everything merges down to a single point, the surface would curl under the edges of the part, actually crossing the plane of symmetry in a very small radius section of the part. As you zoom in on the area, it looks like a dark strip on the wrong side of the surface edge.

Curves Influence

I have to admit that I spent a fair amount of time fiddling with the Curves Influence settings, trying to discern exactly what they do, and how to predict what they do. From that "fiddling," the settings might as well be labeled 1, 2, 3, and 4, because I was not able to find much, if any, correlation between the names of the settings and the resulting shapes. The results did change with the different settings, although some of the setting results tended to look similar. This is not a criticism of the software, but rather of the documentation. Just because I am not able to reverse-engineer the meanings from the results does not mean that there are no meanings.

A SolidWorks employee in the know assures me that the options were named with a purpose and that in the right conditions, the names are descriptive of the actual functionality, but with this (and other) examples I was not able to verify it, so I will not go into the functions of the options in depth. Suffice it to say that the Curves Influence options change the way the curves in a given direction influence the overall result of the boundary surface, and seem to only have an effect when there are multiple curves in either direction.

I have a hunch that even if I had a good answer, it would be one of those answers that can't be put simply into words that describe enough situations to make it a *predictable* set of options. The options can mean the difference between a feature that works and a feature that doesn't work, but the best advice I can give you on how to select one of the options is simply to try them all and see which one looks best to you.

Adding more Direction2 curves might be a better solution than trying to just use one curve and connectors. That would clear up some of the U-V directional mess, and keep the cross section more consistent.

Notice also that the Direction2 curve is made up of an arc and a spline, and that it is in a shared sketch with the Direction2 curve for the first Boundary feature. Shared sketches work out fine, especially with the SelectionManager. The only problem I see in doing what I have done here is if you wanted to move one of the sketch profiles in a direction normal to the sketch plane, and wanted the other one to stay put. In the end, "best practice" still says that you should put sketches like this in separate sketches, but in this case, editing the two at the same time saved a bit of leaving one sketch and going to another. It is the same "speed versus stability" discussion that rages throughout SolidWorks, and beyond to life in general.

The 3D sketch

Jumping out of sequence here, I would like to talk a little about the 3D sketch used in the second lobe. In the first lobe, the ridge is on the center plane, but in the second, the ridge is on a curl. It would be very difficult or impossible to make the ridge of this curl using my favorite 3D curve technique, the projected curve.

I can think of two other techniques to create this curve that do not have the limitations of the projected curve. One is the direct 3D sketch spline that I took. To draw this spline as a 3D sketch, I adjusted the view to the Front plane, and just drew it as if it were a 2D spline. Then I tilted the view 90 degrees and pulled individual spline points to the required heights. The idea is that when dragging unconstrained points in 3D space, SolidWorks moves the points in a plane parallel to the screen, so if you are looking at it from the Right view, the points should be moving in the direction of needed depth. You have to do this all the way around the spline. Getting the taper back down to the pointed ends is not easy. You should probably use the tangency direction handles to give the last portion of the spline some curvature. Resist the temptation to move the points in an oblique view, because although the motion may look right from your point of view, it will likely look wrong when seen from another point of view.

Figure 19.18 shows the 3D sketch against the backdrop of the sketch picture. It is difficult to visualize the 3D curvature of the spline without seeing at least two points of view, but if you open the part from the downloaded material, you will see it more clearly. The 3D curve was actually the first sketch made after the sketch picture, which is why it does not show up with any other geometry as reference.

FIGURE 19.18

The 3D spline sketch

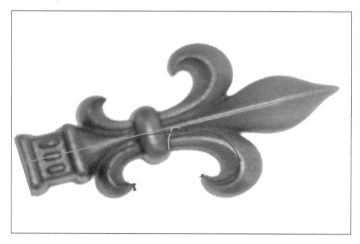

A more constrained approach to making this 3D curve is arguably the better one. Sketch a planar spline in a 2D sketch, extrude the sketch as a surface, and then make a Spline On Surface. This method has the advantage of segmenting the curve almost as if it were a projected curve. You only have to worry about one direction at a time. Spline On Surface can be difficult to control if you aren't used to working with it, but I don't believe it is any worse than a 3D spline.

The belt

The next feature is the belt that goes around the midsection of the flower. This could be created in many different ways, but I chose a loft, and then closed in the sides with a couple of Fill surfaces.

The Fill surface technique has a feature in it that I would like to mention. When you use a Fill feature on an open gap, as in this part, you can use the Fix Up Boundary setting to enable Fill to use an open ring of edges rather than the usual requirement of a closed loop. When using the Fix Up Boundary option, Fill often makes an extra-large pancake-shaped appendage of some sort just to cover the opening. I don't know if this is intentional or what is going on, but it usually cures me of my laziness. I try to get away with not closing in the gap, but that extra material on the Fill surface would just be too difficult to get rid of. So I might as well do it right, because "fast" alone isn't going to get me where I need to go.

Curve Through Reference Points

It is always important to watch other people model. Cross-pollinated ideas seem to be the best ones. I picked up this method for closing off open areas that still qualifies as lazy, but has the added bonus of actually working well in many situations.

The largely forgotten Curve Through Reference Points turns out to be a handy tool to close a gap by picking two points. Activate the Curve Through Reference Points, select two endpoints or vertices, and you are done. Now you can use the new curve, which looks like a straight line, in your Fill feature with the rest of the surface edges.

So, in this case, with a big C-shaped gap, just use the Curve Through Reference Points to select both ends of the C, and create a two-point spline (straight-line curve) that you can use to turn the C into a D.

Mirror and Trim

From here, getting a solid made of the flower body is relatively easy. Use mirror to create the rest of the part, and then perform a Mutual Trim to enclose it. You might even use the Try To Form Solid feature, just to see if your "lazy luck" is working today. In my case, I used a Thicken feature.

The base

The base of this part was far easier to model than the rest of it. These "apple core" decorative shapes still show up on lighting fixtures and furniture, as well as more expensive cast-iron outdoor fencing and other items.

The base begins with a simple solid loft transitioning from an ellipse to a circle. The circle is the start of the revolved base with all of the apple core features. A construction sketch established the angle between the sketch planes. Figure 19.19 shows sketches to create a loft. Each set of sketches creates half of a small feature. The round edges of the solid model are used as guide curves.

FIGURE 19.19

Lofting the apple core features

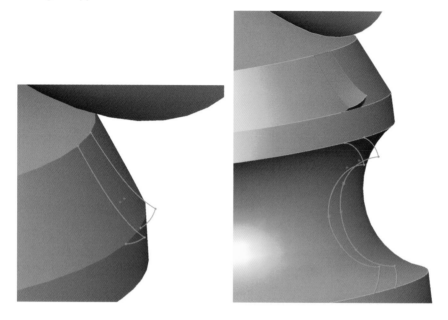

From there, I mirrored the small lofts, and then patterned the original with the mirror to enclose the two areas. Remember that you can set your open surface edges to have a different color. Blue is the default, as shown in Figure 19.19.

Next comes a Knit feature, selecting the bodies from the Surface Bodies folder. Some revolved dots are added to the base for a texture.

To integrate the patterned apple core work into the solid, you have several options. I had some difficulty with my first option, and so I'll show you my second option. For reference, the first option was to add planar caps to each of the apple core rings, make them solid, and then try to combine them with the revolved solid. Instead, I removed the faces from the revolved solid that would sit under the apple core features, leaving the base as an open surface model. Now the apple core rings fit in perfectly, and it all knits together as a tight solid model.

Another approach you could try here would be a Replace Face. I guessed that this more brute-force method had a better chance of working. The Replace Face function in my estimation has a high likelihood of failure.

Add some finishing fillets, and the model is complete. The finished model is shown in Figure 19.15.

Modeling a Scroll

The lantern shown in Figure 19.20 has some very interesting features on it. Because the previous section discussed the apple core feature, here I will discuss one of the scroll features.

Scroll features are not all that difficult to model, but they can be difficult to visualize the first time you have to work with one. The first time I worked out how to do one, the hardest thing to do was to visualize how to trim the surface features to wind up with a solid model.

Open the file from the downloaded data for Chapter 19 called Chapter 19 – Lantern.sldprt. Use the filter at the top of the FeatureManager and search for Surface-Loft5. Roll back the model to the Surface-Loft5 feature, and follow along with this discussion.

A model of a lantern with spiral scroll features

To begin the scroll, you might expect that a tapered helix is in there somewhere, and you would be correct. I started the scroll with a tapered helix, and then used Convert Entities to project the tapered helix back down to the sketch plane. This provides a "shadow" of the helix on the plane.

From this combination of a sketch and a curve, I lofted them together to produce a spire-like surface. Figure 19.21 shows the combination of sketch and curve, as well as the resulting lofted surface.

FIGURE 19.21

Lofting a surface from a sketch to a curve

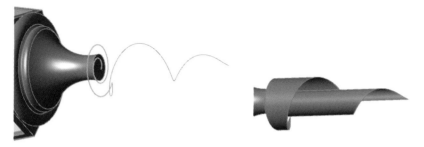

To cap this surface, you need to create a Sweep feature. The path of the sweep is a straight line that runs along the axis of the helix. The profile is another straight line that is pierced on one end by the straight-line path and on the other end by the tapered helical edge of the lofted surface. When you create this sweep, the result is as shown in Figure 19.22.

FIGURE 19.22

Capping the scroll

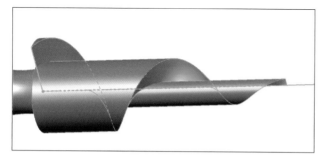

Next, create a Mutual Trim between the lofted scroll surface and the swept cap surface. Keep the surfaces on the outside, and remove anything on the inside.

This still leaves two openings on the surface body. There is the big one at the bottom, and a long rectangular one at the end of the scroll surface. In this case, I used Planar surfaces to shut off both of these holes, and then knit the surfaces together. From that point, I added Extrude and Revolve features to complete the geometry.

Modeling a Botanical Shape

Some shapes are more successful than others. Still, with a leaf shape that, all things considered, could have been more successful, there are yet things to be learned from the technique while leaving the actual shape out of the discussion.

This particular model makes use of several small tools that can be effective in shape creation. These tools are possibly under-represented in the body of work that you see created by end users. It could also be that they are under-represented because they are also under-developed. The tools that will be discussed in this section are the Spline On Surface, Deform, Freeform, and Ruled surface. The tools used to produce this leaf-like shape are valid and useful. Figure 19.23 shows the model used as an example here.

A model of a leaf

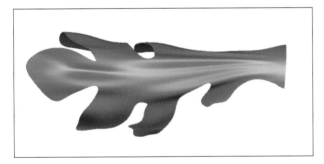

This model began as a simple two-section surface loft with some end conditions to give it a little shape. Botanical shapes do not look very realistic when they have the smooth, CAD-like perfection that we usually strive to achieve, and so in order to "perfect" this model, I followed some steps to rough it up a bit.

From the original shape, I wanted to get a bit of an outward curl to the end of the leaf. I couldn't get what I was looking for with a simple two-profile loft, and so, rather than complicating the loft, I introduced a Deform feature to alter the original shape. This falls into the category of "direct modeling," which enables the user to directly manipulate the shape of existing geometry without using sketches or parameters stored in a feature history. This was made possible with the Deform tool. I assigned an existing curve, and then made a target curve, and asked SolidWorks to deform the shape of the 3D part from the old to the new.

Figure 19.24 shows this transformation. The new curve was created by taking an Intersection Curve, removing the sketch relation, and using the Simplify Spline tool to add spline control points back to it. This was changed slightly from an identical Intersection curve.

FIGURE 19.24

Altering the leaf with a Deform feature

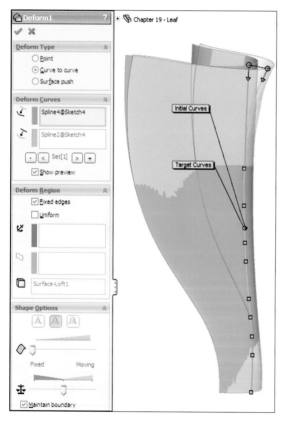

The next step was to create the basic outline of the leaf on this still somewhat idealized shape. Because the shape wraps around and needs to be asymmetrical, the outline of the leaf could not be created by projecting a shape from the back or from the side; it had to be created directly, much like the 3D spline in the fleur-de-lis example. Wrap is a nice feature that sort of works, but it works on cylindrical and conical shapes only, and this is clearly a NURBS surface.

That leaves us with a Spline On Surface. Spline On Surface enables you to draw a spline directly on a complex surface, and even to cross-face boundaries, as long as they are continuous. This type of sketching is more difficult than regular 2D sketching, and, depending on your hardware, the shape you are sketching on, and the number of points in the spline, it can become a performance problem. In any case, this is how I created the outline of the leaf. Then I used the Split Line feature to split the surface with the Spline On Surface. The Trim feature also has the capability to trim a surface at the intersection of a Spline On Surface, which can be a very handy, if awkward, tool when you need it.

Figure 19.25 shows the split surface and a highlight of the Spline On Surface used to create it.

FIGURE 19.25

Splitting the outline of the leaf with a Spline On Surface

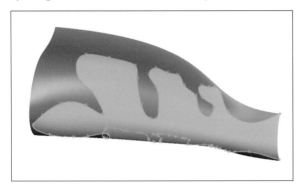

Before making the split, I made a copy of the surface body. This is because I wanted to alter the shape a little more, but I didn't want to do that to the split body. I used the Freeform tool to directly manipulate the shape of the surface model, and Freeform needs a four-sided face to operate on. It would not work on a split face. I will come back to the split leaf body shortly.

The Freeform feature, shown in Figure 19.26, enabled me to tug-and-pull points in the surface to manually edit the shape directly. It allows you to create ripples, pull out a bulge, or create many other effects. This kind of geometry editing takes some practice. People with other modeling software packages do this kind of work frequently, but as SolidWorks users, this tends to be foreign to us.

When I was done tweaking the shape of the copied surface with the Freeform feature, the new shape was significantly different from the old shape, but somehow I had to transfer the shape from one complex surface to another very complex surface.

You don't have much to work with here. No tools exist that do this kind of thing for this kind of shape. Recognizing that the new shape is similar to the old shape within a tolerance of maybe 0.25 inch or so, I saw that I could use a Ruled surface to, in a way, project the edges from the original surface onto the new shape.

FIGURE 19.26

Using Freeform

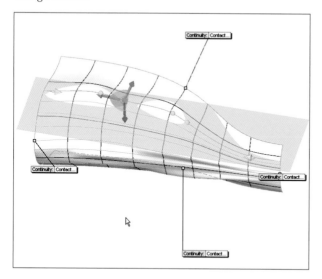

In Figure 19.27, I show the new surface in a transparent green, and the old trimmed surface in a light blue.

FIGURE 19.27

Comparing the new and old surfaces

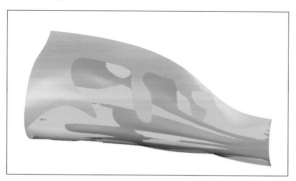

By creating a Ruled surface along the trimmed edge, and making that Ruled surface normal to the face of the old surface, the Ruled surface was sure to cross the new Freeform surface at some point. A Ruled surface is needed on both the inside and the outside because the Freeform did not just displace material to one side, it did it to both. So, Figure 19.28 shows the model with a pair of

Normal To Surface Ruled surfaces on it that intersect the new Freeform surface around the face enough to make a trim. The Ruled surface is shown in red, where dark red is behind the transparent Freeform surface feature.

FIGURE 19.28

Using Ruled surfaces to trim the Freeform

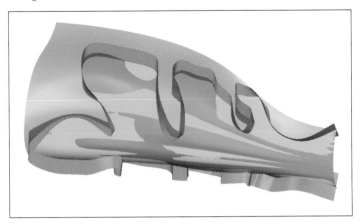

From here, the trim was easy to accomplish, shown in Figure 19.29

FIGURE 19.29

The final trim

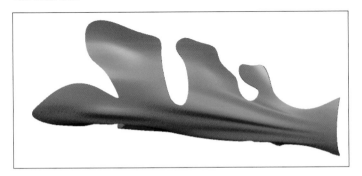

I have often run into situations where a 3D trim fence was required on a highly complex shape. This technique can be applied in many situations, although it may seem a little abstract in this example. It may not be a feature that you use daily, but when you need it, you will remember it.

Summary

SolidWorks has many tools for modelers of complex parts. The tools, however, only get you part way. You cannot go anywhere without some proven techniques to go along with the tools. Rarely in complex modeling are things just handed to you that work perfectly the first time. Learning several different methods to accomplish the same task is necessary in work at this level, because the first couple of things you try may not work at all.

Decorative work is definitely not the kind of work that all complex modeling professionals will get into, but there are still several techniques that anyone can learn from. Decorative modeling is less constrained, which makes it both easier and harder than other types of consumer product-type modeling. This chapter demonstrated several specialized techniques on a range of models in a conversational style.

I encourage you to try modeling some of these shapes and others on your own. The best thing to do to get practice is to look around the house for jewelry, furniture, light fixtures, fireplace accessories, or even architectural details to find things to model. You can also find many examples and images of all sorts of goods on the Internet, which are free for the looking.

Chapter 20

Modeling Overmolded Geometry

Overmolded geometry can be handled in several ways, from the extremely detail-oriented tooling engineer to the somewhat less stringent artistic types. Artistic types may tend to fake in something that looks like an overmold, but engineers and mold designers have to actually model the internal geometry, the interface between the differing materials. In this chapter, I will show a range of approaches, starting with the more stringent engineering approach and following with a couple of quick "looks like" modeling ideas for those who need less structured data.

I have seen several methods for modeling overmolded parts, and the first method that I will show is the most accurate and the fastest that I have seen. This method assumes that the overmolded material is a volume. Other methods assume the overmolded material is a layer, and for those methods, surfacing is a better approach than the solid approach shown in this part. At the end of the chapter, I show other surfacing approaches in which the overmold adds thickness to the outside of the part, rather than remaining flush with the surface of the part, as in the main example.

Because this toothbrush is a nice part to model, and the overmold part of the data is relatively simple, this chapter also goes through the rest of the modeling process on the toothbrush, rather than just covering what turns out to be rather simple overmold modeling.

IN THIS CHAPTER

Understanding the overmold process

Modeling the toothbrush

Understanding the Overmold Process

Overmolds can be made in several ways, but in general, it is a multi-step molding process where one material is molded, then the part is taken out of the mold, and then the part is put into another mold (or in some cases, a piece of the first mold is removed). This allows another shot of a different color or material to be molded on top of the first shot. Essentially, an incomplete part is molded first, and then more material is added by a second molding process, usually in a different machine, although multi-shot molding machines do exist. The toothbrush I have modeled for this chapter uses three separate materials.

Because the part must sit in two different molds, the mold engineer has to model the interface between the first and second shots explicitly. That is what I have done in this part. In order to get a good mechanical connection between the two different shots, you have to have some additional structure inside the part, usually in the form of ribs (for stiffness) and holes for flow-through connections.

The toothbrush I have modeled for this tutorial uses three separate materials.

Because the part must sit in two different molds, the mold engineer has to model the interface between the first and second shots explicitly. That is what I have done in this part. In order to get a good mechanical connection between the two different shots, you have to have some additional structure inside the part, usually in the form of ribs (for stiffness) and holes for flow-through connections.

Modeling a Toothbrush

I started with a real toothbrush, taking pictures and modeling from sketch pictures. I cut the toothbrush up so I could see how the overmolding was accomplished. The model roughly reflects the actual molding scheme used for this real-life, high-volume overmolded part.

1. Open a blank inch template part with the default plane arrangement of Front on the XY plane, Top on the XZ plane, and Right on the YZ plane.

2. Open a sketch on the Right plane, draw a horizontal line from the origin along the positive X axis, and dimension it seven inches.

3. From the downloaded material for Chapter 20, use the image file Chapter 20 – Right.jpg as a sketch picture in the sketch with the 7-inch line. Scale the image down so that the origin is at the virtual sharp of the lower front end of the toothbrush, and the handle is about seven inches long.

   Close the sketch and rename it Side View.

4. Open another sketch on the Top plane, and bring in the image file called Chapter 20 – Top.jpg as a sketch picture; orient and size it according to the first image.

   Close and name this sketch Top View.

5. Open another sketch on the Top plane, and trace one side of the silhouette. Be careful to make good use of spline points and handles if you like to trace the outline in a single smooth, yet accurate, spline. You might also want to check the curvature comb to make sure the convexity does not waver too much, which can be shown by checking for inflection points in areas that should have fairly consistent curvature.

NOTE On the model I made, I found it was an advantage to not make the ends of the top sil-houette curve into the symmetry plane, but rather to leave them largely tangent to their end directions. This technique can be useful when you plan to cap off ends of parts, either with fillets or by some secondary feature, rather than with the primary feature for the part.

6. Open a sketch on the Right plane of the part, and trace the top and bottom silhouettes of the toothbrush with separate splines. The top silhouette will need a secondary spline, as shown in the middle of the toothbrush in Figure 20.1. The big "belly" of the handle exists only to make a smooth transition across the area that will be trimmed out with another surface.

   Exit the sketch and rename it Side View Sketch.

FIGURE 20.1

Tracing the top and bottom silhouettes of the handle

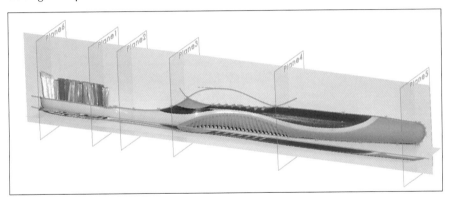

7. Make a series of planes, as shown in Figure 20.1, on which to place loft or boundary pro-files. The planes are parallel to the Front plane, at selected spline points. Notice that more planes are placed where the curvature will change more rapidly.

8. This would be a good time to put together an overall plan for modeling the part.

   The head has squarish corners, and the rest of the brush is very rounded. To me, this sug-gests that the two areas should be modeled as separate features with a zone of transition (a third feature) between them.

   The thumb area will be trimmed out with a separate feature.

   The head end will be capped flat and filleted, because this seems to match the intent of the head area.

   The butt end of the handle will be capped with a Fill feature driven by a sketch point constraint curve.

   This is plan enough for our purposes here.

9. Open a sketch on the Front plane, and sketch three lines and an arc, as shown in Figure 20.2. One construction line goes down the plane of symmetry; the other is vertical from the indicated corner and uses the side silhouette to drive the width of the sketch.

The toothbrush head profile

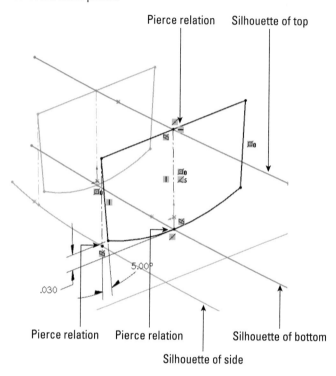

Pierce relation   Silhouette of top

Pierce relation   Pierce relation   Silhouette of bottom

Silhouette of side

10. Copy this sketch to two other planes in the head area, and reconnect the pierce points in the copied sketches.

11. Create a Boundary surface, selecting the three profiles created in Steps 9 and 10 as the Direction1 curves and using the SelectionManager to select the splines of the Side View Sketch as Direction2 curves.

    You will also need to use the Trim By Direction 1 option, or the boundary surface will continue for the entire length of the Direction2 splines.

NOTE   The Trim By Direction X options enable you to control whether the boundary feature ends at the profiles in the same way that a Loft feature works, or whether the profiles are continued to the ends of the curves in the other direction, in the same way that a sweep works.

12. Create four new sketches on the rest of the handle. The sketch closest to the head of the toothbrush is a single spline, but it looks rather four-sided to ease the transition to the more squarish profiles of the head.

    The remaining three profiles are simply ellipses where the height is governed by pierce constraints to the silhouette splines, and the width is governed by another vertical construction line with a pierce on one end.

    Figure 20.3 shows these profiles, with a detail of the four-sided spline.

FIGURE 20.3

More profiles for the handle

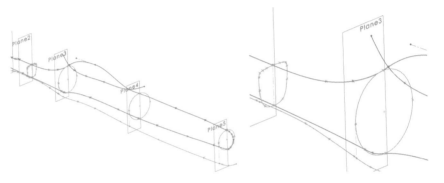

13. Create a Boundary surface using the four profiles as Direction1 curves, and again, the top and bottom silhouettes of the Side View Sketch selected with the SelectionManager as the Direction2 curves, using the Trim By Direction 1 setting.

    This produces the handle section, with a gap between the handle and the head of the toothbrush.

    Part of the reason for this gap is that if the entire shape were made in a single feature, the non-tangencies of the squarish shape of the head would cause edges along the entire length of the handle. Making the head separately from the rest limits those edges to the head and transition areas, leaving the handle free from extraneous edges and possible tangency breaks.

14. The transition from the handle to the head turns out to be more difficult than it looks. I tried several things before I found settings that worked acceptably. Figure 20.4 shows the settings and the results.

    Be aware of the importance of connectors, and their limitations when used in conjunction with the SelectionManager.

    Also note that in this feature, I chose not to use Direction2 curves but instead used the tangency weighting to drive the shape of the two-profile Boundary surface.

FIGURE 20.4

Building the transition

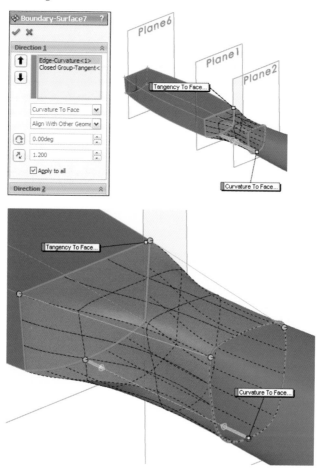

Be especially careful of puckers around the top sharp corners. Relaxing the head end set-ting from Curvature to Tangency helped me to eliminate these.

15. Open a sketch on a plane that crosses the short extra spline in the Side View Sketch, such as Plane 3 shown in Figure 20.5. The short extra spline is shown in purple in the figure.

Sketch an arc, similar to that shown in green in Figure 20.5. Make it wider than the actual handle, but of a larger radius than the surfaces of the handle, such that when you use it to create a Boundary surface, the edges of the Boundary extend outside of the handle surface.

Make sure that the arc actually intersects the purple spline.

FIGURE 20.5

Building the thumb rest area

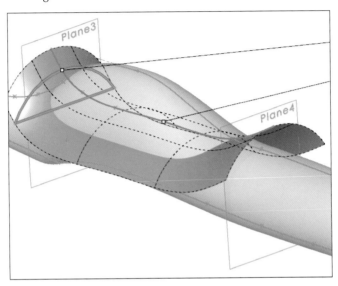

16. Create a Boundary surface from the green arc and the purple spline. Don't use any of the Trim options, because you want the surface to be plenty large to trim away a chunk of the handle.

17. Create a Mutual Trim feature. With this one, you will need to switch the option to select Pieces To Remove, because the piece to keep of the new thumb rest surface is inside the model, and you would have to use Select Other to get to it. Because the pieces to remove present themselves much more readily, it is probably best to go with that choice.

18. Open a new sketch on the Right plane, and create a sketch point approximately 0.15 inch beyond the opening at the butt end of the handle, approximately aligned with an imaginary axis of the handle.

19. Make a Fill feature using the Curvature setting at the single edge, and using the sketch point as a Constraint Curve. The preview and Fill feature PropertyManager are shown in Figure 20.6.

20. Use a Face fillet with the Constant Width option to put a fillet around the thumb rest area. Assign a width value of 0.030 inch.

21. Cap the head end of the brush with a Planar surface, and knit all of the surface bodies of the part together.

Capping the end of the handle

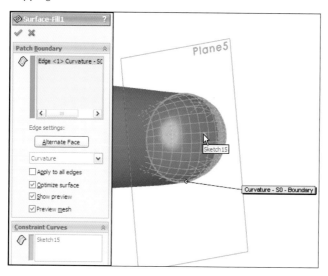

22. Finish the cosmetic geometry with a Full Round fillet on the head end of the brush, a 0.070-inch radius fillet (Face fillet, continuous curvature) on the non-bristle side of the head, and a small 0.015-inch radius fillet on the bristle side.

The finished part should look like Figure 20.7.

The cosmetically finished toothbrush, awaiting overmold treatment

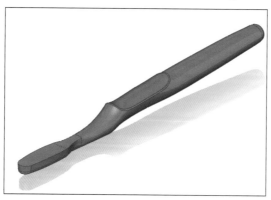

23. To apply the overmolds, I first split the model where I wanted the overmold edges, hid the overmold bodies, and built in some ribs to make some structure inside the part.

    The result of this is shown in Figure 20.8.

FIGURE 20.8

Creating ribs under the overmolds to add structure

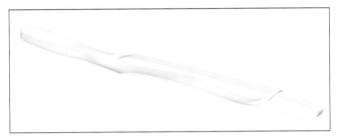

24. I made several through holes in the part and ribs so that the overmold material had something to anchor on mechanically.

25. Finally, I copied the main hard plastic central body (twice), and made Combine/Subtract features, subtracting the main body from each of the overmold bodies. Figure 20.9 shows an exploded view of the model at this point.

FIGURE 20.9

Overmolds exploded from the main body

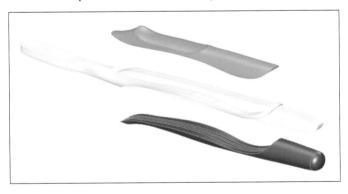

I also promised some quick and easy looks-like overmold modeling tricks. These won't be of any value for modeling for tooling, but they will do for concept models and data to hand to an engineer.

The previous method relied mainly on solid bodies, Split, and Combine. This method relies on surface tools. The resulting geometry is cosmetically somewhat different, mainly to show the thickening advantage of a surface-based technique as opposed to the more literal solid technique.

1. Open the file from the downloaded data called Chapter 20 – easymethodStart.sldprt.

2. Use whatever method you find effective to select all the faces of the model and knit them into a single surface body. (Window select and select tangency are a couple of possible examples.)

3. Use Sketch 17 to trim the new surface body. Keep the pieces to the top and bottom of the pair of splines, and discard the surface in between.

4. Use the Thicken feature to thicken each surface body 0.020 inch to both sides, so that each piece is now 0.040 inch thick. Half of that goes into the original part, and half goes outside of it.

   Be sure to turn off Merge Result in the Thicken PropertyManager before accepting the features.

5. Apply a 0.030-inch radius fillet to the outer edges of both bodies.

6. Use a Move/Copy Bodies feature to copy the overmold bodies.

7. Use a Combine feature to subtract the overmold copies from the main handle body. Figure 20.10 shows the model in this finished state with the overmold parts exploded.

FIGURE 20.10

The result of fast and easy overmold modeling

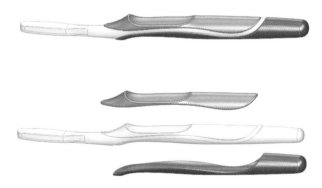

An even simpler method that gives the same external cosmetic results is as follows:

1. Start from the same Chapter 20 – easymethodStart.sldprt part as the previous method.

2. Again, knit all the faces of the model.

3. Again, trim out the center section, leaving the two overmolded face sets.

4. Simply thicken each surface body by 0.010 to 0.020 inch, and fillet the edge.

For the truly lazy, you can just throw some split lines across the part and color the faces.

On the other extreme, overmolds can become even more involved, with a relief or reveal area around the overmold to emphasize the color/material break, assist in tooling, and make imperfections less obvious. Reveal grooves can be added by sweeping cuts or by using the Move Face feature to set faces back from one another.

Summary

Depending on your requirements and position within the product development process, you may need to create highly detailed overmold models or simple looks-like mockups, which only convey where you want material or color breaks in the product. Making the actual geometry is not that difficult, but it does require some body management skills.

Specific requirements for working with different material combinations can be critical to the physical mechanical design of your overmolded parts. It is advisable to consult the tooling engineer of the molder or mold builder you will be working with to produce the parts.

Chapter 21

Working from Digitized Data

igital scanning equipment is getting less expensive every year. The likelihood that you are going to either have a desktop scanner or receive data from some sort of 3D digitization device is always increasing. When you are dealing with complex and organic shapes, that likelihood increases even more. You need to be prepared to deal with this kind of data in its many possible forms.

Digitized data is collected by bouncing laser light off of the object being scanned, reading the reflections, and recording the coordinates of the points using text data. Getting good data from the process is dependent on several factors, including accuracy of the equipment, surface finish or treatment of the object, operator skill, and post-processing factors. While many scanning devices claim an accuracy of 0.005 inch or less, I would not rely on that sort of accuracy for models that need to be very precise. Sometimes the resulting data can be incomplete, with large sections of the part missing. If you must scan a part multiple times from different angles to get all of the faces of the part, you need to be aware of the possibility of scan alignment errors.

All of this is just to say that you need to take the data with a grain of salt. Realize that even though the data is generated by the advanced technology of lasers and computers, the many possible sources of error can result in data that needs to be altered or compensated for in various ways. Reference measurements of critical features and some common sense will help you build an accurate finished model. It often helps to have an expendable original that you can cut into sections and measure.

The data that you receive from a scanning device may come in various formats, including point cloud (*.xyz, *.txt, *.asc, *.vda, *.igs, *.ibl), a mesh format (such as *.stl, *.3ds, *.obj, *.wrl, *.ply), or even a proprietary scanner format. You may get the raw data, or you may get it after it has been post-processed for smoothness, decimation, alignment or merging of separate scans, and so on.

In this chapter, I will lead you through the creation of a couple of parts from 3D digitized data. The items that I have selected are common household items. The first example is an orange juice bottle with some interesting features. The second is a cast iron skillet handle, an example of an antique shape in a modern product.

Working from scanned data requires a completely new set of skills. The data is not presented in "features," it does not distinguish between planar, cylindrical, or complex faces, and there are no edges to subdivide the model for you.

Some reverse engineering software has the ability to automatically create NURBS surfaces directly from the point cloud data. While this technique can be very useful, it is not core to the manual techniques on which this book is centered. The automatic surfacing options differ with the various software packages. In this area, SolidWorks offers ScanTo3D, which is part of the SolidWorks Premium package. If you tried an early version of ScanTo3D, the 2008 release greatly improves the functionality available in this package. Still, the quality of the resulting NURBS surfaces is probably not something you would want to manufacture from.

The goal of this chapter is to focus on the manual techniques that are available to you when working from scanned data, but in order to do that, I will need to prepare some of the data with the ScanTo3D software, and discuss the capabilities that the add-in brings. This chapter is not a user's guide for ScanTo3D. A true guide to the ScanTo3D software would take much more space than a single chapter in a surfacing book, but it seems necessary at least to show a couple of practical examples of why the software is useful for this kind of work.

In the cases where I have scanned my own objects, I have used the NextEngine scanner, with the base ScanStudio Core software that is included with the scanner, and I have done some post-processing and curve generation with the ScanTo3D software.

Creating an Orange Juice Bottle

This bottle is simpler in shape than the bottle modeled in Chapter 18. The corners present a bit of a modeling challenge, but the rest of it is fairly simple. It will give us the opportunity to concentrate more on working with the scanned data than on complex surface modeling techniques. The image on the left in Figure 21.1 shows the original bottle. I painted the bottle a neutral tan color, using a textured spray paint. The neutral tan or gray is a good choice because a scan should stand out from the background, which a scanner would usually see as dark. The image to the right shows the scanned image from approximately the same angle of view.

FIGURE 21.1

A photo and the scanned data of the bottle

 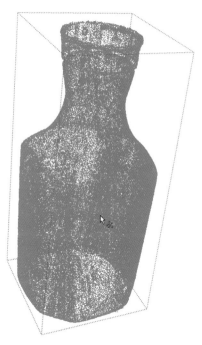

Photograph by Kim Hardy

You may be able to see in the photo that the bottle has some powder on it and some white spots. The powder, like a baby powder or foot powder, gives the surface a matte finish, so that reflections of the laser light bounce back toward the scanning device. The reflected light makes the distance readings possible. The small white dots on the part are used to align scanned data when the object is scanned from multiple angles. For reference, this bottle was scanned from seven different angles to make sure that enough good overlapping data was captured to piece together the entire bottle.

A limiting factor in scans of this kind is the angle between the face being scanned and the face of the device. When this angle, called the angle of incidence, becomes more than, say, 35 degrees on a side, not enough laser light is bounced back to the device to collect data points.

Accessing point cloud data

The data shown in Figure 21.1 came into SolidWorks as an *.xyz file, which is a space-delimited text file where each row of three values corresponds to a point in 3D space. You can only read this type of data into SolidWorks with the ScanTo3D software enabled. If you do not have ScanTo3D, you can import a STEP or IGES file containing point data, but the data comes in as a set of points in a 3D sketch, which could be extremely cumbersome to use if it has thousands of points. Most scans have tens or hundreds of thousands of points, and can have far more, your hardware and patience being the limiting factors. This bottle has a total of 108,724 points.

The biggest problem in using an imported point cloud is that you cannot select individual points of the cloud without using the Curve Wizard in ScanTo3D. This makes point clouds virtually useless unless you are using the automated tools.

ON the WEB   If you are interested in following along with this example and you have ScanTo3D, you can use the file included with the downloaded material for this chapter, called Chapter 21 – ojbottle.xyz, and practice bringing in the *.xyz data. If you do not have ScanTo3D, you can use the file called Chapter 21 – ojbottlepointcloud.sldprt. The PointCloud feature is the only feature in the part.

Options without ScanTo3D

If you do not have ScanTo3D, but need to work with point cloud data, some options exist, although they are not great options. In the downloaded data is an IGES file with the same name as the *.xyz file. This file was created by reading the *.xyz file into Rhino, and exporting an IGES file. Reading this file into SolidWorks takes some time, and results in a single 3D sketch with over one hundred thousand sketch points. As you can imagine, this slows the software down significantly, but it is not completely unusable. Again, the level of usability will depend on the amount of data in your scan and the power of your computer.

This IGES file has the advantage that you can reference individual points to make sketch entities driven by the point cloud data. There is no such tool that is equivalent to the Intersection Curve for use with point cloud data, unless you are using ScanTo3D.

A second method that works, but is inaccurate and potentially frustrating, is the ability, starting in SolidWorks 2008, to use the Section View tool to section surface, mesh, and point cloud data. All that this really does for you is to allow you to section the cloud at the sketch plane, and visually trace over the sectioned cloud. It is only visual, because you cannot select the points, but it is better than nothing, which is what your alternatives amount to.

If it is any consolation, you cannot select individual points after importing an *.xyz file into Rhino either, and the IGES import seems to take even longer.

NOTE   Individual points of the 3D point cloud can be selected when a sketch tool is active in a 3D sketch, and when the Plane PropertyManager is active, as well as in some other situations. The reasons for limiting access to point cloud data are probably related to performance.

Options with ScanTo3D

By now, it should be apparent to you that if you plan to work with scanned data directly, you are going to need some help beyond base SolidWorks. ScanTo3D is the obvious choice because it is part of the SolidWorks family of products, but there are alternatives. Rapidform and Geomagic are two reverse-modeling software packages that provide advanced functionality that surpasses ScanTo3D.

ScanTo3D has several steps that help you condition the data, and then either automatically or semi-automatically create surfaces, or create curves at various sections to enable you to manually build surfaces:

- Mesh Prep Wizard
- Mesh Edit
- Curve Wizard
- Surface Wizard
- Deviation Analysis

The Mesh Prep Wizard helps you to create a mesh from a point cloud. The mesh functions similar to STL data, displayed as triangles between data points. The wizard walks you through repositioning the data, decreasing the noise in the data, trimming out sections of the mesh, simplifying the mesh, smoothing the data, and filling any holes in the mesh. When you are finished with the Mesh Prep Wizard, the software has converted the point cloud to an STL-like mesh. It is preparing the data for creating NURBS surfaces from the mesh data.

Creating surfaces

The Mesh Prep Wizard leads you directly into the Surface Wizard, which gives you the option of choosing Automatic Creation, allowing the software to create NURBS surface patches across the part, or using a semi-automated Guided Creation, which requires you to select the areas to be created as individual NURBS patches. I cannot help wondering what the Automatic Creation will do, and so I usually opt for that first.

The main problem with Automatic Creation is that the patches that it creates are not usually smooth enough (across the edges between patches) for top-notch results. Although Guided Creation enables you to more explicitly lay out the patches of the final NURBS surfaces, it is still true that the smoothness across the patches is still not very good. For example, Figure 21.2 shows the results of both processes.

The crazy faces created by Guided Creation are trying to fit either analytical shapes or a BSpline surface to selected areas of the mesh. You can help it along by specifying face types such as Planar, Conical, and Cylindrical, and even specifying dimensions from which the software will build sketches and parametric surface features. Although this is an interesting approach which seems to have validity as a concept, I was not very successful with it on this particular model.

After going through this, and other exercises like it, you will see that automatic surface creation is a brilliant idea whose time has not yet come. To me, if you are serious about modeling production-quality data from scans of any quality, the choice is obvious. There is nothing quite as effective as good old-fashioned manual work. The ScanTo3D Surface Wizard is not ready to be used professionally at this point.

FIGURE 21.2

The results of Automatic Creation and Guided Creation

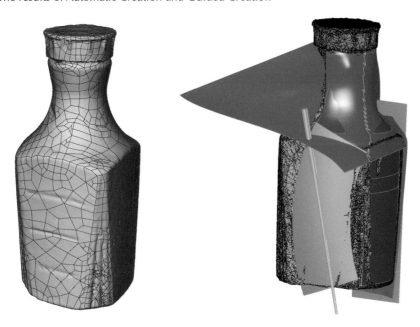

Creating curves

To me, the most useful thing you can use ScanTo3D for is to create curves on your point cloud data, and then to use the curves as reference geometry to build a parametric model. The scan data of the bottle is fairly clean but not perfect. It will be rare for you to find perfect data, especially as the shape becomes more complex.

To create the curves from the mesh data, use the Curve Wizard from the ScanTo3D options. Figure 21.3 shows the Curve Wizard PropertyManager, along with the preview results. The Curve Wizard creates sketches on offset planes.

In the example that follows, I have chosen to use the point cloud as a reference to create curves, and to use the curves as a reference to create parametric sketches, from which to build surfaces. Essentially, I am following a standard surfacing workflow, just using the scanned data as a starting point, and not using any special tools once the curves have been created.

FIGURE 21.3

Creating curves with the Curve Wizard

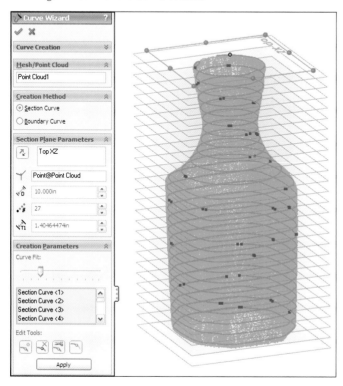

Model an orange juice bottle from a scanned data reference

Next, you will walk through the creation of the bottle, starting from the curves generated by the ScanTo3D Curve Wizard. You do not need to have ScanTo3D installed on your computer in order to use the files or follow these steps.

1. Open the file from the downloaded material named Chapter 21 – ojbottleCurveWizard. sldprt. This part contains the result of the ScanTo3D Curve Wizard, with several cross sections in both directions. The sections are in 3D sketches, and are colored to make them easy to identify.

2. Open a sketch on the Front plane, and draw one horizontal line above the top of the cap, and one below the bottom. Dimension the top line 0.110 inch below the origin, and the bottom line 10.125 inches below the top line.

NOTE Notice that the scan data is not centered on the origin properly. The ScanTo3D Mesh Prep Wizard can move this, but no other tools exist in SolidWorks to help you move the point cloud. In this example, you will create the complete bottle and then move the body to the correct location, with the origin at the center of the bottom of the bottle.

3. Create a plane at an angle (90 degrees) from the Front plane through the top line drawn in Step 2. Rename this plane Top Of Cap.

4. Open a new sketch on Top Of Cap, and sketch a circle, as shown in Figure 21.4. I drew this circle as a best-guess approximation of the center of the axis of the bottle. The data is reasonably good, allowing a fair approximation of the center.

   Draw construction lines to indicate the horizontal, vertical, and 45-degree directions for the bottle.

   This sketch will also assist in moving the finished bottle onto the origin when you have completed it. Rename the sketch as Relocating Sketch.

FIGURE 21.4

Sketching the top of the cap

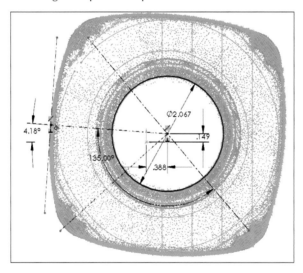

NOTE Through this series of steps, you see that it is much easier if the alignment of the part to the origin is done initially in the scanned data rather than as a part of the modeling process; however, because misaligned data is fairly common, I wanted to demonstrate how to work with it.

5. Create a plane 90 degrees from the Top Of Cap plane through the centerline touching the center of the circle created in Step 4. Rename this plane Bottle Center Plane.

6. Create a second plane perpendicular to the construction line from which the Bottle Center Plane was created. Select the construction line and the centerpoint of the circle,

and choose the Normal To Curve option in the Plane PropertyManager. Rename this new plane Bottle Side Plane.

7. Establish the scheme of how to model the bottle. The cap section will be modeled separately, probably as a Revolve feature with a notch cut into it and patterned around. This chapter does not cover modeling the cap because it is easy and obvious.

   It may be tempting to create the neck of the bottle with a loft along the axis of the bottle, but if you look at it carefully, you will see that a revolve will be the best choice. A revolve is easy to extend in both directions.

   The sides of the bottle will be created oversize and trimmed back to fit.

   Because of challenges between the shell and the fillets, the bottom of the bottle will be created with an Indent feature after the model has been made solid and shelled.

   The detail in the corners of the bottle will be the most difficult feature on the part and can use the horizontal sections to establish the shape. The grooves on two of the side faces will be swept in as surfaces and trimmed out of the larger faces.

8. Start with the part of the bottle that you have the most information about. If the neck is done as a revolve, one of the section sketches already has almost what you need. Unfortunately, ScanTo3D was used to generate the curves for the profile before the scan data was aligned to the origin, and so it is close, but not quite useful.

   Instead, bring the view normal to the Bottle Center Plane, sketch a smooth spline by tracing along the silhouette of the point cloud, and draw a centerline from the center of the circle drawn in Step 4. Make sure the spline extends beyond the face you are creating by at least one spline point. You may want to check your spline with a curvature comb to make sure that it is continuously concave. You do not want the spline to have any inflection points.

9. Add a centerline to the sketch to revolve the surface around.

10. Create a revolved surface from the sketch made in Step 7. Hide the revolved surface before continuing. Rename the revolved surface as Neck Surface.

11. You now need to construct one of the side surfaces. Assume that all four sides are the same except for the grooves on two of the surfaces. Create the side surface using a Boundary surface. To do this, start by making a plane parallel to the Top plane and use one of the spline points of the highest 3D sketch spline that does not touch the neck area. Rename this plane as Top Side Plane. Figure 21.5 shows the preview of the plane.

    The basic scheme for using the Boundary surface to make one of the sides is to use the X layout scheme, so that you can extend the Boundary by making a curve in one direction longer. With a loft, you would have to guess at the profile shape at the extended position, but Boundary can function in some respects like a sweep, which will benefit you in this situation.

12. Open a sketch on the Bottle Center Plane. Use a spline to trace over the silhouette profile of one of the sides, and then examine the curvature comb of the spline. When you do this, you find that the spline curvature varies slightly back and forth across inflection points until it is about an inch from the bottom of the bottle, but the overall tendency is a slight convex bow, where the curvature comb is more or less at a constant height. To me, this suggests that the sides are best modeled by a large radius arc with a short spline at the bottom.

Creating a plane for the side face

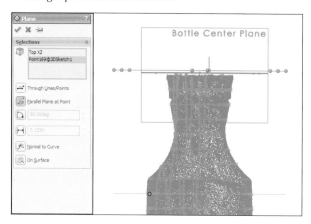

NOTE   The modeling goal with this part is different from some previous examples that this book presents. With this model, you are trying to create a viable model for a real product, not necessarily to exactly replicate the scan data. You cannot interpret the scan data literally; that would result in a part with some questionable modeling.

The spline was sketched just to help you see what type of sketch entity to use to create the side of the bottle. Now that this has been determined, you can delete the spline, but keep the sketch open.

13.   To one side of the point cloud, sketch an arc, and then use three of the spline points to lock the arc into place, as indicated in Figure 21.6. Use a spline with an Equal Curvature sketch relation to cover the section of the side that begins to curve in toward the center of the bottle. Also make sure that the spline extends past the line from the Top and Bottom Layout sketch that denotes the bottom of the bottle.

FIGURE 21.6

Creating a side profile

Arc is coincident to points on silhouette

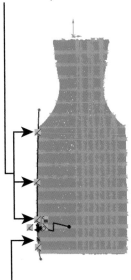

Three point spline with equal curvature

14. The next step is to create a profile on the Top Side Plane created in Step 11. Sketch an arc, and connect the endpoints with a construction line. Make the construction line parallel to one of the construction lines in the Relocating Sketch from Step 4. Place a sketch point on the arc, at about the middle, and then create a Pierce relation between the point and the arc from Step 13. Add one more relation between a spline point from the 3D sketch sections and the arc. You can see these relations in Figure 21.7.

Add one dimension between the construction line and the arc, as shown in Figure 21.7, and exit the sketch when it is complete.

FIGURE 21.7

Adding the second side profile

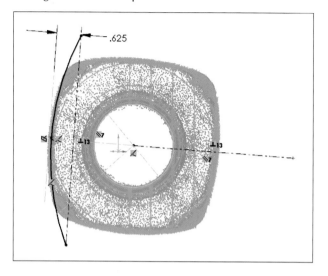

To add a dimension from the construction line to the tangent point of the arc, hold down the Shift key when selecting the arc near the tangent point.

15. Create another plane parallel to the Top plane at the endpoint shared by the arc and the spline from Step 13. Rename this Bottom Side Plane.

16. On this plane, create a sketch just like the arc in Step 14. Give the construction line between the arc endpoints in this sketch an Equal relation with the equivalent construction line in Step 14. This Equal relation serves to make the arc at the top the same width as the arc on the bottom, keeping the U-V lines of the resulting surface relatively straight and uniform.

17. Initiate the Boundary Surface feature, and select the two arc sketches in one direction, and the arc-spline combination in the other direction. Make sure that the Trim By Direction 1 or 2 option is not selected. All other default settings for this feature are shown in Figure 21.8, which shows the PropertyManager for the Boundary feature.

18. Create an axis normal to the Top plane through the center of the circle in the Relocation Sketch.

FIGURE 21.8

Creating the face for the side of the bottle

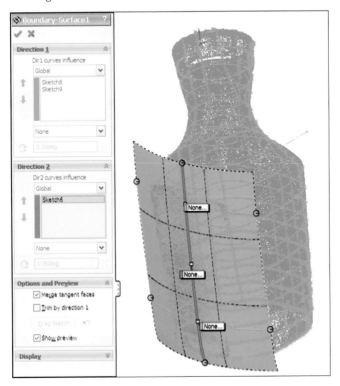

19. Create a circular pattern, using the axis just created to pattern the Boundary surface body four times. Remember to select Boundary surface in the Bodies To Pattern panel of the Circular Pattern PropertyManager.

20. Show the revolved Neck Surface body, and create a Mutual Trim feature, trimming the neck with the four patterned side panels of the bottle.

21. Create a fillet with a 0.625-inch radius on the four vertical edges of the trimmed surfaces, as shown in Figure 21.9.

22. Create a fillet with a 0.25-inch radius that goes around the edges around the trimmed Neck Surface. This is shown in Figure 21.9. The 3D sketch curves have been turned off for clarity in this image.

FIGURE 21.9

Trimming and filleting

R.250

R.625

23. Open a new sketch on the Bottle Center Plane, and sketch the three lines and construction line, as shown in Figure 21.10. The sketch is symmetrical and dimensioned from the origin. This sketch sets up the corners of the bottle that need to be removed to add the decorative features. The trimmed out corners extend to the bottom of the bottle, and nearly up to the fillet around the revolved neck surface. The dimensions themselves are unimportant, but they serve to position the lines relative to the rest of the bottle.

24. Create a Split Line feature, splitting the main bottle face and the vertical fillet faces in both directions.

25. Create a Derived Sketch of the sketch from Step 23 on the Bottle Side Plane (perpendicular to the other sketch), and make another Split Line similar to the feature in Step 24. The resulting edges on the faces of the bottle should resemble Figure 21.10.

26. Create a Delete Face feature, using the Delete option, and delete the faces inside the acute angles in the corners. This is in preparation for the decorative corner detail.

27. Using the Relocation Sketch construction lines, create a plane at 45 degrees to the Bottle Center Plane, and 90 degrees from the Top plane. Name this new plane 45 Degree Plane.

Notching the corners

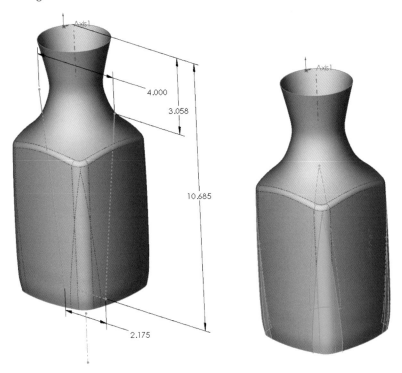

28. Open a sketch on the new 45 Degree Plane, and use Convert Entities to convert the open edges created by the Delete Face feature in one of the corners, as shown in Figure 21.11.

29. Create an extruded sketch using the Up To Body end condition, selecting the main surface body of the bottle. The result is shown in Figure 21.11.

NOTE The instructions for creating features beyond this point may not provide complete information about each individual feature. Sometimes modeling of this type becomes an action of almost instinctive Zen-like stream of consciousness. In the original model, I did not perform the steps in a straight, unbroken line as I present them here, but rather as a series of false starts and workarounds. It is at times like this when you find yourself wishing for a direct modeling system rather than a parametric system.

You may find it most instructive to work with the finished model in rollback as you read the step-by-step instructions. When you are modeling on your own, you should not always expect the first thing that you try to work exactly as you imagine it. You should have enough patience to try a couple of different scenarios for each complex modeling situation.

The results as of Step 29

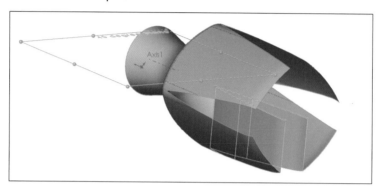

30. Create two more planes parallel to the Top plane, as shown in Figure 21.12. The upper plane uses a model vertex, and the lower plane uses a spline point from the next-to-lowest 3D sketch spline.

Creating planes for corner decorative detail

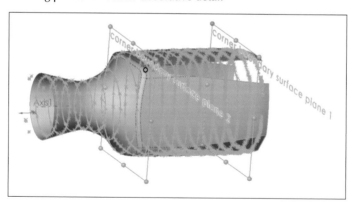

31. The sketch on the top plane is a single straight line, at a 45-degree angle to the Bottle Center Plane, 0.125 inch long, and set inside the model by 0.020 inch, as shown in the image to the left in Figure 21.13. Place a sketch point at the midpoint of the line.

32. The sketch on the lower plane captures the three-hump shape of the decorative detail, as shown in the image to the right in Figure 21.13. Place a sketch point at the midpoint of the middle arc.

     The sketch is shown under-defined. When modeling subjective shapes like this, dimensions are often of small benefit.

FIGURE 21.13

Building the decorative corner detail

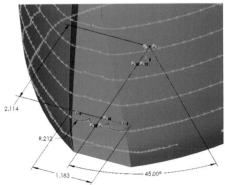

33. Open a sketch on the 45-degree plane that runs through the axis of the bottle and the corner in which you have sketched the last two sketches. Draw an arc between the sketch point on the short line at the top and the sketch point on the middle arc on the bottom, and give the arc a bulge of 0.085 inch (the distance from the construction line between the endpoints and the tangent point of the arc).

34. Start a Boundary feature, selecting the short line and the three-arc sketch for one direction, and the long arc for the second direction. Accept the default settings.

35. Use the Extend feature to extend the big end of the new Boundary surface past the bottom of the bottle.

36. Knit together the extruded surface from Steps 28 and 29 with the main bottle body.

37. Create a fillet with a radius of 0.035 inch on the two edges between the surface bodies that were knit together in Step 36.

38. On the plane that you sketched on in Step 33, sketch an angled line, as shown in the image to the left of Figure 21.14. The bottom point of the line should be coincident with the bottom edge of the main bottle. Extrude this line MidPlane wide enough to extend outside of the main bottle surface body.

39. Create a Mutual Trim between the extruded surface, the extended surface, and the main body of the bottle. There may be some small bits of the extruded surface that you need to select as well, and so you may have to look carefully for the pieces to keep.

40. Open a new sketch on the Top plane, and using the Relocating Sketch construction lines that extend beyond the boundary of the part, draw a pair of perpendicular lines aligned with the bottle directions, not the part. The lines should have the decorative detail you just modeled inside the 90-degree angle.

41. Use the sketch to extrude a surface through the entire height of the bottle. Then use the extruded surface to trim away three-quarters of the part, leaving the corner that you have been working on.

FIGURE 21.14

Drawing an angled line

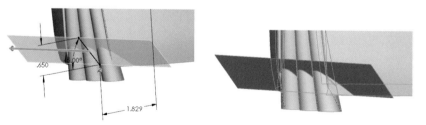

42. Open a new sketch on the Bottle Center Plane, and use Convert Entities to convert the top and bottom lines from the Top and Bottom Layout sketch at the top of the tree. Extend these lines larger than the bottle, and extrude this sketch so that it is oversize and creates the top and bottom faces of the bottle.

43. Use a Mutual Trim with all of the surface bodies just created to block out a quarter section of the bottle. The Trim feature should result in a closed volume.

44. Use a Thicken feature to make it into a solid.

45. Apply a 0.020-inch fillet to the four inside corners of the decorative feature, and a 0.200-inch fillet to the bottom edges of the bottle, as shown in Figure 21.15.

FIGURE 21.15

Applying pre-shell fillets

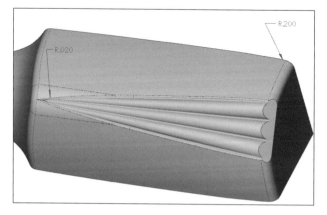

46. Shell the model to 0.010 inch, removing three flat faces, the two forming the 90-degree angle, and the top.

47. Apply fillets around the 45-degree face at the bottom of the decorative detail, with a 0.20-inch radius to the inside of the shell and a 0.030-inch radius to the outside.

48. Use the axis created earlier in the part to create a circular pattern, patterning four instances of the quarter of the bottle, and then use Combine to merge them into a single solid body.

49. Revolve a solid body to use as an Indent feature tool body to create a dome on the bottom of the bottle. Use Indent to push up the dome in the bottom of the bottle, adding a little thickness to the Indented area with a 0.020 inch Indent thickness. Indent is a nice tool to add features to an already shelled plastic part.

You can see that adding some detailed features to a surface-modeled part significantly adds to the work. It is also difficult to "fake it" when surface modeling in SolidWorks.

You may want to take on the task of finishing the bottle, including adding a real neck area with threads, as well as creating a separate cap for the bottle from the scanned data.

Creating a Cast Iron Skillet Handle

In the example of this cast iron skillet handle, you are provided with incomplete scan data, and there are no cross sections. All you have is half of the raw point cloud. Even without ScanTo3D, this is sufficient to make a model. It may be less accurate than with the complete data, and it may be more difficult to extract the needed information, but you can still accomplish the task.

In modeling this part, the following steps treat the scan data as if it were simply a 3D image to be traced over, like you would trace over a sketch picture. Also, notice that I have renamed the default planes slightly. The Right and Top planes have been swapped. The named views have not been changed, however.

1. Open the file from the downloaded material called Chapter 21 – SkilletHandlePointCloud. sldprt.

2. Open a sketch on the Top plane, and sketch the outline of the point cloud data. Make sure that at the Right plane, the spline handle is set in a direction perpendicular to the Right plane so that the tangency across the symmetry plane works out. You may want to use the curvature comb to keep the spline smooth. This sketch represents the parting line around the outside of the handle.

3. Open a new sketch on the Right plane, and sketch the parting line of the cast iron handle. The parting line location may be difficult to discern, but place it approximately in the middle of the height of the handle, as seen from perpendicular to the Right plane. Make sure that both of these splines are the same length. Do this with sketch relations in the second spline sketch. Both sketches are shown in Figure 21.16. These sketches will be used to create a projected curve.

4. Initiate the Projected Curve feature, and select the two previous sketches. Make sure the option is set to Sketch On Sketch.

5. Adjust the view to look normal to the Right plane, and sketch a spline across the bottom of the handle. Make sure that the end of the spline at the end of the handle stops at the end of one of the sketches from the previous steps.

FIGURE 21.16

Sketches for first projected curve

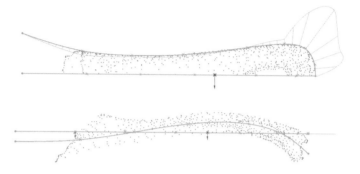

6. Initiate a Boundary surface feature, and select the projected curve and the sketch from Step 5 as curves in Direction 1. Set the Tangent Type for the sketch to Normal, and for the projected curve, set it to Direction Vector, with the Top plane as the vector, and an angle of five degrees representing casting draft. Also set the tangency weighting for the curve to 1.5 to make the curvature of the surface fit the data better. All other settings remain at default. Figure 21.17 shows the preview for this feature.

FIGURE 21.17

The preview for the first Boundary feature

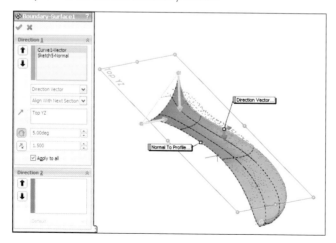

7. Open another sketch on the Right plane, and use a spline to trace over the top side of the handle up to the thumb rest. Also sketch an arc to trace the front side of the thumb rest. Make sure there is some sort of a point at the intersection of the spline and arc. You will need to reference this point later on. The point could be a separate sketch point, a spline point, or an endpoint. Figure 21.18 shows this sketch for clarity.

8. Initiate another Boundary feature, selecting the edge of the first surface, and the spline from the sketch in Step 7. You will need to use the SelectionManager to select the spline. Figure 21.18 shows the preview for this feature.

FIGURE 21.18

The preview of the second Boundary feature

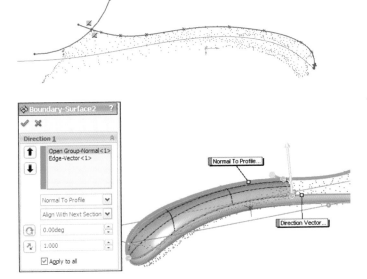

NOTE The edge is much longer than the spline. The Boundary feature allows you to pull back the connectors on the ends to trim back the size of the feature, and so you do not need to use the entire length of either the spline or the edge. Pull both connector handles back to slightly more than half way along the spline, as Figure 21.18 shows.

9. Open a sketch on the Right plane, select the spline that forms the top of the handle, and click Convert Entities. Then place a Split Entities point on the spline, and assign a coincident sketch relation between the Split Entities point and the open corner of the Boundary surface on the plane of symmetry. Turn the section of the spline that follows the top Boundary surface into construction geometry.

10. Extrude this short spline away from the rest of the part a short distance. You will use this section of surface as a construction surface.

11. On the Top plane, sketch a short line that crosses the open edge of the Boundary surface you just made. Use the Projected Curve to project the sketch onto the top handle surface.

    This step is a workaround because I could not get a sketch to make a relation to a surface edge. This kind of workaround is unfortunately necessary from time to time simply because of limitations in the software. Your model may be slightly different and may not require the workaround. The problem seems to stem from an edge that would project into the sketch plane as a self-intersecting spline, and so SolidWorks does not allow you to project (convert) it or to make a relationship to it (a relationship to a 3D edge from a 2D sketch projects the edge into the sketch plane).

12. Figure 21.19 shows an orange spline and a blue one. You will project these sketches to create a 3D curve representing the edge of the thumb rest. The orange spline is on the Top plane, and the blue one is on the Right plane. The endpoints have coincident relations to the projected curve workaround from the previous step. After the coincident sketch relation is created for each spline, drag the endpoint as far to the edge of the surface as it will go. The endpoint should stop dragging at the end of the projected curve. This is by no means perfect, but it does work.

FIGURE 21.19

Making sketches for the thumb rest

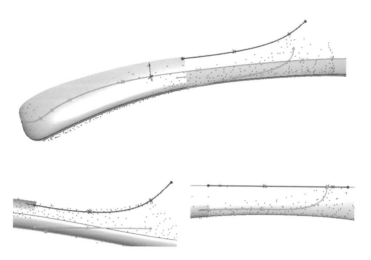

13. Create a Sketch On Sketch Projected Curve using the two sketches from Step 12.

14. Make a Boundary surface between the projected curve, the short construction surface for the Direction 1 curves, and the edge of the top Boundary surface.

> **NOTE** Because the projected curve intersects the edge of the top Boundary surface in the middle of the edge rather than at a vertex, you have to use the **Trim By Direction 1** option, which is in the Options and Preview panel for the Boundary PropertyManager. This setting trims off the Boundary surface to the last curve in Direction 1.

15. Open a sketch on the Right plane, and show the sketch created in Step 7. Use Convert Entities to copy the arc to the new sketch. Drag the upper end point of the arc back to the point at the intersection of the arc and the spline.

16. Extrude this sketch the same way as the sketch in Steps 9 and 10, to be used as a construction surface.

17. Create a Knit surface feature to merge the three Boundary surfaces on the screen. Don't merge the extruded construction surfaces.

> **NOTE** Part of the reason for knitting at this point is to isolate the open portion of the long bottom Boundary surface. You only want the section of this surface that is not adjacent to the surface of the top rear of the handle. Merging the surfaces breaks the long edge of the bottom surface.

18. Make a Ruled surface along the open edge of the handle bottom Boundary surface, using the Tapered To Vector option, with the Top plane the vector, and five degrees the taper. The angle should represent the draft on the top half of the part.

19. Create a plane parallel with the Front plane at the open end of the construction surface created in Step 16.

20. On this new plane, sketch a two-point spline, setting the end near the construction plane tangent to the edge of the surface, and using the tangency direction handle at the other end using a Tangent relation to an Intersection Curve on the Ruled surface. You can see this spline on the right end of the Fill feature in Figure 21.20.

21. Initiate a Fill surface, and select all of the edges around the open gap. Be sure to get the edge of the Ruled surface rather than the Boundary surface immediately behind it. Apply a Tangent edge condition to the Ruled surface; apply Curvature to the back top boundary, None to the thumb rest area, Tangent to the extruded construction surface, and None to the sketched spline. Figure 21.20 shows the preview of the Fill surface feature, along with its PropertyManager.

22. Use the plane created in Step 19 to trim off the extra portion of the bottom Boundary surface with the Trim surface feature.

23. On the Top plane, open a new sketch and draw a two-point spline, with both spline endpoints to the left of the origin, as shown in Figure 21.21. Use vertical sketch relations on the end tangency handles to create half of an egg shape. Trim the bottom side of the handle, removing the surface inside the egg shape.

FIGURE 21.20

Filling the area around the thumb rest

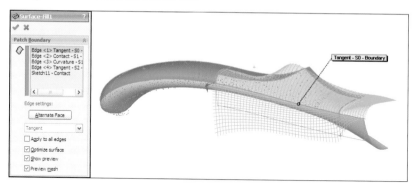

24. Copy the sketch from Step 23, and paste it again onto the Top plane. Edit the sketch and move the big end of the egg further from the origin, making the egg longer. Use this new sketch to trim the top side of the handle. The result is shown in Figure 21.21.

FIGURE 21.21

Trimming out the hook area of the handle

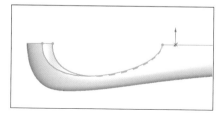

25. Sketch another egg-shaped two-point spline inside the two trimmed shapes. This one should be smaller and moved closer to the end of the handle.

26. Create a Projected Curve using this new sketch and the first parting line sketch used for the first projected curve feature (this is Sketch3 in the finished part provided).

27. Create Boundary surfaces between this new projected curve and the trimmed edges. Use Curvature settings at the trimmed edges and Direction Vector at the projected curve end. The results are shown in Figure 21.22.

NOTE   You may have to pay special attention to the use of connectors with these Boundary features. Every time I have worked with a feature of this shape with a Boundary feature, the connectors have had to rescue me from ripples in the surface. You might remember similar problems with the detergent bottle handle area from Chapter 18, which had a very similar shape.

FIGURE 21.22

Creating the inside of the hook area

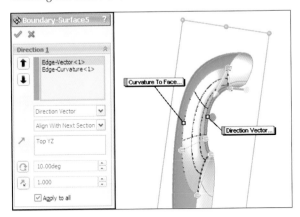

28. Mirror all of the surface bodies around the Right plane.

29. Orient the view to the Back view, so that you can see the rounded end of the handle.

30. Open a sketch on the Front plane, and draw an ellipse that will trim out the area around the point at the end of the handle where the four surfaces come together. Make the ellipse as big as possible without forcing the trim to bleed over to other surfaces.

31. Make the trim. It may be useful to switch the selection option to Pieces To Remove, so that pieces are kept by default.

32. Use a Fill feature with Curvature setting to smooth over the gap.

33. Make a Planar surface on the end of the handle nearest the skillet. This was trimmed by a plane, and so a planar surface should work.

34. Use Knit to merge all of the surface bodies. Do not use the option to try to make a solid.

35. The two faces that comprise the thumb rest area are not very smooth. Use Delete Face with the Delete option and remove them.

36. Use a Fill surface with a Curvature setting for the back end of the handle and the None setting for the ridge going around the thumb rest. Also use the Merge Result and Try To Form Solid options. After you have exited out of the feature, make sure that the Fill feature actually created a solid.

37. Apply a 1-mm fillet around the ridge of the thumb rest.

38. Use Hide or Delete Bodies to remove the construction surfaces (two extruded surfaces and a ruled surface).

39. Save and close the file. Figure 21.23 shows the finished skillet handle model.

FIGURE 21.23

The finished skillet handle

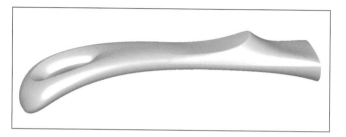

Summary

Many types of digitized data exist, and if you have some help with the data, you may not need fancy tools to do great work. If you can get a few well-placed cross sections of the data and get the data properly oriented to a coordinate system, things should work well.

Without ScanTo3D or an equivalent from another vendor, working with digitized data is less precise, and involves more guesswork. Remember that the only times you can actually select points within the point cloud are when placing points (spline points, end points, sketch points) in a 3D sketch, or when creating a reference plane or axis—strangely, you cannot select a point cloud point when creating a reference point.

Chapter 22

Using Master Model Techniques

The term *master model* typically refers to a single model that drives other models. You might choose to do this kind of modeling for one of several reasons. One of the most common reasons is that you are working on a product that has a complex shape that spans several actual parts, and you want to have a single location to make global shape changes. So, for example, changes to the shape of an alarm clock top that encompasses five or six individual plastic parts is all done in the master model, but detail changes to features like mounting bosses or reveal edge effects between parts are done at the lower-level part document.

In this chapter, I use an alarm clock as an example. The clock has a nice shape to it, and the various buttons, top and bottom covers, and the front bezel all blend in with the overall shape.

Understanding Master Model Tools

You can use master models in several ways, and SolidWorks provides several tools to make this happen. In SolidWorks 2008, SolidWorks has reworked some of these tools to avoid some of the serious shortcomings of the tools in previous versions of the software so you can control them more completely.

A fair amount of confusion tends to follow these tools, first because they are not among the most widely used tools in the software, and second because four tools exist that do roughly the same thing. In previous versions, each of the four tools had different strengths and weaknesses, so there was no clear winner that you could recommend all of the time. The differences between them were subtle, but important in specific situations.

The four tools in SolidWorks that you can use with master model techniques are as follows:

- Split
- Save Bodies
- Insert Part
- Insert Into New Part

These four tools operate in two different ways. Split and Save Bodies push the body out to another part, and Insert Part and Insert Into New Part pull a body or entire part into another part. The push and pull terms were introduced in the Advanced Surface Modeling official SolidWorks training manual that I helped write for SolidWorks 2007.

You may hear the overall master model technique referred to using various names that SolidWorks once used in place of the current Insert Part term. "Base Part" and "Derived Part" are legacy feature names that still find common use, particularly among SolidWorks users with more than a few years of experience. The original confusion between Base and Derived Parts has carried over and expanded into even more features and has created confusion about the tools.

In an attempt to pull together information about all of the available tools, I developed a comparison chart for the Advanced Surface Modeling training manual for 2007. SolidWorks has not updated the chart in the training books to reflect the changes in SolidWorks 2008. Table 22.1 has different information in it from the chart in the training books, and, of course, I believe this table is the more useful of the two.

Before we get into the individual tools, I want to compare them in Table 22.1.

TABLE 22.1

Comparing Push and Pull Operations

	Push Operations		Pull Operations	
	Split	Save Bodies	Insert Part	Insert Into New Part
Solid bodies?	Yes	Yes	Yes	Yes
Surface bodies?	No	No	Yes	Yes
Solids and surfaces simultaneously?	No	No	Yes	No
Sketches and reference geometry?	No	No	Yes	No
Use existing part as child?	No	No	Yes	No
Initiated from?	Parent – Menu/Toolbar	Parent – RMB Bodies Folder Only	Child – Menu/Toolbar	Parent – RMB Bodies Folder or RMB Body in Folder

	Split	Save Bodies	Insert Part	Insert Into New Part
Creates feature in parent?	Yes – Split	Yes – Save Bodies	No	No
Creates feature in child?	Yes – Stock	Yes – Stock	Yes – Part	Yes – Stock
Specify location in parent history?	Yes	Yes	No*	No*
Specify configuration?	Yes	Yes	Yes	Yes
Create assembly?	Yes	Yes	No	No

* You cannot specify the location in the parent history from which the bodies are taken, but you can specify a configuration; you could therefore use configurations to suppress features to alter the state of the inserted part or body.

What differentiates the push from the pull is the fact that two of these techniques create features in the parent document, which pushes updates out to the child. The other two have no marker in the parent file, and so if a change is propagated, the child has to go looking for the actual change and pull the change in. Even though Insert Into New Part is initiated in the parent document, the data still has to be pulled from the child, and so it is classified with the pull operations.

Differentiating Multi-body Parts and Assemblies

Before we talk about master model techniques in depth, I want to emphasize a couple of thoughts about the differences and similarities between multi-body models and assemblies. Master model techniques most often use multi-body modeling and very often are created to model assemblies. You should be careful not to try to replace assemblies with multi-body parts. They are not equivalent, and multi-body parts are not necessarily a quick shortcut for an assembly.

Speaking of real physical parts, an assembly is made of individual, separate parts. If you are modeling parts that are separated in that way, it should be reflected in your CAD data as a real SolidWorks assembly. If you are making an inseparable subassembly — like captive hardware, pressed-in PEM fasteners, threaded inserts for plastic parts, or overmolded elastomeric parts — it makes sense to make them as multi-body parts.

Multi-bodies are typically a midway point between states of the model. Sometimes bodies are used as reference geometry. Sometimes you need to bridge between two areas of a solid. Sometimes it is most convenient (or even at times it is the only possible way) to pattern or mirror multiple bodies instead of patterning or mirroring features.

An assembly file enables you to do things that you can't do in a multi-body part file. Possibly the most important difference between an assembly and a multi-body part is that your feature lists for each part are separate when you have individual parts, but they are all jumbled together if you have a multi-body part. If you have an error in a multi-body part, all of the bodies inside that file may be affected. If you want to reuse a part, that is extremely difficult to do if the part is modeled

417

as a single body among several other bodies. Assemblies allow dynamic assembly motion, and parts do not. Assemblies enable exploded views, while multi-bodies do not. In an assembly you can just drag parts around the screen and rotate them easily. When you have individual parts, you can get individual mass properties and assign different materials to different parts. You can easily replace one part with another in an assembly but not in a multi-body file. You can also move a part to a different subassembly if it is not in a multi-body part.

Some uses of multi-body parts are valid, and some of these have already been mentioned. Multi-body parts can sometimes be an effective way to avoid in-context weaknesses, especially when it comes to combining in-context and configurations. This in-context workaround is the only time I recommend replacing assembly techniques with multi-body techniques, and only because of the limitations with in-context type work.

I do not want to frighten you from using multi-body parts, but I do want you to respect the difference between multi-bodies and assemblies. Do not form bad modeling habits with the over-use of multi-bodies simply to avoid assemblies. Many inexperienced users discover multi-body modeling and proclaim it a great way to avoid file management problems. This may seem true initially, but modeling indiscriminately in multi-body would be jumping from the frying pan into the fire.

Understand and respect the differences between multi-bodies and assemblies. Use individual parts and assemblies unless you can articulate a specific reason for using multi-bodies.

Using Push Type Master Model Tools

Push master model tools are the features that send data from a parent document to a child document. These tools leave a feature in the FeatureManager of the parent document that enables you to position it in history so the body is pushed out at a particular state of the model. For example, you initiate the Save Bodies feature from a part (which becomes the parent part), and from it is created another part (known as a child part). A Save Bodies feature is also left in the tree, and you can drag it up or down the tree so that the data sent to the child has either more or fewer features in it.

Using the Split feature

The Split feature is two features in one. The primary function of the Split feature is to split solid models into multiple bodies. The secondary function is to save bodies out as individual parts. Split can use sketches, planes, or surface bodies to split solids. Split cannot split surface bodies into multiple bodies. In fact, there is no feature in SolidWorks that can take a surface body and split it into two bodies. You can trim a body, you can put split lines on a body, and you can copy, move, and delete bodies, but you cannot split a surface body. Enhancement request, anyone?

Figure 22.1 shows a solid part that I have split into several bodies using multiple Split features. While a single Split feature can use sketches on planes that face multiple directions, I tried to be more organized about it and only created related splits in a single feature.

FIGURE 22.1

An alarm clock as a single body and, after the split, as multiple bodies, with multiple Split features in the FeatureManager

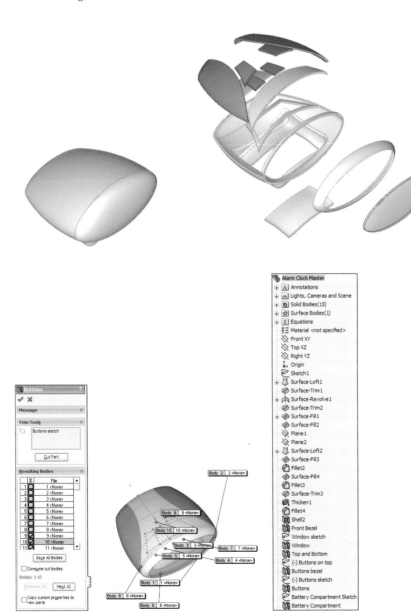

> **NOTE**   The image in Figure 22.1 seems to show an exploded view, but multi-body parts cannot use exploded views; that is only allowed in assemblies. Instead, I used the Move/Copy Bodies feature to position the bodies.

This usage of the Split feature is just to break out the individual bodies that will later be used as parts. To take the next step, and make individual parts out of all the bodies, you can click the Save All Bodies button at the bottom of the Split PropertyManager, shown in Figure 22.1. The default naming for the files will be Body1.sldprt, and so on. This is probably not good enough for real work, but as you can see from Figure 22.1, you have 15 parts to rename. The callouts for each part are not always exactly clear as to what they are pointing to, and often point to the edge between parts. You may choose to just accept the default names, and then as you open each individual part, rename it using a Save As. This should maintain the links.

Details concerning the Split feature

In SolidWorks 2007 and previous, the Split feature was much maligned by advanced users. This is because, if the number of bodies in your part prior to the Split feature changed, the Split could fail or lose track of which body was which. This caused any dependent features inside the saved-out parts to be lost. Also, if you redefined a failed Split feature, it would overwrite all of your parts with new copies of the bodies, so you would lose any dependent features in the individual parts. There was a workaround to avoid losing all of that data, but although it saved a lot of work, it was an ugly hack, and required that you catch the situation before it happened, rather than after.

Fortunately, SolidWorks has addressed this situation in the SolidWorks 2008 release, and the Split feature is no longer the pariah it has been for several releases now. Still, if you look at the chart comparing the four techniques, Split can only transmit solid bodies, not surfaces, and not reference geometry or sketches. It may work well for splitting your solid part into bodies, and it may be convenient for saving the bodies out to parts, but it may not be able to do what you need it to do.

Using the Split feature to create assemblies

Another attractive aspect of the Split feature is that once you have created the Split and saved bodies out to individual parts, you can then right-click the Split feature in the FeatureManager and select Create Assembly from the list. This option does just what it says and assembles the parts made from the Split back into the proper spatial orientations in an assembly. Because each of the parts is made from bodies from the same part, they all share the same origin, so when the parts are put back together in an assembly, they just fall together into the correct locations, simply by aligning the origins of each part. This is very fast and convenient.

Using the Save Bodies function

The Save Bodies function is really just the second half of the Split feature. The Save Bodies PropertyManager looks identical to the lower half of the Split PropertyManager. Save Bodies has no menu selection, nor does it have a toolbar icon. It is only available through the right mouse button (RMB) menu on the Solid Bodies folder. You cannot use it on surfaces or on individual solid bodies. When a Save Bodies feature appears in the FeatureManager, it has the same icon (but a different name) as the Split feature. You can even use it to make an assembly of the saved-out solid bodies in the same way as the Split feature.

So, although this is a separate function, initiated from a separate location, I will not mention the Save Bodies function again, because it is materially the same as Split. You'll notice in Table 22.1 that all of the characteristics of the two features are identical.

Using Pull Type Master Model Tools

The big functional difference between the push and pull tools is that the push tools have a built-in where-used function, so you can find the child from the parent. Pull functions do not leave any trace of the link in the parent document, so you can only find the parent from the child, not the other way around.

A second major difference is that the push tools enable the user to decide at which point in the history of the parent part it should be sent to the child. The pull tools always pull from the end of the FeatureManager. To overcome this limitation, pull tools can specify which parent document configuration they are pulling from. You can specify the configuration by right-clicking the feature with the external reference (denoted by "->"), selecting List External References from the list, and picking the configuration from the drop-down box in the upper center of the dialog box.

 The names of the two pull tools, Insert Part and Insert Into New Part, give the impression that the differences between them are trivial, but that is not really the case, as you will see next. An additional feature called Mirror Part is not usually associated with master model tools but has specific functionality for making mirror image parts. Mirror Part has also received a major upgrade in 2008 and is very closely related to the Insert Part functionality, so I will examine them together.

Using Insert Part and Mirror Part

I treat Insert Part and Mirror Part as essentially the same function, with Mirror Part having the obvious addition that it also mirrors the inserted body. In fact, when you use the Mirror Part feature, SolidWorks displays the Insert Part PropertyManager.

Insert Part is probably the most widely used of the master model operations, and it has received a substantial upgrade in SolidWorks 2008. In versions prior to 2008, Insert Part was only able to bring forward solids, surfaces, planes, axes, and cosmetic threads, but now it is also able to bring with it sketches, custom properties, and coordinate systems, and it can even break the link back to the parent part.

NOTE   SolidWorks 2008 has fixed a bug in the previous version's ability to bring in planes. Before 2008, any planes you brought in would come into the origin. You could not use the planes as mate references if you moved the model on Insert. Now you can. The limitation is that the Inserted planes cannot be autosized; that option is unavailable for the inserted planes.

Figure 22.2 shows the Insert Part PropertyManager in the image on the left. The image on the right shows how an inserted part is shown in the FeatureManager when the link is broken back to the parent document.

FIGURE 22.2

The Insert Part PropertyManager and the FeatureManager

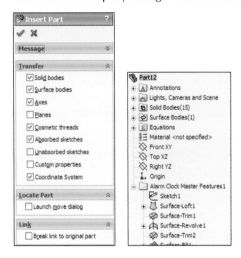

It is interesting that curves are still excluded from the list of items to bring forward. This may have something to do with the fact that SolidWorks still cannot mirror curves. Curves have also been excluded from significant enhancements for the past several releases.

Another thing to notice with this function is that if you insert a part into another part that already has geometry in it, SolidWorks does not display the Link panel. So, SolidWorks is assuming that if you already have geometry in a part, you do not want to position the inserted geometry. Of course, you can always resort to the Move/Copy Bodies tool to position inserted or mirrored geometry.

Details concerning inserted parts

Insert Part, when used as a master model tool, has a tendency to be effective, but inefficient. It is nice to be able to bring in all of the types of data that are in the parent model, but it requires you to bring forward all of the data. Take the alarm clock model as an example. If I wanted to make an individual part of one of the buttons, I would still have to insert the entire model, and then delete all the rest of the bodies.

The Delete Bodies function is not a true delete function in the way we are used to thinking of delete. When you delete something, you expect it to be gone, but when the delete function becomes a history-dependent feature, it means that whatever you delete is actually still there. So, if you insert 15 bodies, and delete 14 of them, the geometry data for all of the bodies is still stored in the part file. You just have to roll back before the Delete Bodies function to see it.

This inefficiency is usually overlooked in favor of the other strengths of Insert Part, but if you are converting a lot of bodies into parts, the manual process and inefficiency might be more than you care to deal with. For this reason, some users choose one of the more selective methods, such as Insert Into New Part or a push technique.

Details concerning mirrored parts

Although the interface and most of the behavior of mirrored parts are identical to inserted parts, mirrored parts have a few distinguishing functions that you need to know about. First, a Mirror Part feature has to be initiated from the parent document; it cannot be initiated from the child document the way an Insert Part feature can.

Second, the PropertyManager for Mirror Part does not allow you to position the new body (the Locate Part panel is missing). It is not clear to me that this is an intentional omission. I'm not sure why you would want to exclude locating the body as a possibility when using Mirror Part, when it is an option with Insert Part.

Third, when you mirror a part and check the option to Break Link To Original Part, SolidWorks brings in the entire feature tree in a folder in the new part and places a Move/Copy Bodies feature at the end of the tree. The Move/Copy Bodies feature doesn't have any of the options that come with normal Move/Copy Bodies PropertyManagers, but it is clearly mirroring the contents of the part. Why does it not use a Mirror Bodies feature? One reason might be the need to delete the original body, which you wouldn't have with a Move/Copy feature, but then the normal Move/Copy feature cannot mirror geometry. Something is obviously going on behind the scenes here.

The mirror functionality can be achieved manually by copying the file, placing a Mirror feature at the end of the tree, and deleting the original body. The functionality is somewhat puzzling and not exactly in keeping with normal SolidWorks practice.

Using Insert Into New Part

The Insert Into New Part function name is somewhat disingenuous. It is similar enough to Insert Part that you could be excused for not recognizing it as a separate function. The only distinction that gives any advantage to Insert Into New Part is that you can use it to pull individual bodies from a parent part, instead of inserting all of the bodies and then culling out the unneeded ones.

One downside is that you can pull solids or surfaces but not both at the same time. Another downside when compared to Insert Part is that you cannot use Insert Into New Part to insert anything into an existing part.

Tutorial

In this tutorial, I walk you through splitting up the alarm clock into separate bodies, and then using some of those bodies to add detail features.

1. Open the part from the downloaded data for Chapter 22 called Chapter 22 – tutorialStart.sldprt.
2. Use the Section View tool to look at the part in cross section. Notice that the part is shelled out and hollow inside. You could do this with a completely solid part as well, adding Shell features to the individual parts if you chose to do that instead.

NOTE   Notice that I created the Shell feature without selecting any faces to remove. This makes
an airtight part with a solid thickness but no opening. This use of the Shell feature is not
that common, but it is useful in some situations, such as roto-molded parts; it is also useful when you
need to shell the assembly as a solid, and break the individual detail parts out after the operation has
been performed on all parts.

3. Initiate the Split feature. It is available from the Feature toolbar or from the menus under
Insert ➪ Features ➪ Split. Select the front plane as the Trim tool, and click Cut Part.

4. Put a check mark in both of the boxes in the Resulting Bodies panel. Checking these
boxes means that you want to make that particular cut, which is why the scissors are
above the column of check boxes. Figure 22.3 shows the Split PropertyManager in use
with a feature preview in the graphics window. In this case, only checking one box would
lead to exactly the same result, because cutting one body means that the other body has
to be cut as well. In some more complex situations with more bodies or more complex
cutting tools, there may be situations in which you do not want to make some of the
available cuts. A later step shows an example of this.

FIGURE 22.3

Selecting the bodies to cut using the PropertyManager and the graphics window

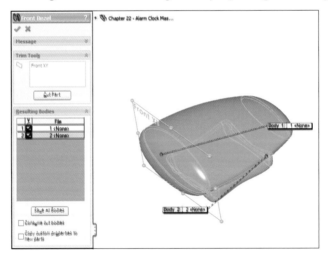

Clicking the Save All Bodies button automatically assigns filenames to each body and pre-
pares the bodies to be saved out as individual parts. You can also save bodies as parts by
assigning a name and a path in the callout flags in the graphics window. Do not save
these bodies as parts yet; you will get to that in a later step.

Click the green check mark to accept the results when you are satisfied.

Body Naming Conventions

The figure that follows shows what happens to body names when you change the names of the features that last touch them. Notice that at the top of the list are Window[1] and Window[2]. These are the two features touched by the Window Split feature. If you were to add a fillet to any of the existing bodies, the body that the Fillet feature acted on would be renamed to the fillet name, for example, Fillet2.

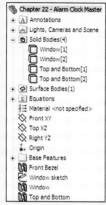

SolidWorks body naming conventions

You can also manually rename bodies to help you remember the intended usage for particular bodies. In older versions of SolidWorks, renaming bodies was a source of some frustration to many users, because when a body was renamed manually, that name would be replaced by the next feature that affected that body, and so the name of a single body would change at various places in the history of the part, even if it was manually renamed. In SolidWorks 2008, any manually assigned name is maintained, even through the addition of features to that body.

5. Rename the resulting Split feature as Front Bezel.

6. Initiate another Split feature; this time, pick the Front Window Sketch, and use it to only split the smaller front piece. This will create the plastic bezel around the clear lens but will not cut the housing half of the part.

   Accept the feature when you are satisfied, and rename the new Split as Window.

7. Initiate another Split, and use the Top plane to split the housing body in half without splitting either the lens or the bezel. Rename this feature Top And Bottom when complete.

8. Initiate another Split, this time using the Top Panel Layout Sketch. This one is a little tougher than the others. SolidWorks makes it tough to select which bodies you want to cut. You can't select them from the graphics window, and the bodies don't do any dynamic highlighting. The only way to do it is by trial and error. Click a box, and if it's not what you want, clear it and repeat.

   When you are done, the entire top of the clock is the selected color (pink in this case), and you should have seven new bodies from the top cover.

   Click the green check mark when complete, and rename the feature as Buttons Bezel.

9. Initiate another Split feature, using the Buttons Split Sketch to split one of the panels created in the last step into four buttons. Rename this feature as Buttons.

> **NOTE** You may notice that these split sketches are not as carefully drawn as they could be. As long as a sketch entity doesn't cross a part boundary or another sketch entity used in the Split feature, it will not create an unwanted split. For production data, you may want to be more careful about how you sketch and dimension things like this.

10. Initiate the last Split feature, using the Battery Compartment Sketch. The battery compartment is on the bottom of the clock.

    Use the callout flags in the graphics window to assign filenames to the Bottom Cover and Compartment Cover parts. Assign drive paths where you will be able to find the parts later so that they won't interfere with other work.

    Accept the feature, and name it Battery Compartment.

11. Right-click the Battery Compartment Split feature, and select Create Assembly from the menu.

    Name the assembly and place it in the same folder as the parts. The assembly will open and the Bottom Cover and Compartment Cover parts will appear in the assembly, placed in the correct locations, but without any of the other parts.

12. Open the Compartment Cover part in its own window, and change the color of the part.

    Also add a Move Face feature to the inside face of the cover with the Offset setting, moving the face by 0.010 inch to make the part thinner.

    Add a 0.035-inch chamfer around the outside edges of the part.

    Extrude a thin feature wall by sketching a rectangle on the Top plane and extruding Up To Next with an offset of 0.875 inch and a wall thickness of 0.050 inch, as shown in Figure 22.4.

13. Save the battery door and the lower housing assembly and return to the original part file window.

14. Open a new part and save it with a name of Top Side Panel.

FIGURE 22.4

Adding a wall to the battery compartment door

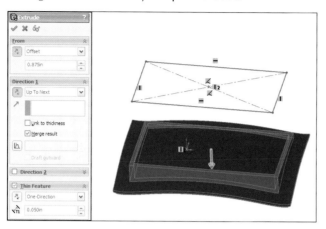

15. Click Insert ➪ Part, and browse to the clock model. Insert solids, surfaces, planes, and unabsorbed sketches.

16. Initiate a Delete Body feature, and select all of the solid bodies except for one of the top side panels.

17. Tile the windows, and drag the Top Side Panel into the Bottom Cover Assembly. If you drag from the top of the Top Side Panel FeatureManager to the origin in the graphics window of the assembly, the part should snap right into place with a Fixed constraint.

18. Return to the main part window, and type **Sketch2** in the Filter at the top of the FeatureManager. Select Sketch2 from the list of remaining features, double-click it, and double-click the 3.500-inch dimension in the graphics window. Change it to 3.25 inches, and click the Rebuild symbol in the Modify dialog box.

19. After the model rebuilds, click the green check mark to dismiss the Modify dialog box, and go back to the Bottom Cover Assembly to see that the parts that were made through different processes update properly.

20. Save and close the parts and assembly.

Summary

You might be tempted to look at this chapter with open-mouthed befuddlement, and honestly, I wouldn't blame you. The options, differences, similarities, nuances, and limitations with the Split, Save Bodies, Insert Part, Insert Into New Part, and Mirror Part functions are so similar, and at the same time contradictory, that it leaves you wondering why SolidWorks couldn't just have made a single tool that manages all inter-part relations. The Fillet tool is a single tool that manages disparate and even incompatible types of fillets all in one location, so why can't we have a Share Bodies tool that manages all types of relationships, without being so difficult to understand?

Beyond the wish for a brighter tomorrow, the existing tools do cover a wide range of functionality. If you want to share surface data between parts, you are limited to the pull tools. If you want to share both solids and surfaces in the same part, you are limited to Insert Part. The Split feature still exceeds the others in terms of speed and convenience when distributing solid bodies to individual files.

Chapter 23

Post-Processing Data

Making beautiful models is not all there is to it. Sometimes you have to communicate with the outside world. There are various forms of communicating, and you have to use several factors to come up with the right format for the right group of people. SolidWorks allows you many ways to communicate with people in different parts of the design process who have different needs. While this single chapter overview of several communication tools will not make you an expert at any of them, it can give you some idea of applications for each one.

What kind of presentation can you do if the boss has just showed up at your desk with no warning and is looking over your shoulder with an investor and four guests from China? What do you do with 15 minutes' warning? An hour? A week? Unlimited preparation time? Obviously, you will prepare differently, depending on how much time you have. Being aware of the possibilities is the first step to pulling off a fantastic impromptu demo of a product that does not exist yet.

Presenting Ideas with PhotoWorks

Getting good-looking images out of PhotoWorks is a field of study all its own, and I am not going to try to add anything to that discussion here in this brief chapter. What I am going to try to do is to give you some ideas for how to present ideas with PhotoWorks, or really any photo renderer.

Selecting where you are on the continuum

Several different types of people are reading this book on a continuum from the highly technical to the highly artistic: engineers who have to create complex shapes for technical projects, engineers who have to re-create shapes for production manufacturing models, CAD jockeys who have to translate from an artistic concept to a real 3D model, and artists who have to create their own 3D solid models, either for concept or actual production.

Because of the range of readership, I have to offer a range of solutions for presenting ideas visually. Doing a PhotoWorks rendering means different things to different people. To some, it will mean at least a day of work, creating a background with careful attention to details, adding items in the view, modeling parts for a background, setting the lights, or searching the Web to find just the right HDRI (high dynamic range images) environment, textures, materials, decals, and so on. The final rendering might take eight hours to actually run, after a day or more of test shots.

On the other hand, some people will be satisfied with flipping on RealView, assigning a graduated background and a reflective material, turning on shadows, and just saving out a screen capture. You have to make the call as to what is important to you, and how important it is.

Investing time

How much time do you have to invest in an image? Who is your audience? What is your audience going to use the image for? You wouldn't go to a meeting with an outside advertising firm with straight screen shots from SolidWorks, and you wouldn't waste a couple of days making a nice rendering to do a review with the shipping department. Here are some things to consider when deciding how much time you have and how much rendering you can do in that time.

The "we gotta have it now" image

This happens more often than any of us will admit. You have to just print it and go. No time for finesse, just show us what you have right now — we can use our imaginations. When you are in a situation when there isn't any time for anything fancy, there are still a few things you can do to make the image a little clearer and easier to understand for people who do not stare at a CAD tube all day.

Perspective

The first thing you can do is to turn on perspective display. This takes no time at all if you have it available right there on the toolbar. Non-CAD users and non-engineers are not used to looking at images that do not use perspective. This comes as a surprise for a lot of engineers. How can otherwise visually intelligent people not be able to see what is going on? Many types of product design professionals are actually offended by non-perspective images. It's a simple button push for you and will do so much for their well-being.

Figure 23.1 shows the difference between the SolidWorks roadster model with perspective and without perspective. The effect is even more pronounced on products with straight edges.

FIGURE 23.1

An image with and without perspective

It is a big enough difference for you to notice, and, believe me, these artist types will notice. eDrawings automatically uses perspective because part of the purpose of using eDrawings is to communicate with non-technical types, and the technical folks would never even consider turning it on because we see no need. It looks perfect just the way it is.

Shadows

Shadows are another thing that CAD users are accustomed to not seeing, but the rest of the world is usually far more aware of their absence. I am not saying that you have to model with perspective and shadows, although for some people that is exactly what they do; SolidWorks sketches and dimensions do not like perspective, but if you have a minute to print out a screen shot, surely you can turn on shadows.

Here are a couple of hints about shadows so that when the time comes, you will be able to deal with them. First, you can turn shadows on or off at View ⇨ Display ⇨ Shadows In Shaded Mode. You can also find that feature on the View toolbar if you want fast access to it.

The second hint is that if you are going to use shadows, make sure the shadows are under the part. If you are presenting information to a visual artist and you have shadows beside something, they will be led to believe that the object is mounted on the wall. To change the direction of the shadow, first turn off the shadow, then orient the part such that the bottom (where the shadow will go) is toward the bottom, and then turn shadows back on. Figure 23.2 shows how an incorrect shadow can really turn the world on its ear, so to speak.

FIGURE 23.2

Direction of shadows is important

Again, it's so simple, but displaying the correct shadows may be the difference between confusing and communicating.

Edge Display

Personally, I really like edge display in shaded mode. It helps me to select faces, distinguish fillets from the rest of the part, and so on. Unfortunately, not everyone feels that way. If you have cut out a section of a model and replaced it with a Fill feature, this is going to show extra edges that do not convey any sort of meaning to anyone who did not build the model.

Non-CAD folks tend to use the word "cartoony" when they see a shaded model with the HLR edges shown. A button for Edge Display is on the View toolbar. If you've got a minute to print out something, you can quickly rotate the model to a good view, and hit these three buttons: Perspective, Shadows, and Edge Display.

The five-minute warning

Maybe you've been given a reprieve, and instead of one minute, you have five minutes. If you are prepared, you might be able to get out a very quick rendering in five minutes, but you would have to have it all set up and ready to go to both render and print it and still get down to the corner office in five minutes, so let's leave out the possibility of doing a quick rendering.

In five minutes, you can do a lot with RealView. First you have to make sure you have the hardware for it. In SolidWorks 2008, the hardware requirements for running RealView have changed dramatically, so if you are unsure, you should check with the SolidWorks Web site to determine if a video card upgrade is in your future.

RealView allows you to use reflective environments, reflective materials with texture on your parts, a reflective floor, and shadows that not only cast on the floor, but also onto the part itself — for example, on interior surfaces of the part.

Figure 23.3 shows clearly enough the difference between RealView and CAD. It is the difference between product visualization and looking at a CAD model.

FIGURE 23.3

The RealView difference

Quick renderings

Quick renderings require some setup beforehand, but in return, they allow some spontaneity on the field of battle. Quick renderings make sense if you have several templates set up for different types of renderings, with the backgrounds, lighting, settings, HDRI images, and all of that type of thing already set up in an assembly file. All you would have to do is insert your part into the assembly, orient it properly, and render. You could have files already set up for typical types of renderings: indoor, outdoor, on a tile floor, and so on. Rendering template files is a great idea that I picked up from a fellow presenter at a regional user group event (Devon Sowell).

Renderings have a couple of simple advantages over RealView images. The first is that the quality of the lighting and shadows can be much better in a real rendering. This is because PhotoWorks has the ability to do multiple light bounces and can light indirectly from image backgrounds.

Another option where PhotoWorks is an improvement over RealView is in antialiasing. Antialiasing is the smoothing out of jagged diagonal lines in computer images and displays. RealView is unable to antialias the SolidWorks display unless the HLR edges are shown in shaded mode.

As a caution, if you are trying to make a five-minute rendering, antialiasing can really increase the render time in PhotoWorks, easily doubling or tripling it for very high antialiasing settings.

A more considered rendering

Of course, if you have unlimited time or at least more than a few minutes, you can work more magic. You can bring many elements together to make an effective rendering.

Subject matter

The best subject matter to render is a part or assembly that has some curvature and a little reflectivity. Curvature makes the light rise and fall smoothly, and reflectivity helps you see the curvature by distorting the background somewhat. Many non-artistic renderers overlook curvature and reflectivity as a source of image quality. If you have a sheet metal part, it may be difficult to add curvature to that, but making it somewhat reflective can add immensely to the finished rendering.

One aspect of subject matter modeling that is often overlooked is to apply small fillets to the edges of most objects. If you have a part that fits in your hand, you should have corner radii no smaller than 0.005 inch on every sharp, unless it is a knife edge. Rounded corners help the light reflect in a more realistic way. In the real world, very few parts actually have corners sharper than a 0.005-inch radius.

Environment

Placing the subject in a familiar environment can show your audience that you understand the piece that you are working with. For example, if you are modeling components for an outboard motor, placing a boating magazine in the image can help your audience believe the rendering.

The environment can also help give a feeling of scale. For example, putting a penny or a mechanical pencil somewhere in a rendering gives an impression of small scale, but putting your part in proximity to a tree might help give a sense of larger scale. Scale is important in making people believe that your rendering is more than a cartoon.

You can also choose a sterile studio background, such as a simple white background; try to integrate your subject into a more complex background, such as a kitchen counter; or — what I consider to be the most difficult — integrate a product into a human environment. This is very tough to do convincingly.

Lighting

Lighting is probably the one thing you can do after selecting the subject matter to make a rendering look lifelike. You should try to use the HDRIs that PhotoWorks can use to light a scene. You can use these in conjunction with additional lights, such as spot or point lights. HDR images wrap around 360 degrees, and the light spots in the image act as the lights. This is effective both for indoor shots where pictures including fluorescent light panels can light a room, and outdoors where the sun or bright clouds can light a scene, while simultaneously providing a reflective background.

HDRI lighting automatically turns on indirect lighting, which is the most realistic lighting available in PhotoWorks. You can find special HDR images in Web searches, and these should work with PhotoWorks.

Realistic materials

Realistic materials help parts look convincing. Plastics with a little roughness, sheet metal with a grain direction or finish marks, glass or clear polycarbonate with some refraction and reflection — all can make a product seem more real. Textures can be downloaded from many sites on the Web, and other properties can be assigned to generic PhotoWorks materials to enable you to create your own custom materials, finishes, and bump maps.

Shadow quality

Default shadows in PhotoWorks are very sharp, as if all of your light comes from a single point source, but in the real world, light bounces from all around, and shadows are typically not razor sharp. Smoother, higher-quality shadows definitely cost some extra rendering time, but are usually worth it.

Depth of field

One of the distinguishing marks of a computer-generated image is that the entire image is perfectly in focus, without any depth of field. Computer-generated images become much more believable when the background is blurred somewhat, and that can be done in PhotoWorks with the use of a Camera and the Depth Of Field option in the camera settings.

Communicating with eDrawings

eDrawings is a 2D and 3D viewer and mark-up application for SolidWorks files, as well as many other formats such as DWG, DXF, STL, Pro/E, and dedicated eDrawings formats. eDrawings publishing software is available for SolidWorks, Pro/E, AutoCAD, Inventor, CATIA V5, Unigraphics, Solid Edge, and PTC CoCreate OneSpace.

The eDrawings application window is shown in Figure 23.4.

FIGURE 23.4

The eDrawings application window

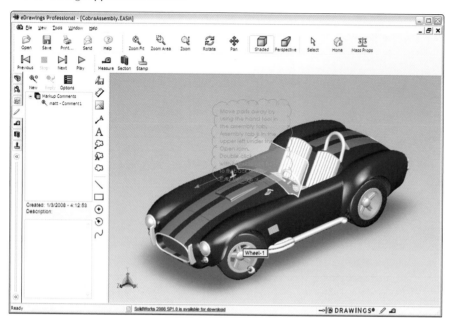

Choosing the appropriate format for your data

eDrawings data can be saved in several formats, depending on your needs:

- **eDrawing format (*.eprt, *.easm, *.edrw)** — This is the format to send to people who have the free eDrawings viewer (downloadable from the SolidWorks Web site) and are mainly interested in a small file size.

- **Executable file (*.exe)** — This is the format to send to people who do not have the eDrawings viewer. It contains both the viewer and the data in a file size that is reasonable for e-mailing. EXE files will not make it through many virus filters or firewalls.

- **ZIP file (*.zip)** — This is an attempted workaround to get an EXE file through a virus filter by putting it inside a ZIP file.

- **HTML file (*.htm)** — This file is just like a Web page, but it requires a plug-in for your browser, which is automatically downloaded and installed the first time an eDrawing of this type is opened on your computer.

I have provided one of each type of file for you to examine, with some sample annotations and dimensions to get you started. These files are called eDrawingsSample.* and are located in the downloaded data for Chapter 23.

While SolidWorks is not available for Apple operating systems, the eDrawings application is.

eDrawings may be created from SolidWorks in two different ways. You can use the Save As command from the menu, which simply deposits a file where you specify. This only enables you to choose a native eDrawing format, not an *.exe, *.zip, or *.htm format. For the additional formats, you can have the eDrawings toolbar active, which starts the application with the current document open in it.

Applications for eDrawings

The eDrawings application from SolidWorks is one of those tools that would change my business if it did not exist. In the modeling phase of a project, I have to communicate electronically with several types of people, some of whom are technically literate, and some not. Sometimes I have to communicate with people who are barely computer-literate, but the communication is completely electronic, which poses a challenge. If I had to communicate in 3D with these people, I would be hard pressed to come up with an alternative. The new 3D PDF is a good tool, but it is not as widely accepted as eDrawings, and is also more expensive.

eDrawings plays several roles in the design communication world. You can use it as a viewer of SolidWorks files for people who do not have SolidWorks installed on their computers. In fact, PDMWorks Workgroup uses eDrawings in this capacity for PDM users who do not use SolidWorks. You can use it to measure, mark up, section, rotate, take assemblies apart, and put them back together, view, print, and so on.

The markup functionality enables you to do remote, non-simultaneous design reviews where everybody still gets to comment. The word "collaboration" is used a lot with eDrawings.

One of the original applications for eDrawings that is sometimes forgotten is that it can cycle through the views of a drawing, animating the view change between views, including detail and section views. Oftentimes, this is a nice option for non-mechanical types who are not adept at reading mechanical drawings.

Finding the functionality

Applying dimensions is part of the markup capability, not part of the measure. All of the options are on the tabs to the left side of the window. Listed from the top tab to the bottom, the icons are as follows:

- **Components (Assemblies)** — Enables you to see the parts or subassemblies in the assembly, as well as to hide, show, or make them transparent. Remember, if you want to do something, try to right-click.

- **Configurations and Display States** — Select configurations and display states used in SolidWorks to display versions of an assembly or make different sets of parts visible.

- **Reorder Views** — Used for when animating through the views.

- **Markup** — Draw simple shapes, add annotations, and place dimensions. Everything is added to the manager panel to the left, with your Windows login name.

- **Measure** — Allows you to enable or disable measuring (in the Pro version), along with selection filters.

- **Section** — Controls how cross sections are displayed.

- **Stamps** — Places various stamps on the drawing.

One of my favorite things about eDrawings is that it can include animations created in Animator, and even Cosmos results. Both of these applications are beyond the scope of this book, but are certainly part of post-processing design data and communicating with other parts of the product design chain.

eDrawings does not make it particularly easy to display photo-quality renderings, but it does give the recipient the ability to see your geometrical layout and the assemblage of components, while making comments.

Using 3D Instant Website

The 3D Instant Website feature uses some of the same technology as eDrawings, but it is completely Web-based. You publish your document to a SolidWorks server (or a local server if you so choose) from your computer through an easy-to-use template-based wizard. You can assign passwords and expiration dates, and you can give people the option to collaborate back and forth with comments and markup data. Then you can send invitations out to recipients in the form of a link within an e-mail.

To use 3D Instant Website, you need to activate it from your Tools ⇨ Add-ins list. You also need to be using Windows XP Pro or Vista Business (or higher, with on-line meeting capability) in order to be able to publish the data properly through SolidWorks. On the receiving end, the operating system does not matter, as long as it is a Windows OS.

Figure 23.5 shows 3D Instant Website in action. This is a cool application to use when you have several people who have to review something, and you want all of the comments to be public, or at least public within your group. It is not complicated or very sophisticated, but it works for the intended purpose.

A tool such as 3D Instant Website can be extremely valuable when you are dealing with multiple locations in different areas, such as China or India. This puts everyone literally on the same Web page, if not necessarily speaking the same language.

FIGURE 23.5

The 3D Instant Website feature in action

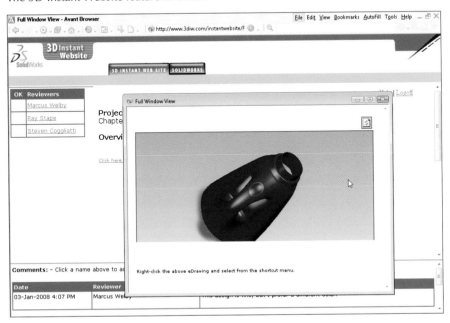

Using PowerPoint as a Communication Tool

PowerPoint is an amazing communication tool. It is sometimes maligned because of over-use in the corporate world and the tear-inducingly boring presentations that the application makes possible.

One of the reasons I like PowerPoint so much is because it makes it so easy to place and organize information visually in a computer screen-ready format. It is the one tool that makes it easy to combine visual information with text and symbols.

For example, when working on one project, I had to communicate several geometrical problems to the client, and do it along with a bit of a narrative so that all of the pictures made sense. Screen captures are easy to get from SolidWorks directly (although I use the SnagIt application, which enables image capture, video capture, text capture, and rolling window capture) and paste from the clipboard directly to the PowerPoint window. Put in a couple of circles and arrows to identify specific items, and then some explanatory text, and I've communicated the point even better than I could have in person.

Another extremely powerful part of communicating with PowerPoint is the power of animation. More often than not, the animation used to simply move text and images on or off the screen provides more distraction than value, but effects like fading from one image to another one that is similar allows you to make a comparison between two different or similar concepts. This can be very effective. In particular with SolidWorks models, you can show the same part with different options, with features moved from place to place, or subtle differences that can only be noticed when the images are literally on top of one another.

Revealing bullet points line by line can be an effective communication tool, limiting the information you give out in each line. On the other hand, you may have a message to convey that does not lend itself to being reduced to bullet points.

Text on its own can be misleading and misunderstood. Images on their own do not tell the full story. Combining text and images enables you to point out something specific, and then tell its story. An early version of this book, believe it or not, was written in PowerPoint specifically because it was well suited to presentation on the computer screen and offered an excellent way to combine images with text.

Once I even made a PowerPoint presentation instead of a 2D drawing for a vendor. Even I could not believe what I was doing, but in this case, it really did make more sense to communicate the product requirements through more pictorial means than to do a formal 2D drawing. I had never done that before, and will likely never do it again, but that one time it seemed appropriate.

Writing effective PowerPoint presentations is a bit of an art form all its own. You have to be able to balance the visual and textual data. If the text becomes overwhelming, you should have just printed it out; if the images take over, I think the words are not there to focus attention on the desired aspect of the image.

Another aspect of PowerPoint that sets it apart as the centerpiece of even technical presentations is that it is an incredibly dynamic document type. You can embed documents directly into the PowerPoint file, or more commonly use hyperlinks to link to any type of file, regardless of whether it is on the local computer or on the Web. You can even embed an eDrawings file right into PowerPoint! Hyperlinks bring a presentation to life. When showing SolidWorks data, I frequently link a PowerPoint file to a SolidWorks document, so I can just click the link in the presentation, and the part opens up in SolidWorks.

With all of this said, it is still too easy to create really bad PowerPoint presentations. One of the most common mistakes is to get carried away with the background. Backgrounds that are too busy or too loud or too...RED...just distract from the content of the presentation. Using too much pointless clipart is another distraction. Sometimes I find myself looking at the clipart image of shaking hands and I wonder if there was any real reason for putting that there, or if the author just felt naked without some sort of an image... and by that time, I've missed what he had to say about the rest of the slide.

I have also seen presenters get out of control with text fonts. "Creative" fonts can be difficult to read, and trying to place too much information on a page can lead to fonts that are too small to read.

PowerPoint is so powerful because it can become a central hub for any type of presentation, whether technical, artistic, or business. You can even print it out to a PDF document, or send it in a *.pps" slide show format for which you can get a free viewer.

The next time you have to communicate a visual concept and need to include symbols or words, do not hesitate to make a quick PowerPoint presentation. You may be surprised by how much information you can convey quickly.

Rapid Prototyping

Should digital prototyping not be enough for you, rapid prototyping is sure to please. Rapid Prototyping, or RP for short, has come to signify an entire range of additive polymer processes that produce an ever-expanding range of materials, from very strong, to very flexible, to very metallic looking. Many products can be prototyped and delivered to you in a couple of days and for just a couple of hundred dollars, directly from your SolidWorks or other 3D format files.

With an industry that is changing so rapidly, any specifics that I write here would be out of date by the time the book is printed. You should contact a local RP firm to see what materials and processes are available. Depending on the volume and the part properties you need, they may have some surprising suggestions. Most RP houses can do short-run plastic casting for more realistic materials and surface finishes. Even short-run, quick-turn metal parts are not out of the question.

Some of the processes that are available include laser sintering of layers of powder, laser curing in a vat of liquid, ink jet-like spraying of liquid polymer to build a shape, UV flash-curing layers of liquid polymer, laying down a long bead of continuous semi-molten plastic, laying down layers of paper and trimming them away with a laser, and probably a half-dozen other processes that I've left out. Each process has materials and properties that may be unique to it, so you will probably need some help in choosing both a process and a material for your application.

For a small number of industries, hand prototyping is still cost effective. Industrial designers frequently hand-fabricate mockups out of foam or fiberboard. This is fast and effective and allows the designer to keep tweaking the design in its physical form. For most industries, however, this kind of model building is a fading or fully forgotten art form.

You need to know a couple of things when designing for RP processes. First, parts should be thin-walled. You don't want to have to pay for a large volume of RP materials, so don't model parts with thick, solid sections. At the same time, you don't want to model the parts too thin either, because the RP materials are generally not as strong as regular injection-molded parts.

Second, if you are modeling a blow-molded or roto-molded part — parts that are typically large and hollow but may not have a great way to get out something that is inside the part — you want to provide a place for any excess material inside the part to escape.

Third, take into account the accuracy of the process. If you have a detail on your model that is 0.005 inch, and the accuracy of the process is only 0.005 inch, do not expect that detail to show up on the finished parts. Some realism is required.

Lastly, RP models are usually priced by time on the machine and the amount of material used. If your parts can be created flat to the bed of the machine, without much height in the Z direction, you can get a less expensive model.

What about Fully Dimensioned Prints?

Let me just say this right up front, and you can throw rotten eggs if you feel the need. If you are reading a book on complex shapes for a reason, you probably do not need fully dimensioned prints. If your products are in a certain range, and your vendors are requiring fully dimensioned prints, you need new vendors because they are costing you money. Sheet metal parts require 2D drawings. Gaskets require 2D drawings. Assembly documentation usually requires 2D drawings. Parts that are fabricated by a guy with a bandsaw require 2D prints.

If you are designing plastic or cast parts, you do not need 2D prints. At the most, you may want to create a simple inspection drawing with maybe half a dozen critical dimensions, and an approximate part weight or volume. If you are fully dimensioning these parts, you are wasting your time because, for most plastic parts, there are many shapes that cannot be dimensioned at all anyway. If you give someone else a dimensioned print and they are re-modeling your part from the drawings, they are wasting your time and money.

This is still a controversial topic, and people across industries typically argue the point back and forth, but fully dimensioned 2D prints of parts that will be fabricated by computer numerical control (CNC), molding, or casting are a waste of money. Inspection can justify 2D drawings, but in higher-volume shops, coordinate measuring machines (CMM) automate that task as well, and do it straight from the solid model, again without the need for 2D paper drawings.

In my day-to-day business, I tell customers that I charge a double rate to make drawings. This is mostly facetious, but I partially mean it. I don't do drawings. I've modeled plenty of plastic parts that are sent off to be made without ever seeing paper. I don't even own a printer that can print any larger than B-sized sheets.

For the types of products listed above, and some additional ones, 2D drawings still make sense, but for many industries, it is an unnecessary expense.

Summary

Modern industry affords you many modes of electronic communication. A simple answer as to the best method is probably not possible. Each method has its merits, and is more or less useful in different situations and for different purposes. You will probably need to use a combination of several of the methods outlined here in order to be effective in your business.

Index